P9-COP-885

Making Sense of Criminal Justice

Policies and Practices

G. Larry Mays
New Mexico State University

Rick Ruddell
Eastern Kentucky University

Foreword by
Alfred Blumstein
Carnegie Mellon University

New York   Oxford
OXFORD UNIVERSITY PRESS
2008

Oxford University Press, Inc., publishes works that further Oxford University's
objective of excellence in research, scholarship, and education.

Oxford New York
Auckland Cape Town Dar es Salaam Hong Kong Karachi
Kuala Lumpur Madrid Melbourne Mexico City Nairobi
New Delhi Shanghai Taipei Toronto

With offices in
Argentina Austria Brazil Chile Czech Republic France Greece
Guatemala Hungary Italy Japan Poland Portugal Singapore
South Korea Switzerland Thailand Turkey Ukraine Vietnam

Copyright © 2008 by Oxford University Press, Inc.

Published by Oxford University Press, Inc.
198 Madison Avenue, New York, New York 10016
http://www.oup.com

Oxford is a registered trademark of Oxford University Press

All rights reserved. No part of this publication may be reproduced,
stored in a retrieval system, or transmitted, in any form or by any means,
electronic, mechanical, photocopying, recording, or otherwise,
without the prior permission of Oxford University Press.

ISBN 978-0-19-533244-5

Printing number: 9 8 7 6 5 4 3 2 1

Printed in the United States of America
on acid-free paper

Contents

Section I
Criminal Justice Policy

Chapter 1
The Politics and Policy Dichotomy

Chapter 2
Crime Control Versus Due Process

Section II
Law Enforcement Issues

Chapter 3
The Search for a Guiding Philosophy of Policing

Chapter 4
Police and the Use of Force

Chapter 5
Gun Control

Section III
Justice for All, or Just for Some?

Chapter 6
Sentencing

Chapter 7
Race, Ethnicity, and Justice

Chapter 8
Gender and Justice

Chapter 9
Wrongful Convictions

Section IV
The Challenges of Correcting
Law-Violating Behavior

Chapter 13
Juvenile Crime and Violence

Section V
Public Safety and the Future

Chapter 14
Living in a Post-9/11 World

Chapter 15
Making Sense of Criminal Justice

Foreword

I t is striking how many issues of conflict in our democratic society involve matters of concern to the criminal justice system. This is reflected in the fact that fully half of the first ten amendments comprising the Bill of Rights are explicitly directed at the criminal justice system: II (gun control), IV (on search and seizure), V (double jeopardy and self-incrimination), VI (speedy trial by jury), and VIII (bail, fines, and cruel and unusual punishment). Thus, our Founding Fathers appreciated fully the inherent tension between society's desire to impose punishment for wrongdoing and its need to restrain that desire in order to preserve individual dignity and rights.

Mays and Ruddell cover this tension in a wide variety of ways. They start with the tension between the crime control model and the due process model, articulated so well by Herbert Packer. The police represent the initial locus of that conflict. The large majority of police officers are quite sensitive to the restraint they must exercise in dealing with the public and with offenders in particular. Too often, however, there are individual officers who fail to exercise that restraint, especially in dealing with the less powerful among us. This can lead to a breakdown of police authority, a reduction of the legitimacy police inherently need, and considerable conflict with the many members of that broader community.

One other realm of tension involves the Second Amendment and its interpretation regarding the right to bear arms. In the 1990s, there was broad recognition of the considerable havoc created by the widespread availability of guns in the hands of people who had no right to have them and a number of efforts to keep guns from such people. However, there is a large U.S. population with a strong sense of concern about potential limitations on its right to have guns, and many of them express those concerns rather vigorously, especially at election time. In the presidential election of 2000, Al Gore was defeated in the states of Tennessee (his home state) and Arkansas (Bill Clinton's home state), and the issue of gun control was an important factor in that election. Undoubtedly as a result, virtually no voice has been raised in favor of any form of gun control by any politician since that time. The only exceptions seem to have been big-city mayors (such as Mayor Michael Bloomberg of New York City) who recognize that the intense opposition to gun control comes largely from rural areas.

Another area of strong tension between punitiveness and restraint has been the area of sentencing policy. For at least 50 years, until the early 1970s, the United States had maintained an impressively flat incarceration rate of about 110 per 100,000 population. A similar pattern was displayed in a number of other countries. That homeostatic pattern was maintained by decisions within the criminal justice system. In the 1970s, however, the political system came to recognize that advocating more punitiveness helped them get elected, and so began a process of escalating legislative sentences involving mandatory-minimum sentences, "three strikes" sentences, "truth in sentencing" laws, and various other means of augmenting punishment. This resulted in an annual increase in the incarceration rate of about 6–8 percent, resulting in an incarceration rate that is now the largest in the world and is almost five times the rate that prevailed for the previous 50 years. Unfortunately, the Eighth Amendment spoke against excessive bail and excessive fines but said nothing about excessive sentences, only that they not be "cruel and unusual." Perhaps if they had anticipated the direction in which sentencing has come, they might well also have prohibited *excessive punishment*, and many of the current sentencing policies would have been found unconstitutional.

The tension is also reflected in the inevitable concern about error in the criminal justice system. This concern has been highlighted by the large number of exonerations of people on death row through invoking recent DNA technology to review cases of people sentenced before that technology was widely available. The concern over error is strongest in cases of capital punishment. At this writing, we have not yet seen a case where a truly innocent person was erroneously executed, but one is almost certain to show up in the future. These concerns prompted Governor Ryan of Illinois to commute all the death sentences in his state. If many demonstrated errors show up in capital punishment cases, where one would expect the maximum of diligence, then the error rate in less serious cases would likely be much larger.

One issue that permeates the criminal justice system has nothing to do with the Bill of Rights but rather with the post-Civil War amendments XIV and XV, in their attempts to undo the damage of slavery. Subsequent Supreme Court decisions have been much stronger in making racial discrimination unconstitutional. This issue of race pervades the criminal justice system from policing through courts to corrections. It is reflected in the fact that the incarceration rate of African Americans is about eight times that of whites. Furthermore, it has been estimated that one third of African American males aged in their 20s are under the control of the criminal justice system: in prison, jail, probation, or parole. This widespread involvement of African Americans in the criminal justice system is clearly a matter of considerable concern, partly because it is a distressing reflection of the broad scope of the criminal justice system throughout society. This tends to diminish the deterrent effect of punishment because the stigma effect is minimized when all one's peers have been so stigmatized. Perhaps most important, such a high incarceration rate can too easily be interpreted as attributable to racial discrimination within the criminal justice system. There is strong evidence that this difference in incarceration rate is attributable much more to differential involvement in the kinds of crimes that get one into prison than to discrimination itself, but it does highlight the importance of the concern about discrimination that follows from the disproportionate involvement.

The tension between governmental control and individual liberty has been exacerbated by the response of the Bush administration to the threat of a terror attack following the events of September 11, 2001. These intrusions were initiated as secret activities and were subsequently revealed by press reports and then challenged. In some cases, these intrusions received widespread public support, reflecting public fear of further terrorist attacks. In some cases, they even received congressional endorsement, but have seen only limited judicial review. These issues highlight the importance of the presence of the Bill of Rights in the Constitution as an ultimate restraint that might be violated under conditions of temporary duress but that will ultimately be restored under conditions of stability.

These are the tensions that Mays and Ruddell have articulated so well in this volume. They represent the essential tensions that pervade the criminal justice system of police, courts, and corrections. But because these tensions go well beyond the criminal justice system, the volume serves more broadly as a window on many of the conflicts that pervade a democratic society. Thus, while it serves admirably as a text for a course in a program on criminal justice, it is also a most useful text on the tensions of civics in many other contexts. ✦

Alfred Blumstein
University Professor and J. Erik Jonsson Professor
of Urban Systems and Operations Research

H. John Heinz III School of Public Policy and Management
Carnegie Mellon University

About the Authors

G. Larry Mays is Regents Professor of Criminal Justice at New Mexico State University. He served as a police officer in Knoxville, Tennessee, for five years in the early 1970s, and he holds a Ph.D. in political science from the University of Tennessee. Dr. Mays taught at East Tennessee State University and Appalachian State University before coming to New Mexico State University in 1981. He has published over 70 articles in refereed journals, in addition to numerous practitioner publications, encyclopedia entries, and book chapters. This book is his fifteenth, and he most recently has been a coauthor with L. Thomas Winfree, Jr., of *Essentials of Corrections*, third edition (Wadsworth), and *Juvenile Justice*, second edition (Waveland Press).

Rick Ruddell will be joining the Correctional and Juvenile Justice Studies Department at Eastern Kentucky University in August, 2007. An Associate Professor of Political Science at California State University, Chico, Dr. Ruddell has extensive experience as a supervisor and manager within the Department of Corrections and Public Safety in the Province of Saskatchewan, Canada. His research has been published in 35 scholarly articles and focuses upon criminal justice policy, imprisonment trends, juvenile justice, jails, lethal violence, issueless college-town riots, and firearms fatalities. He is the author of *America Behind Bars: Trends in Imprisonment, 1952 to 2000*, recently published by LFB Scholarly Press, and coeditor with Mark Tomita of a forthcoming book on issues in correctional health. ✦

Introduction

Have you ever taken a course and felt like you knew less when you finished than when you started? How about the course where the instructor told you all of the theories, policies, or practices that did not work, but little of what has worked? We have heard these complaints from students over the years, and this book, in some ways, is a response to such laments.

This book is also designed for criminal justice and other social science courses that fall into one of two categories: (1) the capstone course (sometimes called senior seminar) and (2) policy-oriented courses. It is aimed at an upper-division undergraduate and graduate market, so all of you taking this class should have completed a wide variety of fundamental courses in your major.

The chapters are organized somewhat like in an introductory textbook, with the standard police/courts/corrections treatment. However, a quick glance at the table of contents will show you that we have chosen to focus instead on a range of issues that continue to confront the criminal justice system.

We have made the assumption that most of you will choose a career in the criminal justice field or in one of the areas allied with criminal justice. We acknowledge that this may not be true for some students, and a group of you may never work in criminal justice. However, as "good citizens" and active consumers of justice processes and services, all students can benefit by understanding what is working and what is not working in the criminal justice arena.

The authors of a book approach their project with certain assumptions in mind, and we feel that you will understand this book better once you understand our assumptions. First, the administration of justice is an inherently political process, and the criminal justice system in the United States (and in other nations as well) is a part of the country's political system. All of the laws enacted and all of the policies developed have at their very core a political dimension.

Second, all of our worldviews are shaped by our experiences, morals, values, ethics, and a host of other factors. Whether you are a Democrat, Republican, or Independent—liberal or conservative—your values (and our values) color the picture we see of the world. In terms of this book, that means that there are not necessarily "right" answers. In fact, there may be many more questions than there are answers. Our desire is that you will be tolerant of the viewpoints of others and able to ask better questions than you were asking when you first entered college. Even if you ask good questions, you will need to be willing to live with a certain degree of ambiguity in relation to the answers that are available.

Third, an endless supply of issues or controversies could be addressed in a book like this one. Many of the ones that we have chosen provide fruitful areas of debate. Some we chose because we are the ones writing the book. Others were suggested by some of our reviewers. We take all of the blame for what is missing and what may not be adequately explained. At the end of this section, we provide you with contact information. We would like to hear from you (as we so often hear from our students and former students) about your experiences with this book. In large measure, if this book is successful, it will be because of you and not because of us.

Finally, a key assumption for us is that this course is one that will help you bring together bits and pieces of information gleaned from your other classes. At this point, it is not the instructor's responsibility to help you make sense of the criminal justice system in the United States; it is your responsibility. Good luck.

Acknowledgments

Although only the authors' names appear on the cover of a book, preparing a manuscript is a team effort, and many people supported us to complete this work. First, both authors would like to acknowledge the assistance of Claude Teweles, President and Publisher of Roxbury Publishing Company, who helped us refine some of the major points in this book. Second, we thank the reviewers, Jeremy Ball (Boise State University), Jeff Bumgarner (Texas Christian University), Kathleen Contrino (Buffalo State College), Scott Decker (Arizona State University), Terry Gingrich (Western Oregon University), Marie Hansen (Husson College), Laura Myers (Prarie View A & M University), Dan Okada (California State University, Sacramento), Nicole Piquero (University of Florida), Rebecca Paynich (Curry College), Wendy Perkins (University of Cincinnati), Joy Pollock (Texas State University), Gayle Rhineberger (University of Northern Iowa), Lisa L. Sample (University of Nebraska at Omaha), and Lynn Urban (Central Missouri State University), who read the first version of the manuscript and were able to provide excellent suggestions about making this a stronger textbook. In addition, we thank the editors and staff, including Monica Gomez and Scott Carter, at Roxbury who made this process much less painful than it could have been.

Larry Mays would like to acknowledge his wife Brenda for her infinite patience while he is working on a book (especially since he swears that every one will be "the last one"). Further, he would like to note the research assistance of Kathy Movsesian, his graduate assistant and tireless researcher for this project. Rick Ruddell would like to thank his colleagues, family, and friends for their support while researching and writing this book. Special thanks to his biggest supporters, Alister and

Lucie Sutherland, Renu James, and Eric Owen. He would also like to thank Larry Mays for inviting him to participate in this project: It was a great learning experience. ✦

Contact Information

G. Larry Mays
New Mexico State University
glmays@nmsu.edu

Rick Ruddell
Eastern Kentucky University
rick.ruddell@eku.edu

Chapter 1

The Politics and Policy Dichotomy

Introduction

W hy would a book about understanding the criminal justice system in the United States begin with a chapter on politics and policy? What do these two notions have to do with the operations of criminal justice agencies and the organizational environments within which criminal justice personnel function? The short answer is, everything.

Quite often people will say something like this: "We need to get politics out of the administration of justice in the United States." Or perhaps they will say it this way: "Politics should play no role in the criminal justice system." As we will see, politics is very much a part of the policymaking process in this country. In fact, the following section outlines the essential role that politics plays in every facet of policymaking, and this includes criminal justice policy.

The Role of Politics in the Administration of Justice

Most people have an idea of what *politics* means, or at least the use of the word conjures up certain images in the minds of virtually everyone. From the world of political science, Robert A. Dahl (1991, 1) has said that politics is "an unavoidable fact of human existence. Everyone is involved in some fashion at some time and in some kind of political system." He added that a political system is "any persistent pattern of human relationships that involves, to a significant extent, control, influence, power, or authority" (Dahl 1991, 4). Another political scientist gave politics a shorthand definition. He said that politics essentially is "who gets the cookies" (Sego 1977).

In a democratic society such as the United States, politics is all about decision making by the public, typically through their elected representatives. Therefore, to fully understand the critical role that politics

---

Box 1.1
What Is Politics?

Currently, a variety of definitions are available for the word *politics*. Some authors see politics as a struggle within society to see who gets certain benefits and who is excluded from those benefits. They also include the dimensions of power and influence in their definition (Bardes, Shelley, and Schmidt 2006). Other authors pose a related definition that politics is about resolving conflicts in society and about who should receive different kinds of benefits (Sidlow and Henschen 2007). Finally, another group of political scientists views politics as the way we as a society decide who will govern and the types of policies that result from that government (Magleby, O'Brien, Light, Burns, Peltason, and Cronin 2006). ✦

---

plays in our form of government, and eventually the connection to the criminal justice system, it is best to think of a series of concentric circles (see Levine, Musheno, and Palumbo 1986, Figure 1.1).

In the outermost circle is the **social system** of the United States. We could say that this circle represents all that we are as a nation. Moving inward, the next circle represents the **political system** of the United States. This system is composed of all of the various forms and types of governments at all levels (Hojnacki 2000). The political system includes

Figure 1.1
The U.S. Criminal Justice System as It Relates to Other U.S. Systems

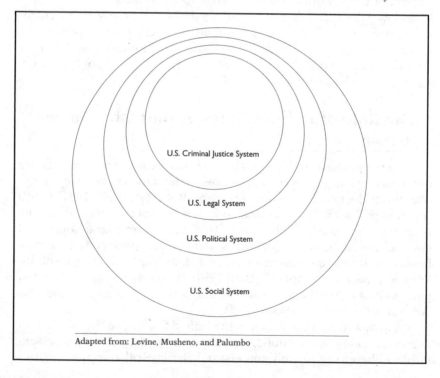

U.S. Criminal Justice System

U.S. Legal System

U.S. Political System

U.S. Social System

Adapted from: Levine, Musheno, and Palumbo

mayors and town or city councils; county executives of many types and county courts or commissions; governors and state legislatures; and finally, the President of the United States and the United States Congress. Most of these groups and individuals are elected, and ultimately they answer to the electorate.

The next circle as we move inward is the nation's **legal system.** Here legislative bodies are once again represented along with courts and other adjudicative entities. The legal system includes the lawmakers and the law deciders.

The innermost circle is the **criminal justice system.** Traditionally, it is described as having three principal components: police, courts, and corrections. Law enforcement agencies operate at local (city and county), state, and federal levels. Today there are 17,784 state and local law enforcement agencies of various types, plus those at the federal level. Additionally, the most recent data from the Bureau of Justice Statistics (2005) indicate that there are 796,518 sworn law enforcement officers at all levels. The court system in reality is 51 court systems, those of the federal government and the states. Further, many jurisdictions also operate city and county courts. Finally, correctional agencies and organizations also operate at all three levels of government. Jails and similar detention facilities represent local institutional corrections, with state and federal prisons rounding out the picture. There are also a number of community-based correctional programs, including probation and parole, group homes, and reintegration centers or halfway houses that provide support for prisoners returning to the community.

Thus, the criminal justice system in the United States is part of the legal system. The legal system is part of the political system, and the political system is part of the larger social system of the nation (see Calvi and Coleman 2004). This illustration demonstrates the connection between politics and the policymaking process and operations of the criminal justice system. Historically, criminal justice activities were seen as a local concern, and they were influenced primarily by local politics. In the past four decades, state and federal governments have become increasingly involved in justice systems. In the following chapters, we explore some of the implications of this trend and the reasons for these changes.

Sources of Law and Policy

In the United States, there are numerous sources of law, and fundamentally, each source and type of law is an expression of policy. Although you have studied most of the sources and types of law in other courses, we briefly review these in this section to set the stage for the discussions that follow.

At the highest level in this country is **constitutional law.** We have the Constitution of the United States of America, and each of the 50 states has its own unique constitution. The U.S. Constitution declares

Box 1.2
What Is Policy?

Unlike the word *politics*, for which definitions abound, definitions for *policy* are a little more elusive. At its core, policy is a course of action or a direction established by one of the three branches of government—executive, legislative, or judicial—or by administrative agencies. *Black's Law Dictionary* (1991, 801) defines *policy* as the "general principles by which a government is guided in its management of public affairs, or the legislature in its measures."

As this chapter demonstrates, policies arise from a number of governmental entities. These policies are developed through the political process, and their implementation and enforcement set criminal justice agencies on certain courses of action. In reading through this text (particularly Chapters 3–14), keep in mind the policy development, implementation, and enforcement processes. Ask yourself the following questions as you read each chapter:

(1) What is the primary policy that is designed to address this problem?
(2) When was the policy developed?
(3) Who were the major players who favored or opposed the policy?
(4) Has the policy been implemented as it was envisioned?
(5) Has the policy achieved the desired effect(s)?

Engaging in this exercise will help you make better sense of the sometimes chaotic world of criminal justice policies and processes. ✦

that it is the "supreme law of the land." This means that every statute and every court decision at every level must square with the dictates of the Constitution.

The **Bill of Rights,** the first 10 amendments to the Constitution, are of particular importance, and the Fourth, Fifth, Sixth, and Eighth Amendments define many of the protections related to the criminal justice process. These amendments spell out the guarantees that citizens have from unreasonable intrusions into their rights by the government. The protections provided by state constitutions often mirror the U.S. Constitution, and some states provide for even more extensive rights.

A second source of law in this country is **common law.** We inherited the common law traditions from England, and 49 of the 50 states (Louisiana is the exception since it operates under a civil law, or Napoleonic Code, tradition), as well as the federal government, have legal systems that are influenced by common law. In England, the common law was unwritten, judge-made law based on local mores and customs. As the common law system of jurisprudence matured, court decisions were based on the decisions that had gone before, and the notion of precedent became a strong value in common law countries such as the United States.

It is important to remember that the common law is not static; it changes over time. For example, if college students decide as a rite of spring to run naked on the campus, they might be arrested and charged

Box 1.3
The Bill of Rights and the Criminal Justice System

We outlined four constitutional amendments that deal principally with criminal justice processes in the United States. These are the Fourth, Fifth, Sixth, and Eighth Amendments. To better understand the impact of these amendments on criminal justice policy, we describe them and briefly discuss the significance of each amendment on making sense of criminal justice.

Fourth Amendment

The right of the people to be secure in their persons, houses, papers, and effects against unreasonable searches and seizures, shall not be violated, and no warrants shall issue, but upon probable cause, supported by oath or affirmation, and particularly describing the place to be searched, and the persons or things to be seized.

This amendment is especially important in situations where the police must obtain a warrant to make an arrest or in situations where they intend to search for drugs, weapons, or other fruits or instrumentalities of crime. There are several exceptions to the search warrant requirement, and the police will employ these when possible (for example, incident to arrest, plain view, exigent circumstances, and consent searches). However, the courts often view warrantless searches as presumptively unreasonable. This means that the courts—especially appellate courts—will engage in policymaking by defining and redefining for the police the acceptable parameters of legal searches.

Fifth Amendment

No person shall be held to answer for a capital, or otherwise infamous, crime, unless on a presentment or indictment of a grand jury . . . nor shall any person be subject for the same offense to be twice put in jeopardy of life or limb; nor shall be compelled in any criminal case to be a witness against himself, nor be deprived of life, liberty, or property, without due process of law; nor shall private property be taken for public use, without just compensation.

The Fifth Amendment allows states some flexibility in the filing of criminal charges. While the federal courts employ grand juries to establish probable cause, only about half of the states use them.

One area that creates some confusion in the criminal justice system is the protection against double jeopardy. For instance, if an individual robs a bank and state authorities file armed robbery charges and the FBI files charges for robbing a federally insured institution, is this double jeopardy? The answer is "no" because of the legal doctrine of *difference of sovereigns*. How about a case in which an individual appeals a conviction for murder and the appellate courts overturn the conviction and order a new trial. Is this double jeopardy? Again, the answer is "no." Suppose an individual robbed several men in a neighborhood poker game, and he was tried and acquitted of robbing one of the men. Could he then be tried for robbing the others? The U.S. Supreme Court in the case of *Ashe v. Swenson* (1970) held that since all of the robberies were part of a single event, this did constitute double jeopardy.

The Supreme Court also articulated one of its most famous policy statements in *Miranda v. Arizona* (1966) when it said that the police must warn suspects in custodial interrogations that they have the right to remain silent (Fifth Amendment) and that suspects have the right to an attorney during questioning (Sixth Amendment).

Sixth Amendment

In all criminal prosecutions, the accused shall enjoy the right to a speedy and public trial, by an impartial jury of the state and district wherein the crime shall have been committed . . . and to be informed of the nature and cause of the accusation; to be confronted with the witnesses against him; to have compulsory process for obtaining witnesses in his favor, and to have the assistance of counsel for his defense.

This is often considered the trial amendment, and it represents two important policy dimensions. First, it provides for a speedy and public trial. As a result of the ambiguity over the meaning of a *speedy trial* (see, for example, *Barker v. Wingo* 1972), in 1974 Congress passed a speedy trial law (18 U.S.C., Sect. 3161) requiring that federal criminal defendants be indicted within 30 days of arrest, arraigned within 10 days of indictment, and tried within 60 days of arraignment, absent court-granted continuances. Since 1974, all states have followed suit and dictate that criminal defendants be brought to trial within 90 to 180 days, depending on the specific state. Obviously, such legislation has an impact on the courts and the speed with which they can move their criminal dockets, given their limited resources.

The second policy consideration arising out of the Sixth Amendment is the right to counsel. Originally, this provision was understood to include only federal cases, and if the defendant could afford a lawyer, he or she was entitled to be represented by one. However, a series of U.S. Supreme Court cases—including *Powell v. Alabama* (1932), *Gideon v. Wainwright* (1963), and *Argersinger v. Hamlin* (1972)—established the right to counsel for indigent state defendants. This means that states now must provide some system of defense for the nearly 60 percent of criminal defendants who cannot afford their own attorney.

Eighth Amendment

Excessive bail shall not be required, nor excessive fines imposed, nor cruel and unusual punishments inflicted.

Eighth Amendment issues have been raised with increasing frequency in the past 20 years. Of special concern has been the use of pretrial or preventive detention (see *Schall v. Martin* 1984 and *United States v. Salerno* 1987). Part of the policy debate in this area centers around whether the Eighth Amendment provides for the right to bail, and when and under what circumstances judges should be able to deny bail to criminal defendants. At this point, the courts have refused to recognize an absolute "right to bail," and judges still have the option of setting high money amounts of bail to prevent detainees from being released.

The "cruel and unusual punishment" clause of the Eighth Amendment has surfaced in regard to two different—although somewhat related—issues: the death penalty and prison conditions. Prison inmates have raised a number of concerns regarding the death penalty, but to date, the U.S. Supreme Court has upheld the constitutional validity of capital punishment.

By contrast, inmates have been successful in challenging the conditions of confinement under which they are held. These suits have dealt with crowding, food services, recreation, the quality and number of security staff members, medical treatment, and a variety of other concerns. The courts have been somewhat sympathetic to prisoners' rights litigation, and more than 30 states have had all or parts of their prison systems under court order to improve conditions of confinement. ✦

with common law lewdness even though there was no specific law prohibiting running naked. In truth, today most common law offenses
have been supplanted by statutes.

Statutory law is what most people envision when they think of the
concept of law. Legislatures enact criminal and civil statutes, as well as
substantive and procedural statutes. Statutes are created by local, state,
and federal law-making bodies. City councils and county commissions,
state legislatures, and the U.S. Congress develop statutory laws as a series of written codes that are systematically compiled and published in
regularly updated volumes. Most university and public libraries have
copies of your state's codes, as well as the criminal and civil codes of the
federal government. If you are not familiar with these volumes, now is a
good time to take a trip to the library to thumb through them.

Case law, as a source of law, is related to both constitutional law and
statutory law. Case law results from the decisions of state and federal
appellate courts. In most instances, when these courts decide cases, the
judges or justices issue written opinions that are published in volumes,
which often are called "reports" or "reporters." Although your college
or university may not have a law school, your library might have copies
of some of the regional or federal reporting series, or you can find key
cases through commercial legal services such as LEXIS/NEXIS© or Web
sites such as findlaw.com.

Appellate courts are referred to as collegial courts because cases are
decided by groups of judges rather than by a single judge as in the initial
trials. When appellate judges hear cases, they must decide what the Constitution provides, what the relevant statutes say, and what all of this
means. Therefore, case law clearly illustrates the notion of judicial interpretation and, to a very large extent, demonstrates the policymaking
power of judges. However, it is essential to emphasize that case law will
apply only to the level of government for which the particular court has
jurisdiction. This means that cases decided by a state supreme court are
binding only on the courts and citizens of that particular state. By extension, cases decided by the U.S. Supreme Court apply to all federal courts,
all state courts, and all U.S. citizens.

A final source of law and a clear source of policy in the United States
is **administrative law,** sometimes called **regulatory law.** State administrative or regulatory agencies can be the source for some of these
laws, but the most visible sources are the federal regulatory agencies.
Most of these agencies are part of the "alphabet soup" of the federal
government, and they include the Federal Communications Commission (FCC), the Federal Aviation Administration (FAA), the Interstate
Commerce Commission (ICC), the Securities and Exchange Commission (SEC), the Food and Drug Administration (FDA), the Occupational
Safety and Health Administration (OSHA), the Environmental Protection
Agency (EPA), and many others. These agencies have rulemaking powers
that border on law creation. They can propose regulations that apply to

individuals, businesses, and organizations and publish these proposed regulations in the *Federal Register*. After an appropriate period of publication, review, and comment, these regulations become administrative laws unless challenged in court and overturned by a judge.

It is essential for us to fully understand these sources of law and the roles they play in law and policymaking in our society. In the following section, we examine in greater detail how the legislative process creates laws and otherwise defines the operations of the criminal justice system.

Politics and Legislative Processes and Functions

While legislatures operate outside of the domain normally associated with the criminal justice system, much of what legislative bodies do impacts criminal justice operations. For example, legislatures enact both substantive and procedural laws. The laws created by legislatures give the criminal justice system and its agents more procedural rules to follow and laws to enforce. As previously mentioned, legislatures enact civil laws and criminal laws. Within the category of criminal laws, offenses are designated as either felonies or misdemeanors. Legislative bodies can even make further distinctions by establishing different levels of felonies (first-, second-, and third-degree felonies, for example), and they can categorize misdemeanors by degrees or as petty misdemeanors or simply as misdemeanors.

Legislatures also are responsible for creating many types of courts, including new specialized courts such as gun courts, drug courts, and mental health courts. The exceptions to this statement, of course, are the so-called Article III courts of the United States. These courts are covered in Article III of the U.S. Constitution, and they provide most of the federal judicial branch with some independence from the other two branches of government.

Even in this realm, however, Congress can establish new federal court districts and can create new federal circuit courts of appeals.[1] Additionally, state legislatures and the U.S. Congress can modify the jurisdictions of courts from time to time. For example, at the state level, legislatures have removed some of the most serious offenses, such as murder, from the jurisdiction of the juvenile courts and have placed the jurisdiction for these cases in adult courts. In a few states, juvenile courts and adult courts may have concurrent jurisdiction over certain offenses, which means that prosecutors can file charges in either juvenile or adult courts. Less serious crimes, such as traffic law violations, also may be removed from juvenile courts and placed in the adult courts that hear similar cases.

Finally, legislative bodies appropriate or disperse the funds that pay for the salaries, equipment, training, and other costs associated with operating criminal justice agencies. This is a major expenditure for most levels of government in the United States. For example, the Bureau of Justice Statistics reported that $185 billion were spent in the United States on justice system expenditures in 2003 (Hughes 2006). It is interesting that in 2003 almost 2.4 million people worked in all facets of the criminal justice system in the United States, accounting for a one-month payroll of approximately $9 billion. The majority of justice system employees work for local (city and county) governments, and most of them provide police protection. About one third of the justice system employees work for state governments, and 62 percent are employed in corrections. The remainder (11 percent) work for the federal government, most in law enforcement-related duties (Hughes 2006). All of these numbers indicate something of the magnitude of justice system expenditures in the United States, and legislative bodies are obligated to provide the funding necessary to meet the needs of police, court, and correctional agencies.

This section demonstrates that the U.S. legislatures at both the state and federal levels play a major role in defining criminal justice policy. Legislative bodies establish laws, as well as create regulatory agencies that exercise oversight of certain industries, such as transportation, aviation, and environmental protection, on behalf of the legislature (Calvi and Coleman 2004). In addition, the legislative branch holds the purse strings for all aspects of the criminal justice system in the United States. The allocation of funding clearly is one way legislatures can define and redefine policies.

Policymaking and Criminal Justice

Before we close this chapter, it is important to consider the world of public policy and how policy is related to the political process. Hojnacki (2000, 6) says there are four characteristics of government activity that define public policy:

(1) Only governmental entities and actors or agents of government can "make and implement public policy."

(2) Policies are deliberate acts "designed to achieve some predetermined goals and objectives."

(3) Policies involve what is done, not just what might be intended to be done (however, as we will see, there still can be a gap between what was intended and what was accomplished).

(4) Policies should be consistent and predictable in their application and not left to the interpretation of individual governmental agents.

He adds that "[p]ublic policy is the product of the political system" and is "whatever the government chooses to do or not to do" (Hojnacki 2000: 6, 19).

Levine, Musheno, and Palumbo (1986, 8–9) described six stages of the policymaking process that are related to criminal justice (or any other public agencies, for that matter):

(1) The first stage is *agenda setting*. This is where a problem becomes apparent enough that some governmental action seems warranted.

(2) The second stage is *policy formulation*. Alternatives are developed for dealing with the problem, and compromises often are worked out.

(3) The third stage involves *policy implementation*. Administrative agencies formulate a specific program or plan of action to tackle the problem.

(4) *Policy impact* is the fourth stage of the policymaking process. Impact is concerned with the extent to which the policy that has been implemented addresses the initial problem.

(5) *Policy evaluation* is the fifth stage in the process. Here there is an analysis of whether and how the policy has achieved its goals.

(6) The sixth and final stage is *termination*. A policy will be ended if it has not achieved the intended goals and objectives.

To more fully appreciate the policymaking process, let us examine each of the six stages more carefully.[2] To do this, we take the specific example of driving while intoxicated (DWI) or under the influence (DUI) to illustrate what can happen. First, the problem is identified in the agenda-setting stage. This may occur after the appearance of news media accounts of notorious cases. The public often shows a growing concern, particularly when someone has been arrested 20 times for DWI or a family is killed on Christmas Eve by a drunk driver. Some famous person also could be involved in these situations either as a victim or an offender, which Walker (2006) called "celebrated cases." Additionally, **public interest groups** such as Mothers Against Drunk Driving (MADD) help to set the legislative agenda.

The second stage—policy formulation—typically takes place in the legislative arena. This may occur at the national, state, or local levels. However, all three branches of government (legislative, executive, and judicial) may be involved, and often the result is a new law or a modification to an existing law (making penalties for certain crimes more severe, for example). Box 1.4 discusses the importance of funding, budget formulation, and priorities that arise in the legislative process.

The policy implementation stage can be problematic for a variety of reasons. For example, we must emphasize that laws do not necessarily change human behavior, and again, drunk driving is a good example.

Box 1.4
The Money Game

State legislatures and the U.S. Congress spend a lot of their time considering bills that are proposed by the executive branch of government (the governor or the President), as well as bills that arise from legislators themselves. Eventually, for most legislation, the question seems to be: What is this going to cost? As a result, every legislative body in the country has a budget or finance office that will provide some estimate on the price tag for a particular piece of legislation (for example, in New Mexico, the legislative body that performs this function is the Legislative Finance Committee).

The budgetary process involves politics like in every other stage of arriving at legislation. Legislators try to persuade one another that certain bills are worthy of passage and funding. In the process, there can be trade-offs. In effect, one legislator says to another (or to others), "You vote for my bill, and I'll vote for yours." The result is a budgetary "Christmas tree" with something for everyone. However, this does not ensure that problems are approached in a systematic and comprehensive manner. Much of the legislative process addresses matters in a piecemeal fashion, and therein lies some of the problems in dealing with a social issue such as crime. We may end up doing what is popular (most state legislators really like bricks-and-mortar projects such as new prisons) or politically expedient, not necessarily what is "best."

The most appealing pieces of legislation are the most likely to pass and to receive significant funding. In effect, the dollar amounts attached to particular bills say something about where these items fit in the executive or legislative (or both) list of priorities. Again, some legislation is very partisan (associated with one political party or the other), and some is bipartisan (supported by both political parties), but it is all political. ✦

New laws and stiffer penalties may or or not reduce drunk driving. Even threatening repeat offenders with prison terms will not stop some people from driving while intoxicated. Furthermore, the agencies charged with implementing the laws (the police, for example) may modify the aims of the legislation to fit their own goals or missions, and resource limitations (for example, money, personnel, and/or equipment) may make some laws or policies difficult to implement.

To illustrate how funding can influence legislation, we return to our example of DUI. In the 1980s and 1990s, many states established blood alcohol levels of .10 (10 grams per 210 liters of breath) as the legal benchmark for driving while intoxicated. The federal government, however, tied the granting of billions of dollars in federal highway funding to the stipulation that states must establish a blood alcohol level of .08 as the standard for intoxication. Although states were able to maintain the .10 standard, they would suffer significant financial consequences for not adopting the lower level. As a result, the .08 blood alcohol content is now the standard in all 50 states.

An example of policy implementation involves the issue of drunk driving (see Box 1.5). When we look at the problem of drunk driving, we clearly can see issues related to policy impact. Quite often politicians,

Box 1.5
Why Good Ideas Go Bad or Bad Ideas Go Good

There are many reasons why a particular policy may fail. The concept may be flawed from its inception, it may be poorly implemented (or not implemented at all), or the program or policy may suffer from lack of evaluation or follow-through. Of all of these, implementation is the most critical factor. Briefly, let us consider the problems associated with poor implementation.

First, legislatures may ask criminal justice agencies to do the impossible. For instance, no law, policy, or program will stop some people from driving while intoxicated. If legislators think that adding 50 more state police officers (or highway patrol officers, depending on the state) will significantly impact the DWI problem, they may be disappointed. Furthermore, there is no guarantee that an increase in the number of officers (without a specific legislative mandate) will result in an increased police presence on the highways. Some of these officers may be diverted to equally pressing functions within the department.

Second, agencies may not know specifically what the legislative intent is for passing a bill. The legislature may enact a tough seatbelt law (after receiving lobbying pressure from the insurance industry), but there may be no indication of whether officers should employ "active" enforcement (looking for motorists who are not wearing seatbelts) or "passive" enforcement (merely citing motorists for seatbelt violations when they are stopped for other infractions).

Finally, sometimes new laws are passed with no additional resources. New responsibilities may fall into the all too familiar "other duties as assigned" category, and as a result, there may be little implementation of the new law given employees' already busy schedules. This can be seen in some jurisdictions where judges regularly impose restitution orders on probationers, with the assumption that probation officers (POs) will be the enforcers. POs simply may ignore this part of the sentence because they are unwilling or unable to be collection agents.

By contrast, some ideas are politically appealing and are implemented very effectively. Nevertheless, that does not mean that such ideas will have the intended policy results. Let us look at a few examples.

First, consider gun control, a topic we examine more fully in Chapter 5. A quick search of one of the legal sites on the Internet reveals that the United States is a nation of gun laws. In fact, when all of the federal, state, and local laws are combined, the total is several thousand. How much impact have these laws had on gun violence in the United States? The answer is probably very little. Several points seem especially relevant here:

- An estimated 238 to 276 million firearms are in circulation in the United States. If no other firearms were manufactured or sold from this day forward, the existing stockpile of weapons would last into the twenty-second century.
- Most of the firearms owned in the United States are used very seldom, and nearly all are used legally.
- Most of the illegal use of firearms is by people who may not legally own or possess weapons in the first place.
- Most criminals obtain firearms through "straw purchases" (someone lawfully purchases a weapon for another person who cannot buy one legally; this

---

practice is a violation of federal law), theft of weapons in burglaries, or in black market sales.

Additional laws and stepped-up enforcement by agencies such as the Bureau of Alcohol, Tobacco, Firearms, and Explosives (ATF) might have some impact on firearms and criminal activity (especially violence), but probably very little (see Kleck 2004).[3]

Second, consider get-tough sentencing, such as the three-strikes laws adopted by almost half of the states. We examine sentencing changes in Chapter 6; but for the moment, let us look at the unintended consequences of these politically popular sentencing changes.

When the first "three-strikes and you're out" laws were passed, the assumption by the general public was that the aim was incapacitation of violent offenders. However, quite often these offenders are incarcerated for long periods of time for their crimes, and it may become mathematically impossible for them to qualify for a third strike. If we look at the sentencing records of states such as California, what we see is that persistent nonviolent offenders are most likely to qualify for enhanced sentencing (25 years to life) under the three-strikes provision. Therefore, on the one hand, the public may be no safer as a result of greatly enhanced sentences; and on the other hand, a situation has been created where the scarce and expensive commodity of prison space has been filled with nonviolent property offenders (Mays and Winfree 2005; Kovandzic, Sloan, and Vieraitis 2004). There is also the possiblity that these very long sentences will result in injustice from the imposition of disproportionately harsh punishments.

These areas illustrate some of the difficulties associated with policy implementation. Some good policy ideas are poorly implemented or not implemented at all, and other policies of questionable value are implemented fully but with unintended consequences. In either case, the end result involves some dimension of policy failure. ✦

---

members of the general public, and public interest groups will ask, "Why don't the laws stop drunk driving?" The answers are as complex as the problem. Perhaps the best way to respond is through another series of questions. Has the law been fully implemented? Do the police have the resources (or the knowledge) to apprehend a significant proportion of drunk drivers? Are we making correct assumptions about human behavior? For example, does punishment really serve as a deterrent? Are we dealing with a driving problem or a drinking problem (alcoholism)? Asking these questions helps us develop a better appreciation for the difficulty in addressing many social problems.

Evaluation research increasingly has become a key component related to criminal justice policies. In fact, many of you taking this course have been required to take a research methods class, and you still are not sure why. Perhaps we can answer that for you now. A variety of answers help explain this question, but for our purposes, one use of research—program evaluation—is especially appropriate.

Evaluation often is mandated when state and federal governments give agencies money to implement a certain program. Evaluation research determines how funds were used and the degree to which a program could be termed a success. However, it is important to emphasize that success is not the only criterion for program continuation. For example, we might have an anti-DWI program that does not seem to have much impact but continues because it is popular with politicians and the police. Often we find government programs outliving their initial mandate simply because they are politically popular. An illustration of criminal justice programs that have continued to exist, in the face of negative research findings, is correctional boot camps. When boot camps began to appear in the early 1980s, a number of states jumped on the bandwagon to create such programs. Within a decade, research had demonstrated little efficacy of boot camps (MacKenzie and Shaw 1990; MacKenzie, Shaw, and Gowdy 1993). Nevertheless, they appealed to politicians and members of the general public who saw them as dispensing "real" punishment.

This brings us to the issue of program termination. We find with many criminal justice projects that programs may be ended because of, in spite of, or without careful evaluation (see Levine, Musheno, and Palumbo 1986, 18). As previously noted, some programs continue because they are politically or publicly popular (the Drug Abuse Resistance and Education or DARE program comes to mind here). By the same token, effective or successful programs may not flourish because they do not have political support or constituencies that lobby for them. Prison industries programs come to mind as an example. Although prison industries can generate income and provide inmates with valuable work experience, the public strongly believes that inmates are less deserving of such opportunities than the least deserving members of free society. In addition, some private companies protest prison industries despite the fact that they provide inmates with jobs and save state governments money. One notable example is an office furniture company that protests that government contracts for furnishings often go to prison industries.

As we have noted, policies are made in a variety of ways. We previously pointed out that the "political" branches of government (the executive and the legislative branches) are explicitly in the business of policymaking. The President and state governors enact policies through cabinet-level officials, and they articulate their policy directions through the budget-making process. For example, during the Presidency of Bill Clinton, one of the major national priorities was adding more law enforcement officers to state and local police agencies. The Justice Department created the Office of Community-Oriented Policing Services (COPS) "to help law enforcement agencies implement and enhance community policing" (COPS 2005). It was to provide federal funding for 100,000 new police officers nationwide. Although this goal has not been reached to date, there has been a significant net increase in the number of U.S. police officers, especially at the local level. We return to the topic of community policing in Chapter 3.

Under Republican Presidents Nixon, Ford, and Reagan, the federal government initiated and supported a "war on drugs" (actually a series of such "wars"). Money was poured into increased law enforcement efforts and, to a lesser extent, education and treatment programs. Again, these and various other anticrime programs illustrate the role the federal government has played in developing and articulating crime control policy.

Congress aids in the policy process by conducting hearings, passing legislation, and—as previously discussed—providing the funding to implement such programs. However, Congress can on its own initiative develop crime control policy as well. Members of the House of Representatives or the Senate may receive requests from justice agencies in their home states to aid in providing funding or new laws. For example, the recent debate over immigration reform has seen state and local law enforcement agencies along the U.S.-Mexico border lobbying members of Congress for help in "securing the border." At times, the President and the Congress may be developing legislative proposals that are parallel to one another. In other instances, these two branches of government may create proposals that are in conflict.

Although the executive and legislative branches most often are thought of in regard to the creation of policy, it is important to acknowledge once again that the judicial branch certainly has an impact on the policy process. Several recent Supreme Court rulings clearly illustrate this point. First, in the cases of **Blakely v. Washington** (2004), and in **United States v. Booker** and the companion case of **United States v. Fanfan** (2005), the Supreme Court ruled that the Federal Sentencing Guidelines, developed by the U.S. Sentencing Commission and enacted into law by the U.S. Congress, could not be imposed in a mandatory fashion on federal judges. Judges could use the guidelines in an advisory manner, but the specific sentences could not be prescribed for federal judges. Congress could establish broad sentencing parameters, but judges had the ultimate authority to decide what a particular sentence should be. Second, in the case of **Roper v. Simmons** (2005), the Supreme Court struck down the death penalty laws of 19 states as they applied to 16- and 17-year-olds tried as adults for murder. Using the notion of "evolving standards of decency," the five-member majority held that states may impose life sentences (even without parole) for 16- and 17-year-olds convicted of murder, but that the direction taken by the majority of states and the weight of world opinion were against executing such individuals. Without a doubt, these recent cases demonstrate the ability of the courts (and especially the Supreme Court) to affect the policy process.

Conclusions

The criminal justice system in the United States is intimately linked to the political system. That is both a good news and a bad news situation. It is good news because criminal justice policy should reflect the popular will of the citizens. Criminal justice policy is influenced by political elites, politicians, public interest groups, the general public, business interests, and the news media. In some cases public opinion leads public policy, and in other cases it follows public policy; however, these policies should be openly debated and developed in an atmosphere that allows for public scrutiny and comments. This means that criminal justice policy is linked to the political processes and political agendas of a broad range of groups and individuals. The bad news about this is that policies such as the "war on drugs" and the "three-strikes-and-you're-out" laws of the 1980s and 1990s have remained publicly and politically popular. However, this does not mean that they will have the effect that was envisioned for them. At best, some of these policies might turn out to be ineffective. At worst, they might produce an opposite outcome of what originally was envisioned.

As you read the following chapters that address current issues in the criminal justice system, keep in mind the role politics plays in the development of policy. Each of these issues represents a major policy dimension within the criminal justice system, and each illustrates the ways in which politics can affect policies.

Notes

1. This was done most recently when Congress split the U.S. Court of Appeals for the Fifth Circuit, which extended from Florida to Texas, and established the new U.S. Court of Appeals for the Eleventh Circuit, comprising Alabama, Georgia, and Florida. Texas, Louisiana, and Mississippi remain in the Fifth Circuit. There also has been much discussion of late about dividing the Ninth Circuit (considered by many to be the most liberal of the circuits), which currently includes Arizona, California, Nevada, Oregon, Washington, Idaho, and Montana.

2. Much of this discussion is based on the framework developed by Levine, Musheno, and Palumbo (1986, 8–18).

3. ATF has gone through a history of reorganization and redefinition. Originally, it was called the Alcohol Tax Unit (ATU) of the Treasury Department, when it was created during Prohibition (the period of the "Untouchables"). During the late twentieth century, the name was changed to add firearms enforcement to the agency's mandate. In the wake of the 9/11 attacks on New York and Washington, federal law enforcement was substantially reorganized. Many of ATF's responsibilities were transferred to the Justice Department, and "explosives" was officially added to the list of agency duties. In Chapter 14, we address some of the significant changes that occurred in federal law enforcement after the 9/11 attacks.

Key Terms

administrative law   *Barker v. Wingo*   case law
Argersinger v. Hamlin   Bill of Rights   common law
Ashe v. Swenson   *Blakely v. Washington*   constitutional law

criminal justice system	*Powell v. Alabama*	statutory law
Gideon v. Wainwright	public interest groups	*United States v. Booker*
legal system	regulatory law	*United States v. Fanfan*
Miranda v. Arizona	*Roper v. Simmons*	*United States v. Salerno*
political system	*Schall v. Martin*	
politics	social system	

Critical Review Questions

1. A fellow student in one of your classes makes this statement: "Politics has no place in the U.S. criminal justice system." How do you respond and why?

2. What is the relationship between the political system and the criminal justice system in the United States?

3. The fact that criminal justice processes are spread over three levels of government (local, state, and federal) and three branches of government (legislative, executive, and judicial) contributes to some sense of inefficiency. Why do we have a criminal justice system that is arranged in such a fragmented and decentralized way? What would be the "costs" associated with having a more efficient system? (You might want to revisit this question after you finish Chapter 14.)

4. In many high school civics classes, students are taught that the legislative branch of government "makes the laws." Is this an accurate statement? Why or why not?

5. What do we mean by the common law and how does it compare with modern statutory law? You might want to make lists of the features of each.

6. Is case law really "law"? Explain.

7. Are "politics" and "policy" two distinct notions or simply parts of something bigger? Explain your answer.

8. Make a list of the reasons why a new, tougher law aimed at curbing drunken driving might not be effective.

References

Ashe v. Swenson, 397 U.S. 436 (1970).

Argersinger v. Hamlin, 407 U.S. 25 (1972).

Bardes, Barbara A., Mack C. Shelley, and Steffen W. Schmidt. (2006). *American Government and Politics Today: The Essentials*. Belmont, CA: Wadsworth.

Barker v. Wingo, 407 U.S. 514 (1972).

Black's Law Dictionary. (1991). St. Paul, MN: West.

Blakely v. Washington, 542 U.S. 296 (2004).

Bureau of Justice Statistics. (2005). "Law enforcement statistics." Retrieved July 24, 2006, from: *http://www.ojp.usdoj.gov/bjs/lawenf.htm*.

Calvi, James V., and Susan Coleman. (2004). *American Law and Legal Systems*, fifth edition. Upper Saddle River, NJ: Prentice Hall.

Community-Oriented Policing Services, Office of. (COPS) (2005). "About COPS funding." Retrieved July 24, 2006 from: *http://www.cops.usdoj.gov*.

Dahl, Robert A. (1991). *Modern Political Analysis, fifth edition*. Englewood Cliffs, NJ: Prentice Hall.

Gideon v. Wainwright, 372 U.S. 335 (1963).

Hojnacki, William P. (2000). "The public policy process in the United States." Pp. 5–21 in *Public Policy, Crime, and Criminal Justice*, second edition, edited by Barry W. Hancock and Paul M. Sharp. Upper Saddle River, NJ: Prentice Hall.

Hughes, Kristen A. (2006). *Justice Expenditures and Employment in the United States, 2003*. Washington, DC: U.S. Department of Justice, Bureau of Justice Statistics.

Kleck, Gary. (2004). "The great American gun debate: What research has to say." Pp. 470–487 in *The Criminal Justice System: Politics and Policies*, ninth edition, edited by George F. Cole, Marc G. Gertz, and Amy Bunger. Belmont, CA: Wadsworth.

Kovandzic, Tomislav, John J. Sloan, and Lynne Vieraitis. (2004). "Unintended consequences of politically popular sentencing policy." Pp. 456–469 in *The Criminal Justice System: Politics and Policies*, ninth edition, edited by George F. Cole, Marc G. Gertz, and Amy Bunger. Belmont, CA: Wadsworth.

Levine, James P., Michael C. Musheno, and Dennis J. Palumbo. (1986). *Criminal Justice in America: Law in Action*. New York: Wiley.

MacKenzie, Doris L., and James W. Shaw. (1990). "Inmate adjustment and change during shock incarceration: The impact of correctional boot camp programs." *Justice Quarterly* 7 (1), 125–150.

MacKenzie, Doris L., James W. Shaw, and Voncile Gowdy. (1993). *An Evaluation of Shock Incarceration in Louisiana*. Washington, DC: U.S. Department of Justice.

Magleby, David B., David M. O'Brien, Paul C. Light, James MacGregor Burns, J. W. Peltason, and Thomas Cronin. (2006). *Government by the People*, twenty-first edition. Upper Saddle River, NJ: Prentice Hall.

Mays, G. Larry, and L. Thomas Winfree, Jr. (2005). *Essentials of Corrections*, third edition. Belmont, CA: Wadsworth.

Miranda v. Arizona, 384 U.S. 436 (1966).

Powell v. Alabama, 287 U.S. 45 (1932).

Roper v. Simmons, 543 U.S. 551 (2005).

Schall v. Martin, 467 U.S. 253 (1984).

Sego, Michael A. (1977). *Who Gets the Cookies III: A Realistic Look at American Government*. Brunswick, OH: Kings Court Communications.

Sidlow, Edward, and Beth Henschen. (2007). *America at Odds*, fifth edition. Belmont, CA: Wadsworth.

United States v. Booker (and United States v. Fanfan), 543 U.S. 220 (2005).

United States v. Salerno, 481 U.S. 739 (1987).

Walker, Samuel. (2006). *Sense and Nonsense About Crime and Drugs: A Policy Guide*, sixth edition. Belmont, CA: Wadsworth.

Recommended Readings

Cole, George F., Marc G. Gertz, and Amy Bunger. (2004). *The Criminal Justice System: Politics and Policy*, ninth edition. Belmont, CA: Wadsworth.
   This reader contains elements of traditional introduction to criminal justice textbooks in that it covers police, prosecution, courts, and corrections. However, the theme around which the book is organized is the interaction of politics and policy in the administration of justice. The first section of the book (which contains the two models

developed by Herbert Packer that are discussed in the next chapter of this text) is called "Politics and the Administration of Justice." The final section, called "Policy Perspectives," deals with a number of the issues discussed in this text.

Hancock, Barry W., and Paul M. Sharp. (2000). *Public Policy, Crime, and Criminal Justice*, second edition. Upper Saddle River, NJ: Prentice Hall.

Hancock and Sharp organize their reader around three major headings: "Public Policy and Crime," "Public Policy and Criminal Justice," and "Trends in Public Policy, Crime, and Criminal Justice." Part II of the book deals with the standard police, courts, and corrections issues, although Hancock and Sharp have been very selective in choosing topics for the book. Chapter 1, entitled "The Public Policy Process in the United States" (cited in this chapter), provides a foundational view of how public policy is made in a number of administrative and governmental arenas.

Marion, Nancy E., and Willard M. Oliver. (2006). *The Public Policy of Criminal Justice*. Upper Saddle River, NJ: Prentice Hall.

This new text takes a political science/public policy approach to examining criminal justice. In Chapter 3, the authors analyze the public policy process in depth, and in Chapters 4–7, they look at what each branch of government brings to the development of criminal justice policy. Three chapters in this book are particularly noteworthy: Chapter 8, which considers the influence of public opinion and the media; Chapter 9 on interest groups; and Chapter 14, which develops a case study of criminal justice policy. ✦

Chapter 2

Crime Control Versus Due Process

Introduction

A number of different models have been used to explain criminal justice operations in the United States. Two models that are frequently encountered in introductory criminal justice courses were proposed by **Herbert Packer.** In 1968, Packer published an insightful book, entitled *The Limits of the Criminal Sanction,* which described the two models—crime control and due process. They are the focus of this chapter and should provide you with a clear way of making sense of criminal justice policies as you read the remainder of this book.

One of the first points to emphasize about Packer's models is that they are prototypes or ideal types. In other words, in the real world you might not find them in their pure form. They are abstractions of reality and not reality itself, just as a model train is an oversimplified representation of a real train.

Second, Packer himself was quick to emphasize that the two models do not represent the "is" versus the "ought to be," or the "real" versus the "ideal." They are not intended to be representations of the way a perfect criminal justice system would operate. They simply provide us with *two different viewpoints* for interpreting why the system operates the way it does and, in turn, the way criminal cases are processed.

These two views sometimes are characterized as "conservative" versus "liberal," and it is these descriptions that provide a simple and usually correct labeling system (see Walker 2006; Wylie-Marques 2002). However, we cannot merely assume that the crime control model is conservative without question and that the due process model is liberal. That would present an oversimplification or a generalization that might be hard to defend. In reality, many criminal justice policies in the United States contain elements that are both conservative and liberal. They frequently serve multiple and, unfortunately, competing purposes. With these caveats in mind, let us turn to examining the features of Packer's two models.

The Crime Control Model

At the most basic level, the crime control model operates from a viewpoint that protecting the welfare of the majority of citizens is more important than the rights or liberties of any single individual. Public safety becomes a principal concern for advocates of the crime control model, and fundamentally they believe that if we are not safe as a society, then individuals are not safe either.

This means that the **crime control model** supports the suppression of crime in society. The police should be able to prevent some crimes; however, in the absence of crime prevention, they will respond in a reactive way to investigate crimes and to apprehend suspects. Such actions by the police and the vigorous prosecution of accused offenders are thought to promote the law's deterrent effect. In a sense, the efficiency of the crime control model should demonstrate to all the swift, sure, and accurate operation of the legal system and the punishment of offenders.

In terms of criminal justice operations, the crime control model relies heavily on the operations of the police and prosecutors. Law enforcement agencies often are characterized as the "thin blue line" that stands between civilization and anarchy. To the extent that this is true, the police carry the bulk of crime control responsibilities. Crime control, then, is predicated on the fact-finding and criminal investigative functions of law enforcement agencies and prosecutors at various levels in the United States. Adherents of the crime control model trust the police and prosecuting attorneys to do an adequate job of gathering evidence and screening for legal sufficiency in order that there can be an arrest and eventual conviction of people who violate the law.

One of the ironies of focusing on the police in the crime control model centers on the view that a significant amount of police time and a number of resources are devoted to crime fighting. As most students of criminal justice quickly learn in their first year of course work, the vast majority of the typical police officer's time is concentrated on order maintenance and public service. This leaves crime control as a relatively minor—though symbolically significant—part of the job.

The operations of the crime control model are built around notions such as efficiency, coupled with swift and final resolution of cases. Packer (1968, 159) stated, "There must then be a premium on speed and finality. Speed, in turn, depends on informality and on uniformity; finality depends on minimizing the occasions for challenge." This "emphasis on speed favors plea bargaining, prosecutorial discretion, and mandatory sentencing in which occasions for legal challenge are minimized" (Wylie-Marques 2002, 377). Therefore, similar types of cases are lumped together and are treated similarly. This means that the crime control model operates much like an assembly line with "routine and stereotyped procedures" (Packer 1968, 159). **Assembly-line jus-tice** is based on this characterization.

Assembly-line justice is a label applied to the rapid and routine han-dling of cases, particularly by the lower-level criminal courts in the United States. Holten and Lamar (1991, 64) noted that the lower-level (or infe-rior) courts have been faulted for

> their capriciousness, their arbitrariness, their ignorance of the law and
> of proper procedure, their denial of fundamental rights to some liti-
> gants and defendants, their subservience to local political cliques, and
> their concern with generating fines and fees for themselves and their
> towns or counties.

However, rapid and routine processing of cases is not only confined to the inferior courts but also apparent in most criminal justice opera-tions. Welch (2002, 77) said that within the crime control model, as-sembly-line justice "stresses efficiency, reliability, and productivity, as measured by increases in arrests, convictions, and incarcerations." In other words, like a factory assembly line, the justice assembly line aims at handling the maximum number of cases, in the shortest time possi-ble, with the lowest expenditure of resources.

One element that must be factored into assembly-line justice is the operation of the **courtroom work group** (Eisenstein and Jacob 1977). The courtroom work group is composed of a changing cast of charac-ters, but at its core are the judge, prosecutor, and defense attorney. This group pursues a number of organizational goals, among which are foster-ing cooperation and expediting case processing (see Eisenstein and Jacob 1977; Neubauer 2005). The foundation of this approach is a shared under-standing of the most appropriate sanction ("the going rate") for a given offense within that court. This means that it is in the best interest of all members of the courtroom work group (but perhaps not the defendant) to limit arguments on a case as long as the proposed sanction is within the range of those normally imposed. Thus, through its interactions, the courtroom work group actually may facilitate the crime control model and promote assembly-line justice.

The final feature often associated with the crime control model is what Packer (1968, 160) named a "**presumption of guilt**," sometimes called **factual guilt.** In the criminal justice system, we are accustomed to hearing that a person is innocent unless and until the state can prove him or her guilty. Nevertheless, the presumption of guilt assumes that the vast majority of defendants are guilty. If a person is innocent or if there is a problem with the case, it will be kicked off the assembly line by the agents responsible for quality control. Therefore, the presump-tion of guilt is a "prediction of outcome," meaning that it is likely the person is guilty and will be found guilty. The farther the case progresses along the assembly line, the higher the level of guilt presumed by members of the news media, most agents of the criminal justice system, and even some potential jurors.

One way to understand factual guilt or the presumption of guilt is to examine a hypothetical case. Assume the police receive a burglar alarm call to a school building late at night. A search of the building turns up a suspect hiding under a desk in one of the classrooms. It is safe to assume that a high level of factual guilt—that is, a presumption of guilt— attaches to such a person. The police believe (they would say they really "know") that he is guilty. The prosecutor handling the case believes that the person is guilty, and if a jury hears the facts, they may agree that the suspect or defendant is guilty as well. However, it is essential to emphasize here that even the person caught in *flagrante delicto* (in other words, red-handed) has the right to insist on a trial and to make the state *prove* him or her guilty. As we will see later in this chapter, the practical effect of the presumption of guilt is to keep the assembly line moving through the use of plea bargaining.

As you read through the remainder of this book, ask yourself if the topics being presented and the policies being examined can be classified as crime control. (As a note of warning, some issues are much more easily classified than others.) Do they promote efficiency within the criminal justice system, along with the processing of offenders in a rapid and routine manner? Policies that on their surface are aimed at increased public safety are, by definition, crime control oriented.

The Due Process Model

The concept of due process is found in the Fifth and Fourteenth Amendments to the U.S. Constitution, and while the Constitution does not define *due process*, the Supreme Court consistently has emphasized that *due process* means "that which is fundamentally fair." **Substantive due process** provides that laws not only be fair but also promote some legitimate governmental purpose or function. By contrast, **procedural due process** defines the ways in which the government must go about applying laws in a just and evenhanded manner (see Kelly 2002). Taken together, these two elements of due process mean that the federal and state governments can, and often do, intrude into the lives of citizens in various ways, but that they must do so in a way that is fair.

The **due process model** is based on the protection of the individual accused of crime, as outlined in the Constitution of the United States, along with state constitutions and federal and state statutes. Due process is the idea that the government must pursue legitimate purposes (substantive due process) and it must do so in a fundamentally fair way (procedural due process).

This model is much more concerned with formal fact-finding procedures than is the crime control model. This fact finding typically occurs in the give-and-take of the criminal trial. It rejects the goals of speed and efficiency in disposing a case and instead stresses getting at the truth. Efficiency and finality take a back seat to trying to eliminate errors. Packer (1968, 165) noted, "The aim of the process is at least as much to protect the factually innocent as it is to convict the factually guilty." The phrase "It is better for 10 guilty people to go free than for one innocent person to go to prison" illustrates the values associated with the due process model.

In terms of the two models we are considering here, Wylie-Marques (2002) said that the due process model is the opposite of the crime control model. However, Packer (1968) emphasized that the two models are simply different ways of viewing criminal justice processes. Whereas the roles of the police and prosecutors tend to dominate discussions of the crime control model, the courts—and especially the appellate courts—take center stage in the due process model.

Finally, while the crime control model operates on a presumption of guilt (or factual guilt), the due process model is based on the notion of **legal guilt.** Legal guilt (or the **presumption of innocence**) tells criminal justice officials how they are to proceed in processing a case, and it is not "a prediction of outcome" (Packer 1968, 161). Saying that defendants are presumed innocent does not mean that they likely are innocent or that it is likely they will be found innocent. It means that guilt is not to be assumed. Therefore, guilt can exist only when the state has proven the defendant guilty beyond a reasonable doubt and the jury has returned a verdict of guilty.

The due process model frequently is characterized as being supported by liberals. However, a more accurate characterization is that it is supported by civil libertarians, and not just those who belong to civil liberties groups. It stresses the fundamental fairness and procedural regularity with which the government should behave toward those individuals suspected of criminal activity. In the end, due process protects not only those people accused of criminal activity, but also it protects all of us.

The Practical Differences Between the Models

Now we need to ask the question So what? In other words, what difference does it make which model of the criminal process we prefer or which one may be in operation at any one time? Answering the "so what" question often is not that easy, and in the end many walk away from this discussion largely unsatisfied. Nevertheless, we should examine the development of criminal justice policy in the United States since the 1960s, particularly in light of Packer's two models.

Many of you reading this chapter will immediately identify at a fundamental level with some or all of the tenets of either the crime control model or the due process model. This says something about your perspective or world-view. As you will see, you are not alone in holding a particular perspective. Quite often politicians, policymakers, and members of the general public will share your perspective. Yet, one should keep in mind that history has repeatedly demonstrated that what is popular is not always right, nor is what is right always popular.

For example, conservatives or crime control advocates often stress the idea that people commit crimes as a result of rational choices, or their own free will. As a result, the response is that offenders should be held fully culpable for their acts, and they should be punished accordingly. By contrast, liberals may take the position that everyone in society is subject to a variety of influences, and none of us is totally a free moral agent. Therefore, we need to take into consideration the social, psychological, and biological factors that influence people to engage in a variety of behaviors (including crime). These perspectives help different people make sense of why people behave in certain ways—for example, why people commit crimes or why some people commit certain crimes. We often call these various perspectives *theories*, although that is sometimes a word from which students recoil. For our purposes in this text, it is important to remember that criminal justice policies in the United States frequently are enacted with one of these two theoretical viewpoints in mind.

Crime Control Model Policies

As mentioned previously, the crime control model is assumed by most people to represent a conservative orientation toward controlling law-violating behavior (Walker 2006; Wylie-Marques 2002), and the due process model illustrates a liberal (or civil liberties) view. If this is correct, what has been the dominant philosophy guiding criminal justice policy in the United States in recent years?

It is safe to say that since the late 1960s, the United States has been in a protracted period of enacting crime control policies. Richard Nixon used crime as a major political issue in his 1968 presidential campaign. Once elected, Nixon began his Presidency promising to get tough on crime and to appoint federal judges who were conservative or who held a nonactivist orientation in their judicial decision making. This change was significant because before the 1960s, crime was considered a local matter and federal politicians had little interest in "street crime." Beckett and Sasson (2000) contend that the only way the federal government could get involved in fighting street crime was to increase drug enforcement.

One of the first pieces of legislation that passed under Richard Nixon's Presidency was the Omnibus Crime Control and Safe Streets Act of 1968.[1] This law provided substantial federal funding for state and local law enforcement agencies in order for them to better train and equip their officers through the Law Enforcement Assistance Administration (Mabrey 2005). This legislation also created the Law Enforcement Education Program (LEEP) that would pay part of the costs for police officers to attend college. As a result of the LEEP program, the number of colleges offering law enforcement (and later criminal justice) degrees—from the associate's degree through the doctorate—increased from a few dozen to over 1,200 (see Morn 1980; Ward and Webb 1981). Some people have compared the impact of the LEEP program in the 1960s and 1970s to the GI Bill after World War II in spurring college attendance.

In case it seems that the crime control orientation has been linked only with Republican Presidents (although this is largely true), during the Presidency of Bill Clinton, two clear examples of crime control legislation were signed into law (Mabrey 2005). In 1994, President Clinton signed the Violent Crime Control and Law Enforcement Act, and in 1996, he signed the Antiterrorism and Effective Death Penalty Act (AEDPA). These two pieces of legislation expanded the death penalty in federal cases, as well as limited appeals by prison inmates.

Crime control policies have been manifested in other ways as well. For example, Richard Nixon's "war on crime" of the 1960s and 1970s eventually gave way to a "war on drugs" waged by both Presidents Reagan and Bush in the 1980s. Increasing amounts of federal money were poured into the interdiction and apprehension efforts of law enforcement agencies, especially those at the federal level. The Drug Enforcement Administration became the front-line agency in America's "war on drugs," and while some monies were earmarked for drug education and treatment, the lion's share of funding went into law enforcement and suppression efforts.

The 1970s and 1980s also saw changes in state and federal sentencing policies. At this time, there was much debate over sentencing purposes in the United States. Both liberals and conservatives were dissatisfied with the system of **indeterminate sentences** that had been in place for nearly 100 years. This system, along with discretionary parole (as created by legislative bodies), gave state parole boards and correctional officials considerable discretion in how much time an offender would serve in prison (Champion 1989; Knapp and Hauptly 1989). The work of people such as David Fogel (1975) and others provided the philosophical justification for the development of **determinate sentences,** and a number of states (led by Maine in 1976) moved to eliminate discretionary parole (see Anspach, Lehman, and Kramer 1983). By eliminating parole, it was said to add **truth in sentencing,** so that offenders would serve most of their sentences (less any "good time" credits earned). The result was a movement toward not only determinate sentences but also more predictable sentencing through the use of **sentencing guidelines.** Sentencing guidelines provide a prescriptive plan by which judges determine the appropriate sentence, given the offender's present offense and criminal history. The guidelines typically are developed by a government commission and then enacted into law by the appropriate legislative body. In most instances, the guidelines become binding on all judges within the particular jurisdiction (such as a state).

In the end, the results were more people incarcerated and longer average sentences for offenders, a goal that was supported by crime control model advocates (see DiIulio 2001; Wright 2004). For example, from yearend 1990 until midyear 2005, the number of people held in federal and state prisons nearly doubled, from 1,148,702 to 2,186,230 (Harrison and Beck 2006). This growth in inmate population occurred at the same time that crime rates were decreasing. Crime control advocates argued that the increase in incarceration resulted in the decrease in crime rates. Others (see Donziger 1996; Tonry 1999) argued that the two trends operate independently of one another and that there are other explanations for the increase in imprisonment rates, such as changes in public opinion, partisan politics, political fragmentation, and the rise of the prison-industrial complex in the United States (Ruddell 2004).

Although we will consider juvenile crime more fully in Chapter 13, it is important to note at this point that the crime control model also has influenced the operation of the juvenile justice system in the United States. Beginning in the early 1980s, several states instituted policy changes to get tough with what was perceived as a substantial juvenile crime wave (Bernard 1992). Among the measures that were enacted were lowering the age at which youngsters could be tried as adults from the age of 16 in many states to 15 or even 14 years. Also, the number of offenses that qualified for transfer was expanded (Butts and Mears 2001). Additionally, many states legislatively excluded certain young offenders from juvenile courts and automatically transferred them to adult court jurisdiction. For example, many states now exclude youngsters who have committed offenses that call for life in prison, including homicides and other serious personal offenses such as rape, armed robbery, or kidnapping (Gardner 2003).

In addition to making it easier to transfer teenagers to adult courts, state juvenile codes were also amended to transform juvenile sentences from indeterminate to determinate, and a small number of states implemented sentencing guidelines for juveniles that closely paralleled those of their adult counterparts (Mears 2002). Juvenile court hearings became increasingly formal, and while many youngsters still were diverted from the formal system of adjudication, those who remained faced harsher penalties (Butts and Mears 2001; Fox 1996). Altogether these changes mark a trend similar to the decreasing emphasis on rehabilitation for adult offenders.

Illustrations of get-tough, crime control-oriented penalties imposed on juveniles involve adult prison sentences and the death penalty. A limited number of states (New Mexico among them) have developed what are called **blended sentences** (Torbet, Griffin, Hurst, and MacKenzie 2000). This approach allows for either juvenile sentences or adult sentences (including prison time) to be imposed on youngsters. Under New Mexico's blended sentencing scheme, **youthful offenders** do not know whether they will receive juvenile or adult sanctions until their case is adjudicated and the judge decides which set of penalties seems most appropriate (Mays and Gregware 1996). For those youngsters who meet statutory age and offense criteria, adult penalties—including incarceration in the state's adult prisons—are very real possibilities. Occasionally, the response by crime control advocates is that "if you're old enough to do the crime, you're old enough to do the time."

The ultimate sanction for any offender is the death penalty. In the case of *Furman v. Georgia* (1972), the U.S. Supreme Court ruled that the death penalty, as it was imposed, was arbitrary and capricious. When Georgia and a number of other states rewrote their death penalty laws, a challenge was again mounted; however, the Supreme Court ruled, in *Gregg v. Georgia* (1976), that the revised capital punishment statutes were constitutional. Every year since 1976, the Supreme Court has received challenges to the death penalty, and while the Court has issued rulings that have refined the circumstances under which executions are imposed (and the people who should qualify for execution), the Court has never shown an indication that it was willing to declare capital punishment, in-and-of itself, as a violation of the Eighth Amendment's prohibition of cruel and unusual punishment.[2] By contrast, in 1996 Congress passed the Antiterrorism and Effective Death Penalty Act that restricted the time limits and the bases for appeals by state and federal inmates. The restrictions imposed by AEDPA limit *habeas corpus* appeals by prisoners and also restrict the time limits within which all appeals (including those arising in capital cases) must be filed.

Due Process Model Policies

After reviewing the previous section, it would be easy to conclude that after two decades of dominance by the crime control model that the due process model is dead or at least dying. Perhaps the response by Mark Twain to premature newspaper reports of his death is appropriate here: "The reports of my death have been greatly exaggerated." In the same way, it is premature to report the death of the due process model in the criminal justice system in the United States.

Arguably, the golden era of the due process model was during the time period when Earl Warren was Chief Justice of the U.S. Supreme Court (1953 to 1969). In the first half of the 1960s, the Warren Court issued rulings in such historic cases as *Mapp v. Ohio* (1961), *Escobedo v. Illinois* (1964), *Gideon v. Wainwright* (1963), and *Miranda v. Arizona* (1966).[3] These decisions articulated or expanded the due process rights of adult criminal defendants and similar rights also were extended to accused delinquents in decisions such as *Kent v. United States* (1966), *In re Gault* (1967), *In re Winship* (1970), and *Breed v. Jones* (1975).[4]

The "due process revolution" of the 1960s led groups such as the John Birch Society to begin an "Impeach Earl Warren" campaign. While there have been criticisms of some of the procedural due process cases decided by the Supreme Court, a great deal of the Warren Court's legacy remains intact. In fact, among the three branches of government, the Supreme Court (even in its current, largely conservative, configuration) seems the most committed to notions of due process. For example, in the relatively recent case of *Kyllo v. United States* (2001), the Supreme Court ruled that an exterior scan of a house with a thermal scanning device, in order to detect the heat signature of "grow lights" to allow indoor cultivation of marijuana, constituted a search and required officers to obtain a search warrant. Also, in *Missouri v. Seibert* (2004), the Court held that it was unconstitutional for the police to interrogate a suspect without giving the *Miranda* warnings. In this case, the police deliberately did not give the *Miranda* warnings and questioned a suspect until a confession was obtained. Then they questioned the suspect again after giving *Miranda* warnings and tried to use the second confession.

Although the U.S. Supreme Court generally has retained a due process orientation, even with a fairly conservative plurality on the Court, there have been concerns in some states that the Court has retreated from the standards established during the Warren Court era. Therefore, some state supreme courts (and not just those of more "liberal" states) have taken the stand that the Court sets the *minimum* due process constitutional standards, but that state supreme courts can apply state constitutional provisions that establish even greater personal protections.[5] This means that in areas such as Fourth Amendment search and seizure cases, state supreme courts may decide cases based on their state constitution that are more restrictive than decisions provided by the U.S. Supreme Court.

For example, Hayes (1999) said that there was a concern in some states that the U.S. Supreme Court "was retreating in its protection of individual rights." At the same time, the Supreme Court seemed to encourage "state courts to utilize state constitutions as the basis of their rulings concerning constitutional rights." Thus, in *State v. Gomez* (1997), the New Mexico Supreme Court did not support some warrantless searches by the police that might be permitted by the U.S. Supreme Court (Hayes 1999). In simplest terms, this demonstrates that the efficacy of the due process model does not depend solely on the U.S. Supreme Court and that other state and federal courts apply this model as well.

It is also important to ask what other evidence we might have today of the vitality of the due process model. At least three illustrations come to mind. First, as discussed, the use of determinate sentencing is a way to promote truth in sentencing. Several states have adopted sentencing guidelines with the explicit purpose of limiting or eliminating sentence disparities (see Mays 2004). A review of court rulings over the past three decades demonstrates that similarly situated offenders often did not receive similar sentences. Under indeterminate sentencing schemes, judges were permitted to consider or ignore a wide array of factors in deciding on the appropriate sentence. Legislatures gave them that authority, and it was exercised with a great deal of discretion. Sentencing guidelines normally consider only two factors—present offense and criminal history—in determining the sentence. Under the determinate sentencing system, factors such as race, gender, drug use, and employment history are supposed to be irrelevant, and sentence disparities should all but disappear. While human nature still plays a role in the sentencing process, most states with mandatory sentencing guidelines have found that the degree of disparity among cases has been reduced among various racial and ethnic groups and between males and females.[6]

Second, addressing disparity in the juvenile justice system has become an explicit priority of the Office of Juvenile Justice and Delinquency Prevention (OJJDP), a division of the U.S. Department of Justice. One of OJJDP's national priority goals is to identify, address, and remedy **disproportionate minority contact (DMC)** among juvenile offenders.[7] State juvenile authorities are challenged to examine every stage of the processing of juvenile offenders to determine if African-American, Hispanic, American Indian, and Pacific Island youngsters (among others) are overrepresented at any stage of the handling of accused delinquents. For OJJDP's purposes, the population at risk includes those 10 to 17 years old.

Research to date shows that at virtually every stage, from arrest through adjudication and incarceration, minority youths are overrepresented in juvenile justice processes (see Dean, Hirschel, and Brame 1996; Devine, Coolbaugh, and Jenkins 1998; Pope and Feyerherm 1995). Therefore, the DMC initiative by the federal government has clear due process dimensions. In Chapter 7, we address the topic of race and incarceration and the mistrust that many minority groups have of the criminal justice system. It has been speculated that ensuring just and fair outcomes in justice systems may actually increase the likelihood that citizens will follow the law (Tyler 2006).

Third, as a result of the identification of individuals wrongfully convicted of crimes, many states now are requiring testing of DNA evidence in cases such as murder or rape.[8] In fact, many states have passed laws allowing convicted defendants to have their cases reopened to allow for DNA testing of evidence that was obtained before DNA testing was available.[9] Although DNA testing is somewhat expensive and time-consuming, it represents another technicality or potential detour in the obstacle course that is procedural due process, but the expanding use of DNA evidence may minimize the likelihood of wrongful convictions (see Huff, Rattner, and Sagarin 1996; Mays, Purcell, and Winfree 1992; Purcell, Winfree, and Mays 1994).

Conclusions

Herbert Packer's models of the criminal process give us two ways to view the processing of criminal cases in the United States. However, in a broader context, these models also tell us something about the development of criminal justice policies and the orientations of politicians and policymakers at all levels of government. In examining the underlying assumptions of the crime control and due process models, several conclusions become apparent.

First, it is difficult to find either the crime control model or the due process model in its purest form almost anywhere. The two models exist as something of hybrids in most jurisdictions across the United States. In fact, it probably is most accurate to think of the two models as existing along a continuum. Therefore, moving from one state or locality to another, from one level of government to another, or among the various branches of government will move us toward one end of the continuum or the other.

Second, the U.S. Supreme Court clearly operated in the due process domain for much of the 1960s and even into the 1970s. At the same time, virtually every president elected since 1968 has had a more or less crime control orientation. Among these presidents, perhaps Jimmy Carter had the least overt law-and-order orientation, and Ronald Reagan seemed to be the most focused on crime control issues. Regardless of one's political office or party affiliation, however, no politician wants to be labeled "soft on crime."

Third, even today—with the crime control model still dominating state and federal policies—elements of the due process model can be found throughout the system. Therefore, we are left to ask, Which model will hold sway in the next decade, and what social, political, or economic issues will cause a society to shift from one of these models or paradigms to another?

Notes

1. In reality, the Omnibus Crime Control and Safe Streets Act had been proposed, but not passed, during the end of Lyndon Johnson's Presidency.

2. While the Supreme Court has never ruled that capital punishment is unconstitutional *per se*, recent cases have illustrated the Court's increasingly restrictive view of who should be eligible for the death penalty. Cases such as ***Atkins v. Virginia*** (2002) and ***Roper v. Simmons*** (2005) have held that capital punishment should not be imposed on mentally retarded individuals or on people under the age of 18 at the time they committed their crimes.

3. *Mapp v. Ohio* extended the exclusionary rule first articulated in ***Weeks v. United States*** (1914) to the states. *Escobedo v. Illinois* and *Miranda v. Arizona* addressed the issue of right to counsel during police custodial interrogations, and *Gideon v. Wainwright* extended the right to counsel to state felony defendants in noncapital cases.

4. *Kent* was concerned with the right to a transfer hearing for juveniles who faced trial as adults, as well as the right to counsel at transfer hearings. *In re Gault* addressed a wide range of due process issues such as the notification of charges, the right to confront and cross-examine accusing witnesses, protection against self-incrimination, and the right to counsel during delinquency adjudications. Some of these decisions spilled over from the 1960s into the 1970s during a period when Warren Burger, a "strict constructionist," was Chief Justice of the Supreme Court.

5. A hard-and-fast rule that certain state supreme courts are liberal is somewhat difficult to establish. However, on issues like privacy, the medical use of marijuana, same-sex marriages, and the right-to-die, supreme courts in California, Connecticut, Hawaii, New York, and Oregon have developed reputations that they are more liberal than supreme courts in many other states.

6. However, see the recent Supreme Court cases of ***Blakely v. Washington*** (2005) and ***United States v. Booker*** and ***United States v. Fanfan*** (2005) striking down the mandatory nature of the federal sentencing guidelines based on the degree of departure allowed judges in imposing sentences.

7. This is a concept to which we will return in Chapter 6.

8. According to the Innocence Project (2007), 188 wrongfully convicted people had been freed based upon DNA evidence by January 2007.

9. See, for example, *New Mexico Statutes Annotated*, Section 31-1A-2, which provides, in part, "A person convicted of a felony, who claims that DNA evidence will establish his innocence, may petition the district court of the judicial district in which he was convicted to order the disclosure, preservation, production and testing of evidence that can be subjected to DNA testing."

Key Terms

assembly-line justice	*Furman v. Georgia*	presumption of guilt
Atkins v. Virginia	*Gideon v. Wainwright*	presumption of inno-
Blakely v. Washington	*Gregg v. Georgia*	cence
blended sentences	*habeas corpus*	procedural due process
Breed v. Jones	indeterminate sentences	*Roper v. Simmons*
courtroom work group	*In re Gault*	sentencing guidelines
crime control model	*In re Winship*	*State v. Gomez*
determinate sentences	*Kent v. United States*	substantive due
disproportionate minor-	*Kyllo v. United States*	process
ity contact (DMC)	legal guilt	truth in sentencing
due process model	*Mapp v. Ohio*	*United States v. Booker*
Escobedo v. Illinois	*Miranda v. Arizona*	*United States v. Fanfan*
factual guilt	*Missouri v. Seibert*	*Weeks v. United States*
flagrante delicto	Packer, Herbert	youthful offenders

Critical Review Questions

1. Compare and contrast the various elements of Packer's two models of the criminal process. Where in the criminal justice system are we most likely to find the two different models at work? Explain.

2. Are politicians correct when they assume that the public demands increasingly harsher sanctions for criminal offenders? Is this a figment of the politicians' imaginations, or do they have substantial evidence of the punitive orientation of the public?

3. How do substantive due process and procedural due process differ? Which of these is more likely to be associated with the public's perception of technicalities in the processing of criminal cases?

4. What are the differences between indeterminate sentencing and determinate sentencing? Which (if either) of these is more consistent with the crime control model? Which with the due process model? Do sentencing guidelines fit with either of the two models? Explain.

5. Do we have any evidence that the death penalty serves as a deterrent to would-be killers? What has been the general trend since the mid-1970s in the rulings by the U.S. Supreme Court in regard to the death penalty? What about the Court's recent decision in *Roper v. Simmons*, 543 U.S. 551 (2005) prohibiting the death penalty for offenders younger than 18 years of age? Does this signal a new direction?

References

Anspach, Donald F., Peter M. Lehman, and John H. Kramer. (1983). *Maine Rejects Indeterminacy: A Case Study of Flat Sentencing and Parole Abolition.* Washington, DC: National Institute of Justice.

Atkins v. Virginia, 536 U.S. 304 (2002).

Beckett, Katherine, and Theodore Sasson. (2000). *The Politics of Injustice: Crime and Punishment in America.* Thousand Oaks, CA: Pine Forge Press.

Bernard, Thomas J. (1992). *The Cycles of Juvenile Justice.* New York: Oxford University Press.

Blakely v. Washington, 542 U.S. 296 (2004).

Breed v. Jones, 421 U.S. 519 (1975).

Butts, Jeffrey A., and Daniel P. Mears. (2001). "Reviving juvenile justice in a get-tough era." *Youth & Society* 33 (2), 169–198.

Champion, Dean J. (1989). "The U.S. Sentencing Guidelines: A summary of selected problems and prospects." Pp. 231–239 in *The U.S. Sentencing Guidelines: Implications for Criminal Justice,* edited by Dean J. Champion. New York: Praeger.

Dean, Charles W., J. David Hirschel, and Robert Brame. (1996). "Minorities and juvenile case dispositions." *Justice System Journal* 18 (3), 267–285.

Devine, Patricia, Kathleen Coolbaugh, and Susan Jenkins. (1998). *Disproportionate Minority Confinement: Lessons Learned From Five States.* Washington, DC: U.S. Department of Justice, Office of Juvenile Justice and Delinquency Prevention.

DiIulio, John J., Jr. (2001). "Prisons are a bargain, by any measure." Pp. 119–120 in *Debating Crime: Rhetoric and Reality,* edited by David W. Neubauer. Belmont, CA: Wadsworth.

Donziger, Steven R., editor. (1996). *The Real War on Crime*. New York: HarperCollins.

Eisenstein, James, and Herbert Jacob. (1977). *Felony Justice: An Organizational Analysis of Criminal Courts*. Boston: Little, Brown.

Escobedo v. Illinois, 378 U.S. 478 (1964).

Fogel, David. (1975). *". . . We Are the Living Proof. . ." The Justice Model for Corrections*. Cincinnati, OH: Anderson.

Fox, Sanford J. (1996). "The early history of the court." *Future of Children* 6 (3), 29–39.

Furman v. Georgia, 408 U.S. 238 (1972).

Gardner, Martin R. (2003). *Understanding Juvenile Law*, second edition. New York: Matthew Bender/LexisNexis.

Gault, In re, 387 U.S. 1 (1967).

Gideon v. Wainwright, 372 U.S. 335 (1963).

Gregg v. Georgia, 428 U.S. 153 (1976).

Harrison, Paige M., and Allen J. Beck. (2006). *Prison and Jail Inmates at Midyear 2005*. Washington, DC: U.S. Department of Justice, Bureau of Justice Statistics.

Hayes, Curtis. (1999). "The new federalism: New Mexico's experience with independent state constitutional analysis of Fourth Amendment rights." Paper presented at the annual meeting of the Southwestern Criminal Justice Association, September 30–October 2, Ft. Worth, Texas.

Holten, N. Gary, and Lawson L. Lamar. (1991). *The Criminal Courts*. New York: McGraw-Hill.

Huff, C. Ronald, Arye Rattner, and Edward Sagarin. (1996). *Convicted but Innocent: Wrongful Conviction and Public Policy*. Thousand Oaks, CA: Sage.

Innocence Project. (2007). *http://www.innocenceproject.org/*.

Kelly, William E. (2002). "Due process." Pp. 586–589 in *Encyclopedia of Crime and Punishment*, edited by David Levinson. Thousand Oaks, CA: Sage.

Kent v. United States, 383 U.S. 541 (1966).

Knapp, Kay A., and Denis J. Hauptly. (1989). "U.S. Sentencing Guidelines in perspective: A theoretical background and overview." Pp. 3–18 in *The U.S. Sentencing Guidelines: Implications for Criminal Justice*, edited by Dean J. Champion. New York: Praeger.

Kyllo v. United States, 533 U.S. 27 (2001).

Mabrey, Daniel. (2005). "Homeland security funding, strategies, and needs." *Telemap Bulletin* 12 (2). Huntsville, TX: Bill Blackwood Law Enforcement Management Institute of Texas, Sam Houston State University.

Mapp v. Ohio, 367 U.S. 81 (1961).

Mays, G. Larry. (2004). "Sentences and sentencing guidelines." Pp. 1502–1505 in *Encyclopedia of Criminology*, edited by Richard A. Wright and J. Mitchell Miller. Hampshire, U.K.: Taylor & Francis.

Mays, G. Larry, and Peter R. Gregware. (1996). "The children's code reform movement in New Mexico: The politics of expediency." *Law & Policy* 18 (1 & 2), 179–193.

Mays, G. Larry, Noreen Purcell, and L. Thomas Winfree, Jr. (1992). "DNA (deoxyribonucleic acid) evidence, criminal law, and felony prosecutions: Issues and prospects." *Justice System Journal* 16 (1), 111–122.

Mears, Daniel P. (2002). "Sentencing guidelines and the transformation of juvenile justice in the 21st century." *Journal of Contemporary Criminal Justice* 18 (1), 6–19.

Miranda v. Arizona, 384 U.S. 436 (1966).

Missouri v. Seibert, 542 U.S. 600 (2004).

Morn, Frank. (1980). *Academic Disciplines and Debates: An Essay on Criminal Justice and Criminology as Professions in Higher Education*. Chicago: Joint Commission on Criminology and Criminal Justice Education and Standards.

Neubauer, David W. (2005). *America's Courts and the Criminal Justice System*, eighth edition. Belmont, CA: Wadsworth.

Packer, Herbert. (1968). *The Limits of the Criminal Sanction*. Stanford, CA: Stanford University Press.

Pope, Carl E., and William Feyerherm. (1995). *Minorities and the Juvenile Justice System.* Washington, DC: U.S. Department of Justice, Office of Juvenile Justice and Delinquency Prevention.

Purcell, Noreen, L. Thomas Winfree, Jr., and G. Larry Mays. (1994). "DNA (deoxyribonucleic acid) evidence and criminal trials: An exploratory survey of factors associated with the use of 'genetic fingerprinting' in felony prosecutions." *Journal of Criminal Justice* 22 (2), 145–157.

Roper v. Simmons, 543 U.S. 551 (2005).

Ruddell, Rick. (2004). *America Behind Bars: Trends in Imprisonment, 1950-2000.* New York: LFB Scholarly Press.

State v. Gomez, 122, N.M. 777, 932 P. 2d 1 (1997).

Tonry, Michael. (1999). "Why are U.S. incarceration rates so high?" *Crime and Delinquency* 45 (4), 419–437.

Torbet, Patricia, Patrick Griffin, Hunter Hurst, Jr., and Lynn Ryan MacKenzie. (2000). *Juveniles Facing Criminal Sanctions: Three States That Changed the Rules.* Washington, DC: U.S. Department of Justice, Office of Juvenile Justice and Delinquency Prevention.

Tyler, Tom R. (2006). *Why People Obey the Law.* Princeton, NJ: Princeton University Press.

United States v. Booker, 543 U.S. 200 (2005).

United States v. Fanfan, 543 U.S. 200 (2005). [Companion case to *U.S. v. Booker.*]

Walker, Samuel. (2006). *Sense and Nonsense About Crime and Drugs,* sixth edition. Belmont, CA: Wadsworth.

Ward, Richard H., and Vincent J. Webb. (1981). *Quest for Quality.* Chicago: Joint Commission on Criminology and Criminal Justice Education and Standards.

Weeks v. United States, 232 U.S. 383 (1914).

Welch, Michael. (2002). "Assembly-line justice." Pp. 77–80 in *Encyclopedia of Crime and Punishment,* edited by David Levinson. Thousand Oaks, CA: Sage.

Winship, In re, 397 U.S. 358 (1970).

Wright, Richard A. (2004). "In support of prisons." Pp. 249–263 in *Criminal Justice in America: Theory, Practice, and Policy,* third edition, edited by Barry W. Hancock and Paul M. Sharp. Upper Saddle River, NJ: Prentice Hall.

Wylie-Marques, Kathryn. (2002). "Crime control model." Pp. 376–380 in *Encyclopedia of Crime and Punishment,* edited by David Levinson. Thousand Oaks, CA: Sage.

Recommended Readings

Abadinsky, Howard (2003). *Law and Justice: An Introduction to the American Legal System,* fifth edition. Upper Saddle River, NJ: Prentice Hall. Abadinsky's book provides an overview of the legal system in the United States, including the roles of judges, prosecutors, and defense attorneys in the system. However, throughout the book, he deals with the concept of due process, and the chapter on history especially highlights the notion of civil liberties and the "civil rights revolution." This chapter also addresses some of the due process decisions that came out of the U.S. Supreme Court during the time that Earl Warren served as Chief Justice.

Fogel, David (1975). ". . . *We Are the Living Proof . . ." The Justice Model for Corrections.* Cincinnati, OH: Anderson. A number of people contributed to the intellectual development of the justice model or just deserts approach to criminal justice, but Fogel's book brought most of this material together for the first time. This notion became the driving force behind much criminal justice policy in the 1980s and 1990s.

Packer, Herbert L. (1968). *The Limits of the Criminal Sanction.* Stanford, CA: Stanford University Press. Although they are now nearly 40 years old, the materials discussed by Packer are still relevant today. In fact, this book has become a standard point of reference for many introductory textbooks in the field of criminal justice, and it remains one of the most influential works ever published on this topic. It provides the framework for this chapter, and it should be required reading for all students of criminal justice. ✦

Chapter 3

The Search for a Guiding Philosophy of Policing

Introduction

Traditionally, in the United States the police have been characterized as performing three functions: order maintenance, public service, and law enforcement. Order maintenance focuses on maintaining peace and civility in a community. Order maintenance requires police to deal with loud music or noisy parties, barking dogs, and other types of activities that might disturb the tranquility of a neighborhood. Public service is something of a catchall, and it may involve a lost child, animals running loose, overgrown lots and abandoned cars, or even a dented trash can. Public service involves any type of action in which citizens do not know whom else to call about a particular problem. Law enforcement duties include traffic citations, crime reports, and arrests for misdemeanors and felonies. Other responsibilities could be added to the list, but fundamentally all police duties fall into one of these three categories.

Order maintenance was one of the first justifications for creating civilian law enforcement agencies and that, along with public service, continues to consume a great deal of police time and resources. Ironically, many police officers view their primary function as law enforcers. This perspective is reinforced by the amount of initial training devoted by recruits to law enforcement topics (often over 80 percent).

This image is perpetuated by some police departments, and the public has come to expect police officers to be crime fighters. In fact, the crime-fighting orientation attracts some people to the field of policing, and the news and entertainment media seem to be fascinated with the crime-fighting image. This view is consistent with the crime control model (see Chapter 2). However, research (Harris 1973; Wilson 1968) shows that police officers often spend fewer than 20 percent of their working hours devoted to law enforcement duties, even broadly defined. Therefore, is it realistic for us to believe they can have a significant effect on crime? We must acknowledge that there are crime-related factors (outside of the reach of government) that may be beyond the ability of the police to address.

In this chapter, we review the historical bases for policing in the United States, beginning with developments in England that were transferred to this country. We also examine some of the phases through which policing in the United States has passed. This will provide the foundation for our inquiry into the contemporary search for a paradigm or model to guide policing. This search not only affects current approaches to policing, but also influences the nature of police work as we progress into the twenty-first century.

Some observers have suggested that U.S. law enforcement agencies are relatively static or stagnant and are oriented toward maintaining the status quo. They view police departments as highly resistant to change; for example, they say many departments make changes only when extreme conditions require them to do so. However, a quick review of policing in the United States shows that throughout history, although admittedly sometimes very slowly, law enforcement agencies have adapted their methods to fit the times and changing demands placed on them by society.

English Roots of Policing

We must return to England to discover how policing, as well as other elements of the U.S. criminal justice system, was transferred to the North American colonies and how it evolved here. The basic elements of policing in England are still easily detected in contemporary police agencies in the United States.

In the earliest manifestations of law enforcement in England, the apprehension of people suspected of violating the law was dependent on a **mutual pledge system.** The citizens of a community were expected to raise the **hue and cry** in order to alert others that a particular person was wanted for a crime (see Uchida 2002). Thus, each local community initially was involved in the law enforcement effort, and all citizens were bound together in the pledge system to assist in enforcing the laws. To provide a greater sense of cohesion (and to make the collection of taxes easier), groups of 10 families were organized into **tithings** (sometimes spelled tythings). Within these groups,

> [e]ach person was responsible for the behavior of everyone in his tything. If any member committed a crime, the other members were expected to hold him for trial in the local court, or, if they failed to do that, they were required to make compensation. (Johnson 1981, 2)

Ten tithings then were clustered together to form a **hundred,** and the hundreds eventually became **shires** or what today we would call counties. The king or a local nobleman would appoint a chief law enforcement officer for each of the shires, and this person was known as the **reeve.** From the combination of the words *shire* and *reeve,* we eventually got the office of **sheriff.** The early English sheriffs were less concerned about enforcing the law than they were about collecting taxes and protecting the property and possessions of the landed classes.

To protect the king's peace, reeves typically appointed assistants who were known as **justices of the peace.** In England, these officials carried out law enforcement-like duties, but when the position by this name was adopted in the United States, it evolved into a judicial office. The justices of the peace needed help in carrying out their duties, and often they employed **constables** as their primary enforcement agents. Champion (2005, 57) wrote that originally constables were "favored noblemen of the king who commanded neighborhood groups" and, as such, they were "the forerunners of modern-day police officers."

The office of constable exists as the basic law enforcement position in England today. Additionally, in contemporary policing in the United States, "constables are comparable to county sheriff's departments, doing patrol and criminal apprehension. They may be local officials with limited police powers" (Champion 2005, 57). U.S. states such as Alabama, Arizona, Pennsylvania, Tennessee, and Texas have retained the office of constable as an elected law enforcement position, primarily with the duty of process serving, or serving court papers such as summonses and court orders (see Connell 2005; DEAauctions 2005; Walker 1998).

The first full-time law enforcement agency in England was a private policing organization developed by **Henry Fielding.** Fielding was a magistrate whose office was on Bow Street in London. When he took over as magistrate, he found that of the 80 constables employed at the time by the Bow Street court, only 6 were honest and reliable. He kept these 6 and dismissed the rest, and in 1749 he created the **Bow Street Runners** (eventually called the Bow Street Horse and Foot Patrol). These constables were hired to provide basic security and investigative services to those who could afford them, and initially they were paid from reward monies plus bonuses provided for successful prosecutions (Devon and Cornwall Constabulary 2005a).

When Henry Fielding died in 1754, his brother John took over responsibility for the Bow Street Runners. Both Henry and John were zealous advocates of law enforcement, and they supported the idea of a national police agency in England. While this idea proved unpopular, in 1792 Parliament did pass a law creating more constabulary offices based on the Bow Street model and allowing other parts of England to call on the services of the Runners (Clark 2004).

The Fielding brothers were followed in English public service by **Patrick Colquhoun.** Colquhoun believed that policing should be a governmental function and, like Henry Fielding, Colquhoun's influence largely spread as a result of his writings. In fact, in the 1790s he wrote two influential books on police reform, which laid the foundation for the work of **Sir Robert Peel** and others who were to follow (Johnson 1981, 13–15).

From the late 1700s to the early 1800s, there continued to be calls for the creation of a governmental police agency, leading to the first public law enforcement agency in England, the **London Metropolitan Police.** In 1822, at the age of 34, Sir Robert Peel was appointed British Home Secretary. At the time of his appointment, he found 450 law enforcement officers scattered in a variety of London policing agencies (such as the Bow Street Runners and the Marine Police). These groups were not especially well trained, nor were they particularly efficient in carrying out their jobs. There also was very little coordination among these groups. As a result, Peel proposed a bill to Parliament for the creation of a governmentally funded police agency. In 1829, Parliament enacted the bill entitled "An Act for Improving the Police in and Near the Metropolis," or simply the London Metropolitan Police Act. This act provided a uniformed and investigative police force of 1,000 officers for London. Other cities throughout England followed London's example and created their own police departments (Devon and Cornwall Constabulary 2005b).

Samuel Walker (1998) noted some of the characteristics of Sir Robert Peel's first constables. He said

> uniforms were designed to enhance the officers' visibility and, presumably, their deterrent effect. To coordinate the widely dispersed patrol force, Peel adopted a military command structure, including military-style ranks and a hierarchical, authoritarian chain of command. Thus, Peel established the quasi-military features that have dominated modern police administration to the present. (Walker 1998, 53)

Box 3.1 includes the principles upon which Peel based his philosophy of policing. It is interesting to note that the initial orientation toward the mission of the police ("to prevent crime and disorder"), as well as Peel's concerns over the use of force by his officers (Principles 4 and 6), are relevant issues today.

While London's Metropolitan Police found a highly centralized and tightly controlled organization, the historical development of policing throughout England led to a decentralized organizational pattern, and each community had its own police organization. This pattern continues today. Unlike many of the other nations in Europe—and even their island neighbors in Ireland—English policing always has been locally organized and administered. There is no national police agency in England as there is in France, Italy, and Spain. Although this places the control of the police in local hands, it creates problems with investigations that cross jurisdictional boundaries.

One of the byproducts of decentralization is **fragmentation.** English police agencies exist in various locations and maintain a division of responsibility among all of the agencies. Again, there is no overarching organizational structure that helps coordinate the activities of different agencies. In this regard, policing in England is similar to policing in the United States.

Box 3.1
Sir Robert Peel's Principles of Policing

(1) The basic mission for which the police exist is to prevent crime and disorder.

(2) The ability of the police to perform their duties is dependent upon public approval of police actions.

(3) Police must secure the willing cooperation of the public in voluntary observance of the law to be able to secure and maintain the respect of the public.

(4) The degree of cooperation of the public that can be secured diminishes proportionately to the necessity of the use of physical force.

(5) Police seek and preserve public favor not by catering to public opinion but by constantly demonstrating absolute impartial service to the law.

(6) Police use physical force to the extent necessary to secure observance of the law or to restore order only when the exercise of persuasion, advice and warning is found to be insufficient.

(7) Police, at all times, should maintain a relationship with the public that gives reality to the historic tradition that the police are the public and the public are the police; the police being only members of the public who are paid to give full-time attention to duties which are incumbent on every citizen in the interests of community welfare and existence.

(8) Police should always direct their attention strictly towards their functions and never appear to usurp the powers of the judiciary.

(9) The test of police efficiency is the absence of crime and disorder, not the visible evidence of police action in dealing with it. ✦

Source: Peel (n.d.) on New Westminster Police Web site (2005). Retrieved July 26, 2006 from: *http://www.newwestpolice.org/peel.html*.

According to *magnacartaplus.org*: "Because many early police archives have been destroyed, it is not certain Peel did compose these nine principles."

Finally, one of the major distinctive characteristics of policing in England—started with Sir Robert Peel's first "Bobbies"—is the fact that constables do not carry firearms on a routine basis (see Thurman 2002a). Some officers in every police department are specially trained and designated as firearms officers. Their services are called on in extreme situations, but the average police officer in England may never carry a firearm in the course of duty. While this may seem unusual to Americans, the English initially were opposed to deploying an armed paramilitary force because they considered this a threat to democracy (Malcolm 2004).

Brief History of U.S. Policing

The history of the United States includes a very distinctive tradition of policing as well. Our initial model of policing was inherited from England, but over the past two and one-half centuries, policing in this country has evolved significantly. Today we are faced with the question of which model—or to use the popular word from the corporate world, paradigm—will guide us as we progress into the twenty-first century.

During the colonial period of the seventeenth century, most communities had no organized law enforcement efforts. Like the tradition in England, every male citizen was expected to take his turn serving as constable or watchman (Johnson 1981, 5). This worked while communities had small populations and people lived in close proximity to one another. As cities began to develop, however, law enforcement service became a less appealing civic duty.

The first law enforcement officers in the United States—sheriffs, town constables, or marshals—often had titles that were borrowed directly from England (see Uchida 2002; Walker 1998). Originally, these officers were appointed—first by colonial governors and later by local governing bodies. In the nineteenth century, as a result of Jacksonian democracy, jurisdictions increasingly elected law enforcement officials. Today throughout the United States, we find elected sheriffs, and still in some states elected constables as well.

Major cities, such as New York and Boston, created the office of night watch in the 1700s, and these offices continued well into the 1800s. The individuals who served as part of the night watch frequently were called "rattle-keys" for the noise they made with large rings of keys as they made their rounds. They were to check for open doors or windows on businesses and to be on the lookout for fires, a major problem of the period. With the advent of gas lights, the night watch also became responsible for lighting and extinguishing these lamps.

The next stage in the development of policing in the United States came as a result of urbanization and industrialization in the period leading up to, during, and just following the Civil War (Johnson 1981: 17, 25–28). These two trends motivated cities to create daytime police departments focused on crime prevention to supplement the job of the night watch (Walker 1998). Citizens of the emerging major cities in the east and Midwest were concerned about the increasing presence of Irish immigrants, labor unrest, and the growth in personal and property crimes.

There is some debate over which city was the first to have a unified preventive police department, combining the night watch with daytime policing. Cities such as Boston and Philadelphia created police departments between 1838 and 1854. However, some of these early departments were disbanded and later reconstituted as a result of urban riots and other such disturbances (Walker 1998, 1999).

Johnson (1981: 26, 27–28) said that "New York was the first American city to adopt a lasting version of a preventive police" and that

New Orleans and Cincinnati adopted plans for new police in 1852; Boston and Philadelphia did so in 1854, Chicago in 1855, and Baltimore in 1857. By the 1860s, preventive policing had been accepted in principle, properly modified to meet American conditions, in every large city and in several smaller ones.

As the nation expanded westward, policing moved with it. The role of the sheriff especially became a dominant one in the new southern and western states. Western states and territories also came to rely upon local marshals and the services of an office created during George Washington's Presidency in 1789: the U.S. Marshal. When we compare policing in the United States with that of England, a number of similarities as well as some major differences are relevant. Like policing in England, law enforcement in the North American colonies, and eventually in the new United States, was locally controlled, decentralized, and fragmented. Each new community and each new state created one or more law enforcement agencies (Uchida 2002). The same was true of law enforcement development at the federal level: New problems brought about new agencies.

Originally, police officers in many American cities, like their English counterparts, were not armed. In fact, some cities prohibited the police from being armed until the late nineteenth century (Walker 1999, 24). During this era, when cities did not allow the police to carry firearms, some officers bought and illegally carried their own weapons. In other jurisdictions in the United States, law enforcement officers have carried firearms from the earliest days. Perhaps this can be attributed to their "settling the frontier" orientation, or perhaps it can be attributed to our fight for independence from England as represented by the U.S. Constitution. But, for whatever the reason, the United States historically has had a widely armed citizenry and an armed law enforcement service.

Stages of Police Development

The development of U.S. policing can be categorized into several stages. There are no exact lines of demarcation for these stages, and some observers have even objected to such a characterization. Nevertheless, we use several general periods or eras to describe the evolution of policing in this country.

First, according to George Cole and Christopher Smith (2005), policing in the United States has gone through three stages of development: (1) the **political era**—1820s to 1940s, (2) the **professional era**—1940 to 1970, and (3) the **community policing era**—1970 to the present (see also Hartmann 1988; Kelling and Moore 1988; and Thurman 2002a). We discuss these three eras, along with some transition periods, in the following sections.

The Political Era (1820s–1940s)

During the political era, major cities created police departments, which were developed alongside the new political machines of cities such as Boston, Chicago, and New York (Walker 1998). To get a job as a police officer, a man (they were all men then) would approach his city councilman, alderman, or the local political ward boss and make an appeal for appointment to the force. Uchida (2002, 92) noted that "police officers were recruited and selected by political leaders in a particular ward or precinct." Virtually no training was provided, and the officers' responsibilities were learned on the job, typically from veteran officers. New officers might be required to purchase their own uniforms and firearms, and often there was a conspicuous lack of uniformity in both. Pay, while good for the times, was still meager, and corruption was ignored or tolerated.

During the political era, the politicians took advantage of the police, but the police often tried to exploit the politicians as well. The politicians controlled the types of laws the police could enforce and the groups against whom they could enforce laws. Police ignored or gave tacit approval to certain types of vices, and in return, politicians supplemented the income of the poorly paid officers. The two grew up together and practically were inseparable. It was as if *policing* and *politics* were the same word, with a slightly different pronunciation.

We addressed the issue of the involvement of politics in criminal justice systems in Chapter 1, and the political era represents the worst of the marriage between the political and justice systems. This era was marked by corruption and brutality by the police, and districts had few legal restrictions and still fewer policy restrictions on what the police could do. As a result, "the lawlessness of the police . . . was one of the paramount issues in municipal politics in the late 1800s" (Uchida 2002, 93). Because of the brutishness and poor quality of U.S. police services, there were calls for police reform during the Progressive Era (beginning in the late 1800s and extending into the early 1900s).

Reform Transition (Late 1800s–Early 1900s)

The Progressive Era brought about social changes, such as the first juvenile court, child labor laws, and compulsory school attendance laws. Social reformers, such as Upton Sinclair in his novel *The Jungle,* wrote about the poor quality of the U.S. food supply, and many cities experienced a surge in reforms, which eventually came to be called the "good government" movement. As a result, during this period police reformers such as Theodore Roosevelt (who was the New York City Police Commissioner), **August Vollmer,** and **O. W. Wilson** started to have an impact on the way Americans viewed the police and how the police viewed themselves (Thurman 2002a). This time of reform was a transitional period between the political era and the era of police professionalism that was to follow (Uchida 2002).

The Professional Era (1940–1970)

The professional era of policing came about largely as an outgrowth of early police reform efforts by men such as Vollmer and Wilson.

Vollmer's primary influence came about during his tenure as chief of police in Berkeley, California. He pioneered the notion of college education for police officers and worked to develop a college-based policing program at the University of California. The professional era developed further with Wilson's days as chief of police in Wichita, Kansas, and through his attempts to reform the Chicago Police Department. However, many mark the high point of the professional era as existing during **William Parker's** tenure as chief of police in Los Angeles, California, from 1950 to 1966 (Uchida 2002).

Parker became chief of the Los Angeles Police Department (LAPD) in a relatively unique way. He did not rise through the ranks from the position of patrolman to chief. Parker had earned a law degree in the 1930s, and after having served in the military during World War II, he returned to the department first as an inspector in the traffic division and later as deputy chief overseeing internal affairs. Once he was appointed chief, he implemented a variety of innovations that increased the department's efficiency and public reputation. For example, to increase patrol presence, Parker moved the department to one-man patrol cars. He also instituted an extensive training program and rigorous recruit screening. Under Parker's leadership, fewer than 10 percent of the applicants were accepted as LAPD officers. Throughout his career, Parker stressed reform and innovation (Johnson 1981, 119–121; LAPD 2006).

The professional era of policing was marked by a number of distinctive features. First, departments began the creation or expansion of formal training for police officers. No longer did they rely upon veteran officers to train rookies on the job. Cadets finished a prescribed period of training at the police academy before they were assigned to patrol. Second, while police officers clearly possessed human emotions, they were expected to perform their duties in a businesslike, dispassionate manner. William Parker and his successors carefully cultivated this image through television shows, such as *Dragnet* and *Adam 12*.

Third, to reduce the amount of corruption experienced by some departments, professional policing emphasized rotating officers through many different patrol beats or sectors and also rotating their assignments (especially in areas such as narcotics and vice). To reemphasize the issue of integrity by officers, larger departments created internal affairs divisions, and some cities established police commissions or civilian review boards.

When combined, all of these factors, along with the increased use of automobiles for patrol, insulated and isolated the police from the public they were sworn to serve. As a result, the police frequently lost touch with the values that the citizens cherished, such as the ability to approach an officer. In the end, the professional era suffered its greatest challenges from increasing crime rates, along with the civil rights movement, anti-Viet Nam War protests, and the urban riots of the 1960s (Uchida 2002).

Before leaving our discussion of the professional era of policing, we should note a factor that is often overlooked. The reform movement was simply one force within policing in the United States. Not all departments were reached by this movement, and not all embraced ideals such as high personnel qualifications and preservice training prior to beginning police work. The fragmented nature of policing in the United States meant that the impact of reform also was fragmented. Some departments exhibited high levels of reform and professionalism, and others were totally untouched by reform.

Days of Protest—Another Transition (Mid-1960s–Mid-1970s)

Cole and Smith (2005) characterized the 1970s as the beginning of the community police era, but the late 1960s and early 1970s clearly were a time of transition from the preceding era. The period from about 1965 to 1975 saw an increase in social unrest in the United States. Minority groups—especially African Americans—lobbied for full participation in the political processes of the nation. Activists staged civil rights protests in many cities. In places like Selma and Birmingham, Alabama, these protests were witnessed on national television with local police agencies often playing the parts of the villains. George Wallace, Governor of Alabama, blocked the doorway for admission of African-American students to the University of Alabama, and federal troops and U.S. Marshals were called in to enforce the integration order. Demonstrations against the Vietnam War, draft card burning, and the assassination of Martin Luther King, Jr., brought the police into conflict with groups of college students (and others) who took to the streets to express their displeasure over the nation's state of affairs. The police were called upon to perform jobs they were not trained to do—deal with social unrest and act in a large group, unified fashion—and often they failed in their missions. The major result of this era of protest and transition was a great deal of soul-searching by the police and by society in general. Eventually, there was forward movement by the police as agencies began to embrace the concept of professional public service.

During this era, questions were raised about the reactive nature of most police functions and the crime-fighting orientation that officers had carried over from the professional era. Groups within and outside of policing began to ask questions about what the police *could* do and what they *should* do. The result was the search for a new paradigm.

The Community Policing Era (1970—Present)

Community policing did not originate as such. In fact, during the early 1970s, several movements began that eventually provided us with the concept of community policing. For instance, one of the earliest efforts began in Cincinnati, Ohio, and Boston, Massachusetts, with an approach called **team policing.** Team policing was designed to identify distinct neighborhoods and to assign a group of officers to police those neighborhoods on an ongoing basis. The underlying philosophy or approach was that the officers were to reconnect with the citizens they served. These teams of officers were to interact with the people who ran the businesses and those who lived in residential neighborhoods. They were to get out of their patrol cars and walk around often so they could speak to people and the public would feel comfortable approaching them. The team concept also was designed to help officers share information with each other about trouble spots in their patrol areas, and it was designed to somewhat flatten the hierarchical, military-style organizational pattern that had developed in police agencies during the professional era (Kelling and Moore 1988).

Generally speaking, team policing won the praise of both neighborhood residents and the officers who served on the teams. However, Cordner, Fraser, and Wexler (1991, 355) noted that team policing worked against "what was then a new professional model according to which the measures of increased productivity were more calls taken, shorter response time, less time on each call for service, and decreased reported crime." In the end, team policing was less than fully successful because the decentralized model "was threatening to patrol and investigative divisions as well as to senior administrators" (Cordner, Fraser, and Wexler 1991, 356). This meant that the key elements associated with the concept of team policing (decentralization and greater autonomy for line officers) were also the features that made it difficult to implement on a wide-scale basis. Nevertheless, some of the key elements that were a part of team policing did take root in departments, and these elements provided the foundation for the community policing movement that was to follow.

One of the key elements to emerge from team policing strategy was the importance of **police-community relations.** The idea was that officers needed to listen to citizens, not just talk to them (or sometimes at them). Departments approached the notion of community relations in a variety of ways. As a result of team policing and similar efforts, some departments operated with the philosophy that community relations was the responsibility of every officer every day. Other agencies employed nonsworn personnel to perform community relations functions, or they designated special community relations officers. Frequently, in these agencies, there was a clash of values between the "real" police, who were committed to crime fighting, and the community relations officers, who were seen as holding the hands of the citizens to soothe whatever might be troubling them. An us-versus-them attitude prevailed in such departments. While there always has been some degree of tension within law enforcement concerning the importance of community relations, the soul-searching that has gone on over such concepts has caused agencies to examine their roles in interacting with the community.

In addition to team policing, the work of Herman Goldstein on **problem-oriented policing** and the very influential article written by George Kelling and James Q. Wilson (1982) brought to the forefront the notion of community disorder and its impact on crime and other quality-of-life issues.[1] In their article, Kelling and Wilson introduced the idea of "**broken windows.**" Champion (2005, 32) noted that *broken windows* is a term "used to describe the role of the police as maintainers of community order and safety and the view that police attention to disorder (low-level offenses such as drunkenness or prostitution) will prevent or forestall acts of more serious crime."

In some ways the concept behind broken windows is related to **social disorganization theory** (Cloward and Ohlin 1960; Cohen 1955; Shaw and McKay 1942), and it becomes a shorthand reference for any type of disorder that affects the quality of life in a community. Kelling and Wilson said that in a neighborhood with broken windows left unrepaired, the message is that no one cares. Social disorganization, fear, and crime take over as citizens give up control of their neighborhoods to the elements of disorder. Therefore, to fight the forces of social disorganization, the police and neighborhood residents must band together and forge working relationships that help citizens "take back the streets."

Walker (1998) noted that urban decay and social disorganization encouraged cooperation of police and politicians around the theme of community policing. The initial publicity on the community policing movement "seemed to promise everything: revitalized neighborhoods, reduced crime, and close police-community cooperation" (Walker 1998, 238). However, the question remains whether community policing promised too much. Did the community policing movement prematurely raise the hopes of both the police and the community? We will examine this question in the following section.

Community Policing

Community policing has been described by some as a different philosophy or a new method or approach to policing. It is, as we have mentioned elsewhere in this chapter, a different paradigm than that presented by the reform or professional eras in U.S. police history. While sometimes it is difficult to decide what is and what is not community policing, we can refer to the 10 principles articulated by Kappeler, Gaines, and Bucqueroux (1998) in Box 3.2 as being central to any community policing program. It is important to emphasize, however, that community policing is not a firmly established program or prescription for policing. It is much more a philosophy of or orientation toward delivering police services; thus, it can take many different forms depending on the community.

As we mentioned in the previous section, concepts such as team policing that originated in the period from the mid-1960s through the mid-1970s laid the foundation for what was to become community po-

Box 3.2
The Ten Principles of Community Policing

(1) Community policing is both a philosophy and an organizational strategy that allows the police and the community residents to work closely together in new ways to solve the problems of crime, fear of crime, physical and social disorder, and neighborhood conditions.

(2) Community policing's organizational strategy first demands that everyone in the department, including both civilian and sworn personnel, must investigate ways to translate the philosophy into practice.

(3) To implement true community policing, police departments must also create and develop a new breed of line officer, the Community Policing Officer (CPO), who acts as the direct link between the police and people in the community.

(4) The CPO's broad role demands continuous, sustained contact with the law-abiding people in the community, so that together they can explore creative new solutions to local concerns involving crime, fear of crime, disorder, and community conditions with private citizens serving as unpaid volunteers.

(5) Community policing implies a new contract between the police and the citizens it serves, one that offers the hope of overcoming widespread apathy [while,] at the same time, it restrains any impulse to vigilantism.

(6) Community policing adds a vital proactive element to the traditional reactive role of the police, resulting in full-spectrum police service.

(7) Community policing stresses exploring new ways to protect and enhance the lives of those who are most vulnerable—juveniles, the elderly, minorities, the poor, the disabled, the homeless.

(8) Community policing promotes the judicious use of technology, but it also rests on the belief that nothing surpasses what dedicated human beings, talking and working together, can achieve.

(9) Community policing must be a fully integrated approach that involves everyone in the department, with the CPOs as specialists in bridging the gap between the police and the people they serve.

(10) Community policing provides decentralized, personalized police service to the community. ✦

Source: Kappeler, Gaines, and Bucqueroux (1998, xi–xiii). ·

licing. In fact, Cordner, Fraser, and Wexler (1991, 354) observed that while team policing and community policing (or **community-oriented policing**) "are similar in overall objective, they differ sharply in the ways they have been integrated into departments."

However, while we can identify a number of precursors to community policing, it is difficult to trace the beginnings of this concept. One of the reasons is that community policing, as such, did not spring fullblown onto the policing scene. Instead, it developed over a couple of decades in several incremental steps. Nevertheless, by the 1980s several police departments across the United States had adopted the philosophy articulated by Robert Trojanowicz and his colleagues at Michigan State University under the label of community policing or community-oriented policing.

Trojanowicz and Bucqueroux (1990, 5) saw community policing as "a new philosophy of policing, based on the concept that police officers and citizens working together in creative ways can help solve contemporary community problems related to crime, fear of crime, social and physical disorder, and neighborhood decay."

Building upon this definition, Quint Thurman (2002b, 116) noted that

> community policing might be defined as *the guiding philosophy for the delivery of police services that relies upon positive interactions among police, other public servants, and community representatives to serve local needs regarding crime control, crime prevention, and crime-related quality-of-life issues.*

Thurman suggested both an external focus to community policing—namely building partnerships with the community that will create "safer and better places to live"—as well as an internal focus that deals with equipping officers to perform community policing responsibilities (Thurman 2002a, 273).

In further describing community policing, Thurman listed four dimensions and five perspectives. The first dimension is philosophical. This dimension is related to the values of the particular police department and the kinds of activities in which the members believe the department should be engaged. Second, is a strategic dimension. Thurman labeled this as the "operational" version of the philosophy present in a given department. Third, is the tactical dimension, or the daily operations of the department. Finally, the organizational dimension is concerned with the structure of the department, including management and the evaluation of its employees (Thurman 2002b, 114).

Thurman's five perspectives of community policing have been expanded upon by the Police Executive Research Forum (PERF). PERF lists the first one as the *deployment perspective.* This is the idea of moving officers into closer contacts with citizens. Closer contact could come through community meetings to discuss citizen concerns, or it could come about through the use of foot patrols, bicycle patrols, or community-based offices that would allow for walk-in traffic. The second perspective involves *community revitalization.* Efforts in this area are related to preventing the physical decay of the community ("broken windows") and the implementation of programs designed to reduce citizens' fear of crime. The third perspective addresses *problem solving.* This is one of the principal concerns of community policing because it helps identify problems and provide solutions (see also Goldstein 1990a, 1990b, 1993; Roth and Ryan 2000). Viewing the *citizen as a customer* is the fourth perspective. Police departments need to listen to the concerns expressed by citizens and establish policing priorities based on citizen input. This sends the message that the police have heard community concerns and are willing to do something about them. Finally, *legiti-*

macy represents the fifth perspective. The police must act in an impartial and unbiased manner, and they must be viewed as fair in performing their duties, particularly by minority communities.

Walker (1999) commented that, in some ways, community policing is a return to the early English roots of policing. Therefore, "[t]he community policing movement is an attempt to restore and develop the role of citizens as co-producers of police services" (Walker 1999, 11). However, one of the contemporary scholars of community policing has asked this question: "Is community policing new wine, or is it old wine in new bottles?" (Thurman 2002a, 270). Thus, in this section we will examine community policing in an effort to understand the impact it has had both on how the police view themselves and how they are viewed by their communities.

Goldstein (2002, 102) maintained that in response to community policing, there have been increasing public expectations that "community policing will provide an instant solution not only for problems of crime, disorder, and racial tension, but for many of the other acute problems that plague our urban areas as well." He warned that we should be patient even though we have not been able to develop the perfect model of policing. In our pluralistic, changing society, the best we can hope for is that the police will be "committed to protecting and extending democratic values" (Goldstein 2002: 103, 110).

Where Are We Now and Where Do We Go From Here?

Now that we have had about two decades' worth of experience with community policing in the United States, what can we say about the effectiveness of the most recent policing paradigm? First, neither community policing nor any other approach will solve all of the social problems presented to the police or assure reduced crime through police-citizen interactions. Peter K. Manning (1992, 7) has said that "as long as police exercise authority and force in the name of the state, they will be feared and loathed by some segments of the community."

Second, whatever the specific programs employed, no doubt the rhetoric of community policing has had an effect on police executives in the United States. For example, a report done for the National Institute of Justice found that from 1993 to 1997, the number of police executives who thought that community policing was an effective approach to delivering police services increased from 76 percent to 86 percent. Furthermore, most police executives saw community policing as not just the responsibility of a few officers but also the function of all law enforcement agency personnel (Rosenthal et al. 2001).

Third, community policing has become a priority of the federal government; and over a six-year period, Congress appropriated about $9

billion to back a variety of programs under the label of community policing. Federal dollars were provided to fund up to 100,000 new state and local police positions in agencies around the country, as well as to improve
problem solving, foster community interaction, encourage innovative policing programs, and develop new police technologies (Mabrey 2005; Roth
and Ryan 2000). While departments have increased the number of personnel hired, they have not met the goal of putting another 100,000 officers
"on the streets." Furthermore, the community partnerships that were
supposed to have been developed remain somewhat elusive. In fact,
Roth and Ryan (2000, 17) concluded that "true community partnerships, involving sharing power and decision making, are rare at this
time, [and are] found in only a few of the flagship departments."

Fourth, there is some evidence of crime reduction because of moving
toward the community policing approach, especially as a result of the
funding available from the federal Community Oriented Policing Services (COPS) program. Zhao and Thurman (2004, 1) examined grant
awards made from 1995 to 2000 in 5,659 law enforcement agencies,
and they found that "COPS hiring and innovative grant programs are
related to significant reductions in local crime rates in cities with populations greater than 10,000 for both violent and nonviolent offenses";
cities with populations less than 10,000 did not experience significant
crime reductions. However, a word of caution must be given relative to
possible contaminating factors in this and other evaluations of police
operations. Although Zhao and Thurman used the mid-1990s as the
baseline for their research, some cities had started to experience drops
in crime rates as early as 1990. Additionally, New York City, which saw
one of the biggest drops in crime rates, attributed the positive changes
to implementation of the COMPSTAT program rather than community
policing *per se*. In fact, Lyons (2003) reported that many people credited
COMPSTAT with causing a "decade-long decline in New York City's
crime rate as authorities used technology to pinpoint problem areas
and saturate troubled neighborhoods with cops" (see also McKay 2003;
for a slightly different view see Willis, Mastrofski, and Weisburd 2004).

Fifth, any shift in the policing paradigm is likely to be met with skepticism and resistance by the police and, interestingly, by the public as
well. Therefore, fundamental changes to the way policing services are
delivered in the United States will require both time to plan the changes
and to implement them ("Community policing" 2003). In fact, when
looking at police departments of various sizes around the United
States, we see that some have embraced the community policing concept, while others continue in the traditional, reactive manner of delivering police services. Furthermore, Pelfrey (2004), in examining the
"inchoate nature of community policing," found that the concept has
not been embraced by all of the officers even in agencies that suppos-
edly have adopted community policing. The Philadelphia Police Department, for example, was found to have two groups of officers, but

the "community policing officers are not radically different from traditional patrol officers in several regards." In fact, both groups (community police and traditional patrol) continue to believe in the value of traditional law enforcement practices (Pelfrey 2004, 596).

Finally, since no single paradigm of policing can last forever, we must ask about the next model likely to come along. One possibility offered by the Futures Working Group of the FBI and Police Futurists International is **neighborhood-driven policing** (Jensen and Levin 2005). Advocates say that neighborhood-driven policing differs from traditional, reactive (or combat) policing, and community-oriented policing in the following three ways. The first is control. In combat-oriented policing, decision making is centralized. By contrast, in community-oriented policing, control or decision making is decentralized with community input. Neighborhood-driven policing is controlled by the neighborhood with police input.

The second area of difference in the three types of policing is structure. Combat-oriented policing is hierarchical. Community-oriented policing has a flatter hierarchy than that of traditional departments, but it is nonetheless hierarchical. Neighborhood-driven policing has a structure determined by the particular neighborhood.

The final area of difference involves the method of operation. Combat-oriented policing operates with a reactive response; the police are mobilized after a crime has occurred or after a problem has been identified. Community-oriented policing is geared toward identifying and solving community problems. Neighborhood-driven policing has methods determined by the neighborhood itself (Cowper 2005, 28).

As with the other policing paradigms discussed in this chapter, neighborhood-driven policing clearly is a work in progress. Maybe it is one more in a long line of different models that has been implemented by some police departments and rejected by others, but it could also prove the very model to be embraced by today's change-oriented police executives.

Conclusions

Is community policing the ultimate destination for the delivery of police services in the United States, or is it merely another stop along the road in the evolution of the police role? Different scholars, policy makers, and practitioners answer this question in different ways. Some see community policing as fundamentally changing the way police officers perform their jobs. These changes have become so institutionalized that we can never return to the reactive, call-chasing days of the professional policing era (see Peak and Glensor 2004).

In addition, David Bayley (1998), a scholar with a long-standing research interest in policing, has outlined six changes over the past few decades that have shaped American policing (see Box 3.3). While not all police scholars would agree with his assessment, several of these changes are noteworthy. Within a very short period of time, for instance, the police have transformed themselves from a "blue-collar" occupation that was both "pale and male" to an increasingly sophisticated, professional, and diverse workforce. In a federal government study of police agencies, Hickman and Reaves (2006) found that 33 percent of personnel now work in departments that require a college degree for new officers, almost triple the number in 1990. In terms of diversity, the investigators found the percentage of female and minority officers also continues to grow. This is an issue we address more comprehensively in Chapter 8.

Anybody who doubts the added sophistication of American policing has not had the opportunity to spend much time with officers lately. Bayley (1998) contended that chiefs are increasingly ambitious and wish to stamp their influence on their agencies. To do so, these executives are more frequently surrounding themselves with highly educated commanders, who are versed in COMPSTAT, geographic information systems (GIS) to facilitate crime mapping, and crime and data analysis. Moreover, larger departments have automated everything from shift scheduling to vehicle maintenance. These values are transmitted to everybody in the organization, from patrol officers to personnel administrators, and those officers who want to be promoted are investing in their formal and informal education.

Bayley (1998) speculated that forces external to police departments would shape the types of services delivered in the twenty-first century, and he was correct. The 9/11 tragedy, the proliferation of Central American gangs in some places, changes in patterns of crime (for example, the emergence of identity theft), and drug use (the increasing proliferation of methamphetamine) were all but unforeseeable a decade ago. One can only guess what the future will bring. Regardless of the chal-

---

Box 3.3
Significant Changes in American Policing

- The intellectual caliber of the police has risen dramatically.

- Senior police administrators are more ambitious for their organizations than they used to be.

- The standards of police conduct have risen.

- Police are remarkably more diverse in terms of race and gender than a generation ago.

- The work of the police has become more intellectually demanding, requiring an array of new specialized knowledge about technology, forensic analysis, and crime.

- Civilian review of the police discipline, once considered anathema, has gradually become accepted by the police. ✦

Source: Bayley (1998). Retrieved July 24, 2006 from: *http://www.policefoundation.org.*

lenge, however, the police are better suited to respond to these problems than at any other time in the past two centuries, in part due to the value that many organizations place on professionalism, education, scientific knowledge, and diversity.

Other scholars are not so optimistic; and in fact, a few are downright pessimistic. They see community policing as facing a number of problems. First, to truly operate in a community-policing fashion, a great deal of change may be required of the police. Second, some agencies have espoused a community-policing philosophy, but they have never really embraced the concept. Third, particularly among line officers, an inherent resistance can be seen within the police occupational subculture. And finally, this trend may be viewed as a passing fad and an attempt by police executives and police agencies to co-opt the public as an ally (see Thurman 2002b, 119). If this is the case, then community policing is nothing more than a public relations ploy with very little substance. In fact, Walker (1998, 239) concluded that after about a decade of development, "community policing programs increasingly became conventional anticrime and antidrug programs." Thus, there remain serious questions about "whether community policing represented a new era in policing, as its advocates claimed, or whether it was simply the latest in a long line of overpublicized fads" (Walker 1998, 239).

Most approaches to community policing have been fashioned on the philosophy of making the police more accessible to the community. One group of scholars, however, contend that some police agencies used their federal community policing funds to deploy special weapons and tactics (SWAT) teams in full combat gear to patrol communities in armored vehicles (Kopel 2000; Kraska and Kappeler 1997). While many police scholars do not support Kraska and Kappeler's contention about the increasing militarization of the police, the fact remains that community policing has taken different forms—and that some departments might actually engage in "community policing" practices that alienate officers from the communities they serve.

Another challenge that community policing was supposed to tackle was reducing the distance between the police and the communities they serve. Thomas and Burns (2005, 71) examined survey data from 12 cities and found that

> [d]espite intentions to improve police-minority relations, community policing most strongly and positively affects whites' perceptions of neighborhood police. . . . [A]ctual tactics of community policing had a greater impact on white perceptions of the police than they did for Latino and African American views.

Thus, as the police search for a guiding philosophy, they must also struggle with the implementation of these goals and evaluate whether their actions have the desired effects.

For community policing to work, there has to be a perceived need for change from the prevailing model of policing (still the professional model in many agencies). Furthermore, the public has to want the police to change, and this may include paying for the costs associated with a move toward community policing. Finally, the police must want to change their orientation and operations (see Thurman 2002b, 120). Ultimately, then, community policing requires a buy-in by both the community and the police.

Note

1. Not everyone accepts Kelling and Wilson's assumptions about the history of the police in carrying out their order maintenance functions. See also Walker (1984).

Key Terms

Bow Street Runners
broken windows
Colquhoun, Patrick
community-oriented po-
  licing
community policing
community policing era
constables
Fielding, Henry
fragmentation
hue and cry
hundred

justices of the peace
London Metropolitan
  Police
mutual pledge system
neighborhood-driven
  policing
Parker, William
Peel, Sir Robert
police-community rela-
  tions
political era
problem-oriented policing

professional era
reeve
social disorganization
  theory
sheriff
shires
team policing
tithings
Vollmer, August
Wilson, O. W.

Critical Review Questions

1. Traditionally, students have been taught that law enforcement, order maintenance, and public service are the three primary responsibilities of the police. As policing began to take shape in England, what was the rank-order of these three functions? Did that ordering change in the United States in the twentieth century? How?

2. Do we have any community response to policing today that resembles the "hue and cry" in England? Explain.

3. Think about the office of sheriff in your state (and constables as well, if they still exist). What are the qualifications necessary to run for sheriff? Is there a minimum age requirement? Does a candidate need any law enforcement background or experience?

4. What role should the private sector play in providing police services? Is this an example of the broadly defined "community" coop-

erating in crime prevention and law enforcement duties, or is it merely the corporate model of providing a service to make a profit?

5. Look back at the history of English policing (either in books or on the Web) and find the features or characteristics associated with London's first "Bobbies." Which of these elements do we commonly find in police officers in the United States today?

6. As a nation, what would we gain and what would we lose by converting to a national police system? Do changing times (i.e., the issue of homeland security) warrant us rethinking the highly fragmented and decentralized policing system in the United States?

7. As a follow-up to Question 6, at least at the federal level, should all law enforcement functions be unified in one agency? Is this a good idea or not? Give examples based on current events.

8. List one major contribution to U.S. police reform that each of the following men brought to police work: Theodore Roosevelt, August Vollmer, and O. W. Wilson.

9. Can the police become too ingrained in the life and values of the community? Watch the movie *Mississippi Burning* and write a short essay (one to two pages) on the dangers of the police reflecting the values of the community they serve.

10. What do we mean by the notion of "broken windows"? Is this really a shorthand term for a much more complex phenomenon? Can you link it to one theory (or more) used to explain crime?

11. Under the concept of community policing, who has to change the most—the public and its expectations of the police, or police personnel and their orientations toward the public?

12. Is *anyone* really doing community policing? Is *everyone* doing community policing? Explain.

13. Think about the emerging concept of neighborhood-driven policing. You might want to go to your college or university library to see if you can find a copy of the report released by the FBI and the Police Futurists International. Are we seeing a "new and improved" version of community policing, or is this really the next paradigm?

References

Bayley, David H. (1998). *Policing in America: Assessment and Prospects*. Retrieved December 27, 2006 from *http://www.policefoundation.org/pdf/Bayley.pdf*.

Champion, Dean John. (2005). *The American Dictionary of Criminal Justice*, third edition. Los Angeles: Roxbury Publishing.

Clark, Robert. (2004). "Bow Street Runners, 1749." *Literary Encyclopedia*. Retrieved July 24, 2006 from: *http://www.litencyc.com/php/stopics.php?rec=true&UID=1403*.

Cloward, Richard, and Lloyd Ohlin. (1960). *Delinquency and Opportunity: A Theory of Delinquent Gangs*. New York: Free Press.

Cohen, Albert. (1955). *Delinquent Boys: The Culture of the Gang.* Glencoe, IL: Free Press.

Cole, George F., and Christopher E. Smith. (2005). *Criminal Justice in America,* fourth edition. Belmont, CA: Wadsworth.

"Community policing: Then and now." (2003). *National Institute of Justice Journal* 249, 34.

Connell, Jerry. (2005). "History of the office of the constable in the United States." Retrieved July 24, 2006 from: *http://www.jerryconnell.org/history.html.*

Cordner, Gary, Craig B. Fraser, and Chuck Wexler. (1991). "Research, planning, and implementation." Pp. 333–362 in *Local Government Police Management,* third edition, editor William A. Geller. Washington, DC: International City Management Association.

Cowper, Thomas J. (2005). "Network centric policing: Alternative or augmentation to the neighborhood-driven policing (NDP) model?" Pp. 21–28 in *Neighborhood-Driven Policing: A Series of Working Papers From the Futures Working Group,* edited by Carl J. Jensen III and Bernard H. Levin. Washington, DC: U.S. Department of Justice, Federal Bureau of Investigation.

DEAauctions. (2005). "About constables." Retrieved July 24, 2006 from: *http://www. deaauctions.com/about_constable_police.htm.*

Devon and Cornwall Constabulary. (2005a). "The Victorian policeman: The Bow Street Runners." Retrieved July 24, 2006 from: *http://www.devon-cornwall.police.uk/v3/about/ history/vicpolice/bow.htm.*

———. (2005b). "The Victorian policeman: Sir Robert Peel." Retrieved July 24, 2006 from: *http://www.devon-cornwall.police.uk/v3/ about/history/vicpolice/peel.htm.*

Goldstein, Herman. (1990a). Problem-Oriented Policing. Philadelphia: Temple University Press.

———. (1990b). Problem-Oriented Policing. New York: McGraw-Hill.

———. (1993). "The new policing: Confronting complexity." Research in Brief. Washington, DC: U.S. Department of Justice, National Institute of Justice.

———. (2002). "The new policing: Confronting complexity." Pp. 102–110 in *Crime and Justice in America,* second edition, edited by Wilson R. Palacios, Paul F. Cromwell, and Roger G. Dunham. Upper Saddle River, NJ: Prentice Hall.

Harris, Richard N. (1973). *The Police Academy: An Inside View.* New York: Wiley.

Hartmann, Francis X. (1988). "Debating the evolution of American policing." *Perspectives on Policing.* Washington, DC: U.S. Department of Justice, National Institute of Justice.

Hickman, Matthew J., and Brian A. Reaves. (2006). *Local Police Departments, 2003.* Washington, DC: Bureau of Justice Statistics.

Jensen, Carl J. III, and Bernard H. Levin, editors. (2005). *Neighborhood-Driven Policing: A Series of Working Papers From the Futures Working Group.* Washington, DC: U.S. Department of Justice, Federal Bureau of Investigation.

Johnson, David R. (1981). *American Law Enforcement: A History.* St. Louis, MO: Forum Press.

Kappeler, Victor E., Larry K. Gaines, and Bonnie Bucqueroux. (1998). *Community Policing: A Contemporary Perspective,* second edition. Cincinnati, OH: Anderson.

Kelling, George L., and Mark H. Moore. (1988). *The Evolving Strategy of Policing.* Washington, DC: National Institute of Justice, U.S. Department of Justice.

Kelling, George, and James Q. Wilson. (1982). "Broken windows: The police and neighborhood safety." *Atlantic Monthly* 249, 29–38.

Kopel, Dave. (2000). "Militarized law enforcement: The drug war's deadly fruit." Pp. 61–90 in *After Prohibition,* edited by Timothy Lynch. Washington DC: Cato Institute.

Kraska, Peter, and Victor Kappeler. (1997). "Militarizing American Police: The Rise of Normalization of Paramilitary Units." *Social Problems* 44 (1), 1–18.

Los Angeles Police Department (LAPD). (2006) "The LAPD: Chief Parker" Retrieved July 24, 2006 from: *http://www.lapdonline.org/.*

Lyons, Brendan. (2003). "Mapping database tracks crimes." Retrieved July 24, 2006 from: *http://www.crime-research.org/.*

Mabrey, Daniel. (2005). "Homeland security funding, strategies, and needs." *Telemap Bulletin* 12 (2). Huntsville, TX: Bill Blackwood Law Enforcement.

Malcolm, Joyce Lee. (2004). *Guns and Violence: The English Experience.* Cambridge: Harvard University Press.

Manning, Peter K. (1992). "Economic rhetoric and policing reform." *Criminal Justice Research Bulletin.*

McKay, Jim. (2003). "Continuing the revolution." Retrieved July 24, 2006 from: *http:// www.govtech.net/magazine/channel_story.php/?id=75035&story_pg=1.*

New Westminster Police (2005). Retrieved July 24, 2006 from: *http://www.newwestpolice.org/ peel.html.*

Peak, Kenneth J., and Ronald W. Glensor. (2004). *Community Policing and Problem Solving,* fourth edition. Upper Saddle River, NJ: Prentice Hall.

Pelfrey, William V., Jr. (2004). "The inchoate nature of community policing: Differences between community police officers and traditional police officers." *Justice Quarterly* 21 (3), 579–601.

Rosenthal, Arlen M., Lorie A. Fridell, Mark L. Dantzker, Gayle Fisher-Stewart, Pedro J. Saavedra, Tigran Markaryan, and Sadie Bennett. (2001). *Community Policing: 1997 National Survey Update of Police and Sheriff's Departments.* Washington, DC: U.S. Department of Justice, National Institute of Justice.

Roth, Jeffrey A., and Joseph F. Ryan. (2000). "The COPS program after 4 years—national evaluation." *Research in Brief.* Washington, DC: National Institute of Justice, U.S. Department of Justice.

Shaw, Clifford R., and Henry D. McKay. (1942). *Juvenile Delinquency and Urban Areas.* Chicago: University of Chicago Press.

Thomas, Matthew O., and Peter Burns. (2005). "Repairing the divide: An investigation of community policing and citizen attitudes towards the police by race and ethnicity." *Journal of Ethnicity in Criminal Justice* 3 (1/2), 71–90.

Thurman, Quint C. (2002a). "Community policing." Pp. 270–275 in *Encyclopedia of Crime and Punishment,* editor David Levinson. Thousand Oaks, CA: Sage.

———. (2002b). "Contemporary policing in a community era." Pp. 111–121 in *Crime & Justice in America,* second edition, edited by Wilson R. Palacios, Paul F. Cromwell, and Roger G. Dunham. Upper Saddle River, NJ: Prentice Hall.

Trojanowicz, Robert, and Bonnie Bucqueroux. (1990). *Community Policing: A Contemporary Perspective.* Cincinnati, OH: Anderson.

Uchida, Craig D. (2002). "The development of the American police: An historical overview." Pp. 87–101 in *Crime and Justice in America,* second edition, edited by Wilson R. Palacios, Paul F. Cromwell, and Roger G. Dunham. Upper Saddle River, NJ: Prentice Hall.

Walker, Samuel. (1984). "Broken windows and fractured history: The use and misuse of history in recent patrol analysis." *Justice Quarterly* 1 (1), 75–90.

———. (1998). *Popular Justice: A History of American Criminal Justice.* New York: Oxford University Press.

———. (1999). *The Police in America,* third edition. New York: McGraw-Hill.

Willis, James J., Stephen D. Mastrofski, and David Weisburd. (2004). "COMPSTAT and bureaucracy: A case study of challenges and opportunities for change." *Justice Quarterly* 21 (3), 463–496.

Wilson, James Q. (1968). *Varieties of Police Behavior.* Cambridge, MA: Harvard University Press.

Zhao, Jihong "Solomon," and Quint Thurman. (2004). *Funding Community Policing to Reduce Crime: Have COPS Grants Made a Difference From 1994 to 2000?* Washington, DC: U.S. Department of Justice, Office of Community Oriented Policing Services.

Recommended Readings

Johnson, David R. (1981). *American Law Enforcement: A History.* St. Louis, MO: Forum Press. Johnson presents a brief, but very useful, history of policing in the United States. He begins with policing during the colonial period and concludes with policing in the twentieth century. The book is organized around three topics (that also happen to coincide with the focus of the present book): (1) "the political framework within which policing developed," (2) "reform," and (3) "historical trends in the nature and extent of crime".

Kappeler, Victor E., Larry K. Gaines, and Bonnie Bucqueroux. (1998). *Community Policing: A Contemporary Perspective*, second edition. Cincinnati, OH: Anderson. This book represents a revision of the text originally written by Robert C. Trojanowicz and Bonnie Bucqueroux in 1990 (Trojanowicz died in 1994 at the age of 52). The authors do a thorough job of tracing the history of policing and connecting that history to the notion of community policing. However, they also deal with the contemporary context of community policing, and especially discuss the role of community policing in dealing with issues such as fear of crime, drugs, and special populations (for example, gangs and minority communities). The beginning of the text provides the 10 principles of community policing discussed in this chapter.

Peak, Kenneth J., and Ronald W. Glensor. (2004) *Community Policing and Problem Solving*, fourth edition. Upper Saddle River, NJ: Prentice Hall. This book brings together a policeman turned academic and a ranking police official who continues to serve in law enforcement, but who also teaches on a part-time basis. Peak and Glensor especially focus on the problem-solving aspects of community policing. They frankly discuss a number of the concerns raised by community policing and evaluate some of the community-policing initiatives. Finally, they examine community policing in other countries and speculate on what the future of community policing is likely to be in the United States. ✦

Chapter 4

Police and the Use of Force

Introduction

In Chapter 2, we saw how the police play a central role in the crime control model through the suppression of crime. In the process of performing their jobs, particularly making arrests, they occasionally are required to exert some form of force. A few groups in society, and especially crime control advocates, picture the police as an organization much akin to a national defense force. Yet, unlike in Europe where national police forces are the norm, U.S. police services are delivered in a fragmentary manner. For example, there were nearly 18,000 local and state law enforcement agencies in 2000 (Reaves and Hickman 2002). The services delivered by these agencies are driven by the agency's history, local political demands, goals of the police leadership, and to some extent, the values, norms, and demographic characteristics of a community.

Historically, some police officers relied on the illegal use of force, and "street justice" (dispensing an assault instead of making an arrest) was regularly applied in many departments. Policing has come a long way since that time, and the use of force has become the exception rather than the norm. Still, Bittner (1990, 10) defined the *police* as society's "or else" mechanism, that is "the potential recourse to coercive means—including physical force—to achieve whatever end is required." Reaves and Hickman (2002) reported that there are some 750,000 sworn officers in the United States, and in the course of their interactions with ordinary civilians and offenders, the use of force is inevitable. We examine the extent of police use of force and the individual, contextual, and policy-related factors that influence this use.

We grant the police authority in discharging their duties that no one else in society possesses: the power to lawfully control the behavior of other citizens. This includes the potential to administer a whole range of force against other individuals (Ashley and Golles 2000). The International Association of Chiefs of Police (IACP) (2001, 1) said that **force** is "that amount of effort required by police to compel compliance from an unwilling subject." A report published by the Bureau of Justice Statistics in 2001 defined the *use of force* by the police as "contacts in which the police officer pushed, grabbed, kicked or hit the citizen. Hitting was defined as striking with a hand or an object held in the officer's hand." *Police force* (or the threat of force) also included "dog bites, spray with pepper spray or a chemical, and a firearm pointed in the citizen's direction" (Langan et al. 2001, 1).

One critical factor that needs to be emphasized early on is that, for the most part, we have an armed citizenry in the United States. In fact, citizens can own many of the same weapons as those used by the police. In some instances, they have more lethal weapons than the police.

We examine this issue further in Chapter 5. For the time being, it is important to note that while definitive numbers are difficult to come by, authorities estimate that between 238 and 276 million firearms are currently in circulation in the United States (Ruddell and Mays 2005). In simplest terms, this means that the typical home within the United States is more likely to have a firearm than not. Therefore, not only are some private citizens armed both inside and outside of their homes, but offenders confronted by the police may be armed as well. As a result, society provides the police with a variety of weapons with which to respond to chaotic and hostile situations.

In considering the use of force by the police, there are three sets of factors to examine: personal, situational, and organizational. Personal factors include the characteristics of the officers and suspects, such as age, education, race, gender, and mental state (for example, intoxication or emotional disturbance). By contrast, situational factors include the time of day, the number of police officers present and the number of subjects being confronted, the circumstances surrounding the confrontation (that is, is this a disturbance, or is a felony arrest being attempted?), and the presence of witnesses. Finally, some of the major organizational factors are the agency's degree of policy restrictiveness, the climate or culture of the agency, and the degree to which administrators allow officers to exercise discretion in certain critical situations. We address all of these factors in one way or another.

Defining the Terms

It is important to remember that the notion of force is much broader than the focus of this chapter. For instance, the mere presence of an officer and verbal commands issued by an officer may represent a minimal level of force. We are concerned here not only with the concept of force but also with the related issues of **abuse of authority, excessive force,** and **brutality (by police).**

We already have provided definitions of *force* utilized by the International Association of Chiefs of Police and the Bureau of Justice Statistics, but what about the other terms? We are using police *abuse of authority* as the most inclusive term. Abuse of authority includes abuse of force, as well as other unethical or illegal actions. This includes misuse of authority in a corrupt way (extortion, bribery, and kickbacks, for example) or for personal gain (such as accepting gratuities or receiving discounts on food or other purchases). Carter (1994, 272) wrote that abuse of authority includes "any action by a police officer without regard to motive, intent, or malice that tends to injure, insult, trespass upon human dignity, manifest feelings of inferiority, and/or violate an inherent legal right of a member of the police constituency." Practically every form of police misconduct falls under the umbrella of abuse of authority.

In terms of excessive force, it is important to remember that a reasonable amount of force is "strictly necessary and . . . required for the performance" of police officers' duties (United Nations 1979). This means that excessive force is "the application of an amount and/or frequency of force *greater* than that required to compel compliance from a willing or unwilling subject" [emphasis added] (IACP 2001, 1). The Office of Community-Oriented Policing Services (2005) suggested that in examining the notion of improper use of force, both the elements of "unnecessary" and "excessive" need to be considered. They added that "[t]he unnecessary use of force would be the application of force where there is no justification for its use, while an excessive use of force would be the application of more force than required where the use of force is necessary."

Flowing from these definitions, the meaning of *police brutality* is excessive force that is deliberately designed to degrade or injure an individual. However, as Carter (1994) noted, while the word *brutality* is used in regard to a variety of police misconduct, it is a subjective concept in that it targets the motives of an officer rather than focusing on the actions of the officer. He believes that *use of force* may be a clearer, more precise term.

It is essential to emphasize that the police are authorized to use force in the line of duty, but this force must be *reasonable* and *necessary*. By definition this means that it cannot be excessive. To the degree that police force is excessive, it becomes an abuse of authority and, like corruption, this is a form of police deviance (Kappeler, Sluder, and Alpert 1994, 146).

The fact that police officers occasionally are accused of excessive force provides the backdrop to this chapter. Two factors are important to consider, however. First, recent research shows that the police use force in about 3.61 out of every 10,000 calls for service. This means that over 99 percent of the time, police officers do not utilize any force (other than their physical presence) in encounters with citizens. Second, in the less than 1 percent of cases where officers used force, excessive force was established in only 0.42 percent of the cases (IACP 2001, iii). Nevertheless, in every known use-of-force case, police officers are scrutinized by someone, and sometimes the public perceives that the use of force was not necessary.

This chapter outlines the constraints placed on the police regarding the use of force. Consideration is given to the circumstances under which force may be used, the types of force employed by the police, and the recourse that citizens may have against the police for excessive force or the unauthorized use of force.

Police and Citizen Interactions

Citizens encounter police officers under a variety of circumstances. A study by the Bureau of Justice Statistics[1] found that in 1999 about 43.8 million people 16 years of age or older had at least one face-to-face encounter with police personnel (Langan et al. 2001, 1). Roughly half of the people who had a personal contact with the police did so in a situation involving a traffic stop. Another 20 percent or so encountered the police in the process of reporting a crime.

In terms of police-citizen contacts that involved force, about 422,000 people—less than 1 percent of those who had personal encounters with the police—reported the use of force or the threatened use of force. About 20 percent of this number indicated that the officer had only threatened to use force. Most confrontations where force was exercised primarily involved the officer pushing or grabbing the citizen, and less than 20 percent of the citizens reported being injured as a result of the use of force by the police (see Adams 2002).

Three of the findings in the Bureau of Justice Statistics report are noteworthy. First, over half of the citizens involved in use-of-force incidents indicated that they had "argued, disobeyed, or resisted the police or that they had been drinking or using drugs at the time" (Langan et al. 2001, 2; see also, IACP 2001, iv). Second, roughly three-fourths of the people experiencing police use of force believed that the amount of force employed was excessive. Third, an overwhelming number (92 percent) maintained that in their particular situation, the police had acted improperly. Taken together, these findings demonstrate that police use of force instances are relatively rare occurrences and that the targets of the force often precipitate a use of force response (see Dunham and Alpert 2002).[2]

One form of police use of force that involves subject provocation has been labeled "**suicide by cop,**" or "victim-precipitated homicide" or "law enforcement-forced-assisted suicide." These situations have started to occur with greater frequency, and they are beginning to gain nationwide attention by the news media, medical officials, and the police themselves. In some circumstances, suicidal individuals have placed themselves in situations—such as pointing a firearm at officers—where the police have no alternative but to shoot them. Hutson and colleagues (1998) examined 437 officer-involved shootings in Los Angeles County, California, from 1987 to 1997 and found 11 percent of them were victim-precipitated. While these incidents have long been recognized by police officers, this study is noteworthy because it was conducted by a group of emergency room physicians. The investigators found that many of the persons who were shot had written suicide notes, told others that they wanted to be shot by the police, or engaged in suicidal behavior at some point in a past incident (for example, had pointed a firearm at their head). In one case, the individual actually thanked officers for shooting him.

Such incidents are a tragedy for all parties, and the officers involved are forced to live with the consequences for the rest of their lives. Hutson and colleagues (1998) found that most of these incidents tended to occur relatively quickly and officers did not learn that the person was suicidal until after the event had transpired. Knowing that some individuals use the police to commit suicide is important in understanding the full picture of the use of force, and this factor should also be taken into consideration when reviewing the annual number of persons shot by the police.

Before we move on to some of the ingredients that influence the police use of force, a number of factors need to be considered. First, a variety of elements have been associated with improper use of force. These include "[s]hortcomings in recruitment, training, and management" (Human Rights Watch 1998), lack of confidence by officers in their ability to control certain situations (Ashley and Golles 2000), and even "burnout, alcohol-related problems, cynicism, or disenchantment" (Christopher 1994, 298). Second, when the police attempt to restrain the freedom of citizens, it is not uncommon to meet with resistance. As Ashley and Golles (2000) noted, "When this happens, officers frequently need to use force to control and perhaps arrest the person in question." Third, suspect age (21 to 30) and mental state (being under the influence of alcohol or drugs and/or emotional disturbance) can affect the level of assaults on police officers that trigger a use-of-force response. Finally, individual officer characteristics, such as age (officers over the age of 40 are involved in fewer use-of-force incidents) and level of education (college education results in less use of force), can influence use-of-force incidence (IACP 2001).

In the following sections, we examine some of the individual, situational, and organizational factors associated with the use of force. We also consider the kinds of actions that police departments and the citizens they serve can undertake to minimize both unnecessary and excessive use of force by officers.

Influences on the Use of Force

Essentially, five factors influence the use of force by police officers: (1) local, state, and federal laws, (2) departmental policies, (3) training, (4) police practices (sometimes called the departmental culture), and (5) the characteristics of individual officers. We will consider each of these in turn.

Laws

On most criminal justice issues, some form of law provides the fundamental basis for the majority of policies. Often the law is written in much broader terms than are police departmental policies. When we address the use of force, it is important to recognize that criminal law, civil law, and constitutional law at various levels all influence when and how officers may use force. In this section, we briefly touch on all three areas of law and how each affects police use of force.

When police officers use excessive force in apprehending and restraining suspects, they can be subject to charges under the criminal law. A good example of this involves the initial charges filed against the four officers from the Los Angeles Police Department who were involved in the videotaped use-of-force incident involving Rodney King. The Los Angeles County District Attorney's Office filed state-level criminal charges of aggravated assault against them. Although all of them were acquitted in the initial trial, they were required to answer to state criminal charges and eventually federal civil rights charges related to the beating of Rodney King (see Kappeler, Sluder, and Alpert 1994; Skolnick and Fyfe 1993).

Perhaps as intimidating, if not more so, to many officers today is the threat of a civil (or civil rights) lawsuit. Many of these suits are brought in federal courts under 42 U.S.C. Section 1983, which is the codification of the Civil Rights Act of 1871. These actions allege that government officials, including police officers, have violated the civil rights of a person (or group of persons) "under color of law." Some of these suits ask for injunctive relief or a stipulation that an officer or agency not engage in a particular action. For example, some agencies were sued to prevent officers from using carotid chokeholds to subdue suspects who resisted arrest. Also, civil rights suits have been filed in cases where asphyxiation deaths have resulted from officers "hog tying" suspects with their hands and feet pulled behind them and placing them on their stomachs. Section 1983 suits may ask for actual and punitive monetary damages from the individual officer, as well as from the officer's supervisors, the department, and the city, county, or state, under the doctrine of *respondeat superior* or vicarious liability of supervisors.[3] Since the 1970s, the number and success of Section 1983 lawsuits have transformed police department practices perhaps as much as any other single legal factor. Departments now routinely train officers in this subject; in 2002, 93 percent of the police academies in the United States provided instructions to police recruits in the areas of an officer's civil and criminal liability (Hickman 2005, 9).

The area of constitutional law has been prominent in the discussions of the police use of force because of one case: ***Tennessee v. Garner*** (1985).[4] Prior to the Supreme Court's decision, 23 states statutorily incorporated the common law standard of the **fleeing felon rule,** and another 12 states allowed officers to use deadly force to apprehend certain fleeing felons (Mays and Taggart 1985). The fleeing felon rule allowed police officers to use deadly force to apprehend a suspected felon who was trying to avoid apprehension (Champion 2005, 103).

The fleeing felon rule came to the United States from England, where under the common law virtually all crimes were felonies and all felonies called for the death penalty (Blumberg 1994; Terrill 2003, 52). As a result, anyone—a private citizen or law enforcement official—could use deadly force to apprehend a known fleeing felon. The English common law tradition was transplanted to the United States, and many states included a provision in their criminal law statutes that police officers could use deadly force to apprehend any fleeing felon. After the Supreme Court issued its ruling in *Tennessee v. Garner,* the fleeing felon rule was held to be generally unconstitutional. Now police officers are authorized to use deadly force only in situations where defense of life (their own or the lives of others) would be an issue, or where they are attempting to apprehend a fleeing felon who has used or threatened to use deadly force.

In summary, any consideration of the police use of force (even definitions of force and when and where force may be utilized) must begin with the law. Laws that exist at the local, state, and federal levels provide broad standards of guidance for police actions. Criminal, civil, and constitutional law all apply to police performance, and they provide the foundation for the development of departmental policies.

Policies

One of the ways that departments can define the parameters for acceptable or unacceptable conduct for officers is through the use of policies. Alpert and Smith (2000, 173) wrote, "Conventional wisdom is that police agencies must exercise strict control over their officers," and, "Creating complex policies, procedures and rules has become the customary method of controlling the discretion of police officers." They warned, however, that "police officials must identify which activities require strict control-oriented policies and which require only summary guidance" (Alpert and Smith 2000, 184).

Today law enforcement agencies of all sizes and at the local, state, and federal levels have extensive written policies that cover many of the situations officers will encounter. In fact, a recent federal government survey found that 95 percent of police departments had policies on deadly force, and 90 percent had policies on nonlethal force (Hickman and Reaves 2006). The same study found that less than 1 percent of all U.S. police officers worked for departments that didn't have policies on deadly force—and these tended to be very small agencies. However, it is essential to emphasize that officers still possess a great deal of discretion over when to act and the possible courses of action they may take.

In this section when we talk about **policies,** we are referring to those administrative regulations that are written by ranking agency officials, distributed to the employees on a regular basis, and published as general orders or in an administrative policies manual (whatever that document might be called). Alpert and Smith (2000) maintain that a policy does not tell officers what to do in certain situations. Instead, "a policy is a guide to thinking" (p. 175). By contrast, procedures give officers guidance in how to apply policies. Departments typically review new policies and procedures with officers, and when policies on topics such as the use of force are changed, administrators may schedule in-service training sessions to review the new policies. Quite often, police policies—much like laws on which many of them are based—will spell out the disciplinary consequences for officers found to have violated departmental directives.

As we have mentioned, departmental policies on the use of force may mirror the broad guidelines established by state and federal laws. However, in most instances police policies and procedures on the use of force are much more restrictive and detailed than provided for by the law (see Blumberg 1994; Manning 2004).

We examine training further in one of the following sections; however, it is important to note that one way for policies to be widely disseminated and consistently explained to officers is during their basic academy training. Additionally, many departments require ongoing, in-service training for veteran officers. Therefore, as a reflection of the training program provided by law enforcement academies and as an extension of that training, agencies frequently have policies—at a minimum—in the areas of (1) the general use of force, (2) the use of firearms and other weapons in the course of duty, (3) regulations for officers being armed off duty, and (4) emergency vehicle operations. In the remainder of this section, we examine these areas and address the degree to which departmental policies can set the tone or direction for operations in these critical areas.

Policies concerning the general use of force typically spell out in detail the circumstances under which the use of force by officers is permissible. Rules and procedures instruct officers on the amount of force that is allowable in each situation. Yet, policies on use of force that appear clear-cut in an academy classroom may be harder to implement when an officer is trying to restrain an uncooperative suspect and has to contend with fear, the very real possibility of being injured or killed, and the knowledge that help from fellow officers may be several minutes away. Further, for some state police officers and rural deputies, the realistic possibility may be that there is no backup.

The following provides a typical general policy statement relating to the use of force:

> This Department recognizes and respects the value and special integrity of each human life. In vesting Officers with the lawful authority to use force to protect the public welfare, a careful balancing of all human interests is required. Therefore, it is the policy of this Department that Officers will use only that force reasonably necessary to effectively bring an incident under control while protecting the lives of the Officer or other person.[5]

The use of **deadly force** particularly arises in situations where the officer's life is in danger, when another person's life is in danger, and in order to apprehend a person who has used deadly force or who is attempting to use deadly force. Unfortunately, in police work, policies and procedures cannot cover every possible situation an officer might encounter.

Nevertheless, police policies must establish that officers are allowed to use force in the performance of their duties, but that such authority is granted with severe restrictions. In most instances, the policy may set forth what commonly is called the **use-of-force continuum.** The use-of-force continuum provides a step-by-step progression of options that officers need to consider when responding to suspects who are resisting. However, it is important to emphasize that an officer may enter the continuum at any point, depending on the situational circumstances with which he or she is confronted. In other words, if a suspect lunges at an officer with a knife, the officer does not have to begin at Level 1 of the continuum. In such circumstances, the appropriate response may be at Levels 4–7, or even Level 8 (deadly force). Box 4.1 presents the use-of-force continuum used by one police department.

Box 4.1
The Use-of-Force Continuum

The following list, taken from the El Paso, Texas, *Police Department Procedures Manual,* (2006) illustrates the use-of-force continuum:

- **Level 1**—this involves the officer's presence and any verbal commands that might be given.
- **Level 2**—this level includes arrests made without physical resistance, where the suspect is apprehended, restrained with handcuffs, and escorted from one location to another.
- **Level 3**—when faced with resistance, officers may employ some combination of physical force (such as come-along holds) to restrain uncooperative suspects.
- **Level 4**—at this level, officers may employ the use of chemical agents such as oleoresin capsicum (OC) spray. Many departments now provide that this is the only authorized chemical agent officers may utilize [see IACP 2001].
- **Level 5**—at this point, officers use hands, feet, elbows, etc. to withstand an assault when lower levels of force have been attempted unsuccessfully.
- **Level 6**—striking or impact weapons such as the side-handle baton or the collapsible baton (or even heavy-duty flashlights) may be used if lower levels of physical force and restraint have been tried but have not worked. For most departments, head strikes with impact weapons are not allowed.
- **Level 7**—police dogs (K-9 units) should be considered as a form of force when used to subdue suspects. As a result of the likelihood of injury to the suspect, given this level of force, departments quite often provide additional policy guidance on the use of K-9 units.
- **Level 8**—this level involves the use of deadly or potentially deadly force. ✦

The use-of-force continuum establishes a progression of force options available to officers. The level of force can range from verbal or vocal compliance, through pain compliance, to less-than-lethal, or even lethal, force. Much of the discussion on the use of force by police officers focuses on lethal force, for obvious reasons, but in one of the following sections, we examine less-than-lethal force as well.

The key in every situation is that officers must use *reasonable* amounts of force, and this acknowledges that anything beyond what is reasonable automatically becomes excessive force or, in the extreme, police brutality. The general standard for the use of force in the policies and procedures of most police departments is that officers may use a sufficient amount of force to overcome any resistance they encounter. In other words, they may meet force with a slightly more-than-equal amount of force.

Policies related to firearms use typically are very detailed in most police agencies today. For example, the following list provides an overview of the types of policies that departments may have relative to the use of firearms by officers:

- Types of weapons (calibers, capacities, and mechanical action— revolvers versus semi-automatic pistols) allowed
- On-duty versus off-duty weapons and the permissibility of secondary or backup weapons
- Use of warning shots
- Shooting at, or from, vehicles
- Shooting dangerous or wounded animals
- Reporting weapons fired in the line of duty, including accidental discharges of weapons
- A schedule for requalification with firearms and the consequences for failing to requalify

These types of policies provide general guidance for officers so that there will be an understanding of when and under what circumstances officers may use force, especially deadly force. Some departments have very restrictive policies in these areas, and this raises the question of whether departments that have restrictive use-of-force policies (especially in regard to firearms use) place their officers in greater peril than those departments with less restrictive policies. Blumberg (1994, 205), in reviewing the research findings from the 1970s and 1980s, concluded that "restrictive firearms policies do not make a police officer's job more risky. They may even contribute to a safer work environment." In fact, restrictive policies may cause officers to consider the alternatives they have to the use of force, or these policies may prevent officers from unnecessarily escalating the level of force in certain instances (see also Fyfe 1979a and 1979b).

This leads us to ask, Can we assume that policies, in-and-of themselves, make a difference? The answer is that it depends. If departments have clearly written policies that are regularly updated and clearly articulated to the officers, and the policies actually are enforced, then policies should make a difference (see Alpert and Smith 2000). To the degree that any one of these elements is missing, or officers choose to ignore them, the policies will be less than effective. Ultimately, police departments are human institutions and policies are reflections of human frailties. Since no policy will be self-enforcing or foolproof, departments must include a significant training component to ensure that officers are fully informed of the policies and the consequences for not following them.

Training

Police officers first encounter discussions regarding the use of force as cadets in the police academy. As part of their training, they are taught to use physical force. This training teaches defensive tactics, restraint techniques or how to subdue aggressive subjects, use of the baton or other striking weapons, and use of mechanical restraint devices such as handcuffs.

We discuss **less-than-lethal force** in a subsequent section in this chapter; however, for present purposes, it is important to note that less-than-lethal force is any measure of coercion that is designed to achieve compliance with the officer without deliberately placing the subject's life in danger. This type of force can be physical or chemical, and it may involve striking (impact) or stunning instruments. In terms of training for less-than-lethal force, a recent report by the Bureau of Justice Statistics found that nationwide, 96 percent of the police academies offered training in the use of batons, 77 percent offered training in the use of chemical agents (almost exclusively pepper spray or OC gas), and a few academies even included training with so-called stun guns (such as Tasers) and the use of rubber bullets (9 percent and 2 percent, respectively) (Hickman 2005, 13).

Academies also routinely provide training in weapons retention, or how officers can keep from being disarmed by suspects during a scuffle. They also teach the use of pressure points, fighting techniques, and speed cuffing. Some of these techniques fall within the realm of what may be characterized as "pain compliance" procedures. Pain compliance is meant to inflict a sufficient amount of discomfort in suspects that they will quit struggling or resisting and submit to the arresting officers.

Police recruits receive firearms training and learn not only techniques of firearms use, but also when and under what circumstances the use of firearms is permissible. They learn that part of the responsibility of being armed—some departments even require officers to be armed off duty—is being technically proficient or accurate. Additionally, exercising good decision-making skills in the process of deciding when to use force is of equal importance. The Bureau of Justice Statistics report on state and local law enforcement training found that 88 percent of the police academies in the United States now provide realistic decision-making scenarios or "shoot-don't shoot" situations as a part of firearms training (Hickman 2005, 14).

One of the focuses of modern police training is in the area of officer liability for excessive use of force. Currently, 96 percent of the state and local law enforcement academies in the United States provide training for officers in the civil and criminal liability that may result if they use excessive force. However, relatively few academies (less than 1 in 10) require officers to participate in simulated use-of-force review boards as part of their training (Hickman 2005, 14).

Training is one of the areas where police departments have been fairly diligent in addressing the skills and knowledge that new officers need to perform their jobs effectively. Hickman and Reaves (2006, 9) reported that the number of hours of basic academy training has increased and that "on average, about three quarters of training hours were state mandated." As part of the initial and ongoing training, many departments regularly review new policies and procedures. Policies in the area of use of force typically receive considerable attention, given the potential liability for individual officers, supervisors, agencies, and the political entities they serve.

Departmental Practice or Police Culture

In the study of police practices in the United States, one of the elements occasionally overlooked is the influence of departmental practices that develop over time, or what might be called departmental culture (Fyfe 1982).[6] The department culture can be influenced positively or negatively by departmental leadership, a commitment to "best practices," the average level of experience, and a host of other variables. Two brief examples illustrate this.

Assume that the "Middleburg Police Department" has a policy that uniformed officers must wear their hats every time they exit the police vehicle or anytime they appear in public. The department has a written policy to this effect, and police cadets are made aware of this policy while they are in the academy. In fact, while in the academy, recruits might receive demerits or other disciplinary actions if they violate this policy. However, when the recruits graduate from the academy and begin working in uniform patrol, they often are told by their field training officers (FTOs) not to worry about wearing their hats during the shift, and that they need to be worn only to and from the police station to make a showing for "the brass." In short order, the rookie officers discover that none of their peers, FTOs, or supervisors wear their hats during the shift. Therefore, this example would show that no matter what the departmental policy says, in practice the departmental culture influences the officers to do something different.

A more positive example might involve a department that does not have a written policy on accepting discounted meals while officers are on duty. While this practice is common in some departments, even those with policies that prohibit it, the culture of the "Northville Police Department" is one that discourages officers from accepting meal discounts. Call it tradition or call it peer pressure, FTOs and other veteran officers regularly convey to the rookies that accepting such gratuities is "unprofessional." In this case, the informal norms of the department can operate in the absence of a written policy.

We can extrapolate from the illustrations about wearing uniform hats and not accepting meal discounts to policies relating to the use of force. Departments can have the most thorough, carefully articulated policies possible, and the departmental culture (fostered by both other officers and the supervisors) can undermine the effects of the policy. This dimension can be surprisingly powerful and very enduring. It tends to be passed on by example and word of mouth from one generation of officers to another, and the influence of departmental culture can be especially apparent when a new chief comes into a department and tries to change things. In one situation such as this, after a heated argument, an officer was heard to say to a new reform-minded chief: "I was here when you got here, and I will be on the front steps waving goodbye when you leave."[7]

Organizational culture in law enforcement can be very powerful. The culture of a given agency can foster deviant behavior, or it can provide an environment that socializes new officers into a strict rule-abiding orientation. We cannot assume that the organizational culture is either all good or all bad in any particular agency. One of the challenges for police administrators is that organizational culture of a department often makes it difficult to enact meaningful changes, at least in the short term. Skogan and Hartnett (1997) have labeled this phenomenon as "cautious inaction" as officers wait to see whether organizational changes or policy changes are real and will be sustained over the long term.

The Characteristics of Individual Officers

In any discussion of the use of force, we cannot ignore the personal values and characteristics that individual officers bring to a given situation. For example, as we indicated at the beginning of the chapter, the use of force is related to three sets of factors: individual (those factors and values associated with the individual officer), situational (the particular circumstance in which the officer is found), and organizational (training, policies, and supervision). In this section we briefly examine individual characteristics to determine the degree to which they influence an officer's use or misuse of force.

A great deal of the research on police use of force over the past four decades has focused on the issue of predicting (or explaining) which officers are most likely to use excessive force (see, for example, Mays and Taggart 1985). This is an important area of inquiry since the Christopher Commission that examined the Los Angeles Police Department in the wake of the Rodney King beating found that 5 percent of the department's officers accounted for 20 percent of the reports involving the use of force (Christopher 1994). As a result, the conduct of a small number of officers may shape the public's perceptions of an entire police department.

While it would be helpful to forecast which officers were most likely to use excessive force, to date studies have not been able to provide us with any degree of predictive accuracy. For example, variables such as the age of the officer, the length of the officer's service, gender, education, and patrol area or assignment should give us some indication of an officer's propensity to be involved in a use-of-force situation. Length of service, gender, and area of assignment have been shown to be related to use-of-force incidents by officers (Christopher 1994). The other factors are inconsistently related, at best (Mays and Taggart 1985).

Nonetheless, some departments have started to implement what they call "**early warning systems**" (Kappeler, Sluder, and Alpert 1994; see also Dunham and Alpert 2004; Walker, Milligan, and Berke 2006). Box 4.2 illustrates some of the variables that might be included in an early warning system.

Documentation of problem behaviors can help police departments determine whether an officer's actions are aberrations or part of an on-

---

Box 4.2
Problem Behaviors and Early Warning Systems

Early warning systems are designed to help police departments identify problem employees early and to track factors such as

- the number of citizen complaints (external) against an officer and the results of investigations of complaints

- departmental (internal) complaints against an officer and the results of the investigations into these complaints

- patterns of misconduct for both citizen and departmental complaints

- the frequency with which an officer files resisting arrest or assault-on-an officer charges

- the characteristics (race, age, gender) of people filing complaints against an officer

- the officer's assignment areas (both geographical and the types of jobs performed by the officer)

- records of discipline and performance appraisals

- commendations and citations for exemplary work

- use of sick leave (especially indications of misuse of sick leave) and the officer's off-duty behaviors, including relations with neighbors and home-life stressors (Kappeler, Sluder, and Alpert 1994, 255–256). ✦

going pattern. Additionally, tracking of the types of factors listed in Box 4.2 can help a department to recognize early in the process when officers may be in trouble in their personal lives and the ways this may spill over into the work environment.

What these individual factors do not tell us is whether the use of force might be instrumental. That is, do some officers use force (even excessive force) in situations where they perceive themselves to be dispensers of justice? There may be circumstances in which officers feel that the formal criminal justice system will not remedy an injustice, so they will do so in an expression of "street corner justice." By the same token, some officers simply may engage in excessive force out of anger, frustration, or an expression of some other emotion. In those circumstances the use of force is noninstrumental. Again, it is important to factor individual officer differences into any equation that considers police use of force.

In concluding this section, we want to reemphasize the role that the personal characteristics of individual officers play in the use of force. These factors can include the personal moral and ethical values held by officers, but they can include personal and professional stressors as well. Some officers seem equipped to handle high levels of stress, but a significant number of life stressors can affect even the strongest, most emotionally stable officers.

High-Speed Pursuits As Deadly Force

Typically, when the use of force by police officers is discussed, most of the focus is on firearms, the baton (or flashlight), and restraint techniques such as the carotid chokehold. However, emergency use of the patrol vehicle—particularly in high-speed pursuit situations—clearly falls within the arena of use of force (see Becknell, Mays, and Giever 1999; Crew and Hart 1999). Furthermore, not only does the automobile become a potentially lethal weapon during a high-speed pursuit, but also the adrenalin-driven, emotional charge associated with a pursuit often leads to excessive use of force on apprehended offenders once the pursuit is terminated.

Police agencies typically defend the use of police pursuits on the grounds that they reduce crime and add to the law's deterrent effect by emphasizing the likelihood of apprehension. However, few systematic studies have been undertaken to establish the degree to which this is true (a notable exception is Crew and Hart 1999). Therefore, it is imperative that we examine the desirability and effectiveness of police pursuit options. Police vehicle operations in the realm of responding to emergencies and high-speed pursuits have become an area of major litigation for many agencies, and while as many as three fourths of the police pursuits result in an arrest, one in three has a negative outcome, such as a traffic accident with property damage, injuries, or fatalities (Crew and Hart 1999, 61).

Emergency vehicle operations involving a number of circumstances are common in police work, and in 2002, 99 percent of the police academies nationwide provided a median number of 36 hours of training in this topic (Hickman 2005, 9). However, it is important to emphasize that not all emergency situations involve high-speed pursuits and that police departments have chosen a number of courses of action designed to limit individual officer and agency liability.

Policies on pursuits by police officers vary from department to department. Typically, in the United States, departments fall into one of three categories relative to pursuit policies:

(1) *Judgmental*—the department leaves the decision to engage in a pursuit (as well as the decision to terminate a pursuit) up to the discretion of the individual officer involved in the situation.

(2) *Restrictive*—departments that employ restrictive policies mandate that certain conditions (road and weather conditions or supervisory approval) must be met before an officer can begin a pursuit.

(3) *Discouragement*—these departments do not prohibit pursuits, but they sternly warn officers against pursuits and permit them in only the most extreme situations (Becknell, Mays, and Giever 1999, 100).

We have addressed the issue of police emergency vehicle operations briefly in the sections on training and policy, but the U.S. Supreme Court also has dealt with this issue. In the case of **County of Sacramento v. Lewis** (1998), the Court held that the appropriate standard for judging officer actions during high-speed pursuits was conduct that "shocks the conscience," not deliberate or reckless indifference. In what was viewed as a pro-police decision, the Court refused to rule against police use of high-speed pursuits, but instead set a relatively high standard for citizens to prove liability on the part of police officers and police agencies. Once again, questions of constitutional law interpreted by the U.S. Supreme Court provided guidance for police officer conduct in the United States.

Additionally, officers may face liability under state **tort law** (see Calvi and Coleman 2004, 241–257). Torts are defined as civil wrongs, and they may provide appropriate remedies for individuals injured in police pursuits. However, it is important to note that states may claim sovereign immunity—which was the case in *County of Sacramento v. Lewis* (1998)—and this can keep them from being sued. This was the reason the plaintiffs in the *Lewis* case brought a Section 1983 civil rights action in federal court. By the same token, some states may waive sovereign immunity in situations involving the negligent operation of a motor vehicle by a public official.[8]

Therefore, what can we conclude about the desirability of permitting or prohibiting police pursuits? A nationwide study of 436 police agencies, published in the late 1990s, examined the areas of pursuit policy restrictiveness, training, and evaluations of pursuit situations. The authors of this study concluded that as policy restrictiveness increased, the numbers of pursuits decreased. They also found that more thorough training of officers and more systematic evaluations of pursuit situations by police agencies also decreased the number of pursuits (Becknell, Mays, and Giever 1999, 105).

Less Than Lethal Force

Given the controversy surrounding the use of lethal force by police officers, and the liability presented by such use of force for police departments, it is apparent why so many agencies have expanded the training and use of less-than-lethal force devices (such as stun guns) for officers. However, before we proceed further, it is important to note that there may be a discrepancy in terminology. Many police officials talk in terms of less-than-lethal force, but a more accurate term may be **less lethal force** (see Ingley 2005). This term recognizes the fact that while officers may not intend death or serious bodily injury when they use physical, chemical, impact, or stun force, there is always the possibility that a suspect could die as a result of unforeseen circumstances. For instance, while stun-gun devices such as Tasers have been used effectively many times by officers, a growing number of suspects have died (Bleetman, Steyn, and Lee 2004). However, what is the real extent of stun-gun deaths? The true figures are somewhat elusive. Consider the following.

The international human rights organization Amnesty International reported that between June 2001 and March 2005, 103 Taser-related deaths occurred in the United States and Canada (see *CBC News* 2004). A Seattle newspaper report said that for a similar period (2000–2004), there were 78 Taser-related deaths (69 in the United States and 9 in Canada). A frequently cited, although not totally substantiated figure, is that to date, there have been 80 Taser-related deaths (see Ingley 2005). *CBS News* (2004) reported that 40 deaths were attributed to stuns by Tasers, and a Cincinnati newspaper reporter said that

> Tasers were a contributing cause of death three times, and were not ruled out three times. In the rest of the 70-something deaths, Tasers were used, but the causes of death were something else: drug overdoses, medical conditions, injuries from violence during arrest or before police arrived, etc. (Bronson 2005)

The Cincinnati report—from a city that has witnessed a fair amount of unrest as a result of police use of force—concluded that Tasers were used by police officers about 100,000 times per year, with only three confirmed and three possible deaths resulting. Thus, Bronson's assessment is that the reports of some Taser deaths, while factual, are grossly exaggerated in number.

Surprisingly, the medical establishment seems to support the use of Tasers by police. While acknowledging that some persons have died after being shocked, there often were contributing factors to these deaths, such as stimulant abuse, excited delirium, and overall poor health (Bleetman, Steyn, and Lee 2004; Clark 2006). As Bozeman (2005), an emergency duty physician, observed:

> use of the devices appears to drastically reduce overall injuries and deaths, largely from a reduction in the use of other more dangerous methods available to police officers, such as striking violent suspects with a nightstick or flashlight or shooting them with a firearm.

Consistent with many other issues in this book, the use of less lethal force will continue to be the subject of controversy. Ultimately, we hope that such debates are settled on what the research demonstrates about use of force rather than political expediency based on speculation and anecdotal accounts of incidents.

Police Officer Deaths and Citizen Deaths

One way to fully appreciate the use of force by police officers is to examine the number of police officers feloniously killed in the line of duty each year (by firearms and other instruments as well) and the corresponding number of citizens killed by the police in the performance of their duties. We can be relatively confident when we discuss the numbers of police officers killed in the line of duty annually. This is a figure that has been part of the FBI's *Uniform Crime Reports* for decades. For instance, Table 4.1 shows the numbers of police officers killed annually over an 11-year time period. These numbers range from a low of 42 in 1999 to a high of 79 in 1994. On average, from a national perspective, annually between one and two officers are killed per state, and about five are killed per month. Are these numbers large or small? It probably depends to a great extent on your perception. Given that there are about 750,000 law enforcement officers at all levels of government in the United States, the annual average of officers killed amounts to less than one-tenth of 1 percent. Nevertheless, every law enforcement officer killed in the line of duty represents a significant sacrifice for the officer, his or her family, and the department that the officer represents.

It would seem reasonable to believe that somehow the numbers of officers killed in the line of duty would be related to the numbers of citizens killed by the police, but there is not a logical relationship. In fact, two issues are apparent when comparing these two sets of numbers. First, the police kill a significantly higher number of citizens annually than the number of police officers killed in the line of duty. The Centers for Disease Control and Prevention (CDC) (2004, 8) classify these deaths as

Table 4.1
Police Officers Feloniously Killed in the Line of Duty, 1994–2005

Year	Number of officers killed
1994	79
1995	74
1996	61
1997	70
1998	61
1999	42
2000	51
2001	70*
2002	56
2003	52
2004	57
2005	55
Total	728

*The 72 officers killed in the September 11, 2001, attacks on the World Trade Center are not included in this total.

Source: Federal Bureau of Investigation (2006).

"legal intervention deaths," which they define as deaths that occur "when the decedent was killed by a police officer or other peace officer (persons with specified legal authority to use deadly force), including military police, acting in the line of duty."

Second, we may not have the same level of confidence about the numbers of citizens killed by the police as we have with the numbers of police officers killed. In fact, some researchers (for example, Sherman and Langworthy 1979) have speculated that, because of different (or totally absent) reporting standards, there may be twice as many citizens killed by the police each year as are reported. In a contrasting perspective, the International Association of Chiefs of Police (IACP) (2001), in assembling its National Police Use of Force Database, found that from 1999 to 2000, only three suspect deaths were reported nationwide by the agencies supplying police use-of-force data.[9]

Table 4.2 lists the numbers of felons killed by the police in what are classified as justifiable homicides for the 14-year period from 1989 to 2002. Unfortunately, the years for statistics in Tables 4.1 and 4.2 do not exactly correspond, but there is overlap for eleven years (1994–2004), and these years show somewhere between five and six times as many citizens killed by the police as police officers killed in the line of duty.

Several observations can be drawn from the numbers in Table 4.2, as well as from other government sources dealing with justifiable homicides by the police. First, since 1976, the modern high point for justifiable homicides by the police was in 1994 with 459 (1980 was second with 457, and 1993 was third with 453). Second, since the mid-1990s,

Table 4.2
Felons Killed by the Police in Justifiable Homicides, 1989—2004[10]

Year	Number of justifiable homicides*
1989	363
1990	385
1991	367
1992	418
1993	455
1994	462
1995	389
1996	356
1997	366
1998	367
1999	308
2000	309
2001	378
2002	341
2003	371
2004	368
Total	6,003

*Note: The vast majority of these deaths (typically between 98 percent and 99 percent annually) is a result of police use of firearms.

the annual trend generally has been downward, although the Centers for Disease Control and Prevention showed slightly increasing numbers from 1999 to 2003 (see note 10). Third, research from the Bureau of Justice Statistics (1998 and 2006) showed that most of the people killed by the police were killed with firearms. Fourth, most of the justifiable homicides attributable to the police were the result of attacks on an officer or officers (Bureau of Justice Statistics, 2006). Finally, the issue of race must be addressed in any shooting by the police. Research consistently has found that African Americans and Hispanics are overrepresented as targets of police shootings (see Walker 1999, 223–224 for an extended discussion of this issue). While this is true, recent figures from the Centers for Disease Control and Prevention (CDC) (2003) indicate that from 1999 to 2003, the percentage of white suspects killed by the police ranged from 64 percent to 73 percent (consistently in the range of two-thirds).

Remedies for Unauthorized Use of Force

We have discussed many of the situations in which officers might use force in the performance of their duties, but what can or should be done in situations where officers are not authorized to use force or where they use more force than is necessary? David Carter (1994) proposed a list of seven "differential containment strategies" by which departments can deal with police abuses of authority:

(1) *Personnel selection*—the emphasis should be on factors such as "intelligence, honesty, stability, and reliability," instead of some of the traditional qualities or characteristics on which police departments have focused.

(2) *Training*—there should be less emphasis on the historical crime-fighting orientation and a greater focus on the service duties and responsibilities actually carried out by police officers.

(3) *Performance evaluations*—departments should place greater emphasis on evaluating the quality of service provided by police officers rather than simply quantifying the number of arrests, tickets written, and crime reports filed.

(4) *Open complaint and internal investigation system*—there should be an easy mechanism for citizens to file complaints against police officers, and there should be a perception that complaints will be taken seriously and investigated fully.

(5) *Public information/education*—the public should be adequately educated on the true nature of police work, including the situations under which officers are authorized to use force as well as the types of force that are appropriate in a given situation.

(6) *Troubleshooting/preventive programs*—departments should develop early warning systems [see, for example, Dunham and Alpert 2004], and they should respond to problematic officers with both treatment and punishment, not just punishment.

(7) *Policies, procedures, and organizational control*—organizational guidelines should clearly spell out the nature of officer misconduct and provide officers and supervisors with directions on how to respond to misconduct most appropriately. (Carter 1994, 281–284)

Many of these strategies have been discussed in one form or another in this chapter. Most of these elements are internal to police agencies, but a few are external. Nevertheless, as Carter (1994) suggested, taken together all of these factors contribute to a more thorough approach to preventing and responding to abuses of authority, including the misuse of force.

Conclusions

In a given year, many citizens will encounter the police in a variety of circumstances. For some, it will be in the process of receiving a traffic ticket for a moving violation. For others, the encounter will be prompted by the citizen reporting a crime. For an additional group of people, the interactions will be based on police officers making arrests of persons suspected of having committed a crime. In the vast majority of these cases (over 99 percent), police officers will use little to no force, and the situation will be resolved quickly and quietly. In other circumstances, the police may confront armed suspects, or they may meet with resistance in the process of trying to apprehend or arrest a suspected offender. How will the officers respond? One answer is that, in most cases, force will not be necessary.

Applying the use-of-force continuum as an analytical device, researchers recently discovered some interesting results. For instance, in cases involving resisting suspects, officers escalated their responses (that is, moved up the use-of-force continuum) in about one of five situations. By contrast, when confronted with resisting suspects, officers successfully de-escalated them in three of four use-of-force situations (Terrill 2005).

Most police officers seldom will have to use extreme force in the line of duty, and a relatively small number ever will have to use deadly force (Dunham and Alpert 2002). Although they remain unresolved, a few issues must be mentioned at the end of this chapter. First, in many cases when the police have to use force, they are completely justified in the force they employ to apprehend and subdue suspects. Force is called for and it is reasonably used. Second, a small number of officers use force frequently and, unfortunately, occasionally unjustifiably (see Christopher 1994; Kappeler, Sluder, and Alpert 1994). Some departments act decisively to discipline or dismiss officers who seem to engage in excessive force, but other departments ignore or even reward officers who carry out their duties in an aggressive manner (see especially Chapter 4 on "Police Brutality and Abuse of Authority" in Kappeler et al. 1994). Finally, even when police officers act in a reasonable and justifiable way in the use of force, they are likely to be second-guessed and criticized, not only by those against whom force has been used, but also by members of the general public as well.

Notes

1. This section is largely based on a Bureau of Justice Statistics report, entitled *Contacts Between Police and the Public: Findings From the 1999 National Survey* (Langan et al. 2001).

2. In a recent BJS study, Hickman (2006, 2) reported that citizen complaints about use of force in large law enforcement agencies were "6.6 per 100 full-time sworn officers responding to calls for service" and that rates tended to be higher in large municipal police departments. This study also revealed that approximately 8 percent of cases (where the results were known) resulted in disciplinary action against the officers—meaning that very few use of force complaints were sustained.

Hickman, however, suggests that the number of citizen complaints is often a function of the characteristics of the agency. Law enforcement agencies that make it easy to file a complaint, for instance, will likely have a greater volume of citizen complaints.

3. Champion (2005, 218) stated that this is "a doctrine under which liability is imposed on an employer for the acts of his or her employees that are committed in the course and scope of their employment."

4. The *Tennessee v. Garner* case arose out of a call to the Memphis, Tennessee, Police Department reporting a suspected burglary. When officers arrived at the scene, 15-year-old Edward Garner fled from the home and was ordered to halt by officers. When he attempted to scale a fence to escape, one of the officers fired a shot that hit Garner in the head, instantly killing him. In this case, the Supreme Court was asked to decide whether the long-standing fleeing felon rule was still constitutionally permissible.

5. Policies quoted or referred to throughout this section come from the most recent edition (2006) of the El Paso, Texas, *Police Department Procedures Manual*. These statements are similar to those of many large law enforcement agencies in the United States.

6. Although somewhat dated at this point, the books *Police in Trouble* by James Ahern (1972) and *The Ambivalent Force* by Abraham Blumberg and Elaine Niederhoffer (1985) provide timeless and insightful views of the nature and influence of police organizational culture. A more recent book that explores this topic thoroughly is *Understanding Police Culture* by John Crank (2004).

7. Larry Mays, the senior author of this book, had the privilege of working with the part-policeman, part-philosopher officer who was involved in this exchange.

8. See, for example, *New Mexico Statutes Annotated*, Section 41-4-5.

9. The IACP compiled its report based on contributions from 564 agencies that represent a total population of almost 150 million people. From 1991 to 2000, these agencies reported nearly 46 million calls for service from which there were 177,215 use-of-force incidents and 8,082 use-of-force complaints (IACP 2001).

10. The CDC (2003) reported slightly different numbers of "legal intervention deaths" for 1999–2003: 1999 (398), 2000 (359), 2001 (396), 2002 (384), 2003 (423), and 2004 (372). Data for 2004 were retrieved January 1, 2007 from: *http://www.cdc.gov/ncipc/wisqars*.

Key Terms

abuse of authority	excessive force	less-than-lethal force
brutality, (by police)	fleeing felon rule	policies
County of Sacramento v.	force	suicide by cop
Lewis	legal intervention	*Tennessee v. Garner*
deadly force	deaths	tort law
early warning systems	less lethal force	use-of-force continuum

Critical Review Questions

1. In England, police officers are not armed on a routine basis. Should the police in the United States be armed? Is our situation different from that of England and some other nations? How? Why?

2. Define the terms "abuse of authority," "excessive force," and "police brutality." Which of these terms is the broadest and most encompassing? Which term (or terms) would be most useful in a study of police use of force?

3. How do you respond to the statement: "All brutality is excessive force, but not all excessive force is brutality?" Justify your answer.

4. When does reasonable force become excessive force? Is there an easy line of demarcation for the police and the public to recognize when force becomes excessive?

5. What are the most common ways in which the public encounters the police? When police officers interact with the public, what are some of the stressful factors that result in such interactions leading to the use of force?

6. Carefully examine the five influences on the use of force by the police that were discussed in the chapter. Which of these is most likely to influence the use of force by officers? Why?

7. One social critic was quoted as saying the police in America have two trigger fingers, one for African Americans and another for whites. Is there any evidence to support such a contention, or is this merely political rhetoric?

8. Should police departments forbid all high-speed pursuits by officers? Why or why not? What would be the consequence of a "no pursuit" policy?

9. Why do a small number of officers account for the majority of complaints about the use of force in most departments? Why do some departments have a disproportionate number of use-of-force complaints?

References

Adams, Kenneth. (2002). "What we know about police use of force." Pp. 130–144 in *Crime & Justice in America,* second edition, edited by Wilson R. Palacios, Paul F. Cromwell, and Roger G. Dunham. Upper Saddle River, NJ: Prentice Hall.

Ahern, James F. (1972). *Police in Trouble: Our Frightening Crisis in Law Enforcement.* New York: Hawthorn Books.

Alpert, Geoffrey P., and William C. Smith. (2000). "Developing police policy: An evaluation of the control principle." Pp. 173–186 in *Public Policy, Crime, and Criminal Justice,* second edition, edited by Barry W. Hancock and Paul M. Sharp. Upper Saddle River, NJ: Prentice Hall.

Ashley, Steven D., and Laura Golles. (2000). "The effect of police officer confidence on officer injuries and excessive force complaints." Retrieved July 24, 2006 from: *http://www.sashley.com/articles/effectofpoliceofficerconfidence.htm*.

Becknell, Conan, G. Larry Mays, and Dennis M. Giever. (1999). "Policy restrictiveness and police pursuits." *Policing: An International Journal of Police Strategies & Management* 22 (1), 93–110.

Bittner, Egon. (1990). *Aspects of Police Work*. Boston: Northeastern University Press.

Bleetman, Anthony, Richard Steyn, and Caroline Lee. (2004). "Introduction of the Taser into British policing: Implications for UK emergency departments, An overview of electronic weaponry." *Emergency Medicine Journal* 21 (2), 136–140.

Blumberg, Abraham S., and Elaine Niederhoffer. (1985). *The Ambivalence Force: Perspectives on the Police*, third edition. New York: Holt, Rinehart and Winston.

Blumberg, Mark. (1994). "Police use of deadly force: Exploring some key issues." Pp. 201–220 in *Police Deviance*, third edition, edited by Thomas Barker and David L. Carter. Cincinnati, OH: Anderson.

Bozeman, William P. (2005). "Withdrawal of Taser electroshock devices: Too much, too soon." *Annals of Emergency Medicine* 46 (3), 300–301.

Bronson, Peter. (2005, February 22). "Taser deaths grossly exaggerated." Enquirer Cincinnati.com. Retrieved July 24, 2006 from: *http://www.enquirer.com/columns/bronson/*.

Bureau of Justice Statistics. (1998). *Policing and Homicide, 1976–1998*. Retrieved July 24, 2006 from: *http://www.ojp.usdoj.gov/bjs/pub/pdf/ph98.pdf*.

——. (2006). *Homicide Trends in the U.S.: Justifiable Homicides*. Retrieved July 24, 2006 from: *http://www.ojp.usdoj.gov/bjs/homicide/justify.htm*.

Calvi, James V., and Susan Coleman. (2004). *American Law and Legal Systems*, fifth edition. Upper Saddle River, NJ: Prentice Hall.

Carter, David L. (1994). "Theoretical dimensions in the abuse of authority by police officers." Pp. 269–289 in *Police Deviance*, third edition, edited by Thomas Barker and David L. Carter. Cincinnati, OH: Anderson.

CBC News. (2004). "Taser deaths targeted by rights group." Retrieved July 24, 2006 from: *http://www.cbc.ca/bc/story/bc_amnesty20040526.html*.

CBS News. (2004). "TASER danger?" Retrieved December 31, 2006 from: *http://www.cbsnews.com/stories/2004/10/12/earlyshow/printable648859.shtml*.

Centers for Disease Control and Prevention (CDC). (2003). *Vital Statistics of the United States: Mortality, 2003*. Retrieved July 24, 2006 from: *http://www.cdc.gov/nchs/data/statab/Mortfinal2003_worktable291f.pdf*.

——. (2004). *Coding Manual, National Violent Death Reporting System*. Atlanta, GA: Author.

Champion, Dean John. (2005). *The American Dictionary of Criminal Justice*, third edition. Los Angeles: Roxbury Publishing.

Christopher, William. (1994). "Report of the independent commission of the Los Angeles Police Department (summary)." Pp. 291–304 in *Police Deviance*, third edition, edited by Thomas Barker and David L. Carter. Cincinnati, OH: Anderson.

Clark, John. (2006, Winter). "Is there a proper place for Tasers in the use of force continuum?" *Proceedings of the Large Jails Network Meeting*, pp. 31–35.

Crank, John. (2004). *Understanding Police Culture*, second edition. Cincinnati, OH: Anderson.

Crew, Robert E., and Robert A. Hart, Jr. (1999). "Assessing the value of police pursuit." *Policing: An International Journal of Police Strategies & Management* 22 (1), 58–73.

County of Sacramento v. Lewis, 523 U.S. 833 (1998).

Dunham, Roger, and Geoffrey Alpert. (2002). "Police shootings: Myths and realities." Pp. 122–129 in *Crime and Justice in America*, second edition, edited by Wilson R. Palacios, Paul F. Cromwell, and Roger G. Dunham. Upper Saddle River, NJ: Prentice Hall.

——. (2004). *Critical Issues in Policing*, fifth edition. Long Grove, IL: Waveland.

El Paso Police Department. (2006). *Department Procedures Manual*. El Paso, TX.

Federal Bureau of Investigation (FBI). (2006). *Law Enforcement Officers Killed and Assaulted, 2005*. Washington, DC: U.S. Department of Justice.

Fyfe, James J. (1979a). "Administrative interventions on police shooting discretion: An empirical examination." *Journal of Criminal Justice* 7 (4), 309–323.

——. (1979b). "Deadly force." *FBI Law Enforcement Bulletin* 48, 7–9.

——. (1982). "Blind justice: Police shootings in Memphis." *Journal of Criminal Law and Criminology* 73 (2), 707–722.

Hickman, Matthew J. (2005). *State and Local Law Enforcement Training Academies, 2002.* Washington, DC: U.S. Department of Justice, Bureau of Justice Statistics.

——. (2006). *Citizen Complaints About Police Use of Force.* Washington, DC: U.S. Department of Justice, Bureau of Justice Statistics.

Hickman, Matthew J., and Brian A. Reaves. (2006). *Local Police Departments, 2003.* Washington, DC: U.S. Department of Justice, Bureau of Justice Statistics.

Human Rights Watch. (1998). "Shielded from justice." Retrieved July 24, 2006 from: *http://hrw.org/reports98/police/uspo14.htm.*

Hutson, H. Range, Deirdre Anglin, John Yarbrough, Kimberly Hardaway, Marie Russell, Jared Strote, Michael Canter, and Bennett Blum. (1998). "Suicide by cop." *Annals of Emergency Medicine* 32 (6), 665–669.

Ingley, Stephen J. (2005). "Stun devices." *American Jails* 19 (1), 7.

International Association of Chiefs of Police. (2001). *Police Use of Force in America, 2001.* Alexandria, VA: Author.

Kappeler, Victor, Richard D. Sluder, and Geoffrey P. Alpert. (1994). *Forces of Deviance.* Prospect Heights, IL: Waveland.

Langan, Patrick A., Lawrence A. Greenfeld, Steven K. Smith, Matthew R. Durose, and David J. Levin .(2001). *Contacts Between Police and the Public: Findings From the 1999 National Survey.* Washington, DC: U.S. Department of Justice, Bureau of Justice Statistics.

Manning, Maren. (2004). "Use of force, Vegas style." *Law and Order* 52 (10), 110–112.

Mays, G. Larry, and William A. Taggart. (1985). "Deadly force as a policy problem in local law enforcement: Do administrative practices make a difference?" *Policy Studies Review* 5 (2), 309–318.

Office of Community-Oriented Policing Services. (2005). "Use of force." Retrieved July 24, 2006 from: *http://www.cops.usdoj.gov/print.asp?Item=1374.*

Reaves, Brian A., and Matthew J. Hickman. (2002). *Census of State and Local Law Enforcement Agencies, 2000.* Washington DC: Bureau of Justice Statistics, Office of Justice Programs.

Ruddell, Rick, and G. Larry Mays. (2005). "State background checks and firearms homicides." *Journal of Criminal Justice* 33 (2), 127–136.

Sherman, Lawrence, and Robert Langworthy. (1979). "Measuring homicide by police officers." *Journal of Criminal Law & Criminology* 70 (4), 546–560.

Skogan, Wesley G., and Susan M. Hartnett. (1997). *Community Policing: Chicago Style.* New York: Oxford University Press.

Skolnick, Jerome H., and James J. Fyfe. (1993). *Above the Law: Police and the Excessive Use of Force.* New York: Free Press.

Tennessee v. Garner, 471 U.S. 1 (1985).

Terrill, Richard J. (2003). *World Criminal Justice Systems,* fifth edition. Cincinnati, OH: Anderson.

Terrill, William. (2005). "Police use of force: A transactional approach." *Justice Quarterly* 22 (1), 107–138.

United Nations. (1979). "Code of conduct for law enforcement officials." General Assembly Resolution 34/169, December 17.

Walker, Samuel. (1999). *The Police in America,* third edition. Boston: McGraw-Hill.

Walker, Samuel, Stacy O. Milligan, and Anna Berke. (2006). "Supervision and intervention within early intervention systems." Retrieved July 26, 2006 from: *http://www.cops.usdoj.gov/mime/open.pdf?Item=1671.*

Recommended Readings

Klinger, David. (2004). *Into the Kill Zone: A Cop's Eye View of Deadly Force.* San Francisco: Jossey-Bass. Klinger uses interviews with 80 police officers who have used deadly force, and the results from these interviews shed considerable insight into an officer's split second decision-making process associated with the use of force. This book is well written and gives the reader considerable insight into perceptions of officers who have been involved in shootings—before, during, and after the event.

Rahtz, Howard. (2003). *Understanding Police Use of Force.* Monsey, NY: Criminal Justice Press. This book was partially written in response to allegations of excessive use of force by the police in Cincinnati, Ohio, in 2001 and the subsequent demonstrations and riots. Rahtz deals with many of the issues addressed in this chapter, including definitions, the legal environment of the use of force, the use-of-force continuum, and training police officers to know when and how to use force properly. This short (159 pages) paperback book is useful reading for any serious student of the use of force by the police.

Skolnick, Jerome H., and James J. Fyfe. (1993). *Above the Law: Police and the Excessive Use of Force.* New York: Free Press. Skolnick and Fyfe (a former New York City police officer) begin this book with a thorough review of the beating of Rodney King. However, beyond the first chapter, the authors explore some of the motivations behind the use of force by police officers. Thankfully, they go beyond many of the simplistic explanations offered in the news media about good cops gone bad and examine the occupational culture of policing. Additionally, rather than simply identifying the problems associated with police use of force, the authors also offer a number of remedies or ways to hold the police accountable. They conclude with a discussion of what they call "renewing the police." ✦

Chapter 5

Gun Control

Introduction

For at least four decades, the topic of gun control has been on the political agenda in the United States. The assassinations of John F. Kennedy, Robert Kennedy, and Martin Luther King, Jr., in the 1960s brought this issue to the forefront in U.S. politics. The Gun Control Act of 1968 especially seemed to be spurred on by the 1968 assassination of Presidential candidate Robert Kennedy by Sirhan Sirhan with an inexpensive .22 caliber handgun that many call a **Saturday-night special (SNS).** More recently, during the Presidencies of Bill Clinton and George W. Bush, the topic of gun control has had national focus. The issue has resulted in a variety of national legislation (including both a ban on assault weapons and the **sunset,** or expiration, of that ban 10 years later), but it represents a unique dilemma for crime control advocates. As an issue championed by conservative organizations, such as the National Rifle Association (NRA) and other smaller and less-powerful public interest groups, gun control results in regular efforts to lobby Congress and the President to prevent further restrictions on private ownership of firearms. However, even some of the most ardent firearms enthusiasts recognize that firearms often are involved in the commission of crimes, particularly violent offenses. Therefore, the debate becomes one over whether private ownership of firearms *promotes* criminal activity or whether it *prevents* crimes (see Kleck 1997; Kleck and Kates 2001). Liberals seem to pull one way and conservatives another. Both sides promise that laws can make a difference, but with thousands of gun laws already "on the books," we need to ask, Is it really the laws that make a difference?

Almost everybody has an opinion about gun control, the relationship between guns and violence, and the best way to control the misuse of firearms. Unfortunately, many of our ideas are based on political rhetoric, anecdotal accounts of single incidents, or what we gather from the latest television newscasts. Most people do not have much in-depth knowledge about the history of gun control in the United States, how criminals obtain their guns, how often guns are used in crimes, and the defensive use of firearms. There is considerable debate about the types of legislation that best control firearms misuse or whether gun laws have much impact at all. This chapter provides an overview of firearms mortality and the sources of firearms legislation, and it addresses whether firearms legislation and police interventions are the best strategies for reducing gun violence.

A number of key issues prevail in the debates over firearms, their place in society, and how we should control their misuse. First, because this is an emotionally charged issue, advocates on many sides—liberals and conservatives, as well as groups that want either to place further restrictions on firearms or to oppose such legislation—often rely upon rhetoric rather than factual information about violent crime or the involvement of firearms in violent crime, or in defensive gun use. Second, most of us learn about issues such as gun control from television, and a short news segment does not enable us to learn much about the pros and cons of a given issue. Third, a lot of our perceptions about crime and violence are misleading or wrong.

Throughout many of your classes, you have learned that almost everybody has a strong opinion about the best ways to reduce crime. The dilemma we face is that these opinions are often based on little actual knowledge about the particular offense, the types of interventions that have been used in the past to respond to crimes, how crime control strategies were introduced, and whether interventions were effective. The problem of controlling the misuse of firearms is no exception. To better understand how to control firearms, we need to know more about gun control history, violent crime, the effectiveness of different types of legislation or police interventions that have been used, and the impact of these practices.

Ruddell and Decker (2006) found that while many factors influence the public's perceptions about firearms misuse, the media are by far the worst culprits. Television news agencies, for instance, are often at fault for reducing complex policy issues, especially those about crime and justice, into a report that is only a few minutes long (Kleck and Kates 2001). Further, the films and television programs that we view often sensationalize firearms use, and we watch youngsters with dangerous-looking weapons shooting them indiscriminately and causing all sorts of carnage. Yet, empirical evidence suggests that such events are rare. In addition to the entertainment media, other groups are guilty of distorting our perceptions about firearms use. Different **stakeholders** (people or organizations who have an investment in the particular outcome of an issue), including law enforcement officers and organizations, offer anecdotal accounts about youth or adult gun violence (for example, relating information about rare or sensational incidents as if those cases were normal).

More troubling is that some scholars have deliberately distorted information about firearms use, or the types of firearms that some offenders are likely to use. In a recent case, Michael Bellesiles was alleged to have engaged in shoddy research by deliberately misrepresenting and fabricating data for his 2001 book, entitled *Arming America: The Origins of a National Gun Culture*. Ruddell and Decker (2006) also outlined how academic researchers distort information about juvenile firearms use by categorizing 18- to 24-year-olds as "youths." While we expect that filmmakers will sensationalize information to sell more movie tickets, it is disheartening when academic researchers distort their findings to support a political position or their own personal beliefs.

Altogether, a number of different forces shape our understanding of the world, and there is no shortage of misleading information about firearms use or what is effective at reducing gun violence. Like many other criminal justice topics discussed in this book, the issue of guns and violence poses many questions and offers few simple answers. One hazard in much of the debate over firearms is that our reliance on simplistic solutions ("ban all guns" or "give all teachers guns to prevent school shootings") to explain long-term social problems gives the public unrealistic expectations about solving these complex challenges.

When all of the rhetoric is removed from discussion about firearms legislation, it basically boils down to two different types of interventions. Scholars have called these the supply- or demand-side solutions to the problem. **Supply-side interventions** try to reduce the number of firearms within a jurisdiction (the number of legitimate firearms, certain types of firearms that are thought to be more dangerous, or the number of guns in the hands of unauthorized users, such as juveniles or felons). **Demand-side interventions,** by contrast, attempt to increase the "costs" of illegally using firearms, typically through street enforcement. In addition, educationally-based programs that attempt to change perceptions about illegally carrying firearms would be considered demand-side interventions (see Fagan 2005).

Numerous challenges arise when implementing either approach to firearms control, and liberals and conservatives are not likely to agree on a specific approach. First, the supply side is challenged by the reality that there are some 276 million firearms within the United States, nearly one for every person (Graduate Institute of International Studies 2003). The demand-side argument, by contrast, is challenged by the fact that thousands of federal, state, and local laws already regulate the use of these firearms—from their manufacture, importation, sale and use, to their export.[1] Despite the fact that there are so many laws, some are rarely enforced, and criminals (many of whom are not legally able to possess firearms in the first place) frequently do not abide by firearms laws. Some of these laws are very punitive—such as sentence enhancements for firearms involved in felony offenses or mandatory prison terms for unlawfully carrying concealed guns—but conservatives often ask, Since the existing laws are not enforced, why add more laws that are also unlikely to be enforced?

A central question in the debate over the effectiveness of firearms legislation is whether sweeping national or state legislation will reduce firearms deaths. Many who disagree with this approach argue that the best violence-reduction interventions are demand-side interventions, such as local police-based strategies to reduce unauthorized persons from possessing guns or to apprehend persons possessing firearms illegally. In some jurisdictions, such as Boston, the police, prosecutors, and federal law enforcement officials have worked together to implement interventions that have successfully reduced gun violence (Kennedy 1997). Both approaches have merit, although they both fall prey to the simplistic solutions that politicians often promote.

Many scholars, for example, argue that the most effective solutions to violence reduction are to fix long-standing social problems in areas of greatest disadvantage, such as the inner cities where there is a disproportionate amount of violent crime. While firearms murders occur in all states, they are not distributed equally throughout the nation. Almost half of all U.S. homicides are concentrated in a relatively small number of urban areas, and they seem to occur in places with long histories of concentrated poverty, few positive role models, high drug addiction rates, and other legal problems, such as elevated levels of gang involvement and the drug trade.

Firearms Mortality

Rates of civilian firearms ownership in the United States are higher than almost anywhere else in the world, and much attention has been drawn to the fact that firearms are the primary mechanism of injury in most homicides (Fox and Zawitz 2006). According to data provided by the Centers for Disease Control and Prevention (CDC) (2007), in 2004 some 29,569 Americans died from gunshot wounds, although only just over one-third of that total (11,624) involved homicides. The majority of persons killed by firearms were persons who took their own lives (16,750 cases in 2004), followed by relatively low numbers of accidental firearms fatalities (649 cases in 2004) and police legal interventions (that is, when the police kill a suspect, between 300 and 400 cases per year).

The total costs of firearms violence and unintentional injuries are not trivial. Cook and Ludwig (2000) estimated that nearly $100 billion are spent to repair the harm of gun violence in a given year, although that figure has been disputed because it includes long-term rehabilitative and intangible costs, such as fear of crime or security precautions that people take (see Kopel 2001). To avoid further complicating the issue, our focus here is on the use of guns in crime, where violent crime occurs, and the types of gun control legislation and police interventions that are successful at reducing gun violence.

Altogether, about two thirds of all murders involve firearms, and this percentage has been fairly consistent for decades, even though homicide rates decreased dramatically nationwide between 1993 and 2005. Data from the Bureau of Justice Statistics reveal that the percentage of guns used in murders ranged from a low of 58 percent in 1983 to a high of 70 percent of homicides in 1994 (Fox and Zawitz 2006).

Handguns are used in most firearms homicides. In the late 1970s, approximately 70 percent of all homicides involved handguns, but this had increased to over 80 percent in the early 1990s, at the height of the murder rate. Given these findings, some people ask why we don't regulate handguns more stringently. There are already a large number of laws that have been enacted to restrict the ability of some persons to own firearms, and handguns have been the subject of legislation since the early 1900s. The problem is that no matter what laws we enact, there are still an estimated 276 million firearms in circulation, and they have a service life of one hundred years or more. Short of outright confiscation, the sheer number of firearms within the United States means that there will always be a supply of these weapons.

Many liberals note that in European nations, where it is difficult to purchase guns, rates of firearms homicide are less than in the United States. Conservatives, by contrast, generally point out that rates of violent crime (including firearms crimes) increased in places such as Australia and Great Britain after the civilian use of firearms was greatly restricted throughout the 1980s and 1990s. According to official British Home Office crime statistics for 2004/05, for example, Coleman, Hird, and Povey (2006, 72) observed that "[t]here were 10,964 recorded crimes involving firearms other than air weapons. This is a 6 percent increase over 2003/04, and a 60 percent increase in the five years since 1999/00." Given these statistics, how can we explain the increasing criminal misuse of firearms during times of increasing firearms restrictions in Great Britain?

Kates and Polsby (2000) showed that while the number of firearms circulating within the United States substantially increased between 1973 and 1997, homicides actually decreased during the latter part of this period. Kates (2001, 67) reported that "[e]ach year from 1973 through 1997 the existing stock increased by between 1.7 and 3.7 million new handguns. These increases were accompanied by a long-term decline in murder." The fact that the number of firearms in circulation increased during times of decreasing homicide rates suggests that guns may represent only one factor in the complex homicide equation. For instance, the federal government has reported that recently some 4.5 million firearms have been sold each year within the United States, yet murder rates declined at the same time (Bureau of Alcohol, Tobacco, and Firearms 2000).

Violent Crime

To understand the effectiveness of placing controls on firearms—whether these are legislative or police interventions—one has to understand the distribution of violent crime. Studies of violent crime have revealed a consistent relationship between murder and economic factors, such as poverty, and the social characteristics of a population (Land, McCall, and Cohen 1990). In other words, violence rates increase in areas with high rates of poverty, disorganized families (neighborhoods with a greater percentage of divorced- and female-headed households with children), unemployment, transient populations, or with high percentages of males in the age range of 16 to 19 years who are not attending high school or working. Sherman (2001) observed, for instance, that over half of the homicides in the United States are concentrated in 63 cities that represent only 16 percent of the population.

While nearly anybody can be involved in a violent crime, criminologists generally have found that the typical homicide offender is less likely to be an "ordinary" citizen. Most of the people who commit homicides and many victims are enmeshed in criminal activities. Individuals who actively pursue criminal careers are perhaps the most at risk of lethal violence. Drug dealers are a prime example (Jacobs 2000). Offender populations, residing in disadvantaged communities with significant long-term problems, are at a relatively high risk for involvement in violence. Studies of offender-victim relationships have consistently demonstrated that homicide victims and offenders often participate in lifestyles that expose them to greater risk of victimization (Davis, Lurgio, and Skogan 1997; Miethe and Meier 1994). Many of these people legally are not able to own firearms in the first place. Consequently, increasing the number of firearms restrictions most often affects those persons who would not likely be a problem.

The research outcomes reported in the preceding paragraphs offer some important insights regarding violence and firearms misuse. First, the large number of guns in circulation within the United States suggests that no intervention strategy will realistically remove firearms from the hands of offenders; they are not likely to abide by laws anyway. Second, while rates of firearms use in homicides are high, they decreased significantly between 1993 and 2005, as did unintentional firearms mortality. Third, disproportionate amounts of violence occur in places with high poverty rates, **social disorganization** (a breakdown in social organization and informal social control), and other social problems. Fourth, many of those who commit homicides have prior criminal records, and about half of homicide victims have criminal records as well. Given these facts, one might realistically question whether sweeping firearms legislation would actually lower levels of violence. The following section outlines examples of some key firearms legislation and evaluates the success of some of these initiatives.

Firearms Legislation

To fully understand the firearms violence problem and the use of legislation to reduce gun crime, we need to provide a short history of firearms legislation and the significant local, state, and federal laws that have been enacted to reduce firearms violence. Central to any discussion of legislation is the presence of the Second Amendment's protection for civilian firearm ownership. This Amendment provides that

> [a] well-regulated Militia, being necessary to the security of a free State, the right of the people to keep and bear Arms, shall not be infringed.

Many gun owners believe that the intent of the Second Amendment was to restrict any type of legislation on the use of firearms. This is a controversial position, and there are numerous examples of firearms legislation that were challenged in the courts. In one of the earliest examples, laws that were enacted in 1821 to restrict the concealed carry of firearms were found to be unconstitutional (see *Bliss v. Commonwealth* 1822). A review of early firearms legislation suggests that most of these laws made it illegal to carry concealed firearms. By contrast, little attention was placed on defining persons who should not own firearms or on attempts to reduce firearms availability—strategies that are most common today.

For most of the nineteenth century, there were few state or local laws that restricted firearms ownership. Guns were sold in hardware and retail stores and through the mail, and there were no broad restrictions on purchases. In fact, Thompson submachine guns (the so-called Tommy guns) were available through mail-order catalogs in the 1920s and early 1930s, although they were cost prohibitive for an average wage earner. During the early part of the twentieth century, the number of firearms crimes increased in some cities, and popular support grew to restrict the availability of firearms in some places. For example, in response to an increase in gun violence in New York in 1910, the city enacted the Sullivan law in 1911 that made handgun ownership subject to a license. Since that time, New Yorkers have been restricted from owning handguns.

Part of the increase in violence in the early twentieth century may have been a consequence of the introduction of the Volstead Act in 1919, which made the sale of alcohol illegal and marked the start of Prohibition. Competition for control over illicit production and distribution of alcohol increased organized crime; and several atrocities, such as the St. Valentine's Day massacre, prompted legislators to increase the number of controls on firearms. As discussed in Chapter 1, celebrated cases often drive the enactment of new legislation. Likewise, particularly outrageous crimes seem to lead to the enactment of gun control legislation, after which legislators can report to the electorate that they have taken a meaningful step to reduce future firearms crimes. Researchers, however, have historically done a poor job at evaluating the impact of different justice system interventions; and we speculate that several decades later, most people do not know or they have forgotten why many of these laws were introduced in the first place.

Perhaps the most important gun control legislation within the United States was the 1934 National Firearms Act (NFA). The NFA mandated federal registration of machine guns, short-barreled rifles or shotguns, and silencers. This legislation also made transfers of these firearms subject to a $200 tax, a significant amount of money when a typical wage earner made only a few dollars per day. As each user is taxed when the firearm is transferred, the cost of these firearms increases, creating an economic barrier to ownership. This Act was noteworthy as it was the first time that the federal government became involved in gun control.

The NFA spawned a number of local and state firearms laws, and the number of state gun laws gradually increased over time. The second major piece of federal gun control legislation was the 1968 Gun Control Act (GCA). As mentioned, the GCA was enacted after the assassinations of John F. Kennedy, Robert Kennedy, and civil rights leader Martin Luther King, Jr. This provides another example of a legislative response to celebrated cases. The GCA established higher age limits on firearms purchases and made certain categories of persons ineligible to purchase firearms, including felons, fugitives from justice, persons with mental illness, those addicted to alcohol or drugs, illegal aliens, and dishonorably discharged military personnel. In addition, federal law prohibited the interstate purchase of firearms, and such transactions had to be completed by federally licensed firearms dealers.

Despite these restrictions, ineligible persons met few obstacles in purchasing firearms from gun dealers. The Americans for Gun Safety Foundation (AGS) noted that firearms purchases were made on the "honor system," and purchasers were only obliged to sign a form stating that they were not disqualified from firearms ownership (AGS 2002). In 1993, the Handgun Control and Violence Prevention Act was enacted to make it more difficult for purchases of firearms from licensed dealers. This Act—also known as the **Brady Bill**—is another example of legislation being introduced after a celebrated case. James Brady was wounded in John Hinckley's assassination attempt on President Ronald Reagan in 1981. Ever since this attack, Brady's wife, Sarah, has campaigned extensively for the enactment of tougher firearms laws; and she established Handgun Control Incorporated (which later became the Brady Campaign to Prevent Gun Violence).

The introduction of the Brady Bill promised to reduce the number of firearms purchased by ineligible persons in retail sales. First enacted in 1993 to regulate the purchase of handguns, the legislation was made permanent on November 30, 1998, and it was extended to all cartridge firearms. A federal government study, conducted by Bowling and colleagues (2005) estimated that some 1.2 million applications to purchase firearms have been rejected since the legislation took effect. According to Federal Bureau of Investigation (FBI) records, almost three-quarters of those ineligible purchasers were felons or persons who had been convicted of domestic violence misdemeanor offenses (FBI 2003).

The success of Sarah Brady in developing broad political support for gun control legislation underscores the role of public interest groups in the introduction of gun control legislation—or arguing against such laws. We learned in Chapter 1 that the Mothers Against Drunk Driving (MADD) organization has had a significant role in advocating for tougher DWI laws. There are dozens of interest groups that advocate for tougher gun control legislation, ranging from grassroots movements, such as the Million Mom March, to those operated by public health advocates, such as the Violence Policy Center. Most of these groups disseminate their messages through public speakers and the distribution of press releases and other publications, and they have sophisticated Internet Web sites. Moreover, a majority of these groups provide campaign funding or support to legislators who share their views.

No discussion of interest groups would be complete without an examination of the National Rifle Association (NRA)—one of the oldest, largest, and most influential of the political advocacy groups in the United States. With over four million members, the NRA has the ability to gather significant funding for its political activities, and it has developed an Institute for Legislative Action (ILA) that distributes information about pending state or federal firearms legislation. One of the key activities of the NRA-ILA is to provide campaign donations (1) to support state or federal candidates who support the NRA's political agenda and (2) to mobilize the membership to vote for politicians who share the NRA's goals and ideals. While there are other groups that support the Second Amendment, the NRA is the most well known and professionally organized. The NRA takes a politically mainstream approach to working with policymakers, and in the past, actually has given tacit support for some gun control legislation.

Finally, the manufacturers of firearms have developed a greater political presence over the past several decades. The goal of these corporations is ultimately financial, and most reject placing further restrictions on firearms. Some corporations, such as Ruger and Smith and Wesson, actually have supported certain facets of gun control legislation, but these companies have suffered from a backlash, as hard-core Second Amendment supporters boycotted their products. As a result, most firearms corporations today provide financial support for the mainstream interest groups, such as the NRA.

At the broadest level, firearms laws attempt to control the types of firearms that can be possessed, who can possess them, and how they should be used. The following pages outline whether these strategies are effective at reducing violent crime.

Regulating the Types of Firearms

Some firearms are thought to represent a greater risk to public safety than others. The federal government's enactment of the NFA in 1934 placed restrictions on fully automatic firearms, such as submachine guns, and in many states, ordinary citizens cannot possess these types of firearms. In fact, recent Bureau of Alcohol, Tobacco, Firearms, and Explosives (ATF) statistics show that there are only about 250,000 fully automatic firearms legally registered in the United States. Moreover, federal legislation in the 1980s froze the number of these firearms, and no new fully automatic firearms have been transferred to civilian ownership since that time. The net effect is to create scarcity, and most of these guns now sell for $10,000 or more, well out of the reach of most people. In any case, such registered firearms have rarely been involved in crimes, a fact confirmed by the ATF Director in congressional testimony (Committee on the Judiciary 1986). There is no evidence to suggest that things have changed since that testimony.

Recently, the federal assault weapons ban that was enacted in 1994 was allowed to sunset in 2004. This legislation placed restrictions on the importation and sale of military-style firearms. **Assault weapons** are typically dangerous looking semiautomatic weapons that fire centerfire cartridges in military calibers. These firearms were thought to be at high risk of use in crimes, but unlike depictions in the movies or on television, they rarely have been encountered in criminal offenses. Kopel (1994) found that so-called assault weapons were used in less than 1 percent of crimes before the ban, and a number of federal government studies found that the law had little overall impact on violent crime reduction (see Koper, Woods, and Roth 2004).

Handguns are the types of firearms used most often in violent crimes, and many legislators would like to restrict inexpensive handguns, commonly called Saturday-night specials (SNS). Although definitions of these firearms differ, they typically chamber less powerful ammunition, have short barrels, and are inexpensive (Shine 1998). Information from the Youth Gun Interdiction program of the ATF revealed that 6 of the 10 most commonly recovered firearms from juveniles are in fact SNS (ATF 2002). Some states, such as California and Massachusetts, have also placed various safety restrictions on the types of firearms that can be imported into those states, and this has the effect of limiting the number of SNS that are sold, at least in legal sales. Conservative policy analysts who believe that higher levels of gun ownership reduce violent crime, however, argue that placing barriers to purchasing such firearms has the effect of disarming the poor rather than criminals, and that the poor also should have access to firearms to protect themselves.

One potential policy problem with restricting inexpensive and inaccurate firearms that fire less powerful cartridges is that they may be replaced with more powerful or sophisticated firearms. Ruddell and Mays (2003) found that juveniles who do not have legal access to handguns frequently "sawed off" the barrel and stock of a much more powerful rifle or shotgun as an alternative. Thus, the offender would have a gun that is more lethal than a Saturday-night special. While not advocating for juvenile access to firearms, this is a good example of a **substitution effect,** where the ban of one object causes offenders to replace it with something else. Policymakers often do not consider the unforeseen consequences of a particular piece of legislation, and in some cases it may take years to realize that the unforeseen consequences could be worse than the act lawmakers had initially tried to control.

Some states, most notably California, have proposed to limit crime by placing a serial number on each round of ammunition, which has the effect of increasing the cost of ammunition significantly. Such laws may have a short-term effect, but it is likely that offenders would then import ammunition from other states, reload empty cartridges, or steal their ammunition. As a result, these simplistic ideas to control violent crime are often attractive, but they fail to consider the imagination and ingenuity of offenders, as well as the difficulty associated with implementing such policies (see Jacobs 2002). Because criminal justice legislation sometimes has been a **knee-jerk reaction** of policymakers to a celebrated case—when legislation is quickly passed to respond to an egregious incident—there is an increased possibility of unintended consequences once these laws are enacted.

Legislating Access to Firearms

If regulating the different types of firearms that are available or increasing the cost of ammunition does not seem to be effective in reducing the numbers of firearms crimes, another logical step is to regulate who can own firearms. This was the impetus behind the Brady Bill. The 1968 GCA, for instance, was intended to restrict the access of firearms to persons with mental illness, long-term alcohol or drug users, felons, or other persons who might pose a risk to public safety. There is an intuitive appeal to the notion that screening these ineligible persons might have contributed to the reduction in gun violence. One problem with the GCA, however, is that most states had poor screening mechanisms to evaluate whether a firearms buyer was legally able to make the purchase (AGS 2002).

Yet, the connection between decreases in firearms injuries and homicides and the Brady Bill's introduction is difficult to make. The national decrease in homicide, for instance, predates the introduction of the Brady Bill. In addition, once trends in murder since 1990 are separated on the basis of age, juveniles make a substantial contribution to firearms violence, yet they are not legally eligible to purchase firearms (Ruddell and Mays 2003). Consequently, the relationship between access to firearms and violence is much more complex than controlling for sales on the retail firearms market alone.

In his analysis of the impact of the Brady Bill, Jacobs (2002, 113) noted that while "many rejected purchasers would not have committed gun crimes, [m]any were not left unarmed since they already owned one or more guns. Still other rejected purchasers would have obtained a gun in the secondary or black market." A number of studies have been completed that have examined the relationship between the introduction of more formal background checks on firearms purchasers and fatalities. Ludwig and Cook (2000) examined the relationships between introduction of the Brady Bill and firearms crimes and homicide. They found no association between the legislation and reductions in firearms violence, but they did find a reduction in suicides among the elderly. Ruddell and Mays (2005), by contrast, showed that in states with more sophisticated and comprehensive background checks, there was a statistically significant reduction in firearms homicides.

Other researchers have found a positive impact on various gun control strategies. Wintemute and colleagues (2001), for instance, observed a reduction in violence after California enacted legislation that banned persons with domestic violence convictions from obtaining firearms. Yet, the significance of the study by the Wintemute team has been challenged (see Ludwig and Cook 2003). Moreover, Vigdor and Mercy (2003) examined the influence of state legislation that prohibited those on restraining orders or with misdemeanor domestic violence convictions from purchasing firearms. Using time-series analyses, these scholars found that laws prohibiting persons who were named in restraining orders from purchasing firearms were significantly associated with reductions in intimate partner homicides.

However, none of the studies reported above conclusively established a relationship between reductions of violence and the implementation of Brady-type legislation, and the findings typically have been inconclusive or ambiguous. In fact, a study by the Centers for Disease Control and Prevention found that most of the research to date failed to provide sufficient evidence of the effectiveness of laws intended to reduce firearms violence (Hahn et al. 2003).

Although more complete or thorough background checks should reduce future firearms violence, there are some limitations with this approach. First, most states do not have comprehensive data about persons convicted of misdemeanor domestic violence offenses, dishonorably discharged persons, or commitment of the mentally ill (Jacobs 2002). Second, there are considerable limitations to our society's ability to track illegal aliens or those who are drug addicted (AGS 2002). Last, Jacobs (2002) questioned how we determine whether somebody is alcoholic or drug-dependent and if they should be eligible to purchase firearms once they demonstrate a period of sobriety.

Even if a state's background check is rigorous, there are no guarantees that gun dealers necessarily follow federal or state regulations. Koper (2002, 154) noted how dealers "may engage actively in illegal gun sales, either by selling directly to prohibited users or by colluding with unlicensed, street dealers," or they may engage in "actions that are illegal or otherwise negligent or unethical." So, while state databases that are very comprehensive may be implemented, their effectiveness may be attenuated by unethical dealers or by ineligible persons who obtain firearms through **straw purchases.** Straw purchases involve getting an eligible individual to purchase the firearm from a licensed dealer on behalf of an ineligible person.

Another important factor to consider is the ability of motivated persons to purchase firearms on the secondary firearms market (Ruefle n.d). The secondary firearms market (also called the **"gray market"**) includes guns purchased from nonfederal firearms licensed dealers, firearms borrowed from friends or associates, and those obtained through residential or commercial burglaries. Anecdotal accounts from police officers also point to a gun "rental market," where offenders can rent a gun for a short period of time from other offenders. Analyses of interviews with incarcerated offenders, for instance, suggested that overall, few offenders bought their guns through legitimate firearms dealers; nearly 80 percent of offenders obtained their firearms through friends, family, or illegal (street) sources (Harlow 2001).

Controlling Firearms Use

The third strategy for firearms control is to restrict how firearms may be used. Each jurisdiction has enacted laws that promote responsible firearms use. Most often these regulations are common sense and stipulate that recreational users such as hunters cannot discharge firearms in public places, at night, or if their actions place others at risk (such as hunting at night or firing a firearm near a highway). Most citizens abide by these rules, and the law is not controversial. Yet, some states have placed restrictions on firearms to reduce access to unauthorized users. These are the so-called safe storage or **child access prevention laws.** To promote these policies, many police departments give away gun safety devices, such as trigger locks that make these firearms temporarily inoperable.

Safe storage of firearms seeks to restrict access to unauthorized users, such as children or offenders who might steal firearms. While few people would advocate toddlers and youngsters handling firearms without adult supervision, these laws become controversial as they make law-abiding citizens legally accountable if unauthorized users cause harm with their firearms. Moreover, opponents of gun control legislation argue that locking up firearms effectively disarms a person who would use a firearm for self-defense.

Approximately half of the states currently have some type of safe storage or child access prevention legislation. Despite the fact that such laws have some public support, empirical studies have not found them to be effective at reducing unintentional deaths (Ruddell and Mays 2004). Although child access prevention laws seem to be a commonsense approach to firearms safety, Jacobs (2002, 195) has observed that "[m]ost gun owners are already safety conscious, but those who are currently blasé about loaded weapons in the home may not be easily persuaded to change their behavior." This observation seems particularly crucial in light of the fact that unintentional firearms fatalities have dropped so significantly during the past two decades. It is also possible that mandatory hunter-safety training in most states is responsible for making recreational firearms users more safety conscious.

Thus, we have addressed the efficacy of three types of legislation to reduce the access of firearms to offenders: restricting the types of firearms that are available, restricting who can possess firearms, and placing restrictions on the use of firearms, including child access prevention or safe storage laws.

While many of these legislative initiatives are conceptually appealing, they are limited by the following factors:

(1) The cumulative stock of 238 to 276 million firearms (with a service life of 100 years) ensures a long-term supply on the legitimate and illegitimate markets regardless of what laws are enacted.

(2) Restricting one type of firearm that appears to be more dangerous than others will have no long-term effect on violence reduction.

(3) Rules on safe storage or the responsible use of firearms will have little effect because they tend to be followed by responsible law-abiding persons in the first place.

(4) Conducting background checks may make a short-term contribution to violence reduction or suicide, but probably will not have a long-term effect on keeping firearms out of the hands of offender populations.

(5) A substantial secondary or gray market of firearms exists, and these guns are bought and sold, traded, and sometimes rented by offenders.

Effectiveness of Gun Control Legislation

A number of public health scholars have become involved in the study of firearms violence. The language of those in this discipline is somewhat different than that of the criminal justice literature, and their strategies are often based on **harm reduction.** Many of their recommendations for reducing firearms violence target supply-side strategies, making it more difficult to obtain firearms and reducing the number of firearms in circulation. This group argues that more guns in circulation cause more firearms murders (Wintemute 2000). However, these observations do not seem consistent with the facts reported about the numbers of firearms increasing at the same time as firearms homicides are decreasing. Gary Kleck (1997), for instance, found that rural areas in the United States that typically have the highest rates of firearms ownership have comparatively low rates of firearms crime.

Nevertheless, many advocates of the public health model suggest that firearms laws enacted to screen potential firearms purchases are responsible for some of the decreases in firearms violence (Azrael 2002). Others believe that the widespread availability of firearms within the United States serves as a deterrent to crime, especially offenses such as "hot burglaries," which occur when homes are burglarized while the residence is occupied. Finally, a number of scholars have examined the relationship between carrying concealed weapons and violence reduction. They contend that armed citizens serve as a deterrent to street crime (Lott 2000), although this finding has been criticized (Ayres and Donohue 2002; Kovandzic and Marvell 2003).

What is troubling is that these debates about the effectiveness of gun control legislation, carrying concealed weapons, or defensive gun use often hinge upon the way that a study was conducted: the data that were examined, the variables included in the analyses, the statistical methods used, and the interpretations of the results. Scholars looking at the same data sometimes come to very different conclusions. As a result, it is difficult to place confidence in the results of some studies, especially those that are sponsored or conducted by interest groups.

While there are thousands of local, state, and national firearms laws, a recent study by the Centers for Disease Control (CDC) found that gun control legislation generally did not have a significant impact on violence rates (Hahn et al. 2003). Specifically, Hahn and colleagues (2003, 1) examined the relationship between violence and

> bans on specified firearms or ammunition, restrictions on firearm acquisition, waiting periods for firearm acquisition, firearm registration and licensing of firearm owners, "shall issue" concealed weapon carry laws, child access prevention laws, zero tolerance laws for firearms in schools, and combinations of firearms laws.

The finding was surprising as the CDC typically supports the public health model and many of their scholars advocate reducing the number of firearms in circulation and support legislation that restricts firearm ownership, possession, and use.

A study by the National Academy of Sciences (NAS), released the year after the CDC publication, reported that there was an association between rates of firearms ownership and violence and that illegally obtained firearms are associated with crime (Wellford, Pepper, and Petrie

2004). But answers to more complex questions about the effectiveness of firearms legislation are difficult to explain because we simply do not have enough information and, in some cases, we have no data at all. Furthermore, in the NAS study, Wellford and colleagues suggested that even when we do have the data and use appropriate research methods, there may be other factors that influence gun violence that researchers have overlooked or that we simply cannot measure. Even estimating the number of guns within the nation is problematic as many people are reluctant to disclose to researchers whether they own one or more firearms. Thus, it is difficult to make sweeping conclusions about the effectiveness of gun control legislation even when unbiased results are published.

Given that there are so many firearms in circulation, and that the number increased during periods of decreasing murder rates, other factors must influence gun violence. Violence reduction policies have focused on two dimensions of firearms control: first, supply-side interventions to keep firearms from persons who are not authorized to possess them and, second, reduction of the numbers of illegally carried firearms by lowering demand through law enforcement interventions and punitive sentences. This is the focus of both legislation and police interventions to reduce firearms misuse.

Police Interventions to Reduce Illegal Gun Use

If the police can reduce the numbers of persons who are not legally allowed to possess firearms, or those who are carrying firearms illegally (for example, concealed carrying of firearms without a permit), there should be a reduction in violence. After all, these individuals are likely to be at higher risk of firearms crimes, and they are the target of most gun control legislation. Two well-reported experiments used uniformed police patrols to reduce the number of illegally carried firearms in high-risk Kansas City (Sherman, Shaw, and Rogan 1995) and Indianapolis neighborhoods (McGarrell, Chermak, and Weiss 1999; McGarrell et al. 2006). These short-term experiments demonstrated that violent crime could be reduced through targeted police interventions.

As we noted before, there are places of high risk of violence within the United States, and interventions that target these neighborhoods should decrease violence. Unfortunately, in many cases, these neighborhoods are also the places of highest disadvantage, and often they are populated with high percentages of minority group members. As we discuss elsewhere, there is already considerable concern over police interventions in these communities, and introducing "stop and frisk" programs to reduce the number of guns would have little community support because they would be seen as placing community members under further law enforcement scrutiny (see also Chapter 7 "Addressing the

Race Issue"). As a result, police interventions often focus on target groups at highest risk, such as gang members.

Boston's **Operation Ceasefire,** for instance, has had long-term success in reducing gun violence. This intervention is specifically targeted at reducing violence associated with youth and gang crime. Braga and colleagues (2001) found that less than one percent of all Bostonians under the age of 24 years of age were responsible for almost two thirds of Boston homicides. Police and community groups developed a strategy called **pulling levers** that was based on targeted interventions of this high-risk group. The cornerstone of this approach is cooperative enforcement strategies between prosecutors and law enforcement officers from municipal and federal agencies (Kennedy 1997). The Ceasefire approach emphasized intensive short-term, targeted interventions at individuals or gangs who were violence-prone. After an incidence of gang violence, for instance, law enforcement agencies would engage in saturated patrol and intensive gang interventions.

A number of other jurisdictions have used similar **problem-oriented approaches** to reduce firearms use—especially associated with juvenile gun use. Lizotte and Sheppard (2001), for instance, examined a number of gun violence prevention programs. A common theme in these successful firearms suppression programs was their reliance upon multiple strategies, most often directed at high-risk neighborhoods and populations, such as gang members. Law enforcement strategies were supported by community-based initiatives that offered positive opportunities, such as academic, vocational, or after-school programs. In addition, public information campaigns and mobilization of community leaders in high-risk residential areas attempted to increase resiliency in these places (Lizotte and Sheppard 2001).

One emerging program that directs enforcement at gangs and guns is **Project Safe Neighborhoods** (PSN), a federally-sponsored gun enforcement program that has received a significant amount of federal funding since it was first introduced in 2001. This program has used "lessons learned" from the Ceasefire program, as well as **Project Exile,** an enforcement program that targeted felons who illegally possess or carry firearms, felons with drugs and firearms, as well as domestic violence cases where firearms are involved. Possession of firearms in such circumstances is a federal offense and a cornerstone of the approach is that the resources of the federal government can be used to prosecute and imprison these offenders.

According to Klofas and Hipple (2006, 3), the PSN approach is based on five different elements: "partnerships, strategic planning, training, outreach and accountability." These programs bring together the federal, state, and local law enforcement agencies that use community outreach activities to publicize the message that people violating federal firearms laws will be severely punished. Accountability is a key element of the program; and from 2001 to 2005, the program has increased federal firearms prosecutions by 73 percent. Because the federal penalties for the possession of firearms by unauthorized users are very strict—a minimum of a five-year prison term without the possibility of parole—these types of interventions may be successful at removing the highest-risk offenders from the streets.

One difficulty of any police intervention is that a strategy that is effective in one place may not be as successful when used in another jurisdiction. One noteworthy example is the Minneapolis Domestic Violence Experiment, which demonstrated that mandatory arrest policies were successful in reducing domestic violence (Sherman and Berk 1984). Follow-up studies found that mandatory arrest policies were not effective in other places and actually may have decreased the effectiveness of the police response (see Maxwell, Garner, and Fagan 2001). A significant problem is that many police departments adopted mandatory arrest practices based on the initial success of a single jurisdiction.

In terms of violence reduction programs, a similar lack of success occurred in Los Angeles when the city imported the Ceasefire program (Tita et al. 2005). The Los Angeles Police Department, in conjunction with the prosecutor's office and local, state, and federal law enforcement and correctional agencies, conducted a targeted approach to reduce gun and gang violence. A number of factors, however, made it difficult to implement the Los Angeles Ceasefire interventions in the same manner as the Boston program, including the facts that no community stakeholder group took full ownership of the project and that social programs did not increase to equalize the enforcement nature of the program. As a result, this intervention was not as effective as the results reported in Boston, and despite the best efforts of these agencies, there was no statistically significant reduction in violence (Tita et al. 2005).

This brings us to an implementation issue when examining police interventions that are intended to reduce gun violence and other crime problems: Copycat programs may fail to use all of the elements of a successful program. In some cases, law enforcement officers might not "buy into" the program, and they may only "go through the motions" rather than invest wholeheartedly in the success of the approach. In other places, the demographic or social conditions of the different communities may increase or decrease the success of an intervention. Thus, the approaches that worked in Boston, a city that occupies a relatively small geographical area, were not effective in Los Angeles, a collection of cities that holds a considerably larger population, has different gang dynamics, and has a larger collection of political barriers that had to be overcome (numerous cities were involved rather than a single political jurisdiction).

Conclusions

Even though the rates of violent crime have been dropping since the early 1990s, many Americans remain fearful of crime. Yet individual risk of victimization drops significantly if people are not involved in crime, do not associate with offenders, or do not engage in risky activities. One problem that policymakers must confront is that violence is not distributed evenly throughout the nation. Most suburban and rural counties generally have rates of violent crime or homicide similar to European nations, even though gun ownership rates are relatively high in these areas. Violence is concentrated in America's inner cities, and until fundamental changes occur in the structure of these communities, they will keep American violence and murder rates elevated. As a result, sweeping gun control legislation will have little effect. The people who abide by the regulations are not typically the people who are at risk of involvement in firearms crimes.

It is unlikely that urban America will undergo any type of economic restructuring, so police interventions are the only remaining tactic to reduce gun violence. The integrated approach to removing firearms from the street, as exemplified in Boston's Operation Ceasefire project or Project Safe Neighborhoods, seems to be an important step in the right direction—with local, state, and federal authorities working together to reduce violence.

However, despite the relative success of these different types of firearms intervention initiatives, perhaps long-term changes in public perceptions will be the most successful method of reducing firearms crimes over time. Sherman (2001) observed that public attitudes toward illegally carrying concealed weapons need to change, which is a cornerstone of the demand-side approach. He advocates using sentencing policies as a starting point for changing public perceptions about the seriousness of firearms offenses (Sherman 2001). Through stricter punishments for offenders, we may be able to reduce illegally carried firearms in a manner similar to the way driving while intoxicated was discouraged throughout the 1980s and 1990s.

Many of our ideas about crime and violence, including our notions about the types of guns that criminals use, where they obtain these firearms, and how to prevent offenders from getting guns, come from the media. Most often, the entertainment and news media are guilty of simplifying complex subjects into television reports that sometimes last less than one minute. One problem with this approach is that overly simplistic notions about crime and justice distract the public and policymakers from the complex economic, cultural, and structural conditions that contribute to violent crime within the United States (Ruddell and Fearn 2006).

Students interested in studying gun control will find a fruitful topic to learn about criminal justice policy, the role of interest groups in influencing policy development, and the difficulty of establishing a debate based on what the research reveals about gun crimes, rather than political rhetoric. In addition, an examination of legislative and police interventions to reduce gun crimes suggests that they have often been introduced with little underlying theoretical knowledge about crime, the examination of the success or failure of similar policies, or problems with the implementation of new laws. As a result, many criminal justice interventions, including gun control legislation, fall far short of expectations.

From a policy perspective, perhaps the most promising lesson that we can learn about crime control policies came from the sunset demise of the assault weapons ban in 2004, 10 years after it was introduced. An examination of the effectiveness of the ban revealed that it had little effect on firearms crimes, and there was no broad political support to reintroduce the legislation. Policymakers would be well advised to consider incorporating sunset clauses into other crime control strategies. In cases where laws are discriminatory, ineffective, or produce unanticipated (and possibly adverse) conditions, they would simply expire at a predetermined time; and legislators would not be perceived as being "soft on crime" for actually voting to amend crime control legislation.

Note

1. There is some dispute about the actual number of firearms laws within the United States. Ludwig and Cook (2003) have challenged the commonly-cited number of 20,000 firearms laws.

Key Terms

assault weapons
Brady Bill
child access prevention
    laws
demand-side interventions
gray market
harm reduction

knee-jerk reaction
Operation Ceasefire
problem-oriented approaches
Project Exile
Project Safe Neighborhoods
pulling levers

Saturday-night special
    (SNS)
social disorganization
stakeholders
straw purchases
substitution effect
sunset
supply-side interventions

Critical Review Questions

1. Compare and contrast the liberal and conservative positions on gun control. How are these positions supported in the media?
2. How do stakeholders and interest groups become involved in policy debates about gun control? Should these organizations be allowed to make contributions to political campaigns?

3. What would you suggest is the most effective strategy to reduce firearms violence: federal or state legislation, or changing the activities of police?

4. How can we create better responses to the problem of violence in urban America? Should we attack the root causes of crime, such as addictions, social disorganization, economic conditions, and a lack of positive role models?

5. How do some people increase their likelihood of victimization?

6. Should we regulate certain types of firearms, such as assault weapons, solely because they "look dangerous"?

7. Can you provide an example where a criminal justice policy or practice has resulted in unanticipated results that made the problem worse?

References

Americans for Gun Safety Foundation (AGS). (2002). "Broken records: How America's faulty background check system allows criminals to get guns." Retrieved July 20, 2006 from *http://w3.agsfoundation.com/media/BRReport.pdf*.

Ayres, Ian, and John J. Donohue. (2002). "Shooting down the more guns, less guns hypothesis." National Bureau of Economic Research Working Paper (Number 9336). Retrieved July 20, 2006, from *http://papers.ssrn.com/sol3/cf_dev/AbsByAuth.cfm?per_id=22598*.

Azrael, Deborah. (2002). "Reduction in FFLS: A step in the right direction." *Criminology & Public Policy* 1 (2), 179–182.

Belleisles, Michael A. (2001). *Arming America: The Origins of a National Gun Culture*. New York: Knopf.

Bliss v. Commonwealth, 2 Littell 90 Ky., (1822).

Bowling, Michael, Gene Lauver, Mathew J. Hickman, and Devon B. Adams. (2005). *Background Checks for Firearm Transfers, 2004*. Washington, DC: U.S. Department of Justice, Bureau of Justice Statistics.

Braga, Anthony A., David M. Kennedy, Elin J. Waring, and Anne Morrison Piehl. (2001). "Problem-oriented policing, deterrence, and youth violence: An evaluation of Boston's Operation Ceasefire." *Journal of Research in Crime and Delinquency* 38, 195–225.

Bureau of Alcohol, Tobacco and Firearms (ATF). (2000). *Commerce in Firearms in the United States*. Washington, DC: Author.

——. (2002). *Crime Gun Trace Analysis Reports: The Illegal Youth Firearms Markets in 27 Communities*. Washington, DC: U.S. Department of the Treasury.

Centers for Disease Control and Prevention (CDC). (2007). *Mortality (Fatal Injury) Reports*. Retrieved January 1, 2007, from *http://webapp.cdc.gov/sasweb/ncipc/mortrate.html*.

Coleman, Kathryn, Celia Hird, and David Povey. (2006). *Violent Crime Overview: Homicide and Gun Crime, 2004/2005*. London: Home Office Statistical Bulletin. Retrieved June 6, 2006 from *http://www.homeoffice.gov.uk/rds/pdfs06/hosb0206.pdf*.

Committee on the Judiciary. (1986). *Hearings on H.R. 641 and Related Bills [50965]*. Washington DC: Government Printing Office 50-965.

Cook, Phillip, and Jens Ludwig. (2000). *Gun Violence: The Real Costs*. New York: Oxford University Press.

Davis, Robert C., Arthur J. Lurgio, and Wesley G. Skogan. (1997). *Victims of Crime*. Thousand Oaks, CA: Sage.

Fagan, Jeffrey (2005, November 18). *Attention Felons: Evaluating Project Safe Neighborhoods in Chicago*. Paper presented to the American Society of Criminology

Annual Meeting, Toronto.

Federal Bureau of Investigation (FBI). (2003). *National Instant Criminal Background Check System: 2001/2002 Operational Report.* Washington, DC: U.S. Department of Justice.

Fox, James A., and Marianne W. Zawitz. (2006). *Homicide Trends in the United States.* Retrieved July 26, 2006, from *http://www.ojp.usdoj.gov/bjs/homicide/weapons.htm#weapons.*

Graduate Institute of International Studies. (2003). *Small Arms Survey 2003: Development Denied.* New York: Oxford University Press.

Hahn, Robert A., Oleg O. Bilukha, Alex Crosby, Mindy T. Fullilove, Akiva Liberman, Eva K. Moscicki, et al. (2003). "First reports evaluating the effectiveness of strategies for preventing violence: Firearms laws." *Morbidity and Mortality Weekly Report* 52, 11–20.

Harlow, Caroline W. (2001). *Firearm Use by Offenders.* Washington, DC: U.S. Department of Justice, Bureau of Justice Statistics.

Jacobs, Bruce (2000). *Robbing Drug Dealers: Violence Beyond the Law.* New York: Aldine de Gruyter.

Jacobs, James B. (2002). *Can Gun Control Work?* New York: Oxford University Press.

Kates, Don B. (2001). "Guns and public health: Epidemic of violence or pandemic of propaganda?" Pp. 31–106, in *Armed: New Perspectives on Gun Control,* edited by Gary Kleck and Don B. Kates. Amherst, NY: Prometheus Books.

Kates, Don B., and Daniel D. Polsby. (2000). "Long-term nonrelationship of a widespread and increasing firearm availability to homicide in the United States." *Homicide Studies* 4 (1), 185–201.

Kennedy, David. (1997). *Juvenile Gun Violence and Gun Markets in Boston: Research Preview.* Washington, DC: National Institute of Justice.

Kleck, Gary. (1997). *Targeting Guns: Firearms and Their Control.* New York: Aldine de Gruyter.

Kleck, Gary, and Don B. Kates. (2001). *Armed: New Perspectives on Gun Control.* New York: Prometheus Books.

Klofas, John, and Natalie K. Hipple. (2006). *Project Safe Neighborhoods: Strategic Interventions.* Washington, DC: U.S. Department of Justice. Retrieved June 6, 2006 from: *http://www.psn.gov/pubs/pdf/PSN_CaseStudy3.pdf.*

Kopel, David B. (1994). "Rational basis analysis of assault weapon prohibition. *Journal of Contemporary Law* 20 (2), 381–417.

——. (2001, August, 25, 26) "$100 billion mistake: Loose factoids sink books." *National Review Online.* Retrieved July 20, 2006 from: *http://www.nationalreview.com/weekend/ books/books-kopel082501.shtml.*

Koper, Christopher S. (2002). "Federal legislation and gun markets: How much have recent reforms of the Federal Firearms Licensing system reduced criminal gun suppliers?" *Criminology & Public Policy* 1 (2), 151–178.

Koper, Christopher S., Daniel J. Woods, and Jeffrey A. Roth. (2004). *An Updated Assessment of the Federal Assault Weapons Ban: Impacts on Gun Markets and Gun Violence, 1993– 2003.* Philadelphia: Jerry Lee Center of Criminology.

Kovandzic, Tomislav V., and Thomas B. Marvell. (2003). "Right-to-carry concealed handguns and violent crime: Crime control through gun decontrol?" *Criminology & Public Policy* 2 (3), 363–396.

Land, Kenneth C., Patricia L. McCall, and Lawrence E. Cohen. (1990). "Structural covariates of homicide rates: Are there any invariances across time and social space?" *American Journal of Sociology* 95 (4), 922–963.

Lizotte, Alan, and David Sheppard. (2001). *Gun Use by Male Juveniles: Research and Prevention.* Washington, DC: U.S. Department of Justice, Office of Juvenile Justice and Delinquency Prevention.

Lott, John R. (2000). *More Guns, Less Crime: Understanding Crime and Gun-Control Laws.* Chicago: University of Chicago Press.

Ludwig, Jens, and Philip J. Cook. (2000). "Homicide and suicide rates associated with implementation of the Brady Handgun Violence Prevention Act." *Journal of the American Medical Association* 284 (5), 585–591.

——. (2003). *Evaluating Gun Policy.* Washington, DC: Brookings Institution Press.

Maxwell, Christopher D., Joel H. Garner, and Jeffrey A. Fagan. (2001). *The Effects of Arrest on Intimate Partner Violence: New Evidence From the Spouse Assault Replication Program—Research in Brief.* Washington, DC: National Institute of Justice.

McGarrell, Edmund, Steven Chermak, and Alexander Weiss. (1999). *Targeting Firearms Through Directed Patrols.* Indianapolis: Hudson Institute.

McGarrell, Edmund F., Steven Chermak, Jeremy M. Wilson, and Nicholas Corsaro. (2006). "Reducing homicide through a 'lever-pulling' strategy." *Justice Quarterly* 23 (2), 214–231.

Miethe, Terance D., and Robert F. Meier. (1994). *Crime and Its Social Context.* New York: SUNY Press.

Ruddell, Rick, and Scott H. Decker. (2006). "Kids and assault weapons: Social problem or social construction?" *Criminal Justice Review* 30 (1), 45–63.

Ruddell, Rick, and Noelle E. Fearn. (2006). "Simplistic explanations are the problem: Crime, homicide, and the Zimring-Hawkins proposition." *Criminal Justice Studies,* 19 (4), 323–336.

Ruddell, Rick, and G. Larry Mays. (2003). "Examining the arsenal of juvenile gunslingers: Trends and implications." *Crime & Delinquency* 49 (2), 231–252.

——. (2004). "Risky lifestyles and unintentional firearms fatalities." *Californian Journal of Health Promotion* 2 (1), 49–64.

——. (2005). State background checks and firearms homicides. *Journal of Criminal Justice* 33 (2), 127–136.

Ruefle, W. (n.d.). "No ID, no wait, no questions asked: Classified ads, private gun sales and the Brady Act." Unpublished manuscript.

Sherman, Lawrence W. (2001). "Reducing gun violence: What works, what doesn't, what's promising." Pp. 69–98 in *Perspective on Crime and Justice 1999–2000 Lecture Series, Vol. 4* Rockville, MD: National Institute of Justice. Retrieved October 11, 2006 from: *http://www.ncjrs.gov/pdffiles1/nij/184245.pdf.*

Sherman, Lawrence W., and Richard A. Berk. (1984) "The specific deterrent effects of arrest for domestic assault." *American Sociological Review* 49 (2), 261–272.

Sherman, Lawrence, James W. Shaw, and Dennis P. Rogan. (1995). *The Kansas City Gun Experiment—Research In Brief.* Washington, DC: National Institute of Justice.

Shine, Eva H. (1998). "The junk gun predicament: Answers do exist." *Arizona State Law Journal* 30 (4), 1183–1207.

Tita, George E., K. Jack Riley, Greg Ridgeway, and Peter W. Greenwood. (2005). *Reducing gun violence: Operation Ceasefire in Los Angeles.* Washington, DC: National Institute of Justice.

Vigdor, Elizabeth R., and James A. Mercy. (2003). "Disarming batterers: The impact of domestic violence firearm laws." Pp. 157–201 in *Evaluating Gun Policy,* edited by Jens Ludwig and Philip J. Cook. Washington, DC: Brookings Institution Press.

Wellford, Charles F., John V. Pepper, and Carol V. Petrie. (2004). *Firearms and Violence: A Critical Review.* Washington, DC: National Academies Press.

Wintemute, Garen J. (2000). "Guns and gun violence." Pp. 45–96 in *The Crime Drop in America,* edited by Alfred Blumstein and Joel Wallman. Cambridge, U.K.: Cambridge University Press.

Wintemute, Garen J., Mona A. Wright, Christiana M. Drake, and James J. Beaumont. (2001). "Subsequent criminal activity among violent misdemeanants who seek to purchase handguns," *Journal of the American Medical Association* 285 (8), 1019–1026.

Recommended Readings

Jacobs, James B. (2002). *Can Gun Control Work?* New York: Oxford University Press. Jacobs provides a comprehensive and commonsense interpretation of gun laws and their effectiveness. He examines the disconnect between laws "on the books" and how they are enforced and interpreted and finds that while designing legislation is comparatively easy, new laws often fail in their implementation.

Kleck, Gary, and Don B. Kates. (2001). *Armed: New Perspectives on Gun Control.* New York: Prometheus Books. The authors wade through the policy debate about gun control and focus on the relationships between guns and violence. They examine myths about firearms and gun crimes. Kleck and Kates aim to reduce the exaggerated or inaccurate claims about firearms use and abuse and advocate more accurate and unbiased scientific analyses.

Ludwig, Jens, and Phillip I. Cook (2003). *Evaluating Gun Policy: Effects on Crime and Violence.* Washington, DC: Brookings Institution Press. This edited book is a collection of essays about firearms policy and whether approaches to gun control have had the desired effect. The authors provide examples of liberal gun control interventions that seem to be effective (such as restricting firearms to persons convicted of domestic violence), as well as more conservative approaches (such as enhanced penalties for gun violence). ✦

Chapter 6

Sentencing

Introduction

One of the most significant changes in the way that U.S. criminal justice systems have operated during the past 30 years has been the increased use of incarceration. Figure 6.1 shows the use of imprisonment in the United States from 1925 to 2005. Between 1920 and 1970, prison populations were said to be self-regulating. When admissions increased, officials used parole to release an equal number of inmates. Based on these observations, Alfred Blumstein and Jacqueline Cohen proposed that prison populations balanced themselves and that a stability of punishment existed. They argued that stability was remarkable given the large number of social changes during these five decades. Rates of crime, for instance, increased and decreased, yet federal and state prison systems held approximately the same number of offenders each year (Blumstein and Cohen 1973).

In the mid-1970s, however, the use of imprisonment started to increase dramatically, despite the fact that crime rates were relatively stable at that time (see Savelsberg 1994). The growth in the use of both imprisonment and jail incarceration has remained almost unchecked since then. At mid-2005, American prisons held 488 prison inmates per 100,000 residents, and another 250 were held in local jails (Harrison and Beck 2006). To put this total in perspective, the United States has the world's highest incarceration rate. Ruddell and Fearn (2005) found that the average jail and prison incarceration rate of 19 first-world nations (such as English-speaking, common law nations and European countries) was 97.07 per 100,000 residents in the population, about one-seventh the current U.S. imprisonment rate.

Why do Americans use prisons seven times as much, per capita, as other industrialized nations? With the exception of homicide, crime rates in most European nations are more or less the same as those in the United States, and in some places, crime rates are actually lower than those in the United States (see Farrington, Langan, and Tonry 2004). There has even been some convergence in homicide rates—U.S. rates dropped, while they increased in many European nations. The simple answer is that we sentence more people to prison, and we hold

Figure 6.1
Federal and State Imprisonment Rates, 1925 to 2005

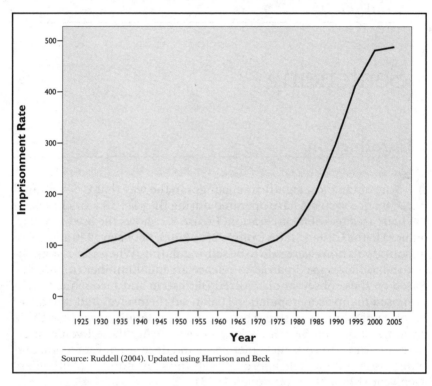

Source: Ruddell (2004). Updated using Harrison and Beck

them longer. However, the reasons for the increased use of punishment are complex. First, America has waged a war on drugs. Approximately 21 percent of all state prison inmates are now held on drug-related offenses (Bureau of Justice Statistics 2006), and 53.7 percent of all federal prisoners were drug offenders in November 2006 (Federal Bureau of Prisons 2007).

In Chapters 1 and 2, we discussed how the federal government provided financial support for states to conduct a war on drugs. The war on drugs has focused primarily on suppression and enforcement, and comparatively little has been invested in treatment. States are now spending more in alternatives to imprisonment for drug offenders, a topic that we address more comprehensively in Chapters 10 and 11. But how much of an impact has the drug war had on overall imprisonment rates? Blumstein and Beck (1999) contended that the incarceration of these offenders had a powerful effect on imprisonment, but we need to take a closer look at the numbers. After subtracting the estimated number of drug offenders (based on federal and state data—about 376,727 prisoners and another 184,639 jail inmates), we find that there were approximately 1,624,864 persons sentenced or held on violent, public order, and property crimes. Even without drug offenders, the United States would have an incarceration rate of 548 persons per 100,000 residents in the population—or greater than five times the average of the 19 other first-world nations described in the Ruddell and Fearn (2005) study.

As a result, the war on drugs has had an effect on imprisonment; but even by subtracting all persons held in jail or prison on drug offenses, the United States would still have the world's greatest imprisonment rate (although Russia would be a very close second place). What makes Americans so punitive? Prison used to be a sanction that was reserved for the "worst of the worst" offenders, criminals who had repeatedly failed to rehabilitate themselves. In the 1950s and 1960s, someone who had been to prison was considered to be a very bad person. This has changed. Bonczar (2003, 1) recently found that "if incarceration rates go unchanged, 6.6 percent of U.S. residents born in 2001 will go to prison at some time during their lifetime." At some point, prison became a more or less normal event in the lives of a number of people. Yet, the increased use of incarceration did not affect all social or racial groups in the same way.

African Americans and Latinos, for example, are at much higher risk of imprisonment than whites. Bonczar (2003, 1) reported that "[a]bout 1 in 3 Black males, 1 in 6 Hispanic males, and 1 in 17 White males are expected to go to prison during their lifetime, if current incarceration rates remain unchanged." Moreover, the imprisonment of women, once very rare, also has increased significantly over the past several decades (Harrison and Beck 2006). Many scholars believe that the war on drugs was responsible for ensnaring more African Americans and Latinos in the criminal justice system (see Blumstein and Beck 1999; Parenti 2000). However, there may be other factors that contribute to higher rates of minority punishment and the increased incarceration of women. We address this issue more comprehensively in our examination of race and justice in Chapter 7.

Getting Tough

Of course, if the public believed that getting tough on crime was undesirable, we probably would not be incarcerating some 2.1 million offenders in jails and prisons as of mid-2005 (Harrison and Beck 2006). In this chapter, we examine the mechanisms that legislators and policymakers use to get tough on crime and some of the political factors that contribute to the increased use of punishment. Like many of the policy shifts we describe, the increased use of imprisonment was a result of political priorities. One important question that we ask throughout this book is whether punishment by itself is the best response to crime. If we believe that drug abusers should be placed in prison, for instance, why do so few of them receive any sort of meaningful drug treatment while they are incarcerated? In a recent BJS study, Mumola and

Karberg (2006, 1) reported that only 15 percent of state prisoners and 17 percent of federal prisoners in 2004 had received drug treatment since their admission to prison (but a greater percentage had participated in "other" addictions-related programs—increasing those percentages to 40 and 49 percent respectively).

At some point, we lost confidence in rehabilitating offenders. Most **penologists** (who study the use of punishment and corrections) believe that two reports that questioned the effectiveness of rehabilitation, and pessimistically suggested that very little worked, were the nails in the coffin of prison rehabilitation programs (see Lipton, Martinson, and Wilks 1975; Martinson 1974). Legislators seized the notion that correctional rehabilitation was not effective and argued that we should return to philosophies of punishment that emphasized deterrence, retribution, and incapacitation.

Such a philosophical shift was supported by politicians who based their electoral campaigns on being tough on crime. Prior to 1968, for instance, crime was seen primarily as a local problem. Politicians and policymakers struck gold when they discovered that criminal bashing made good political sense. After all, what politician really wants to be soft on crime? Like many other ideas about crime and justice, our notions about offenders were shaped by increasing numbers of television programs and movies that portrayed crime and criminals as out of control (see Beckett 1997). Gallup polls conducted between 1950 and 2000 found that the number of people who reported that crime or drugs were the biggest problems facing America increased, especially after the 1970s.

Clearly, some criminals need to be incapacitated, but many penologists question whether we need to incarcerate 2.1 million persons. Few would disagree that **career criminals,** offenders who engage in crimes that place victims at high risk (such as armed robbery) and those who commit many crimes in a given year, should be in prison. These offenders have a significant negative impact upon a community, both economically and in terms of citizen fear of crime. It is much less expensive to incarcerate offenders who do several residential burglaries a week, rather than let them continue their crimes in the community. Locking up the highest-risk offenders (those most likely to commit a large number of offenses or serious offenses) is the principle behind **selective incapacitation.** Some have suggested that today's use of incarceration, however, can best be described as **mass imprisonment** or the wholesale incapacitation of offender populations (see Mauer and Chesney-Lind 2002; Parenti 2000).

Unfortunately, the notion of selective incapacitation is based on an assumption of prediction, and we have not been able to reliably predict who will continue to commit crimes. Sentencing an offender who would not commit any future crimes to a lengthy imprisonment term is a wasteful and expensive intervention. But who are high-risk offenders, how much punishment do they require, and how much of a burden does this place on taxpayers? The example in Box 6.1 outlines the costs of imprisoning a 17-year-old convicted of a violent offense.

Box 6.1
Teenager Gets 32 Years in Gang Shooting

Proclaiming his innocence, a convicted teen-age gang member Friday was sentenced to 32 years in prison for a Chico shooting which seriously wounded a 16-year-old boy.

Teng Yang, who was 17 at the time of the shooting, was convicted by a Butte County Superior Court jury of opening fire with a semi-automatic handgun on a crowd coming out of a teen dance near Bidwell Junior High School last Oct. 12.

The judge sentenced the teen-ager to 5 years in prison on a felony assault count, tacking on 27 more years due to the severity of the victim's injuries and a special finding by the jury that the shooting was an act of "street terrorism" in furtherance of an Asian youth gang called "Menace Boys Crew."

Source: Adapted from Vau Dell, *Chico Enterprise Record*, p. A1.

We hand out lengthy sentences such as this every day, but we do not really know whether these offenders are amenable to rehabilitation, the public often does not know the true costs of housing these offenders, and it is even more difficult to weigh the benefits. Obviously, we cannot have teenagers shooting others (in this case, the victim was shot in the head, but recovered), but would this offender commit further offenses?

For one year, 2005–2006, it cost approximately $34,150 to hold an offender in a California prison, and even if we did not account for inflation, it would cost the state taxpayers approximately $1.1 million dollars to hold Teng Yang in prison until his release (although he will probably be paroled much earlier). Translated into different terms, each California taxpayer paid approximately $2,200 in state taxes in 2002, and it takes about 15 taxpayers to cover Teng Yang's imprisonment. Are we getting a good return on our investment? While it is comparatively easy to estimate the costs, it is much harder to weigh the benefits. ✦

Malcolm Feeley and Jonathan Simon (1992) described how we abandoned **individualized justice** (where each person's strengths and weaknesses are weighed at sentencing) and rehabilitation in favor of a punishment philosophy based on the management of high-risk, unruly, or dangerous populations—what they defined as a **new penology.** Perceptions have shifted away from individual offenders to these dangerous populations that need to be managed. As a result, the role of prison and parole systems have changed from rehabilitation to the efficient management of such groups. Organizational efficiency has become more important than other social goals, such as addressing the causes of crime. Given this perspective, the failure of individuals on parole to successfully re-enter society is entirely predictable. Consequently, the blame shifts from the prison's failure to prepare an inmate for community reintegration to the parolee. Feeley and Simon's (1992) new penology helps us better understand the rejection of selective incapacitation and our reliance on mass imprisonment.

But did justice systems have an alternative to relying on mass imprisonment? Rates of recidivism were high as offenders who were on parole committed new offenses. In a federal study of offenders released from prison in 1983, Beck and Shipley (1989, 1) found that "an estimated 62.5 percent were rearrested for a felony or serious misdemeanor within 3 years, 46.8 percent reconvicted, and 41.4 percent returned to prison or jail." Prisons were failing to have the desired effect (reducing future crime). A follow-up study published a dozen years later found that parolees were even less successful in the 1990s. Langan and Levin (2002, 1) showed that "within 3 years of their release in 1994, 67.5 percent were rearrested . . . 46.9 percent were reconvicted for a new crime . . . and 51.8 percent were back in prison, serving time for a new prison sentence or for a technical violation of their release." Given these statistics, policymakers began implementing a number of different strategies to sanction offenders.

Indeterminate to Determinate Sentencing

For the larger part of the twentieth century, most states and the United States federal government relied on **indeterminate sentencing** systems. These systems were built on nineteenth-century notions pioneered by men such as Zebulon Brockway, who strongly believed in the ability of penitentiaries and reformatories to bring about rehabilitation. As a result of this orientation, governments adopted sentencing arrangements whereby the legislature would establish the minimum and maximum range for the sentence, the judge would impose the sentence, and the actual time served would be determined by a parole board (upon successful rehabilitation).

This approach was based on the belief that offenders could work toward rehabilitation, and that their length of stay in prison would be reduced if they successfully demonstrated positive changes. If inmates completed educational or life-skills programs, were involved in prison work, and conducted themselves in a positive way within a correctional institution, they could be released earlier than if they made less rehabilitative progress. Thus, inmates who were motivated to work toward rehabilitative goals were rewarded with early releases on parole. Inmates who had no rehabilitative goals or were disciplinary problems, by contrast, would stay in prison longer.

Indeterminate sentencing was based on the sentencing of individuals to a variable term of punishment. An offender convicted of burglary, for instance, might be sentenced for a term of 1-to-10 years. In some places, the inmate was eligible for parole at some percentage of the lower range. In the case of a burglar who was sentenced in Texas in the 1970s for instance, he would have been eligible for parole after serving three-quarters of the one year. While few offenders were released from prison at the lower limit, indeterminate sentences gave inmates a positive goal to work toward.

Rehabilitative philosophies are strongly tied to the notion of individualized justice. Each offender was seen to have strengths and weaknesses, and these issues were to be considered by a judge prior to sentencing. For the judge to understand the offender's circumstances, a probation officer often would conduct a **pre-sentence investigation.** The probation officer's report detailed the individual's involvement in the offense, his or her social history, previous contacts with the justice system, and his or her amenability for rehabilitation. Often the individual's potential for rehabilitation was based on education, prior work history, and involvement in substance abuse, as well as family and community supports. Those with more education and job experiences might be perceived by middle-class probation officers and judges as being more amenable to treatment. Thus, it is likely that sentencing based on these **extralegal factors** (factors that have no bearing on the offense, such as race, class, or gender) discriminated against offenders with little prior work experience or poor educational histories.

Pre-sentence reports also outlined the aggravating and mitigating factors about the offense and offender. **Aggravating factors** include whether the offender was paid to commit the crime, if he or she took a leadership role in the offense, if the offense was particularly cruel, or if the victim was vulnerable (such as an infant or senior citizen). A greater number of aggravating factors enhanced the sentence severity. While most of us would probably agree that aggravating factors should be weighed carefully at sentencing, there is less agreement about whether mitigating factors should be considered.

Mitigating factors include whether the crime was the person's first offense, the offender was under duress at the time of the crime, if the person assisted the police, or if the person's involvement in the offense was peripheral. Again, most persons would support reductions in the sentence severity for a first-time offender, one who is immature, or if he or she did not play a central role in the crime. Nevertheless, should a person's good character or reputation, his or her potential for rehabilitation, an honorable discharge from the Armed Services, or the ability to make restitution be considered by a judge as factors that reduce the sentence severity? One important question that we have to ask is: who benefits most from weighing these mitigating factors prior to sentencing?

Whitman (2003) observed that the United States has moved away from consideration of individual factors at sentencing, and the federal government does not recognize mitigating factors.[1] Individualized justice was perceived to encourage judges who were soft on crime to sentence offenders to lenient jail or prison terms. As rehabilitation fell out of favor, the focus was less on the individual's positive characteristics, or one's willingness to make significant rehabilitative changes, and more in favor of determinate sentences. But is it soft on crime to give a short sentence to someone who shows more potential for rehabilitation?

In the 1970s, many states phased out indeterminate sentencing in favor of sentences that were fixed, or **determinate sentencing.** In some jurisdictions, parole was abandoned altogether. For instance, federal parole was abolished for offenders sentenced after November 1, 1987. If we use the burglary offender mentioned previously, his determinate sentence might be fixed at seven years. Most jurisdictions have the ability to grant **good time credits** for inmates who obey the institutional rules, thus providing an incentive for good behavior. In the U.S. Bureau of Prisons, for example, an inmate can earn up to 54 days per year (a 15 percent discount) for good conduct.

To better understand why determinate sentences may actually reduce inmate motivation to rehabilitate themselves, we use the example of two persons sentenced to the same term of incarceration in a federal prison on the same day, for the same offense. One prisoner successfully completes a university degree program during the evening, actively is engaged in the prison's work program, and participates in Alcoholics Anonymous. The other inmate, by contrast, spends all of his free time watching television and is only marginally engaged in some institutional chores. Assuming that both earn the 54 days of good time credit, they both will be released on the same day. Some might question whether the inmate who is more actively engaged in rehabilitation should be discharged earlier. This is one of the difficult considerations about many of the mandatory minimum sentences that we have enacted today: There is little incentive for prisoners to improve their knowledge or skills while incarcerated.

A second challenge that determinate sentences present is that once the inmate is released after serving his or her entire sentence, the justice system has no control over the person's conduct within the community. If prisoners are paroled, by contrast, the parole system still has considerable influence over their behavior, including their place of resi-

---

Box 6.2
Should Prisoners Receive a State-Funded College Education?

Most of the students reading this chapter fund their college educations with part- or full-time jobs, and many will have sizeable student loans to repay after they graduate. Until Congress passed the 1993 Violent Crime Control and Law Enforcement Act and the Higher Education Reauthorization Act of 1994, federal and state prisoners had access to Pell Grants that helped pay for their college education while incarcerated. These acts greatly decreased the ability of prisoners to access higher education.

But should taxpayers pay for prisoners to attend college? Also, will you have to compete with these college-educated prisoners when you are looking for a job after graduation? (When answering this question, remember that while tuition in state-supported schools is increasing, most students pay less than 20 percent of the entire cost of college, and taxpayers pay the rest). Like many of the other issues that we raise, there are no easy answers to these questions. But if these prisoners earn a degree, obtain a job, and pay taxes for the rest of their working lives, is this not ultimately a good investment for society? ✦

dence, curfews, and with whom they associate. Parolees must also submit to police searches, as well as drug or alcohol testing when requested. If parolees violate the conditions of their release, they can be returned to prison on a **technical violation,** such as a failure to abide by conditions of their parole (curfew violation or being in a tavern). Thus, the prison system still can exert some control over offenders while they are reintegrating into the community, a difficult and stressful time for many ex-prisoners.

Sentencing Guidelines

During the 1980s, many politicians believed that sentencing was overly influenced by judges who were perceived to be soft on crime. A second problem was the recognition of racial disparities (an issue we address at length in Chapter 7). To restrict judges from considering mitigating factors and to promote race- and gender-neutral sentences, various types of sentencing guidelines were enacted.

In 1980, the State of Minnesota developed **sentencing guidelines** that prescribed sentences for judges (Lubitz and Ross 2001; Miethe and Moore 1989; Minnesota Sentencing Guidelines Commission 2005). Since Minnesota introduced the first sentencing commission in 1980, 25 other states and the District of Columbia have established sentencing commissions (or advisory commissions), although three of these state commissions are now defunct. Most of these commissions have established sentencing guidelines: seven have voluntary guidelines, while the rest are mandatory (see Rottman and Strickland 2006). The last state to implement sentencing guidelines was Alabama, in April, 2006.

These sentencing guidelines outline a range of possible sentences for offenders based on their prior criminal record and the seriousness of the current offense. Using these schemes, serious current offenses and a greater number of prior convictions result in longer sentences.

Following the example of the states to adopt sentencing guidelines, in 1984 the United States Congress passed the Sentencing Reform Act. The federal sentencing guidelines, which took effect on November 1, 1987, were very much like those in the handful of states that had implemented **guided sentences.** However, the federal sentencing guidelines differed in one critical way. In most states, the determinate or presumptive sentences provided for under sentencing guidelines all but eliminated parole and replaced it with good time credits. Good time credits allowed some fractional reduction in the sentence based on the inmate's good behavior and participation in programming activities. Some states (such as New Mexico) had a fairly generous discount rate of 50 percent, or one day good time credit for each day served. By contrast, the federal sentencing guidelines provided for a 15 percent discount rate, or a maximum of 54 days per year (Mays 1989). This standard became the benchmark for states that moved in the direction of "truth in sentencing," or requiring inmates to serve all or virtually the entire sentence imposed.

Sentencing guidelines provide a range of possible sanctions, but the range tends to be narrowly defined. Judges do have some discretion to depart from the range, but they are often required to justify those sentences, at least prior to the *United States v. Booker* (2005) and *United States v. Fanfan* (2005) decisions. Sentencing guidelines effectively restrict the ability of judges to base decisions on an individual's strengths or weaknesses—most often mitigating factors. State judges, many of whom are elected, who depart from the guidelines too frequently risk the negative attention of an electorate who is unlikely to distinguish between being smart and being soft on crime.

The net effect of sentencing guidelines is that they remove judges' discretion. However, prosecutors are free to file whatever charges they wish, and in some cases, overcharge defendants (charging them with the offense that has the greatest penalty) in order to pressure them into accepting plea bargains (Bibas 2004). Some innocent defendants will plead guilty to a crime that they did not commit to avoid a trial that might result in financial ruin and an onerous sentence if found guilty. Jerome Miller (1996) questioned whether giving prosecutors so much unchecked power is desirable, especially since the prosecuting attorneys in most U.S. jurisdictions are elected politicians who rely upon the electorate in order to keep their jobs. Since they lead these organizations, it is likely that district attorneys who wish to remain on the job ensure that the assistant district attorneys they employ are "tough on crime."

Sentencing guidelines have been called into question by a series of recent Supreme Court decisions, including *Blakely v. Washington* (2004) and the *Booker* and *Fanfan* (2005) decisions. These three cases challenged the factors that judges can consider when imposing sentences and whether federal judges have to adhere to sentencing guidelines. In the *Blakely* case, the Court found that a sentencing judge cannot consider facts (such as aggravating factors) that were not confessed to by the defendant or decided by a jury. In the *Booker* and *Fanfan* cases, the Court found that federal sentencing guidelines are advisory rather than strictly defined criminal sanctions (U.S. Sentencing Commission [USSC] 2005).

These three decisions return discretion to sentencing judges, something that has been advocated by many scholars and jurists. While it is too early to determine the long-term results of these cases, many persons who advocate on behalf of offenders are cautiously optimistic that a degree of rationality will be returned to sentencing decisions, especially in the cases of nonviolent or drug offenders. Yet, there is some debate about whether mandatory minimum sentences, truth in sentencing guidelines, and three-strikes legislation actually created overcrowded prisons, as most of these initiatives were introduced a decade or two after the largest increase in imprisonment use in the mid-1970s (see

Sorensen and Stemen 2002). Still, these sentencing schemes are currently used, and some are very controversial. In the following sections, we review these different types of guided sentences and examine the underlying political factors that led to high imprisonment rates.

Mandatory Minimum Sentences

Mandatory minimum sentences are among the most contentious of sentencing schemes because they impose a fixed penalty on an offender, and judges cannot consider mitigating factors. While mandatory minimum sentences are most commonly associated with drug offenses today, these sentencing practices started as responses to local crime problems. An early example of mandatory minimum sentences was the Massachusetts Bartley-Fox firearms law that called for a prison sentence of one year for persons illegally carrying a concealed firearm. This law, which took effect on April 1, 1975, was a model for gun control legislation in other places. One problem with the legislation, however, was its selective enforcement by the police, and convictions actually decreased after the law was enacted (Walker 2006).

The intent of mandatory minimum sentences is to target and punish behaviors that contribute to high rates of crime or violence. Illegally carried firearms, for instance, have been associated with higher murder rates (Jacobs 2002), as are firearms used in the commission of other crimes, such as robberies. As a result, there is a commonsense appeal that if we enhance penalties for such offenders, the result will be less gun violence.

Perhaps the most controversial aspect of these laws pertains to the penalties for drug possession, sale, or manufacture (Families Against Mandatory Minimums 2005). For instance, in 2002 approximately one-fifth of all state offenders and over half of all federal prisoners were incarcerated on drug-related offenses. The penalties that are imposed on these offenders are strict. Durose and Langan (2004, 3) report that the average federal prison sentence for drug possession was 79 months, compared with the average federal murder sentence of 109 months. We have created a justice system where sentences for drug-offense crimes are almost equivalent to murder, at least if you are in federal court (average state sentences for drug possession are much less severe, and sentences for murder are much greater).

But, are lengthy sentences for drug offenses an inappropriate intervention? The relationship between substance abuse and illegal behavior has long been established. For instance, self-report studies reveal that in 2002, 68 percent of jail inmates reported symptoms consistent with alcohol or drug dependency (Karberg and James 2005). That same study found that over half of the convicted jail inmates were under the influence of drugs or alcohol at the time of their offense, and 16 percent committed crimes to obtain drugs. As jail is the gateway to prison, it is likely that both federal and state prisoners have similar troubles with addictions (see Mumola and Karberg 2006).

Many other crimes are associated with illegal drug use. Perhaps the most destructive offenses are those associated with the distribution of illicit drugs. Street-level dealers, for instance, report being robbed, and these acts often result in violent retaliation because these dealers have no recourse to the law (Jacobs 2000). Often crimes such as residential burglary or robbery are committed to support drug addictions (see Baumer et al. 1998). Addictions also result in countless other tragedies, from child abuse and neglect to car crashes. Addiction costs, in losses due to crime, health problems, and lost productivity are significant.

Some types of drugs—such are crack cocaine—are associated with higher rates of crime and violence. Moreover, the use of crack cocaine by pregnant women has been suspected of producing birth defects. To deter crack users and sellers, the federal government imposed a sentence differential for regular powder cocaine to crack cocaine of 100:1. This means that a person apprehended with one gram of crack cocaine will receive a sentence that is equal to having 100 grams of powder cocaine. As crack cocaine was predominately a drug of choice for African Americans, the penalties that they received were unusually harsh. One problem with this sentencing differential is that crack cocaine and powder cocaine are chemically indistinguishable; they are essentially the same drug but different forms are used by African Americans and whites (Berndt 2003).

The United States Sentencing Commission (USSC) determined that crack might neither have contributed to violence in levels that were initially feared nor resulted in long-term handicaps for children born to crack users (USSC 2002). Moreover, they acknowledged that the sentencing differential impacted minority drug users more than non-minority users who used powder cocaine. As a result, in both 1995 and 2002, they recommended that the sentencing differential be reduced. The recommendations of the Sentencing Commission were ignored. There is little political willingness for any legislator to support such an initiative and be labeled soft on crime. This is a troubling theme: even when criminal justice policies or practices are demonstrated to be ineffective or unjust, there is resistance to making any type of change if these reforms are perceived to be lenient toward criminals.

One of the problems with mandatory minimum sentences is that they are not imposed uniformly, and prosecutorial discretion will lead to some unjust outcomes. In a study of mandatory minimum sentences in Oregon, Merritt, Fain, and Turner (2006, 10) found that prosecutors circumvented this legislation and observed that "new laws, although mandatory, could not ensure either certainty or severity in sentencing." This brings us back to the troublesome issues of getting criminal justice officials to implement policies in the way that they were intended. Historically, it has been difficult to get the officials within the criminal justice system to change established practices, and sometimes they are opposed to very severe sentences.

The trouble is that offenders who commit the same offense will sometimes be treated very differently, as one receives the mandatory minimum sentence, while the other receives a lesser sanction because the prosecutors have the discretion to file lesser charges. Thus, Barker (2006, 39) noted how Oregon prosecutors' decisions about who would be charged under the mandatory minimum guidelines were inconsistent. "What is troubling here is the major strain on uniformity, fairness, proportionality, and equal protection—basic principles of modern justice." As Tonry (2006, 46) contended, "mandatory minimums always produce widespread injustices because they always produce circumvention and seldom significantly augment community safety and welfare."

Research has demonstrated that mandatory minimum sentences have been implemented in an inconsistent manner and typically have produced unanticipated and even unjust results (see Tonry 2006). One of the challenges that we have outlined throughout this book is that new policies, justice system reforms, and other interventions often look "good on paper," but they can be very difficult to implement in a fair and just manner. Three-strikes legislation, for example, was intended to remove the worst offenders from the streets; but in some states, many of the people are sentenced to lengthy prison terms based on nonviolent offenses.

Three-Strikes Legislation

Many people believed that three-strikes legislation was an innovative practice when these laws were enacted in the 1990s. However, a number of jurisdictions already had some form of habitual or persistent offender-sentencing program, and some had been enacted over a century ago (Tonry 1999). We always have recognized the need to sanction the serious repeat offender, but Washington State was the first to label their sentencing program three-strikes when it was introduced in 1993. The intent of three-strikes legislation is to provide a long-term sentence option for repeat offenders, typically those who had been convicted of three serious felonies. Perhaps the only difference between three strikes and previous habitual offender laws was its catchy title.

Other jurisdictions quickly enacted similar legislation, and by 2001, 26 states had adopted these sentencing schemes. Franklin Zimring and his colleagues observed that some states rarely use this sanction, but in California it is used almost daily (Zimring, Hawkins, and Kamin 2001). On September 30, 2006, there were 7,945 inmates with three strikes in California prisons (California Department of Corrections and Rehabilitation 2006). Again, the controversy surrounding such legislation comes not from its presence, but its application. Critics of these policies are concerned that nonviolent offenders are receiving long imprisonment terms under these sentencing programs (Zimring, Hawkins, and Kamin 2001). In fact, a recent California study found that only 37 percent of third-strikers had a violent crime as their last offense (LAO 2005).

In California the prosecutor has the discretion to file some offenses, known as **wobblers,** as either a misdemeanor or a felony. In the 2003 case of *Ewing v. California,* the U.S. Supreme Court upheld prosecutors' ability to consider these crimes as an offender's third strike. In the *Ewing* case, a repeat offender received a 25-year-to-life sentence for the theft of three golf clubs, worth $399 apiece. This offense could have been prosecuted as a misdemeanor, but the prosecutor had the discretion to file the charge as a felony, which led to a 25-year sentence. Like in the Texas 1980 case of *Rummel v. Estelle,* the Supreme Court did not find Gary Ewing's lengthy sentence to be cruel and unusual.[2]

Other problems have been identified with the application of repeat-offender sentencing schemes. For instance, should an offense committed as a juvenile be counted as a strike, even though juveniles do not always have the right to a jury trial? Further, should a significant lapse of time between offenses restrict the prosecutor from pursing a third strike? Last, should judges have the ability to reduce one's prior strikes? One additional concern about imposing a lengthy prison term on a third-strike offender relates to our understanding of the life course and the commission of crime. In most cases, offenders commit fewer crimes as they age and presumably establish more positive bonds with the community, the process that criminologists call **aging out.** If we are imposing lengthy incarceration periods on older offenders (as most three-strikers are—one California County reported that the average age of these felons was 31 years), are we incarcerating them at a time when they pose less risk to society?

Serious and repeat offenders always have challenged justice systems. Supporters of three-strikes-type legislation argue that high-risk or high-rate offenders create a significant risk to the public. The problem is that it is hard to differentiate between a high- and low-risk offender when we do not have the "tools" to predict future criminal behavior. If we incarcerate an offender who is not a risk to society, this represents a significant taxpayer burden. In the United States, it cost an average of $22,650 to hold an offender in 2001 (Stephan 2004), and imposing a 25-year sentence represents an investment of $566,250 (without factoring in inflation) for a single prisoner. Advocacy groups, such as the Sentencing Project, argue that such sentences are both destructive to the individual and squander taxpayer dollars (Mauer 2004).

A 10-year evaluation of three-strikes policies was conducted by the Legislative Analyst's Office (LAO) in 2005, and their report outlined how this legislation had significant impacts on California's courts and corrections systems. Third-strike offenders have increased the number of jury trials in some jurisdictions, increased the percentage of pretrial jail detainees, and contributed to prison overcrowding. Still, the LAO (2005) found that the introduction of this legislation did not have the effect on correctional populations that was initially forecast. The influence on crime rates is more difficult to predict, and the LAO (2005) could not find a significant difference in the decrease of crime rates in counties that had the highest rates of third-strike sentences versus those from the counties with the lowest rates of these sentences.

Such studies are important, as criminal justice policies should be based on what the research demonstrates to be effective or sound policy. Unfortunately, that assumption is naïve, and one of the troubles we repeatedly encounter is that some policies that are not very sound are replicated because there is strong public support for them. In 2004, for instance, California voters had the opportunity to reduce some of the punitive elements of the three-strikes legislation, but the proposition failed (47 percent of the voters supported the amendments). One of the issues that we will address in the following chapters is the public's role in crime control policy: Should experts make the decisions about appropriate interventions, or should the public?

Truth in Sentencing

Somewhat consistent with the mandatory minimum sentences described above, the federal government has funded prison construction in states that hold offenders who have committed violent, Part 1 offenses (murder, attempted murder, aggravated assault, and rape) until they have served at least 85 percent of their sentences. These truth in sentencing laws (TIS) have been adopted in 27 states and the District of Columbia. While these sentencing plans target violent offenders, the people we fear the most, the problem is similar to the problem of three-strikes legislation mentioned previously. Some offenders, even though they committed violent crimes, pose minimal risk of reoffending. Langan and Levin (2002) found that homicide offenders, for instance, were among the least likely of any group to reoffend. However, it is unlikely that there would ever be much support for releasing homicide offenders; and while not advocating the release of all persons convicted of violent crimes, some may be at comparatively low risk to reoffend.

As with other offenders, those who have a stake in the community and benefit from community support in the form of jobs, a place to stay, and a functional family are likely to do well upon release. Contrast that type of offender to a gang member who is released from prison with few supports, few prosocial associates, and a marginal or nonexistent employment history. Even for those who have the best of intentions to succeed, these conditions make the chance of a successful community reentry difficult, an issue we explore further in Chapter 10.

Although TIS came long after the biggest increases in the use of imprisonment, such practices support and maintain high imprisonment policies. It is important to understand that TIS programs undermine the use of individualized justice. In addition, TIS programs tie participating states into a long-term imprisonment program that has significant ongoing costs to the state. While construction of a single prison cell is an expensive undertaking, the annual cost of placing an inmate in the cell is much greater over the long term. One of the problems facing criminal justice administration is that crime-control policies are often implemented without any evidence of their effectiveness. The field of corrections, for instance, has been prone to "quackery" (interventions that have little basis in the research), such as chain gangs or boot camps (Latessa, Cullen, and Gendreau 2002). Another weakness is that few justice system interventions are formally evaluated (Sherman et al. 1998). As a result, even though there is a move toward evidence-based practice, we have very little information about what actually works.[3]

Federal assistance for TIS programs provides important insights into the political support for high-incarceration policies. It is obvious that there is broad political support for tough sanctions on offenders, but where does this political support come from? Some scholars have questioned why the United States, a nation founded on the concept of liberty, would have the world's highest imprisonment rates (Christianson 1998). We find that the use of punishment within the United States is the result of a complex interplay among punitive values, politicians who used crime control as an issue to lure voters, and governments that are less insulated from punitive public opinion than their counterparts in other industrialized democracies.

The Political Context of Imprisonment

It has long been recognized that the use of punishment is inherently political (Garland 2001). A more complex question is why politicians advocate punitive criminal justice practices or policies that are not only expensive but also may have long-term destructive effects on individuals, families, and communities. To understand the get-tough movement, we have to examine the political factors that influence the use of punishment. A common theme through this book is that our criminal justice policies and practices are tightly coupled with political behavior, although that was not always the case. Prior to the mid-1970s, crime was seen as a local problem, and state or federal politicians generally ignored the issue. Ruddell (2004) proposed that a series of social conditions set the stage for the fourfold increase in the use of imprisonment.

Americans experienced a series of social, cultural, and demographic changes starting in the mid-1950s. These changes included the civil rights movement, an unpopular war in Vietnam, changes in the political roles of 18- to 20-year-olds, as well as increasing divorce rates. Mainstream middle-class Americans also became disenchanted with government after the Watergate scandal. Groups with little economic or political power, such as African Americans, Hispanics, and women, fought to increase their status. Not only were such challenges occurring, but television also made these images difficult to ignore. Competition for economic and political power always leads to friction, and some penologists argue that these challenges to the existing social arrangements resulted in the increased use of imprisonment.

Since the 1950s, Americans have become increasingly unhappy and distrustful of politicians (Putnam 2000). Despite the fact that the voting age decreased from 21 to 18 years of age, the voter turnout at elections also decreased (Patterson 2002). A number of national polls during this time captured the public's increasing distrust toward government. The Harris Corporation compiled an *Alienation Index* (HarrisInteractive 2004) from a number of national-level polls conducted since 1966. This index includes a number of measures of public support and trust in government.[4] In 1966, this index had a score of 29, demonstrating general discontent with political institutions; but by 1995 this had more than doubled to 67, revealing widespread public distrust and alienation (HarrisInteractive 2003). National-level polls conducted by the Gallup organization and various news agencies had the same findings: The public was increasingly distrustful of the government and questioned the motives and legitimacy of their political leaders and institutions (LaFree 1998).

Several scholars have outlined how American governments responded to changing conditions and the increasingly political role that government played in the punishment of offenders. Michael Tonry (2004, 21–40) provided a summary of eight different theories of why the use of imprisonment increased so much between the mid-1970s and 2004. Some of these explanations about the increased use of punishment are inherently political, and we will briefly review them.

Tonry (2004) acknowledged the relationships between public demand for punishment and the political willingness to implement high imprisonment policies. Where do members of the public get their ideas about justice? There is some debate about whether politicians respond to public opinion about crime and justice and "get tough," or whether they influence the public to dwell on these issues. Beckett (1997) argued that politicians have contributed to citizen fear of crime, and they generally have led the public to believe that crime is a serious social problem that demands tough government intervention.

Tonry (2004) also observed that conservative political groups have used harsh punishment practices (along with anti-immigration and anti-affirmative action policies) to gain political support of working-class voters. For example, Richard Nixon is widely acknowledged as the first presidential candidate to push the law-and-order issue onto the national agenda in 1968 (Beckett 1997; Beckett and Sasson 2000). Prior to this time, crime always had been seen as a local or state problem. Investigators have examined this proposition, and studies conducted by David Jacobs and Ronald Helms found that there is a positive relationship between Republican governance and punitive justice policies (Jacobs and Helms 1996).

By getting tough on crime and advocating for a law-and-order agenda, governments were able to demonstrate policy success without jeopardizing their political support. Tonry (2004, 24) has speculated that "a wide range of economic, social, and cultural changes have made people anxious, risk adverse, and insecure, and desperate for comforting explanations and easy cures . . . and politicians provided scapegoats. Criminals are among the most vulnerable and viscerally plausible scapegoats." Tonry (2004) also observed that "interactions among crime trends, public attitudes, and policy making shape our sensibilities and through them our thought, policy debates, and policies" (p. 25). From this perspective, the use of punishment follows historical patterns of overreaction to anxiety or insecurity, and moral panics follow this uncertainty.[5]

Tonry acknowledged the contributions of partisan politics, the relationships between public opinion and governance, changing perceptions of risk, and cultural attitudes toward crime and offenders. He suggested that imprisoning offenders has been used to display policy success to an increasingly disaffected public. One way to demonstrate a tangible policy success is to get "tough on crime" as offenders have minimal public sympathy or support. Some have suggested that conservative politicians supported punitive criminal justice policies, and they used them to win elections at offenders' expense (Chambliss 1999; Davey 1998). This argument suggested that the fourfold increase in the use of imprisonment in the United States since the 1970s may be due to growing political disaffection and that politicians responded with policies aimed at "holding the center" and maintaining legitimacy.

In an influential statement, Gary LaFree (1998) argued that governments failed to show much policy success in the 1960s and 1970s. This was an era of runaway inflation, high unemployment, and problematic foreign policy. Moreover, there were high levels of domestic discontent. Consequently, the federal government expanded into roles previously managed by state or local governments (see Caplow and Simon 1999). Despite the fact that government spending increased significantly, the public perceived that governments were not competent, and public trust and confidence in these institutions dropped (LaFree 1998). Increasing domestic political uncertainty during the past four decades required some type of government response to maintain the legitimacy of political institutions. By waging wars on crime and drugs, politicians could show some policy success and distract voters from other issues.

Yet, many first-world nations also had high levels of political disaffection (Pharr and Putnam 1999). Only in America, however, was this disaffection accompanied by the increased use of punishment. Savelsberg (1994) and Sutton (2004) observed that the United States is less insulated against punitive values than European or Scandinavian nations that have strong centralized governments, justice systems that are less politicized, and long traditions of correctional ministries operated by bureaucrats that resist public support for punishment. In essence, because these European nations are less democratic, they punish less (LaFree 2002).

But, should criminal justice policies—including the use of punishment—be shaped by what occurs in other nations? Policies that work well in Japan or Iceland, for instance, may be a consequence of homogeneous populations, where almost everybody shares the same cultural values and beliefs. European nations, by contrast, are likely to have high rates of social spending (on health, education, and welfare programs) that might reduce some crime (although, with the exception of homicide, the crime rates in many European nations are as bad or as worse than those in the U.S.). As a result, we might learn about the practices undertaken in other places, but it is important to acknowledge that America has different cultural values, beliefs, as well as political and economic systems and that these realities ultimately fashion our justice policies.

Conclusions

To achieve a fourfold increase in the incarceration rate, we have sentenced more people to prison and sentenced them to longer terms. Abandoning rehabilitation as a legitimate aim of corrections was the primary philosophical reason behind the increased use of incarceration. We lost confidence in the ability of prisoners to reform themselves; and, instead, governments changed the primary correctional goal to the mass imprisonment of unruly or dangerous groups with little emphasis on changing their attitudes or behaviors. The primary correctional goals became efficiency and incapacitation (Feeley and Simon 1992). This change could only occur with the support of politicians who wanted to get tough on crime and, in some cases, increase their political capital at offenders' expense.

The United States locks up more people per capita than any other nation. Yet, with the exception of homicide, most industrialized nations have property and violent crime rates very similar to America. Advocates of the crime control perspective believe that incarceration is a good investment; by incapacitating offenders, they cannot commit further crimes on the street. Yet, supporters of the due process perspective are apt to argue that sentences for some crimes, such as possession of crack cocaine, are patently unfair. Thus, some have maintained that our drug policies and imprisonment practices are racist (Berndt 2003).

It is important to understand the motivations underlying the increased use of imprisonment, and scholars have identified a number of different reasons (see Beckett 1997; Chambliss 1999; Garland 2001; LaFree 1998; Tonry 2004). Politicians who attempt to increase their legitimacy and political capital—and decrease disaffection—may explain the increased use of imprisonment starting in the 1970s. In the United States, the public supports high-imprisonment policies, but Beckett (1997) and Beckett and Sasoon (2000) argued that the politicians have convinced the public that these interventions are necessary. Yet, support for punishment exists in other industrialized democratic nations as well, and these countries use only a fraction of the imprisonment of the United States.

A number of scholars have argued that one reason our justice systems are more punitive is that the United States is more democratic (LaFree 2002). In many European nations, by contrast, politicians are shielded from public support for punishment by powerful justice-system bureaucracies that have rejected tough on crime practices (Savelsburg 1994; Sutton 2004). Moreover, governments in many developed nations have strong federal and centralized bureaucracies that control the use of punishment, in contrast to the United States, which has strong state-level governments.

This discussion raises an important criminal justice policy question: Should governments rely upon the professional knowledge of long-term bureaucrats, or should we let politicians make decisions about the operations of criminal justice agencies? The disadvantage of the latter is that politicians typically operate from a short-term orientation and cannot afford to support practices that are perceived to be soft on crime, even if these policies have demonstrated effectiveness. In Chapters 10 and 11, we examine these issues more thoroughly. More specifically, we must continue to ask: What are the alternatives to prison, and what are the costs and benefits of high-imprisonment policies?

Notes

1. In the *Mistretta v. United States* decision, the Supreme Court affirmed the constitutionality of federal sentencing guidelines that did not recognize rehabilitative goals or potential for rehabilitation.

2. William James Rummel appealed a sentence of life imprisonment after being convicted of three nonviolent felonies (using a credit card for an $80.00 case of fraud, forging a $28.36 check, and obtaining $120.75 by false pretenses). The U.S. Supreme Court found that, since Rummel had the opportunity to apply for parole after 12 years, the life sentence was not cruel or unusual.

3. There has been more recent emphasis on "what works," including an annual conference on research and evaluation sponsored by the National Institute of Justice, the introduction of the journal *Criminology & Public Policy*, and much more scholarly attention paid to policy-oriented and evaluation research.

4. *The Harris Alienation* index is constructed using the following survey items: The rich get richer and the poor get poorer, what you think does not count very much any more, most people with power try to take advantage of people like yourself, the people running the country do not really

care what happens to you, and you are left out of things going on around you.

5. Moral panics occur when a widespread and exaggerated perception exists that a certain group, in our case offenders, poses a significant problem to society (see Cohen 2002).

Key Terms

aging out	indeterminate sentencing	pre-sentence investiga-
aggravating factors	individualized justice	tion
career criminals	mass imprisonment	selective incapacitation
determinate sentencing	mitigating factors	sentencing guidelines
extralegal factors	new penology	technical violation
good time credits	penologists	wobblers
guided sentences		

Critical Review Questions

1. The United States imprisonment rate is six to seven times the rate of other rich first-world nations. Do you believe that other nations are less punitive because they are less democratic? Should the people of a nation dictate criminal justice policies, or should bureaucrats who better understand the crime problem be responsible for these practices?

2. The U.S. Sentencing Commission has repeatedly found that the 100:1 sentencing ratio of crack cocaine to powder cocaine is harmful and biased. Yet, politicians have not overturned these destructive laws. Why do you believe Congress has failed to act on these recommendations for over a decade?

3. In the 2004 California election, 47 percent of voters wanted to reduce the severity of the three-strikes legislation. Should the public decide the severity of punishment, or should experts who have more knowledge about the costs and benefits of punishment? (Would your answer change if the question were about economic policy, such as inflation control, rather than punishment?)

4. One theory explains that punitive criminal justice policies are a result of governments wanting to demonstrate policy success. What are the strengths and weaknesses of this argument?

5. Not only are there differences in the use of imprisonment in different nations, but there is also considerable variation within individual states. North Dakota has an imprisonment rate of 161 per 100,000 residents in the population, while neighboring South Dakota had an imprisonment rate of 378. Rates of crime in both states are similar, and economic, demographic, and social factors are nearly identical. Given these facts, why is South Dakota more punitive?

References

Barker, Vanessa. (2006). "Deliberating crime and punishment: A way out of get tough justice?" *Criminology & Public Policy* 5 (1), 37–44.

Baumer, Eric P., Janet Lauritsen, Richard Rosenfeld, and Richard Wright. (1998). "The influence of crack cocaine on robbery, burglary, and homicide rates: A cross-city, longitudinal analysis." *Journal of Research in Crime and Delinquency* 33 (3), 316–340.

Beck, Allen J., and Bernard E. Shipley. (1989). *Recidivism of Prisoners Released in 1983.* Washington, DC: Bureau of Justice Statistics, U.S. Department of Justice.

Beckett, Katherine. (1997). *Making Crime Pay: Law and Order in Contemporary American Politics.* New York: Oxford University Press.

Beckett, Katherine, and Theodore Sasson. (2000). *The Politics of Injustice.* Thousand Oaks, CA: Pine Forge Press.

Berndt, Brooks. (2003). "Ritual and racism: A social-historical analysis of the crack sentencing guidelines." *Crime, Law, & Social Change* 39 (2), 175–192.

Bibas, Stephanos (2004). "Plea's progress." *Michigan Law Review* 102 (5), 1024–1043.

Blakely v. Washington 542 U.S. 296 (2004).

Blumstein, Alfred, and Allen J. Beck. (1999). "Population growth in U.S. prisons 1980–1996." Pp. 17–62 in *Crime and Justice: A Review of Research,* edited by Michael Tonry and Joan Petersilia. Chicago: University of Chicago Press.

Blumstein, Alfred, and Jacqueline Cohen. (1973). "A theory of the stability of punishment." *Journal of Criminal Law and Criminology* 64 (2), 198–207.

Bonczar, Thomas P. (2003). *Prevalence of Imprisonment in the U.S. Population, 1974–2001.* Washington, DC: U.S. Department of Justice, Bureau of Justice Statistics.

Bureau of Justice Statistics (2006). *Prison Statistics.* Retrieved June 24, 2006, from: *http://www.ojp.usdoj.gov/bjs/prisons.htm.*

California Department of Corrections and Rehabilitation. (2006). *Second and Third Strikers in the Institutional Population.* Sacramento: Author.

Caplow, Theodore, and Jonathan Simon. (1999). "Understanding prison policy and population trends." Pp. 63–120 in *Crime and Justice: A Review of Research,* edited by Michael Tonry and Joan Petersilia. Chicago: University of Chicago Press.

Chambliss, William J. (1999). *Power, Politics, and Crime.* Boulder, CO: Westview.

Christianson, Scott. (1998). *With Liberty for Some: 500 Years of Imprisonment in America.* Boston, MA: Northeastern University Press.

Cohen, Stanley. (2002). *Folk Devils and Moral Panics,* third edition. London: Routledge.

Davey, Joseph D. (1998). *The Politics of Prison Expansion: Winning Elections by Waging War on Crime.* Westport, CN: Praeger Press.

Durose, Matthew R., and Patrick A. Langan. (2004). *Felony Sentences in State Courts, 2002.* Washington, DC: U.S. Department of Justice, Bureau of Justice Statistics.

Ewing v. California 538 U. S. 11 (2003).

Families Against Mandatory Minimums. (2005). *Smart on Crime: Revisiting America's Approach to Sentencing Drug Offenders.* Retrieved July 20, 2006 from: *http://www.famm.org.*

Farrington, David P., Patrick A. Langan, and Michael Tonry. (2004). *Cross-national Studies in Crime and Justice.* Washington DC: Bureau of Justice Statistics, U.S. Department of Justice.

Federal Bureau of Prisons. (2007). *Quick Facts.* Retrieved January 1, 2007 from: *http://www.bop.gov/about/facts.jsp.*

Feeley, Malcolm, and Jonathan Simon. (1992). "The new penology: Notes on the emerging strategy of corrections and its implications." *Criminology* 30 (4), 449–474.

Garland, David. (2001). *The Culture of Control: Crime and Social Order in Contemporary Society.* Chicago: University of Chicago Press.

HarrisInteractive. (2003). "Modest increase in nation's Alienation Index, according to Harris Poll." Retrieved July 20, 2006 from *http://www.harrisinteractive.com/news/allnewsbydate.asp?NewsID=741.*

——. (2004). "Nation's Alienation Index decreases as fewer people feel powerless and isolated." Retrieved October 9, 2006, from: *http://www.harrisinteractive.com/harris_poll/index.asp?pid=525.*

Harrison, Paige M., and Allen J. Beck. (2006). *Prison and Jail Inmates at Midyear 2005.* Washington, DC: U.S. Department of Justice, Bureau of Justice Statistics.

Jacobs, Bruce. (2000). *Robbing Drug Dealers: Violence Beyond the Law.* New York: Aldine de Gruyter.

Jacobs, David, and Ronald E. Helms. (1996). "Towards a political model of incarceration: A time series examination of multiple explanations for prison admission rates." *American Journal of Sociology* 102 (2): 323–357.

Jacobs, James B. (2002). *Can Gun Control Work?* New York: Oxford University Press.

Karberg, Jennifer C., and Doris J. James. (2005). *Substance Dependence, Abuse, and Treatment of Jail Inmates, 2002.* Washington, DC: Bureau of Justice Statistics, U.S. Department of Justice.

LaFree, Gary (1998). *Losing Legitimacy: Street Crime and the Decline of Social Institutions in America.* Boulder, CO: Westview.

——. (2002). "Too much democracy or too much crime? Lessons from California's Three-Strike Law." *Law and Social Inquiry* 27 (4), 875–902.

Langan, Patrick A., and David J. Levin. (2002). *Recidivism of Prisoners Released in 1994.* Washington, DC: U.S. Department of Justice, Bureau of Justice Statistics.

Latessa, Edward J., Francis Cullen, and Paul Gendreau. (2002). "Beyond correctional quackery—Professionalism and the possiblity of effective treatment." *Federal Probation,* 66 (2), 43–49.

Legislative Analyst's Office (LAO). (2005). *A Primer: Three Strikes: The Impact After More Than a Decade.* Retrieved June 26, 2006 from: *http://www.lao.ca.gov/2005/3_Strikes/3_strikes_102005.htm.*

Lipton, Douglas, Robert Martinson, and Judith Wilks. (1975). *The Effectiveness of Correctional Treatment: A Survey of Treatment Evaluation Studies.* New York: Praeger Press.

Lubitz, Robin I., and Thomas W. Ross. (2001). *Sentencing Guidelines: Reflections on the Future.* Washington, DC: National Institute of Justice, U.S. Department of Justice.

Martinson, Robert. (1974, Spring). "What Works?—Questions and Answers About Prison Reform," *The Public Interest,* pp. 22–54.

Mauer, Marc. (2004). *Lessons of the "Get Tough" Movement in the United States.* Retrieved July 24, 2006 from: *http://www.sentencingproject.org/pdfs/mauer-icpa.pdf.*

Mauer, Marc, and Meda Chesney-Lind. (2002). *Invisible Punishment: The Collateral Consequences of Mass Imprisonment.* New York: New Press.

Mays, G. Larry. (1989). "The impact of federal sentencing guidelines on jail and prison overcrowding and early release." Pp. 181–200 in *The U.S. Sentencing Guidelines: Implications for Criminal Justice,* edited by Dean J. Champion. New York: Praeger.

Merritt, Nancy, Terry Fain, and Susan Turner. (2006). "Oregon's get-tough sentencing reform: A lesson in justice system adaptation." *Criminology & Public Policy* 5 (1), 5–36.

Miethe, Terrance D., and Charles A. Moore. (1989). *Sentencing Guidelines: Their Effects in Minnesota.* Washington, DC: National Institute of Justice.

Miller, Jerome (1996). *Search and Destroy: African-American Males in the Criminal Justice System.* New York: Cambridge University Press.

Minnesota Sentencing Guidelines Commission. (2005). *Minnesota Sentencing Guidelines and Commentary.* Retrieved October 9, 2006 from: *http://www.msgc.state.mn.us/Text%20Only/sentencing_guidelines.htm.*

Mistretta v. United States 488 U.S. 361 (1989).

Mumola, Christopher J. (1999). *Substance Abuse and Treatment, State and Federal Prisoners, 1997.* Washington, DC: U.S. Department of Justice, Bureau of Justice Statistics.

Mumola, Christopher J., and Jennifer C. Karberg. (2006). *Drug Use and Dependence, State and Federal Prisoners, 2004.* Washington, DC: U.S. Department of Justice, Bureau of Justice Statistics.

Parenti, Christian (2000). *Lockdown America: Police and Prisons in the Age of Crisis.* New York: Verso Press.

Patterson, Thomas E. (2002). *The Vanishing Voter: Public Involvement in an Age of Uncertainty.* New York: Knopf.

Pharr, Susan J., and Robert D. Putnam. (1999). *Disaffected Democracies: What's Troubling the Trilateral Countries?* Princeton, NJ: Princeton University Press.

Putnam, Robert D. (2000). *Bowling Alone: The Collapse and Revival of American Community.* New York: Simon and Schuster.

Rottman, David B., and Shauna M. Strickland. (2006). *State Court Organization, 2004.* Washington, DC: U.S. Department of Justice, Bureau of Justice Statistics.

Ruddell, Rick. (2004). *America Behind Bars: Trends in Imprisonment, 1950–2000.* New York: LFB Scholarly Press.

Ruddell, Rick, and Noelle E. Fearn. (2005). "The stability of punishment hypothesis revisited: A cross-national analysis." *International Journal of Comparative Criminology* 5 (1), 1–28.

Rummell v. Estelle 445 U.S. 263 (1980).

Savelsberg, Joachim J. (1994). "Knowledge, domination, and criminal punishment." *American Journal of Sociology* 99 (4), 911–943.

Sherman, Lawrence W., Denise Gottfredson, Doris MacKenzie, John Eck, Peter Reuter, and Shawn Bushway. (1998). *Preventing Crime: What Works, What Doesn't, What's Promising.* Washington, DC: National Institute of Justice.

Sorenson, Jon, and Don Stemen. (2002). "The effect of state sentencing policies on incarceration rates." *Crime & Delinquency* 48 (3), 456–475.

Stephan, James J. (2004). *State Prison Expenditures, 2001.* Washington, DC: U.S. Department of Justice, Bureau of Justice Statistics.

Sutton, John R. (2004, April). "The political economy of imprisonment among affluent western democracies, 1960–1990." *American Sociological Review* 69, pp. 170–189.

Tonry, Michael. (1999). "Why are U.S. incarceration rates so high?" *Crime & Delinquency* 45 (4), 419–437.

——. (2004). *Thinking About Crime.* New York: Oxford University Press.

——. (2006). "Criminology, mandatory minimums, and public policy." *Criminology & Public Policy* 5 (1), 45–56.

United States v. Booker 543 U.S. 220 (2005).

United States v. Fanfan 543 U.S. 220 (2005).

United States Sentencing Commission (USSC). (2002). *Cocaine and Federal Sentencing Policy.* Washington: Author.

——. (2005). *Guidelines Manual.* Washington, DC: Author.

Vau Dell, Terry (2003, August 30). "Teenager gets 32 years in gang shooting." *Chico Enterprise Record,* pp. A1.

Walker, Samuel. (2006). *Sense and Nonsense About Crime and Drugs,* sixth edition. Belmont, CA: Wadsworth.

Whitman, James Q. (2003). *Harsh Justice, Criminal Punishment, and the Widening Divide Between America and Europe.* New York: Oxford University Press.

Zimring, Franklin E., Gordon Hawkins, and Sam Kamin. (2001). *Three Strikes and You're out in California.* New York: Oxford University Press.

Recommended Readings

Parenti, Christian. (2000). *Lockdown America: Police and Prisons in the Age of Crisis.* New York: Verso Press. Parenti argues that criminal justice systems were used to restore stability to a social fabric that was "coming apart" in the 1970s. Parenti finds that punitive criminal justice practices remained in place because stakeholders, including politicians, police and correctional agencies, and corporations all profit from these policies. Ultimately, Parenti argues that we need "less" police intervention, fewer lurid crime stories in the media, and fewer correctional beds in favor of more rational justice policies.

Tonry, Michael. (2004). *Thinking About Crime*. New York: Oxford University Press. Tonry provides a series of explanations about the extralegal factors that have increased the use of imprisonment in the United States. In addition to summarizing eight different propositions, he advances a theory of how punitive criminal justice policies are a result of the short-term orientation of legislators and shifting public opinions about crime and criminals rather than evidence-based criminal justice policies.

Zimring, Franklin E., Gordon Hawkins, and Sam Kamin. (2001). *Three Strikes and You're Out in California*. New York: Oxford University Press. A central theme in this book is that judges and parole boards historically insulated prison inmates from punitive public values. With the abolishment of parole in some jurisdictions and the increased use of sentencing guidelines, offenders became more vulnerable to lengthy prison terms. The authors focus their analysis primarily within California, and this state is unique because of its wholesale use of three-strikes sentences. Their proposition that less democratic nations punish less severely is provocative and calls into question the usefulness of bureaucracies, rather than politicians, to establish limits to punishment. ✦

Chapter 7

Race, Ethnicity, and Justice

Introduction

Emblazoned across the front of the U.S. Supreme Court building is the phrase "Equal Justice Under Law." However, the concept of equality can be very elusive in our system of justice. Various legally relevant factors (such as one's present charge and criminal history) and extralegal factors (income, employment status, or gender) can influence the quality of justice a person might receive. One of the key extralegal factors is race (along with ethnicity), and as Neubauer noted, "in debating crime, all roads eventually lead to issues of race." In fact, "[f]or many Americans, fear of crime is an expression of racial fears" (2001, 135). In the criminal justice system, some policies are applied in a way that creates disparity, and some individual actors in the system may engage in actions that disadvantage certain groups.

Therefore, no discussion of the issues and dilemmas facing the criminal justice system in the United States would be complete without addressing the role that race and ethnicity play in policymaking and everyday decision making. In this chapter, we focus on those features about which we are reasonably sure, as well as the areas in which there is some uncertainty, but where troubling questions remain nevertheless. Much of the discussion is framed by the debate over whether the criminal justice system is racist or not. For some people, this is a settled issue. For instance, Lynch and Patterson (1996, viii) wrote, "We have spent some time examining the issue of racial bias in the criminal justice system, and we believe that the evidence unfortunately weighs in favor of the idea that the system is biased" (see also Mann 1987). Tonry (2002, 71) has added, "Racial disparities in the justice system have gotten worse since 1980." Others, including William Wilbanks (1987), are not so sure.

A few things will become clear to you as you read this chapter. First, we cannot ignore that race and ethnicity impact the operations of the criminal justice system. Race and ethnicity clearly are significant factors in the processing of criminal cases, not only in the United States but also in other nations (Lynch and Patterson 1996). Second, however, it is much less clear why this is the case and what can be done about it. Various arguments are offered, and we explore some of them.

Decision Making in the Criminal Justice System

As we consider the influence of race and ethnicity on criminal justice procedures, six steps in the processing of suspected offenders serve as our key points of focus: (1) arrest, (2) juvenile detention, (3) prosecution, (4) adjudication, (5) sentencing, and (6) punishment.

Arrest

In 2005, 10,974 law enforcement agencies in the United States, representing an estimated population of 217 million people, made almost 10.2 million arrests for all crimes except traffic offenses (FBI 2006, Table 43). Of those individuals arrested, 7.1 million (69.8 percent) were white, 2.8 million (27.8 percent) were African American, and the remaining 2.3 percent represented other races. These percentages compare with national population figures that show that 77 percent of the adult U.S. population is white, 12 percent is African American, and other races account for 11 percent (Durose and Langan 2003).

When examining the eight crimes that compose the Part I Index offenses, it is apparent that significant differences occur in the rates of commission of crimes by race. For example, for murder and nonnegligent manslaughter, 50.5 percent of the arrests nationally were of white suspects and 47.2 percent were of African Americans. Whites were arrested almost twice as often as African Americans for forcible rape (65.1 percent versus 32.7 percent). These numbers closely parallel those for aggravated assault, where 63.3 percent of those arrested were white and 34.3 percent of the arrestees were African American. By contrast, African Americans were arrested more often for robbery than were whites (56.3 percent versus 42.2 percent). For Part I Index property crimes, whites outnumber African Americans in all four categories: Whites comprised 69.9 percent of those arrested for burglary, 69.3 percent of the larceny-theft arrests, 62.8 percent of the motor vehicle theft arrests, and 76.6 percent of the arrests for arson (FBI 2006, Table 43).

In areas other than robbery, whites comprise the majority of arrests in all Uniform Crime Reports (UCR) categories except gambling. If this is the case, why is race an issue in terms of arrests? The simple answer is that the percentage of African Americans arrested exceeds their percentage in the general population in all arrest categories except driving under the influence (9.1 percent) and liquor law violations (10.9 percent). The greatest disparity is in the robbery category, where African Americans constitute the majority of persons arrested.

This means that in virtually all arrest categories, minority group members (particularly African Americans) in the United States are arrested in numbers greater than their distribution in the general population. In fact, they are more likely to be arrested, convicted, and incarcerated. Why is this the case? The two primary explanations offered are (1) that minorities commit more crimes and (2) that they are targeted for official processing by the criminal justice system (Lynch and Patterson 1996, 11).

In regard to the first explanation, some scholars have taken the controversial view that minorities commit crimes because they are somehow biologically predisposed to, or perhaps that they are intellectually inferior to, nonminorities. While there is no credible scientific evidence to support this notion, it nevertheless periodically resurfaces to a new wave of praise or condemnation. Box 7.1 examines one of the most controversial views presented in recent history regarding the relationship between intelligence and social problems.

Box 7.1
The Bell Curve Controversy

In 1994, two conservative scholars—Richard Herrnstein and Charles Murray—published a book, entitled *The Bell Curve: Intelligence and Class Structure in American Life.* An edited book written as a rejoinder said that the book by Herrnstein and Murray "is clearly the most incendiary piece of social science to appear in the last decade or more." The book

> has generated a firestorm of debate, confirming for some their secret belief in the innate inferiority of certain 'races' or ethnic groups, angering many who view the book as an ill-concealed racist manifesto, and worrying untold others who fear the further racial polarization of American society (Fraser 1995, 1, cover).

Almost immediately after it was published, *The Bell Curve* brought to national prominence a discussion of the role of intelligence (perhaps as a substitute for race or ethnicity) in creating a variety of social problems. A number of liberal observers criticized the book based on its methodology, which was characterized as more pseudoscientific than scientific (see Gould 1995; Gardner 1995; see also Fischer et al. 1996). However, conservative scholars also worried about the implications of public policy based on the work of Herrnstein and Murray, and some saw the book as ignoring much of the historical evidence on the concept of intelligence and achievement (Sowell 1995).

Steven Fraser, while noting that *The Bell Curve* focused on class structure in the United States, said that in a subtle way it dealt with race as well. In this regard, the book used low intelligence to explain "not only poverty and unemployment but [also] crime, unwed motherhood, school failure, workplace accidents, welfare dependency, and broken families" (Fraser 1995, 2).

For their part, Herrnstein and Murray claimed that they were not examining race *per se*, but as Fraser (1995, 5) noted, "The fact that [the cognitive underclass] turns out to be disproportionately black is undoubtedly an important political and psychological consolation for some—and it severely weakens the authors' contention that their book is not about race."

Three of the six conclusions related to intelligence that Herrnstein and Murray found to be "beyond significant technical dispute" are relevant to the discussion of intelligence and crime:

(3) IQ scores match, to a first degree, whatever it is that people mean when they use the word intelligent or smart in ordinary language; . . . (5) properly administered, IQ tests are not demonstrably biased against social, ethnic, or racial groups; and (6) cognitive ability is substantially heritable, apparently no less than 40 percent and no more than 80 percent. (Herrnstein and Murray 1994, 22–23).

In terms of race or ethnicity and intelligence, Herrnstein and Murray (1994, 269) asserted that "the average white person tests higher than about 84 percent of the population of blacks and . . . the average black person tests higher than about 16 percent of the population of whites."

While Herrnstein and Murray did not set out to demonstrate that minorities are somehow inferior to nonminorities in the area of measurable intelligence, their book was controversial because of its implications for public policy relating to race and a number of social and behavioral problems. For example, Lynch and Patterson (1996, 8) maintained that the argument offered by Herrnstein and Murray

is raised to justify: (1) lack of general educational and economic success among African American populations; (2) [that it is] an argument for dismantling government programs designed to aid minorities; and (3) the argument [suggests] that minority aid programs threaten a system of meritocracy.

Does all of this explain higher crimes rates for minorities, particularly African Americans? Hardly. Nevertheless, various sociobiological explanations of human behavior surface periodically, and it is important to remember that these explanations may be tied to people or organizations that have certain overt or covert political agendas. In the end, even ideas that lack a scientific basis can influence the debate over public policies in the United States. ✦

Other explanations offered to account for the propensity to commit crimes suggest that because of cultural or structural influences, minorities simply commit more crimes. Structural influences refer to community conditions, such as high rates of poverty and unemployment. Some minority communities have a high percentage of female-headed households and unemployment, few positive role models, and many families who receive some type of welfare assistance. These economic distresses and other factors may be correlated with social disorganization and crime. Bellair and McNulty (2006, 1158) recently investigated the relationships between race and violence and, in particular, the overinvolvement of African American youths in violent crime compared with their white counterparts. They found that:

(1) Community and family contexts are predictive of ability, achievement and violence.

(2) African American more than white children must contend with distressed environments that inhibit healthy child development.

(3) The relative exposure of African Americans over whites to disadvantaged community structures explains the greater involvement in violence among young African American adolescents.

Yet, it is often difficult to separate the cultural characteristics from the structural factors. In such neighborhoods, violating the law may be more common and more commonly accepted.

Stewart and Simons (2006) examined the cultural characteristics of African American adolescents and reported that Elijah Anderson's (1999) "code of the street" explains some violent delinquency. Anderson (1999) proposed that in neighborhoods with high levels of social disorganization and disadvantage, an antisocial or oppositional culture emerges that rejects mainstream values. By adopting the code of the street, neighborhood residents—especially young males—embrace an inflated sense of manhood and involvement in criminal behaviors that ultimately lead to violence.

Other neighborhood-level factors might also increase the way that the police are deployed. Over time, the police start to refer to the neighborhoods where they make a lot of arrests as high-crime areas. Additionally, certain neighborhoods, principally those in which minorities disproportionately live, call for police services more often than those neighborhoods with higher levels of informal social control (where neighbors feel comfortable resolving disputes without involving the police). Since many cities design their police patrol beats or zones in a way to equalize the calls for service, the end result is that the police agencies place larger numbers of officers in these neighborhoods (in response to the high numbers of calls), and once the officers are in the neighborhoods they make arrests. In coming full circle, this means that quite often, minority neighborhoods are identified as high-crime areas, and they are disproportionately policed.

The disproportionate distribution of police services in minority neighborhoods results in the perspective commonly held that the police simply target minorities, particularly young minority males, for arrest. As Reasons, Conley, and Debro (2002, 181) noted,

> The police are the most visible representatives of the criminal justice system in the African American community, and public opinion polls consistently find that African Americans are less likely than whites to trust the police or believe that their communities are treated fairly by law enforcement.

The viewpoint often articulated by minorities is, "Even if you have not done anything, they will arrest you for something." This especially has been alleged in relation to traffic stops and, as a result, questions of **racial profiling** have been raised in regard to the official policies of some police departments, or the unofficial practices of individual officers. Smith and Alpert (2002, 674) say that "racial profiling is one of the most significant issues confronting law enforcement today." However, is it important to define *racial profiling* and to distinguish between racial profiling and simply good police work, if this is possible.

Lange, Johnson, and Voas (2005, 194) said that racial profiling is that idea that "some racial or ethnic groups are being stopped at a rate disproportionate to their representation in the local population." If the stops are based on some objective factor—such as evidence that a crime has been committed—then the police actions are legitimate, but if stops are based on subjective factors—merely having a suspicion based on race or behavior—that may be another matter altogether (Lange, Johnson, and Voas 2005).

In an examination of this issue, John Lamberth (1998) conducted research dealing with traffic law enforcement on the New Jersey Turnpike after hearing complaints from African American motorists about being stopped by New Jersey State Police officers, allegedly for no reason. He found that African Americans were significantly more likely (16.5 times) to be arrested in these highway stops than were nonminorities. Lamberth and others have characterized this phenomenon as "driving while black." Lundman and Kaufman (2003), in examining a national database of self-reported police-citizen contacts, found that the police are substantially more likely to stop minority motorists, whether they are male or female. In fact, they reached five conclusions based on their research:

(1) Nationwide citizens report more frequent stops of African American males than their numbers in the general population would indicate.

(2) Minority motorists (African Americans and Hispanics) frequently believe that the police did not possess a legitimate reason to stop them.

(3) Minority motorists are more likely than white motorists to report that the police acted improperly toward them.

(4) The greatest differences in perceptions by all motorists are between African Americans and whites.

(5) There is a need for further research using multiple methods and measures to determine whether the police are targeting minorities during traffic stops (Lundman and Kaufman 2003, 215).

Russell (2002, 196) maintained that "driving while black" is pervasive in the United States. Her assessment is that in our society being African American is often equated with criminality, and the result is that this "increases the probability that Blacks will be targeted for arrest. This in turn increases the probability that Blacks will be convicted and incarcerated for crimes." Given the fact that arrest decisions have ripple effects that continue throughout the criminal justice process, it would be significant indeed if the police were focusing their efforts on minorities simply because they are minorities.

What can we conclude from the research on the rate at which African Americans are stopped by the police in discretionary traffic stops?

First, regardless of whether there is unfairness in stopping motorists, there certainly is the perception of unfairness (Lundman and Kaufman 2003). Second, while some studies find that racial profiling does occur, a number of scholars warn that we must develop baseline data to properly do the research, and appropriate benchmarks are needed for judging police actions. Some researchers believe that comparing the number of African American motorists stopped with their percentage in the general population may be an inadequate or misleading baseline. For example, Smith and Alpert (2002, 699) concluded, "The current state of research on racial profiling leaves courts and policy makers ill equipped to reach reliable conclusions about the possible unequal treatment of minorities by the police." Furthermore, Engel, Calnon, and Bernard (2002, 250), in reviewing 13 studies on racial profiling, asserted that "the problem with interpreting these findings is that the mere presence of disparity in the aggregate race of stops does not, in itself, demonstrate racial prejudice, any more than racial disparity in prison populations demonstrates racial prejudice by sentencing judges." Does a problem exist? If not, there is still a very strong perception in minority communities that it does.

A position taken by some to explain disproportionality is that the criminal justice system is racist because it exists within a larger American culture that is racist. Reasons, Conley, and Debro (2002, 181) claimed that police practices result from the prejudices of individual officers and the institutional racism that pervades both the criminal justice system and American society. If this is true, then the actors in the criminal justice system are not overtly racists; they merely reflect the racial values held by the large society. Engel, Calnon, and Bernard (2002, 249) countered that the controversy surrounding this area is "overwhelmed by the unsupported assumption that all race-based decision making by the police is motivated by individual officers' racial prejudice." We will return to some of these points later in the chapter when we explore the types of programs and policies that may address racial discrimination and racism in the criminal justice system.

Juvenile Detention

Much of the evidence that we have on detention of minorities comes from the juvenile justice system and the Office of Juvenile Justice and Delinquency Prevention's focus on disproportionate minority contact, or what was originally called disproportionate minority confinement (DMC). Disproportionate minority contact/confinement means that minority group members are represented in greater numbers in short-term detention than their percentages in the general population would predict. The same can hold true at all stages of justice system processing.

We will consider issues relating to juvenile offenders at much greater length in Chapter 13. However, for the time being, it is crucial to note that the same factors and forces that impact juvenile arrestees can be in play for adults as well. On the juvenile side of the ledger, ample evidence demonstrates that minority youngsters are disproportionately detained while they are awaiting court processing (see, for example, Frazier 1989; Maupin and Bond-Maupin 1999; Roush 2004; Schwartz 1991). Again, the question that can be raised is, Why are minority youngsters (and their adult counterparts) detained at rates higher than nonminorities? Several explanations seem plausible.

First, an individual's lack of employment or the family's economic status may make judges reluctant to extend the privilege of bail to minorities, and financial hardships may keep some minority group members from making bail. In this kind of situation, it is not race *per se* that keeps minorities detained awaiting court action; it is socioeconomic status. However, as social scientists have told us for a long time, in the United States, race and socioeconomic status or class are highly correlated (see Cole 2001; D'Alessio and Stolzenberg 2002; Neubauer 2001; Seron and Munger 2002).

Second, other sociodemographic factors may serve as surrogates for race. For instance, the neighborhood in which an individual lives may be considered in pretrial release decisions. For juveniles, family dynamics, such as the number of parents in the home, the age of the parent(s), and the number of siblings, may play a role. Family stability and structure also may enter into the picture. These various elements may have nothing whatsoever to do with race, but taken together, once again they may be highly correlated with race.

Third, prior criminal record—a legally relevant variable—clearly is very important for judges when they are making release decisions (see Burnett 2002). Unfortunately, in this country minorities are substantially more likely to have arrest and detention records than are nonminorities. In fact, Free (2003, ix) noted, "In 2000 there were 188,500 more African American men in prison or jail than enrolled in higher education." Bonczar (2003, 1) added that the imprisonment rate for adult African American males in the United States is twice that of Hispanics and six times that of whites, and that if current imprisonment trends remain unchanged, the lifetime likelihood of imprisonment for a African American male born in 2001 is one in three individuals.

In all likelihood, several of these explanations are at work in the detention decision-making process. The end result is that minority group members potentially find themselves at substantial disadvantages when dealing with agents and organizations within the criminal justice system.

Prosecution

Prosecutors deal with two kinds of factors when considering whether to prosecute a case and what the appropriate charges likely should be. The two factors include those that are legally relevant and those that are extralegal in nature.

Legal factors principally include the current charge and the suspect's criminal history. These are objective criteria that have a basis in law. By contrast, extralegal factors include everything else, such as race, ethnicity, employment status, drug or alcohol use history, education, and income (see Burnett 2002). While such elements might enter the picture at the point of sentencing as mitigating or aggravating circumstances, they should not play a role in determining whether criminal charges should be filed or what the charges should be.

In terms of criminal prosecutions, it is difficult to know whether, or to what extent, various factors (such as race) may enter into the decision to file charges (see Cole 2004). Charging decisions made by prosecutors are virtually without review from any other authority, and most prosecutors would be able to articulate sufficient legal justifications for charging decisions that would be able to nullify questions about whether extralegal variables played a role in the decision-making process. Therefore, individuals making accusations that a prosecutor has acted in a discriminatory way would have to prove a systematic pattern of charging minorities existed in situations where nonminorities have not been charged. For example, in the Supreme Court case of **United States v. Armstrong,** 517 U.S. 456 (1996), a criminal defendant convicted of selling crack cocaine appealed his conviction on the basis that because of his race (he was African American), he had been targeted for prosecution. The notion that a certain person or identifiable group of persons has been selected for prosecution while others similarly situated were not charged is known as **selective prosecution.**

In its opinion in the *Armstrong* case, the Supreme Court held that the burden of establishing a defense of selective prosecution rests with the party bringing the charge. Thus, in Armstrong's case, while he could show that a number of African Americans had been prosecuted for selling crack cocaine, the Supreme Court felt that he could not persuasively demonstrate that he had been targeted for prosecution simply because of his race.

This means that unless prosecutors overtly act in a manner that is racially biased (see the next section on adjudication), it is difficult to identify and correct race-based decision making at this point in the system. Therefore, in most instances, prosecutors still operate with a great deal of unchecked and unreviewable discretion.

Adjudication

Criminal trials involve a wide range of actors with varying motives. Race and ethnicity certainly could play a role in the way lawyers and judges conduct themselves during a trial. However, decision making related to race would seem to be most critical in two activities—the selection and deliberation—of juries.

The **venire** is the pool of potential jurors called for any criminal case. It is not unusual in most jurisdictions to summon from three to four times as many people as necessary to constitute a jury. In most states, individuals are identified for potential jury service from voter registration polls. We know from a variety of sources that minorities are less likely to be registered to vote (for whatever reasons) than are non-minorities. This means that minorities may have a reduced potential for jury service based on this factor alone. To address this deficiency, some states have started to supplement voter roles with lists of licensed drivers.

Furthermore, prosecutors may be wary of minorities serving on juries, particularly when there is a minority defendant. The *voir dire,* or the process of empanelling a jury, allows attorneys for both sides to question prospective jurors about their backgrounds and attitudes toward certain issues. If a prospective juror seems to be problematic, the attorneys can request that the judge excuse that individual from jury service.

Attorneys have two different methods whereby they can excuse or "strike" a potential juror. They always can request that the person be dismissed "for cause." In reality, there is only one cause, and that is prejudice or prejudging the defendant or case. Challenges for cause are based on the answers that prospective jurors give during the *voir dire* process or information they may have provided on the biographical form most courts require. Typically a juror will do or say something that indicates to members of the courtroom work group that he or she has personal information about the case or has decided on some crucial element that the prosecutor or defense will present in the trial. If an attorney can make a compelling case for such challenges, judges will not limit the number of potential jurors that can be excluded.

However, in addition to challenges for cause, attorneys are given a limited number of peremptory challenges. The number of **peremptory challenges** may vary from jurisdiction to jurisdiction and potentially from case to case, depending on the amount of pretrial publicity or notoriety involved. In addition, the severity of the possible sanction also influences the number of challenges. In California, for instance, attorneys in capital cases have twice as many peremptory challenges as other felony cases.

Peremptory challenges can be utilized by attorneys without a stated cause and may result from some uneasiness on the part of an attorney or a "gut hunch" about how a person might perceive a case or might vote. It is the peremptory challenges that have presented the greatest problems racially in criminal cases. For instance, the U.S. Supreme Court was called upon to decide the case of ***Batson v. Kentucky,*** 476 U.S. 79 (1986), in which a prosecuting attorney used peremptory challenges to remove all African Americans from a jury pool in a trial involving an African American defendant.[1] In the *Batson* case, the Supreme Court ruled that since juries should represent a cross-section of the community, prosecutors could not use their peremptory challenges in a racially discriminatory way.

A much more subtle way that juries can be influenced by race simply is by observing the defendant in the courtroom and noticing the way the defendant is dressed or speaks. In these kinds of circumstances, nonminorities, or even minorities of a higher social class, may base their decisions about guilt or innocence on the defendant's race. If race is never raised explicitly as an issue in the jury deliberation process, it might be impossible to know the extent to which race played a role in minds of individual jurors.

Sentencing

We addressed the complex issue of sentencing in Chapter 6. However, it is important to remember that sentencing decisions may be influenced by a number of considerations. In this section, we examine the potential impacts of sentencing systems or structures, the predispositions of judges, and the role that pre-sentence investigation reports by probation officers may play.

First, for the larger part of the twentieth century most states and the United States government relied on indeterminate sentencing systems. These systems were built on nineteenth-century notions pioneered by men such as Zebulon Brockway, who strongly believed in the ability of penitentiaries and reformatories to bring about rehabilitation. As a result of this orientation, governments adopted sentencing arrangements whereby the legislature would establish the minimum and maximum range for the sentence, the judge would impose the sentence, and the actual time served would be determined by a parole board (upon successful rehabilitation).

Indeterminate sentences specify "a term of imprisonment defined by statute as a range of time rather than a specific amount of time" (Mays and Winfree 2005, 425), and this type of sentencing scheme gives judges a great deal of latitude in determining the elements to be considered in the sentencing process. Judges can explicitly or implicitly consider factors such as race or ethnicity, work history, family status, and drug and alcohol use. Under indeterminate sentencing, they also possess a tremendous amount of discretion in deciding the final sentence to be imposed (Benavides 2002). For example, most sentencing laws allow judges to choose between probation and prison, even for very serious crimes such as murder. In terms of prison sentences, indeterminate sentences provide ranges (for example, from 1-to-10 years, or 20-years-to-life) which judges could impose with the understanding that the final sentence actually would be determined by the paroling authority.

These wide grants of discretion have allowed judges to tailor "individualized sentences," but this much discretion has also allowed judges to impose sentences that varied tremendously. In reality, individualized sentences led to **sentencing disparity,** and often disparity worked to the disadvantage of minority group members. Champion (2005, 229) said that sentencing disparity exists when there is "[i]nconsistency in the sentencing of convicted offenders, in which those committing similar crimes under similar circumstances are given widely disparate sentences by the same judge, usually on the basis of gender, race, ethnicity, or socioeconomic factors." Sentencing disparity also can exist where different judges give similarly situated offenders different sentences.

Let us briefly examine some factors that might lead to sentence disparities. First, as we previously have discussed, it is possible that some disparities in the criminal justice system may be related to the more extensive criminal histories of minority group members (see Bonczar 2003; Durose and Langan 2003). If (and this is a big if) minorities have committed more crimes and more serious crimes, then these are legally relevant factors that should explain more severe sentences by judges. However, if we control for the current offense and criminal history, and minorities still are receiving more severe sanctions, then something else is at work (see, especially, Kautt and Spohn 2002; Tonry 2002). If this is the case, how can the system respond in a more racially neutral way? One answer is through a change in sentencing systems.

One of the principal concerns with indeterminate sentences was "the potential for discrimination against disadvantaged individuals" (Steen 2002, 509). As a result of this and other concerns—raised by both liberals and conservatives—beginning with Maine in 1976, states started to move toward determinate sentences, and by 1980, eight states had implemented determinate sentencing and had abandoned or severely restricted parole (Abadinsky 2002; Mays 2004; Walker 2006).

Determinate sentences provide for specific terms (or much narrower ranges of terms) that must be served by persons convicted of crimes (Mays and Winfree 2005, 423; Steen 2002). Nevertheless, even under most determinate sentencing schemes, judges have retained a fairly high level of discretion in deciding whether to grant probation or to impose a specified term of incarceration. As a result of this judicial discretion, continuing concerns over sentencing disparities, and a desire to control prison populations, in 1980 the state of Minnesota developed sentencing guidelines that prescribed sentences for judges (see Minnesota Sentencing Guidelines Commission 2005). As we outlined in Chapter 6, a number of other states followed Minnesota's lead, and the Federal Government introduced their own sentencing guidelines, which came into effect on November 1, 1987.

The federal sentencing guidelines had been in effect only two years when they were challenged in a case that eventually reached the U.S. Supreme Court. *Mistretta v. United States* (1989) was brought by a criminal defendant convicted of selling cocaine. Under the old, indeterminate federal sentencing law, Mistretta potentially could have received probation. However, under the federal sentencing guidelines, a prison sentence was prescribed. Part of Mistretta's challenge was based on the notion that the U.S. Sentencing Commission had usurped the powers of the federal courts in determining the appropriate sentences in criminal cases. In an 8-to-1 decision (with Justice Scalia issuing a stinging dissent), the Supreme Court upheld the constitutionality of the federal sentencing guidelines.

Nevertheless, the *Mistretta* case proved to be a somewhat short-lived victory for the federal sentencing guidelines. In the 2004 case of **Blakely v. Washington,** the U.S. Supreme Court revisited the issue of guided sentences and struck down as unconstitutional the part of sentencing guidelines that allowed federal judges to impose harsher sentences on facts that were not confessed to or found as fact by the jury. The Court was concerned with the disparity that can result when judges are allowed such departures.

It is important to remember that the sentencing systems employed in different jurisdictions explain some of the differences in sentencing processes. However, the judge and the probation officer's preparation of pre-sentence investigation reports (PSRs) also factor into this equation. For instance, given that judges are recruited from the human race, we can assume that they come to the bench with all of the prejudices and predispositions that affect the rest of society. Judges may hold certain views, either positive or negative, about different racial or ethnic groups, and these views may influence the decisions that they render. However, it may not be possible for us to know in a given case what legal or extralegal factors influenced a judge's decision.

Closely related to the predispositions held by judges are those held by probation officers. These perspectives become relevant at the point of preparing pre-sentence disposition reports. Probation officers can include information in PSRs related to family structure, living arrangements, employment history, educational achievement, military service records, and drug and alcohol history. While race may not enter the picture directly, probation officers (who typically are required to hold college degrees) may bring middle-class perceptions and sensibilities into the process of assessing whether a particular individual is deserving of prison or probation. Again, these values may not be open to public scrutiny and may never be explicitly addressed, unless there is an overt pattern of racial discrimination. Petersilia (1997) cited one study that found that judges accepted probation officer recommendations between 66 and 95 percent of the time, suggesting that biases held by probation officers will have a significant effect upon the sentence imposed.

Punishment

The final area in the criminal justice system where race has played a role involves the actual punishments received (beyond the point of sentencing) and the sentences served. This area deals with probation, prison terms, and the possibility of early release through good time credits or parole.

To begin with, what evidence do we have that African Americans and other minority groups are disadvantaged in the process of handing out punishments? One way to answer this is to look at the numbers of felony sentences dispensed by state courts. For instance, in 2000 there were about 924,000 felony convictions in state courts in the United States. Of this number, 54 percent of those convicted were white, 44 percent were African American, and 2 percent were of other races (Durose and Langan 2003, 1). This compares with an adult population in the United States that is 77 percent white, 12 percent African American, and 11 percent other races.

A key measure of punishment disparity is revealed when we look at the percentage of convicted offenders placed on probation. At yearend 2005, about 4.1 million were people on probation in this country. Of that number, over half (55 percent) were white, 30 percent were African American, 13 percent were Hispanic, and 2 percent represented other racial groups (Glaze and Bonczar 2006). While African Americans were more likely to receive probation than their numbers in the general population, they still were less likely to receive probation than were whites. One of the problems with such descriptive statistics, however, is that we do not know enough about the individual case characteristics to determine whether there is some element of bias involved.

Overall, the numbers show that whites still constitute the majority of those convicted of felonies in the United States, and they lead African Americans in all categories of felony convictions except for murder, robbery, drug offenses, and weapons offenses (Durose and Langan 2003, 6). Nevertheless, as the previous figures indicate, African Americans especially are overrepresented in the number of felony sentences handed down and the number of felons sentenced to prison. In fact, of the 1.2 million inmates serving one year or more in prison in 2004, 41 percent were African American, 34 percent were white, and 19 percent were Hispanic (Harrison and Beck 2005, 8). Further, Bonczar (2003, 1) found that if the use of imprisonment is unchanged, for a male born in 2001, 1 of 3 African American males, 1 of 6 Hispanic males, and 1 of 17 white males are likely to go to prison in their lifetimes.

This is reinforced by the numbers on parole as well. For example, at yearend 2005, about 784,000 people were on parole in the United States. Of this number, 41 percent were white, 40 percent were African

American, 18 percent were Hispanic, and 2 percent were of other races (Glaze and Bonczar 2006).

At the most extreme end of punishment scale in the criminal justice system is capital punishment. Here, again, the numbers on race are very interesting. At yearend 2005, there were 3,254 inmates on death row in the United States. Over half (56 percent) were white, yet 42 percent were African American, and 2 percent were of other races. Hispanics accounted for 362 of the prisoners on death row, or about 13 percent (Snell 2006, 1). Furthermore, of those individuals executed between 1977 and 2005, 58 percent were white, 34 percent were African American, 7 percent were Hispanic, and 2 percent were of other races. Both of these figures (number on death row and number executed) show that minorities, and especially African Americans, are overrepresented at the extreme end of the punishment continuum.

All of these numbers taken together strongly suggest that African Americans are disadvantaged in terms of the punishments meted out relative to their white counterparts. This may be a function of some of the disparities in the sentencing process discussed previously. However, what about decisions made in prison once the sentence has been imposed? There also may be administrative considerations that are occurring that might impact the granting of good time credits or parole in a racially disparate manner.

Addressing the Race Issue

In this section, we return to the various processing stages in the criminal justice system and consider the types of programs and policies that might address issues of race and ethnicity in the processing of suspected criminal offenders. At each stage, we consider the types of programs that have been implemented, the effectiveness of such programs, and some of the other options that might be available to us in the future.

Arrest

Given the impact that police procedures have on subsequent processing in the criminal justice system, what can we do to minimize racial discrimination in arrests? Three solutions frequently are mentioned. First, every effort must be made to ensure that the people hired to do police work are not overtly prejudiced. The application and screening process should be designed to minimize selection of those individuals who openly express racially biased attitudes. Second, every effort should be made to hire officers that reflect the racial and ethnic composition of the communities they serve (see, for example, Greene 2003; Nalla and Corley 1996). Brown and Frank (2006) noted that increasing the number of African American police officers has been a priority of many agencies since the 1960s. The basic premise of these efforts is "that increased diversity will improve police-community relations and will decrease biased police behavior, particularly against Black citizens" (Brown and Frank 2006,

96). Third, police conduct should be monitored carefully through the four mechanisms currently available: civil suits (Section 1983 civil rights actions), criminal complaints against the police, internal investigations, and external investigations conducted by civilian review boards (Reasons, Conley, and Debro 2002, 184).

Currently, little evidence shows that police hiring practices can identify recruits who hold subtle but prejudiced, views. These views may be expressed in the course of recruit training, but perceptive individuals may be able to hide strongly held racist views nevertheless. Therefore, the burden for improving police-minority relations would seem to fall on recruiting additional minorities and more closely policing the police. A few brief comments can give us an assessment of how we are doing in these two areas.

In terms of hiring additional minority officers (particularly African Americans), most police departments have made significant gains in the past 25 years. However, "the ratio of black officers to black citizens continues to be low in large cities," and with few exceptions (the Washington, DC, Police Department being one of them), minorities are underrepresented in police employment at all levels (Greene 2003, 208). An important factor to remember, in this regard, is that the number of minority officers employed by a department may make a difference in police-community relations, but minority officers are also likely to be co-opted by the occupational subculture of the department (see the discussion of departmental culture in Chapter 4). As a result, they themselves may treat minorities harshly. In fact, in their research on arrest practices of African American and white officers, Brown and Frank (2006) found that there is little support for the ideas that African American officers behave differently than white officers, or that African American citizens will receive better treatment from African American officers. They concluded, "All else being equal, African American officers are significantly more likely to arrest African American citizens than are White officers" (Brown and Frank 2006, 120).

Therefore, simply hiring minority officers, in-and-of itself, is no guarantee of improving race relations. In fact, recent research on the racial composition of police departments and the differences between the arrest behaviors of African American and white officers found that departments with a larger percentage of African American officers resulted in more arrests of African American and white offenders for simple assault but not more arrests for aggravated assault (Eitle, Stolzenberg, and D'Alessio 2005). These researchers concluded,

> extralegal factors do play a role in criminal justice decision-making, particularly in the contexts in which the police have more discretion. However, the preponderance of evidence gathered from this and other studies generally suggests that the relationship between extralegal fac-

tors and such decisions are complex and sophisticated, not simple and direct. (Eitle, Stolzenburg, and D'Alessio 2005, 54)

When it comes to policing the police, individual officers and the departments they represent have been the targets of federal civil rights actions. The Section 1983 lawsuits have impacted both training and operations in many departments. However, in the area of criminal complaints against the police, this is a section that seldom is used and is seldom effective. Therefore, increased vigilance for most departments means more attention paid to internal investigations.

Additionally, there has been an increase in the number of communities that have civilian review boards. This mechanism for external review may never live up to its full potential as a check on police powers, but civilian review boards do seem to improve community perceptions relative to fairness when it comes to investigating police improprieties (Reasons, Conely, and Debro 2002, 185–186).

Detention

At midyear 2005, nearly 748,000 people were held in just over 3,300 local jails in the United States. Whites constituted 44.3 percent of this population; African Americans, 38.9 percent; Hispanics, 15.0 percent; and other races, 1.7 percent. This means that when all groups are considered together, nearly 56 percent of the nation's one-day jail population is composed of minorities (Harrison and Beck 2006, 8). Interestingly, although the two populations are not equivalent, 60 percent of the jail inmates in the population count also are on pretrial detention status, many of them because they cannot make bail. Therefore, efforts to reduce the pretrial detainee population and to reduce disproportionately minority confinement will have to be directed at the bail process (see Patterson and Lynch 1991).

One effort in this area actually was started in the 1960s. The Vera Foundation began what was known as the Manhattan Bail Reform Project in New York City. The thrust of this project was to reduce the number of people in jail awaiting trial who could not make bail. To do this, the Vera Foundation developed a scoring sheet that pretrial release personnel and judges could use to determine who was most likely to show up for the next scheduled court appearance without having money bail imposed. In effect, the Manhattan Bail Reform Project expanded the use of **release on recognizance** (sometimes called OR or ROR) where detainees gave their word that they would show up for court (Meyer 2002). Research done in the decades following the initial experiment found that while the scoring sheet was not a perfect instrument (for example, David Berkowitz, the infamous "Son of Sam" killer qualified for ROR), it was reasonably accurate in predicting who was likely to make the next court appearance. Furthermore, the failure to appear (FTA) rate for those released OR was no greater than for those released on money bail.

Bail reform has a number of important implications for minorities and nonminorities alike. As previously mentioned, bail reform is likely to reduce the rate of disproportionate minority confinement. Bail reform also is likely to reduce jail inmate populations at some savings to local taxpayers. Finally, conviction rates for those released prior to trial are lower than for those who must wait in jail until their cases are scheduled. One possible reason for this is that criminal defendants who secure pretrial release are able to help their attorneys in the preparation of their defense.

Prosecution

Getting at prosecutorial misconduct that is racially motivated is likely to prove difficult. The one area where the courts have spoken plainly (and very recently as well) is in the use of peremptory challenges to exclude minorities from juries. Previously, we discussed the case of *Batson v. Kentucky*. However, in the 2004–2005 term, the U.S. Supreme Court heard the case of ***Miller-El v. Dretke*** (2005) and reaffirmed and even expanded the ruling in *Batson v. Kentucky* (1986) by making it easier for criminal defendants to raise the issue of improperly constituted juries (see also Fletcher 2005).[2] In the *Miller-El* case, the prosecutor excluded 10 of 11 African Americans from the jury pool, and the jury that was empanelled convicted Miller-El and sentenced him to death. In a 6-to-3 decision, the U.S. Supreme Court held that the lower courts erred in not giving full consideration to Miller-El's claim that the prosecution had violated the Court's standard articulated in *Batson v. Kentucky*. The Court was concerned about the Texas jury selection process that allowed prosecutors to ask different questions to prospective jurors depending on whether they were African American or white; and in its decision, delivered by Justice David Souter, the Court concluded that it was evident that "the selection process was replete with evidence that prosecutors were selecting and rejecting potential jurors because of race" (*Miller-El v. Dretke* 2005). This is one area where application of race to the prosecution of criminal cases is most obvious and an area that seems reasonably easy to remedy.

Adjudication

Like prosecution, adjudication may be a difficult area in which to minimize the effects of race or ethnicity (Farnworth, Teske, and Thurman 1991). Few judges in the United States could be identified as being overtly racist. They may hold negative views toward different racial groups, and at times these may be obvious. Nevertheless, most judges are fairly discrete when it comes to disclosing their personal values on many issues, and this seems especially true of the issue of race.

However, before leaving the discussion of adjudication, it is important to emphasize four points related to the processing of cases.

First, many of the factors related to the adjudication process (such as the offenses charged and the number of counts) are under the control of the prosecutor. Second, prosecutors are the major actors in the plea bargaining process by which most cases are disposed. Third, as more minorities take on the positions of prosecuting and defense attorneys and judges, the potential for racial discrimination may be minimized. But as we have seen with police officers, race may not be as important as the office held or the role played within the criminal justice system. Finally, as we will see in the next section, judges may have their discretion limited by legislatively-mandated sentence structures.

Sentencing

Sentencing disparities have been troubling for many years, and one way to address these disparities is through legislative provision of judicial guidance. We discussed sentencing at length in Chapter 6, but we need to briefly review the impact of race on sentencing.

Guided sentences—including sentencing guidelines, presumptive sentences, and mandatory minimum sentences—restricted judges' discretion in the sentencing process. Steen (2002, 511) noted that sentencing guidelines have as one goal to reduce "racial, ethnic, and gender punishment disparities." The Minnesota Sentencing Guidelines Commission (2005) has as one of its "specific goals" to "promote uniformity in sentencing."

However, while discretion is restricted, it is never fully eliminated. For example, many states still allow judges to depart from the prescribed sentences if they provide written justifications for departures. These departures typically provide grounds for appeal by either side. Now, after three decades of experience with guided sentences, we have some idea of their effect on racial and gender disparities.

For instance, evidence from around the nation has demonstrated that the movement toward determinate sentences (with restricted or no parole) has increased the average prison sentence (Lubitz and Ross 2001). This means that if the same number of people are going to prison, but the average sentence length increases, prison populations will grow. If you add new laws and increased penalties as part of a get-tough orientation, then there is something of a ratcheting effect. Prison sentences increase and prison populations grow exponentially. That is the bad news.

The good news, if you could call it that, is that this effect is occurring for all racial groups; and the disparity between African Americans and whites placed on probation and the average sentence length for each group is narrowing (Lubitz and Ross 2001). Does this mean that the gap has disappeared? Not yet, but it has diminished. However, as Steen

(2002, 511) is quick to add, the disparities continue to appear to be the greatest when judges depart from the stipulated guidelines.

As we will see in the next chapter, sentencing guidelines also have had an impact on the gaps that have existed in sentences for males and females. Generally speaking, throughout our history, females have benefited from leniency extended to them by judges and other officials in the criminal justice system. This may have been because women often have been the primary caretakers for dependent children. It also may have been because judges saw women as weaker and dependent themselves (almost childlike); therefore their criminal activities must have been the result of influences outside of themselves. In other words, boyfriends, husbands, or other family members must have influenced female offenders to have committed their offenses. As states have moved in the direction of guided sentences, women increasingly have been sentenced like their male counterparts. We will return to this discussion in the chapter on gender and justice.

Punishment

One of the most troubling aspects of the criminal justice system, in terms of race, is the disproportionate way minorities are harshly punished. As we have seen in this chapter, minority group members are proportionately less likely to receive probation, more likely to be sentenced to prison, and more likely to be given the death penalty than are nonminorities. Legislatively mandated sentencing guidelines with relatively few grounds for departures may address part of the problem. Furthermore, some states have implemented presumptive parole dates or parole guidelines (Mays and Winfree 2005). Gottfredson (2002, 1476) said that these devices, which act much like sentencing guidelines,

> were developed with several aims: increasing the fairness of parole decisions, that is, reducing uncertainty and unwanted disparity; bring[ing] greater visibility to the decision-making process; enhancing the rationality of decisions; and providing a way to describe decision policy and changing it if desirable.

Thus, implementation of parole guidelines also might reduce (although probably not eliminate) some of the racial disparity that occurs in punishments.

Perhaps the most problematic issue in punishment is the way in which the death penalty falls on minority defendants. Overall, the majority of people sentenced to die and a plurality of the people actually executed since 1977 have been white. Interestingly, most murders in the United States are intraracial (whites killing whites and African Americans killing African Americans). Nevertheless, disproportionate numbers of those executed (both white and African American) had killed white victims, and virtually no whites were executed for killing minorities (see Bohm 1991). It may very well be that as long as we have the death penalty in the United

States, racial disparities will continue to exist. While the U.S. Supreme Court has addressed the issue of racial imbalance in death penalty juries (see **Whitus v. Georgia,** 1967), at the present most of the courts do not seem inclined to deal with this issue.[3]

Conclusions

Now that we have examined some of the evidence concerning the various processing stages in the criminal justice system and the effect of race at each stage, what can we conclude? Do legally relevant or extralegal factors dominate criminal justice policies and decision making? Does the criminal justice system act in a racist manner? Are decisions made, in general, in a racially neutral way? Do we find overt racism, or is it much more subtle and covert, but systemic? Answers to some of these questions should be fairly obvious at this point, but there are some places where the answers are still elusive. For example, racially discriminatory actions may be taken by individual police officers, prosecutors, probation officers, and judges. These actions may have rippling effects throughout the rest of the criminal justice system. By the same token, it may be difficult to separate the actions of individuals from institutionalized policies (such as sentencing systems and drug laws) that have racially disparate effects. However, whether we are dealing with the actions and attitudes of individuals or the policies of agencies and organizations, one fact seems inescapable: Race remains a major issue in the processing of criminal cases in the United States.

Notes

1. In *Batson*, an African American defendant was charged with second degree burglary and receiving stolen goods. During the *voir dire* process, the judge excused a number of potential jurors for cause and then allowed both the prosecutor and the defense attorney to exercise their peremptory challenges. The prosecutor used his peremptory challenges to remove the four remaining African Americans from the jury pool. Defense counsel challenged this move, but the trial judge ruled that attorneys were allowed to use peremptory exclusions any way they wanted to. The U.S. Supreme Court, in a 7-2 vote, held that "[r]acial discrimination in selection of jurors harms not only the accused whose life or liberty they are summoned to try," but also it harms those excluded from jury duty. Therefore, peremptory challenges cannot be used to exclude a "suspect category" group (based on race, ethnicity, or gender, for example) from jury service.

2. In the 2004–2005 term the Court also heard **Johnson v. California** (2005), which did not deal with juries or prosecutorial misconduct but which nevertheless addressed the issue of race. In *Johnson*, the California Department of Corrections had used race as a criterion for the selection of temporary prison cell mates. In a 5-to-3 decision, the Court

said that such practices are subject to strict scrutiny, and it remanded the case to the Ninth Circuit Court of Appeals for review and further consideration.

3. Although they are not death penalty cases specifically, see also *Batson v. Kentucky,* 476 U.S. 79 (1986), and ***Georgia v. McCollum,*** 505 U.S. 42 (1992).

Key Terms

Batson v. Kentucky
Blakely v. Washington
Georgia v. McCollum
guided sentences
Johnson v. California
legal factors

Miller-El v. Dretke
Mistretta v. United States
peremptory challenges
racial profiling
release on recognizance
selective prosecution

sentencing disparity
United States v.
  Armstrong
venire
voir dire
Whitus v. Georgia

Critical Review Questions

1. Is the criminal justice system in the United States (or in other nations as well) racist, or are we dealing with a few individual racists who happen to work in the system? Explain your answer.

2. Go on a little scavenger hunt in your library and see how many definitions you can find for the word *race* as it relates to sociodemographics (*not* related to running). Is there consistency in these definitions?

3. Engage in the same exercise as in Question 2, but look for meanings of *ethnicity.*

4. Are *race* and *ethnicity* the same, related, or different concepts?

5. Look at the explanations why the police arrest some groups more than others. Which one seems to have the most evidence to support it?

6. How do you react to the widely-cited concept of "driving while black"? Have you, your friends, or classmates been subjected to this?

7. Are minorities detained simply because they are minorities? Why or why not? Explain.

8. Jeffrey Reiman (2004) long has maintained that "the rich get richer and the poor get prison." Is it possible to support such an assertion? How could you counter it?

9. Will sentencing guidelines (and/or parole guidelines) solve one of the major problems of racial disparity in the criminal justice system? Why or why not?

10. What impact will hiring more minorities throughout the criminal justice system have on attitudes of racism and actions of racial discrimination?
11. Will anything, short of eliminating the death penalty, reduce the racial disparity that seems inherent in capital punishment? Explain.

References

Abadinsky, Howard. (2002). "Parole." Pp. 1127–1131 in *Encyclopedia of Crime and Punishment,* edited by David Levinson. Thousand Oaks, CA: Sage.
Anderson, Elijah. (1999). *Code of the Street: Decency, Violence, and the Moral Life of the Inner City.* New York: Norton.
Batson v. Kentucky, 476 U.S. 79 (1986).
Bellair, Paul E., and Thomas L. McNulty. (2006). "Beyond the bell curve: Community disadvantage and the explanation of black-white differences in adolescent violence." *Criminology* 43 (4), 1135–1168.
Benavides, Amy. (2002). "Indeterminate sentences." Pp. 875–878 in *Encyclopedia of Crime and Punishment,* edited by David Levinson. Thousand Oaks, CA: Sage.
Blakely v. Washington, 542 U.S. 296 (2004).
Bohm, Robert. (1991). "Race and the death penalty in the United States." Pp. 71–85 in *Race and Criminal Justice,* edited by Michael J. Lynch and E. Britt Patterson. Albany, NY: Harrow and Heston.
Bonczar, Thomas P. (2003). *Prevalence of Imprisonment in the U.S. Population, 1974–2001.* Washington, DC: U.S. Department of Justice, Bureau of Justice Statistics.
Brown, Robert A., and James Frank. (2006). "Race and officer decision making: Examining differences in arrest outcomes between black and white officers." *Justice Quarterly* 23 (1), 96–126.
Burnett, Arthur L. (2002). "Permeation of race, national origin, and gender issues from initial law enforcement contact through sentencing: The need for sensitivity, equalitarianism, and vigilance in the criminal justice system." Pp. 32–47 in *Race, Class, Gender, and Justice in the United States,* edited by Charles E. Reasons, Darlene J. Conley, and Julius Debro. Boston, MA: Allyn and Bacon.
Champion, Dean J. (2005). *The American Dictionary of Criminal Justice,* third edition. Los Angeles: Roxbury Publishing.
Cole, David. (2001). "Race and crime: Does the criminal justice system discriminate against racial minorities?" Pp. 135–137 in *Debating Crime: Rhetoric and Reality,* edited by David W. Neubauer. Belmont, CA: Wadsworth.
Cole, George. (2004). "The decision to prosecute." Pp. 178–188 in *The Criminal Justice System: Politics and Policies,* ninth edition, edited by George F. Cole, Marc G. Gertz, and Amy Bunger. Belmont, CA: Wadsworth.
D'Alessio, Stewart J., and Lisa Stolzenberg. (2002). "Socioeconomic status and the sentencing of the traditional offender." Pp. 251–269 in *Race, Class, Gender, and Justice in the United States,* edited by Charles E. Reasons, Darlene J. Conley, and Julius Debro. Boston, MA: Allyn and Bacon.
Durose, Matthew R., and Patrick A. Langan. (2003). *Felony Sentences in State Courts, 2000.* Washington, DC: U.S. Department of Justice, Bureau of Justice Statistics.
Eitle, David, Lisa Stolzenberg, and Stewart J. D'Alessio. (2005). "Police organizational factors, the racial composition of the police, and the probability of arrest." *Justice Quarterly* 22 (1), 30–57.
Engel, Robin Shepard, Jennifer M. Calnon, and Thomas J. Bernard. (2002). "Theory and racial profiling: Shortcomings and future directions in research." *Justice Quarterly* 19 (2), 249–273.

Farnworth, Margaret, Raymond H.C. Teske, Jr., and Gina Thurman. (1991). "Ethnic, racial, and minority disparity in felony court." Pp. 54–70 in *Race and Criminal Justice,* edited by Michael J. Lynch and E. Britt Patterson. Albany, NY: Harrow and Heston.

Federal Bureau of Investigation (FBI). (2006). *Crime in the United States, 2005: Uniform Crime Reports.* Washington, DC: U.S. Department of Justice.

Fischer, Claude S., Michael Hunt, Martin Sanchez Jankowski, Samuel R. Lucas, Ann Swidler, and Kim Voss. (1996). *Inequality by Design: Cracking the Bell Curve Myth.* Princeton, NJ: Princeton University Press.

Fletcher, Brian. (2005). "Today's argument in *Johnson v. California.*" SCOTUSblog. Retrieved July 24, 2006 from: *http://www.scotusblog.com/movabletype/archives/ 2005/ 04/todays_argument_2.html.*

Fraser, Steven, editor. (1995). *The Bell Curve Wars: Race, Intelligence, and the Future of America.* New York: Basic Books.

Frazier, Charles E. (1989). "Preadjudicatory detention." Pp. 143–168 in *Juvenile Justice: Policies, Programs, and Services,* edited by Albert R. Roberts. Chicago: Dorsey.

Free, Marvin D., Jr., editor. (2003). *Racial Issues in Criminal Justice: The Case of African Americans.* Westport, CT: Praeger.

Gardner, Howard. (1995). "Cracking open the IQ box." Pp. 23–35 in *The Bell Curve Wars: Race, Intelligence, and the Future of America,* edited by Steven Fraser. New York: Basic Books.

Georgia v. McCollum, 505 U.S. 42 (1992).

Glaze, Lauren E., and Thomas P. Bonczar. (2006). *Probation and Parole in the United States, 2005.* Washington, DC: U.S. Department of Justice, Bureau of Justice Statistics.

Gottfredson, Don M. (2002). "Sentencing guidelines." Pp. 1475–1482 in *Encyclopedia of Crime and Punishment,* edited by David Levinson. Thousand Oaks, CA: Sage.

Gould, Steven Jay. (1995). "Curveball." Pp. 11–22 in *The Bell Curve Wars: Race, Intelligence, and the Future of America,* edited by Steven Fraser. New York: Basic Books.

Greene, Helen Taylor. (2003). "Do African American police make a difference?" Pp. 207– 220 in *Racial Issues in Criminal Justice: The Case of African Americans,* edited by Marvin D. Free, Jr. Westport, CT: Praeger.

Harrison, Paige M., and Allen J. Beck. (2005). *Prisoners in 2004.* Washington, DC: Bureau of Justice Statistics, U.S. Department of Justice.

——. (2006). *Prison and Jail Inmates at Midyear 2005.* Washington, DC: U.S. Department of Justice, Bureau of Justice Statistics.

Herrnstein, Richard J., and Charles Murray. (1994). *The Bell Curve.* New York: Free Press.

Johnson v. California 543 U.S. 499 (2005).

Kautt, Paula, and Cassia Spohn. (2002). "Crack-ing down on black drug offenders? Testing for interactions among offenders' race, drug type, and sentencing strategy in federal drug sentences." *Justice Quarterly* 19 (1), 1–35.

Lamberth, John. (1998, August 16). "Driving while black: A statistician proves that prejudice still rules the road." *Washington Post,* p. C1.

Lange, James E., Mark B. Johnson, and Robert B. Voas. (2005). "Testing the racial profiling hypothesis for seemingly disparate traffic stops on the New Jersey Turnpike." *Justice Quarterly* 22 (2), 193–223.

Lundman, Richard J., and Robert L. Kaufman. (2003). "Driving while black: Effects of race, ethnicity, and gender on citizen self-reports of traffic stops and police actions." *Criminology* 41 (1), 195–220.

Lynch, Michael J., and E. Britt Patterson, editors. (1996). *Justice Without Prejudice: Race and Criminal Justice in America.* Albany, NY: Harrow and Heston.

Mann, Coramae Richey. (1987). "Racism in the criminal justice system: Two sides of a controversy." *Criminal Justice Research Bulletin* 3 (5). Huntsville, TX: Sam Houston State University.

Maupin, James R., and Lisa J. Bond-Maupin. (1999). "Detention decision-making in a predominantly Hispanic region: Rural and non-rural differences." *Juvenile and Family Court Journal* 50 (3), 11–23.

Mays, G. Larry (1989). "The impact of federal sentencing guidelines on jail and prison overcrowding and early release." Pp. 181–200 in *The U.S. Sentencing Guidelines: Implications for Criminal Justice*, edited by Dean J. Champion. New York: Praeger.

Mays, G. Larry. (2004). "Sentences and sentencing guidelines." Pp. 1502–1505 in *Encyclopedia of Criminology*, editors Richard A. Wright and J. Mitchell Miller. Hampshire, U.K.: Taylor and Francis.

Mays, G. Larry, and L. Thomas Winfree, Jr. (2005). *Essentials of Corrections*, third edition. Belmont, CA: Wadsworth.

Meyer, Jon'a F. (2002). "Bail and bond." Pp. 93–97 in *Encyclopedia of Crime and Punishment*, edited by David Levinson. Thousand Oaks, CA: Sage.

Miller-El v. Dretke. 541 U.S., 231 (2005).

Minnesota Sentencing Guidelines Commission. (2005). Retrieved July 24, 2006 from: *http://www.msgc.state.mn.us*.

Mistretta v. United States, 488 U.S. 361 (1989).

Nalla, Mahesh K., and Charles Corley. (1996). "Race and criminal justice: Employment of minorities in the criminal justice system." Pp. 139–155 in *Justice Without Prejudice: Race and Criminal Justice in America*, edited by Michael J. Lynch and E. Britt Patterson. Albany, NY: Harrow and Heston.

Neubauer, David W. (2001). "Race and crime: Does the criminal justice system discriminate against racial minorities?" Pp. 135–137 in *Debating Crime: Rhetoric and Reality*, edited by David W. Neubauer. Belmont, CA: Wadsworth.

Patterson, E. Britt, and Michael J. Lynch. (1991). "Bias in formalized bail procedures." Pp. 36–53 in *Race and Criminal Justice*, edited by Michael J. Lynch and E. Britt Patterson. Albany, NY: Harrow and Heston.

Petersilia, Joan. (1997). "Probation in the United States." Pp. 149–200 in *Crime and Justice: A Review of Research*, edited by Michael Tonry. Chicago: University of Chicago Press.

Reasons, Charles E., Darlene J. Conley, and Julius Debro. (2002). *Race, Class, Gender, and Justice in the United States*. Boston, MA: Allyn and Bacon.

Reiman, Jeffrey. (2004). *The Rich Get Richer and the Poor Get Prison*, seventh edition. Boston, MA: Allyn and Bacon.

Reitz, Kevin R. (1999). "The status of sentencing guideline reforms in the U.S." *Overcrowded Times* 10 (6), 9–10.

Roush, David W. (2004). "Juvenile detention: Issues for the 21st century." Pp. 218–246 in *Juvenile Justice Sourcebook*, edited by Albert R. Roberts. New York: Oxford University Press.

Russell, Katheryn, K. (2002). "'Driving while black': Corollary pheonomena and collateral consequences." Pp. 191-200 in *Race, Class, Gender, and Justice in the United States*, edited by Charles E. Reasons, Darlene J. Conley, and Julius Debro. Boston: Allyn & Bacon.

Schwartz, Ira. (1991). "Removing juveniles from adult jails: The unfinished agenda." Pp. 216–226 in *American Jails: Public Policy Issues*, edited by Joel A. Thompson and G. Larry Mays. Chicago: Nelson-Hall.

Seron, Carroll, and Frank Munger. (2002). "Law and equality: Race, gender . . . and, of course, class." Pp. 138–157 in *Race, Class, Gender, and Justice in the United States*, edited by Charles E. Reasons, Darlene J. Conley, and Julius Debro. Boston, MA: Allyn and Bacon.

Smith, Michael R., and Geoffrey P. Alpert. (2002). "Searching for direction: Courts, social science, and the adjudication of racial profiling claims." *Justice Quarterly* 19 (4), 673–703.

Snell, Tracy L. (2006). *Capital Punishment, 2005*. Washington, DC: U.S. Department of Justice, Bureau of Justice Statistics.

Sowell, Thomas. (1995). "Ethnicity and IQ." Pp. 70–79 in *The Bell Curve Wars: Race, Intelligence, and the Future of America*, edited by Steven Fraser. New York: Basic Books.

Steen, Sara. (2002). "Determinate sentences." Pp. 509–512 in *Encyclopedia of Crime and Punishment*, edited by David Levinson. Thousand Oaks, CA: Sage.

Stewart, Eric A., and Ronald L. Simons. (2006). "Structure and culture in African American adolescent violence: A partial test of the 'Code of the Street' thesis." *Justice Quarterly* 23 (1), 1–33.

Tonry, Michael. (2002). "Racial politics, racial disparities, and the war on crime." Pp. 71–84 in *Race, Class, Gender, and Justice in the United States*, edited by Charles E. Reasons, Darlene J. Conley, and Julius Debro. Boston, MA: Allyn and Bacon.

United States v. Armstrong, 517 U.S. 456 (1996).

Walker, Samuel. (2006). *Sense and Nonsense About Crime and Drugs: A Policy Guide*, sixth edition. Belmont, CA: Wadsworth.

Whitus v. Georgia, 385 U.S. 598 (1967).

Wilbanks, William. (1987). *The Myth of a Racist Criminal Justice System*. Monterey, CA: Brooks/Cole.

Recommended Readings

Free, Marvin D., Jr., editor. (2003). *Racial Issues in Criminal Justice: The Case of African Americans*. Westport, CT: Praeger. Free has collected 14 original works concerned with the experience of African Americans and the criminal justice system in the United States. The book is organized around three major themes: (1) the significance of race in American society, (2) criminal justice responses to crime and African Americans, and (3) seeking solutions. Most of the contributors are academics, although a couple of people who have worked as trial consultants in the area of jury selection also participated. Free's goal in editing this text was to "document the significance of race in criminal justice and to provide a vigilant reminder that the criminal justice system is not a value-neutral system that operates without regard to the race or ethnicity of its participants" (p. x).

Lynch, Michael J., and E. Britt Patterson, editors. (1996). *Justice With Prejudice: Race and Criminal Justice in America*. Guilderland, NY: Harrow & Heston. The two editors of this volume bring together a variety of scholars to reflect on a number of issues facing minorities in the criminal justice system. Readings address concerns such as families, media portrayal of minorities, drugs, and the treatment of minority juveniles in the juvenile court transfer process. Additionally, one of the final chapters deals with the employment of minorities in the criminal justice system.

Withrow, Brian L. (2006). *Racial Profiling: From Rhetoric to Reason*. Upper Saddle River, NJ: Prentice Hall. Withrow deals with the relatively narrow, but important, topic of racial profiling. Policing agencies of various types in the United States engage in profiling related to drug trafficking and other, less dramatic crimes. Withrow develops a definition of racial profiling and examines the political and legal dimensions of this police practice. He also examines possible solutions to police operational procedures that may be (or appear to be) discriminatory. ✦

Chapter 8

Gender and Justice

Introduction

In Chapter 7, we began by mentioning the phrase "Equal Justice Under Law," which is inscribed above the entrance of the U.S. Supreme Court building. Ideally, this phrase should mean that everyone coming before the courts in the United States would be treated equally. Race, ethnicity, income, and gender would make no difference. As we learned, race and ethnicity may make a significant difference in the way victims and accused offenders are processed and in the quality of justice that is dispensed. But what role, if any, does gender play in criminal cases? Are men and women treated differently? Do women fare better, worse, or the same as men; and if there are differences in treatment, why do these exist?

Much like the issues of race and ethnicity, the role that gender plays in the administration of justice is both fascinating and complex. Easy answers are not readily available. However, to more fully understand the significance of gender in the administration of justice, we examine three statuses—offenders, victims, and employees. This should help us understand better what we do and do not know about how gender factors into the criminal law's application.

Women As Offenders in the Criminal Justice System

Females 18 years of age and older constituted 51.5 percent of the U.S. population in 2002. In that same year, females represented 17 percent of the individuals convicted of any felony and only 11 percent of those convicted for a violent felony. Additionally, unlike their male counterparts, females are most likely to be arrested, prosecuted for, and convicted of property crimes, especially larceny and fraud (Durose and Langan 2004, 6). When one reviews the literature on offenders in the criminal justice system, it quickly becomes apparent that it is a man's world. Men commit and are arrested, tried, convicted, and incarcerated for the majority of crimes in the United States and most industrialized countries. These gender differences "have held steady, over time, place,

162

and culture" (Fagan 2002, 764–65). In fact, in examining offense patterns in 27 nations, Simon (2002, 1717) found that women's involvement "in criminal activities across nations is much smaller than would be expected by their approximately 50 percent or so representation in the population of nations around the world" and "women still have a long way to go before their criminal activities are commensurate with their numbers in any given country."

Traditionally, there has been something of a rule of thumb in regard to gender distribution and criminal offenders: It is the 10 percent rule. It was assumed that at virtually every processing stage in the criminal justice system, women composed about 10 percent of the population. However, is this estimate accurate? In this section we examine some of the numbers that reflect on women as criminal offenders.

Arrests

One measure of the involvement of women in the criminal process is the number of arrests of female suspects annually.[1] In 2005, there were about 14.1 million people arrested in the United States for all crimes, excluding traffic offenses. About 10.4 million of these arrests resulted in charges being filed, and of that number 7.89 million (76.2 percent) were males and 2.47 million (23.8 percent) were females (Federal Bureau of Investigation [FBI] 2006, Table 42). Therefore, one of the first observations we can make about crime and gender is that females are vastly underrepresented in the population of arrestees. However, to fully understand the picture of female offenders in the United States, we must go beyond the aggregate numbers to look at the specific offenses for which women are arrested. To do this, we use the benchmark of 23.8 percent (the percentage of women arrestees) to see which crimes result in higher numbers of female arrests.

First, in terms of the *Uniform Crime Reports* Part I crime index, females account for 17.9 percent of the arrests for violent or personal crimes and 32 percent of the arrests for property crimes.[2] The only category of Part I offenses for which women are arrested at a higher than average rate is larceny-theft where they account for 329,733 (or 38.3 percent) of all the arrests for this offense.

Second, there are some interesting arrest numbers beyond the Part I index offenses. For example, the crime for which women constitute the highest percentage of arrestees is prostitution and commercialized vice (41,607 arrests or 66.4 percent). This is followed by running away (47,103 arrests, 58 percent), a status offense confined to juveniles, and third is fraud (105,411 arrests, 45.5 percent). The remaining categories (in descending order) where women are arrested at higher than average percentages are embezzlement (50 percent), forgery and counterfeiting (39.7 percent), curfew and loitering law violations (30.4 percent), liquor law violations (26.3 percent), disorderly conduct (25.8 percent), and other assaults (24.6 percent). Taken together, arrests for prostitution, running away, embezzlement, fraud, and larceny-theft account for 21.19 percent of all female arrests, and larceny-theft and fraud comprise the bulk of those arrests (435,144 or just over 17.6 percent of all female arrests). One area where the percentages are not as high as those previously mentioned is drug-abuse violations. Women constituted only 19.1 percent of the persons arrested for drug crimes in 2005, but this accounted for 259,362 persons arrested, or nearly 10.5 percent of all female arrests. This number was second only to larceny-theft for the largest single category of female arrests.

Third, while television and the movies sensationalize women who kill, the reality is that relatively few women are ever charged with murder. The FBI reported that in 2005, only 11 percent of the arrests for homicide and nonnegligent manslaughter nationwide were of women. Most of the women who kill are from the lower socioeconomic classes in society, many have survived a suicide attempt, and often they kill a man who has a criminal record. Clowers (2002, 1734) said that most of the females who commit homicides kill a family member and they do so with something other than a firearm.[3] The largest group of targets for these women is their own children, accounting for 38.9 percent of the homicides. Fox and Zawitz (2006) reported that murders of children decrease with age (the youngest are most vulnerable).

The second at-risk population for women is intimate partners, current or ex-spouses, boyfriends, or girlfriends. These persons were the targets in 36.5 percent of the cases (Clowers 2002). Dugan, Nagin, and Rosenfeld (2003) found that intimate partner homicides dropped between 1976 and 1996, as services for domestic violence victims became more prevalent (such as shelters and other assistance). One unanticipated outcome of their study, however, was that the biggest decrease in victims was the number of males, and Dugan and colleagues (2003, 21) found that the murder rate of married African American males aged 20–44 years decreased 87 percent between 1976 and 1996. While the intention of developing more comprehensive domestic violence services was to reduce the victimization of women, these programs actually decreased the murder rate of men. It is possible that since women have better access to resources, they are now able to escape an intolerable or abusive situation without resorting to violence. In any case, this is one instance of an unforeseen or unanticipated criminal justice outcome.

These arrest numbers highlight a number of features concerning the crimes women commit. First, women are arrested much less frequently than are men. We will explore some of the reasons for this phenomenon shortly. Second, the crimes for which women are arrested overwhelmingly are economic (property, nonviolent) crimes, and they may be related to their economic status. Casey-Acevedo, Bakken, and Welton (2002, 1723) suggested that many women who commit crimes do so to support themselves and their dependent children. Therefore, these women largely commit and are arrested for property crimes as a result of their "economic vulnerability, increased opportunities to commit 'female' crimes, increased formalization of law enforcement, and trends in female drug dependency." Third, four of the crimes for which women frequently are arrested (drug-abuse violations, prostitution and commercialized vice, curfew violations, and running away) may be related to their status as victims of abuse.

During the 1970s, there was much talk about the Women's Liberation Movement and the impact it was having on shaping a "new female offender" (see Adler 1975; Simon 1975). The thought was that as women gained greater freedom, autonomy, and status in society, their offending patterns would change and become more like their male counterparts. However, close examination of the most recent nationwide arrest figures demonstrates that for the most part, women continue to be arrested for the same types of crimes they always have (FBI 2006; Casey-Acevedo, Bakken, and Welton 2002; see also Steffensmeier 1980; Steffensmeier and Cobb 1981).

Again, the observation holds true that, except for a few categories, women are substantially underrepresented in arrest statistics in the United States. However, two notions need to be introduced at this point, concepts that may explain variations in arrest figures by gender. The first concept is **chivalry.** Scholars who support this approach contend that under most circumstances, actors in the criminal justice system are more lenient in their treatment of females who break the law (Pollock 2002; Visher 1983; Winfree and Abadinsky 2003).

There may be a number of reasons that chivalry operates in criminal justice processes. For example, in many instances adult females may be the primary caretakers for dependent children. In fact, a study by the Bureau of Justice Statistics found that roughly 7 of 10 female prison inmates were mothers with 1.3 million dependent children under the age of 18 (Greenfield and Snell 1999). Therefore, if they are arrested and incarcerated for any length of time, their children may have to live with other relatives, be placed in foster homes, or be put up for adoption (Greene 2002). Additionally, police officers, prosecutors, judges, and probation officers may see female offenders as not totally responsible for their actions. They may be perceived as acting under the influence of a male (father, brother, boyfriend, or husband). To the extent this is true, criminal justice system agents may hold the male more culpable than the female.

However, there can be notable exceptions to the idea of chivalry, and this concept must be tempered by the perspective that the criminal justice system's response may change based on whether a female's behaviors comport with society's expected gender roles (Fagan 2002, 766). For example, some observers maintain that when females commit distinctly male-like crimes (for example, murder or robbery), the criminal justice system is likely to respond harshly. Furthermore, women who are lesbians or bisexuals also may receive harsher punishment from the system (see, especially, Belknap 2001). In other words, women who commit "feminine" crimes are the beneficiaries of chivalry, while women who commit "masculine" crimes are not treated so benevolently.

Somewhat related to chivalry is the role that suspicion plays in police-citizen encounters. A recent study of 66,000 traffic stops by the Miami-Dade Police Department found that police officers were "significantly more suspicious of men than of women in traffic-stop encounters, and suspicion was strongly associated with the decision to arrest" (Smith, Makarios, and Alpert 2006, 271). The authors of this study found that officers were more likely to complete field interview cards and request records checks of male drivers, and that they were more likely to search males than females, even though searches of females were as likely to uncover contraband as searches of males. Their conclusion was that "basing suspicion on gender and race is inaccurate and [in]efficient" (Smith, Makarios, and Alpert 2006, 290).

The countervailing force to chivalry in the criminal justice system is **paternalism.** Some scholars argue that girls and women are treated more harshly than men by the justice system to protect them, probably from themselves (see Belknap 2001; Chesney-Lind 1991). Dworkin (2005) said that paternalism "is the interference of a state or an individual with another person, against their will, and justified by a claim that the person interfered with will be better off or protected from harm." In situations of paternalism, groups in positions of power seek to exert their will over the less powerful.

Paternalism often manifests itself in conservative policies designed to protect groups such as juveniles and females. Relative to criminal justice policies and procedures, paternalism means that the system acts in the best interests of those who are presumed incapable of acting in their own best interest. As a result of paternalistic attitudes—sometimes enacted into law—juvenile females who ran away from home or who were suspected of sexual promiscuity were incarcerated "for their own good."

Detention

Unlike the situation with minority males, at midyear 2005 females comprised 94,571 (almost 13 percent) of the nation's 747,529 jail inmates, and this was up from about 50,000 (10 percent) in 1996. Slightly more of them held convicted status compared with nonconvicted status, 7.7 percent versus 4.8 percent (Harrison and Beck 2006, 8; James 2004, 2). Although female jail inmates were less likely than males to be charged with violent offenses, still an increasing number of females were charged with violent crimes, 17 percent in 2002 compared with 13 percent in 1989 (James 2004, 2).[4]

When we compare females detained in local jails with their male counterparts, five facts are significant. First, females are slightly more likely than males to be detained for drug offenses (29 percent versus 24 percent). Second, females are much less likely to have served no previous sentence than males (48.7 percent versus 36.8 percent). Third, in terms of prior alcohol use, in 2002 females were less likely to report regular alcohol use than were males (55.4 percent versus 66.0 percent). Fourth, in terms of drug or alcohol use at the time of their offense, females were slightly less likely than males to have been using drugs or alcohol at the time of their offenses (46.3 percent versus 50.2 percent). Interestingly, the percentage of women using drugs or alcohol at the time of their crimes dropped 12.5 percent from 1996 to 2002 (James 2004, 2). Finally, in 2002 over half (55.3 percent) of the female jail inmates reported ever being physically or sexually abused compared with 18.2 percent of the male inmates. This difference may represent the true difference between the two groups, or it may represent some degree of underreporting on the part of the males.

Therefore, we must ask the question, Even with relatively small percentages, why are these women being held in jail? For the most part, the answer is not that they represent a danger to themselves or to society (although some do); they are there because they cannot make bail to secure their release prior to trial. Many of these women suffer a double or even triple degree of social marginalization: They are female, they are minorities, and they are poor.

Prosecution and Adjudication

As is true of every stage of the criminal process, women are vastly underrepresented in the prosecution and adjudication of suspected offenders. At least four explanations are possible for this underrepresentation in prosecution and adjudication.

First, it is likely for a variety of reasons that females simply commit fewer crimes. They may be socialized by their families and by society generally to behave in certain ways, and delinquency and criminality are viewed as distinctly "unfeminine." Bottcher (2001, 923) offered five factors that contribute culturally to the differences between males and females in regard to delinquency:

(1) Youngsters tend to belong to highly sex-segregated friendship groups, and the nature of these groups support or restrain delinquent behavior.

(2) Males are exposed to more crime-prone daily activities than are females.

(3) Males tend to play the dominant role in practically all adolescent activities.

(4) The timing of the transition into adulthood is different for males and females (with females generally assuming adult roles sooner).

(5) There tends to be less social support for female delinquency than for male delinquency.

As part of their upbringing, females may be taught not to fight or engage in risky behaviors (Bottcher 2001). Even when they are involved in delinquent social groups, such as gangs, they may use gender as a way of tempering their involvement, and this places them at less risk of physical victimization (Miller and Decker 2001; Peterson, Miller, and Esbensen 2001).

Second, as Fagan (2002, 764) reminded us, "gender is likely the strongest predictor of criminal involvement," but we may not know why. However, at least in regard to crimes of violence, it has been suggested that not only does culture play a role but also biology. For instance, the levels of testosterone present in males may contribute to their aggressive behavior. No matter how controversial this may sound, some researchers believe that women may be wired differently biologically, and the biological differences help restrain them from lives of crime.[5]

Third, as we previously have discussed, the justice system may respond in much different ways to women and men who commit crimes. While criminal justice personnel may be less chivalrous today than in the past, we cannot discount the presence of chivalry and the lower levels of suspicion associated with females (Casey-Acevedo, Bakken, and Welton 2002; Smith, Makarios, and Alpert 2006). Finally, as female students are quick to point out in class, women may be more clever than the men, and they do not get caught as quickly or as often.

Criminal Sanctions

In terms of correctional sanctions, in 2005, over 4.1 million Americans were on probation, and women represented 956,200 of the adults on probation. Their percentage of the probation population increased from 21 percent in 1995 to 22 percent in 2000, and to 23 percent in 2005 (Glaze and Bonczar 2006, 6).

In terms of prison inmate populations, Harrison and Beck (2006) reported 1,438,701 persons in prison at midyear 2005. Women comprised 106,174 of these inmates, or about 7 percent nationwide. Of particular note is that the female prison population nationwide continues to increase at a rate faster than that of males. In fact, from midyear 2004 to midyear 2005, the number of women in federal and state prisons increased 3.4 percent compared with an increase of 1.3 percent for males. From 1980 to 2000, there was an eightfold increase in female incarceration rates, and since 1995 the increases for females consistently have outpaced those for males (Greene 2002). Nevertheless, relative to prevalence rates of incarceration, men were 14 times more likely to be sent to prison than were women (Harrison and Beck 2006, 5). Bonczar (2003) noted, for instance, that if incarceration rates are unchanged, a woman born in 2001 has a 1.8 percent chance of going to prison, while males have an 11.3 percent likelihood that they will be imprisoned in their lifetime.

What seems to be driving the increases in women's prison populations? A one-word answer is sufficient: drugs. Casey-Acevedo and colleagues (2002, 1723) maintained, "The increasing use of illicit drugs by women has had a major impact on female arrests. Many female offenders have long histories of drug abuse and are more likely than men to be addicted to drugs." While drug use does not automatically translate into criminality, Greene (2002, 1729) emphasized that conservative policy changes witnessed by "[h]arsher drug laws and mandatory sentences have increased the number of incarcerated women so sharply that some experts have referred to the War on Drugs as a 'war on women.'" This means that much of the increase in the population of female inmates is not the result of increased criminality, but instead it has come about as a result of policy changes, especially drug-control policies (Greene 2002).

To fully understand the world of female offenders, we need to examine the types of women sent to prison and to look at what kind of life awaits them once they arrive. First, we should acknowledge that there is not an equal likelihood of all women going to prison. Building on our discussion of race and ethnicity from Chapter 7, it should be apparent that minority females are overrepresented in U.S. prison populations.[6] In fact, the typical female prison inmate is a racial or ethnic minority, in the age range of 24 to 29, and she has been convicted of a drug or property crime. Many were raised in single-parent homes, and they likely were the victims of sexual abuse and/or they witnessed violence in their homes growing up. These women often are high-school dropouts who use drugs, may have engaged in prostitution, and report (60 percent to 80 percent of the time) having been the victims of some sort of abuse as adults (Greene 2002, 1729). In a word, they are not Martha Stewart. This population presents a number of challenges, and females arrive in prison with a different set of needs than their male counterparts. As we will see shortly, prisons are not always successful at meeting these needs.

Now that we have looked at the profile of the women in prison, it is helpful to turn our attention to the prisons where these women are held. There are a few co-ed (or co-correctional) prisons in the United States, but for the most part female inmates are housed in exclusively female prisons.

The first prison for women was opened in Indiana in 1873 (Casey-Acevedo, Bakken, and Welton 2002). Today, 40 states and the federal government operate a total of 98 female-only correctional facilities. Twenty-one states have a single facility for female inmates, and 19 states (plus the U.S. Bureau of Prisons) operate two or more facilities.

Texas has the most with 11, followed by New York and North Carolina with 6 each, and California with 4 (Mays and Winfree 2005, 334). The other 10 states have only co-correctional facilities or a combination of single-gender plus co-correctional prisons. Roughly one-third of each state's women's prisons are minimum, medium, and maximum security, compared with men's prisons, of which 31 percent are minimum security, 42 percent are medium security, and 27 percent are maximum security (Stephan and Karberg 2003).

Like many of the prisons where men serve their sentences, women's prisons frequently are crowded and typically suffer from tight budgets. Female inmates are much more likely than their male counterparts to live in congregate housing units (dormitories), but both groups of inmates have a variety of treatment needs that prisons may not be able to address. The bright side of the picture for female inmates is that women serve shorter sentences on average than men, and the level of violence is much less in women's prisons than in those for men (Mays and Winfree 2005).

One problem faced by male and female prison inmates is sexual abuse. In men's prisons, when this occurs it most often takes the form of inmate-on-inmate assault. By contrast, in women's prisons, sexual abuse may come at the hands of other inmates or the correctional staff, many of whom are male. McGuire (2005) outlined cases of correctional officers actually "selling" female inmates to male prisoners in facilities where the populations are mixed, such as jails and some prisons. At times, sexual relationships may appear consensual; however, any time one person is in a higher position of power and authority than another, the issue of consent becomes problematic. Therefore, providing a safe environment for female inmates presents an additional challenge for correctional authorities.

Women also are present in the nation's parole population, but again in fairly small percentages. On December 31, 2005, about 784,000 people were on parole in the United States. As Glaze and Bonczar (2006, 8) reported "At yearend 2005 women made up about 1 in 8 adults on parole (93,000)...A greater percentage of women were on parole at the end of 2005 (12 percent) compared to 1995 (10 percent)." In some ways, this is a function of more women being sentenced to prison and thus securing early release on parole.

Finally, a relatively small number of women have received capital sentences in recent years. At yearend 2005, there were 3,254 inmates on death row in the United States. Of this number, 52 (approximately 1.6 percent) were female—33 whites, 16 African Americans, and 3 Hispanics or other races. As Snell (2006, 7) noted, at yearend 2005, "[w]omen were under sentence of death in 18 states and the federal system. More than 6 in 10 women on death row at yearend were being held in four States: California, Texas, Pennsylvania, and North Carolina." Between 1977, when the Supreme Court authorized executions under newly written capital statutes, and yearend 2005, there were 1004 executions in the United States, and this included nine white women and two African American woman, or just over 1 percent of all executions (Snell 2006, 9).

A brief summary seems in order to provide some perspective on the criminal sanctions given to female offenders in the United States. For instance, compared with the fact that they represent 51.5 percent of the adult population, women comprise approximately 13 percent of the nation's jail inmate population, 23 percent of the adult probation population, 7 percent of the prison inmates, 12 percent of those on parole, and about 1.6 percent of the inmates on death row. This means that women are vastly underrepresented in all of these sanctions, are most likely to receive probation (this is true of males and juveniles as well), and are least likely to receive a capital sentence. Nevertheless, although women are underrepresented in the arrest, detention, prosecution/adjudication, and criminal sanctions numbers, this does not necessarily mean that they are treated fairly or equitably by the justice system, relative to their population size or proportionately in comparison with men. The next section explores some of the challenges facing female offenders who are processed by the criminal justice system.

Treatment and Rehabilitation Resources

While women remain a small percentage of those individuals under some form of correctional sanctioning in the United States, two questions remain: Do they receive a proportionate amount of the dollars and programs allocated to correcting criminal offenders; in other words, do they receive their fair share? Furthermore, do they receive the rehabilitative or treatment resources they need to address the problems that confront them?

As noted previously, women comprise about 13 percent of the nation's jail population and 7 percent of the prison population. Taking the total population of incarcerated persons into account, women constitute 9.8 percent of the nation's jail and prison populations and, as we will see in the next section, women often come into the criminal justice system with unique physical and psychological needs. Therefore, to what extent do the nation's prisons and jails address these needs? We will briefly explore the issues of (a) medical and psychological services, (b) drug and alcohol treatment, (c) job training, and (d) family-related issues.

Women obviously have unique medical needs relative to their male counterparts. Past research has indicated that jails and prisons do an inadequate job of meeting these physical needs, particularly in the areas of obstetrics and gynecology (see Greenfield and Snell 1999). Greene (2002, 1730) wrote, "Reports of medical neglect are common. . . . In fact, several deaths have been attributed to inadequate medical attention." As a result, several states have been the targets of lawsuits by female inmates dealing with the issue of medical care. In fact, Schlanger's

(2003) survey of large jails and prison systems found that the number one source of correctional litigation was medical issues.

Additionally, a number of female inmates enter the correctional system with sexually transmitted diseases, including HIV/AIDS, typically contracted through heterosexual contacts, intravenous (IV) drug use, or both. In this area, the difference between male and female inmates may be more a difference of degree (that is, a higher percentage of females with these problems) than a difference of kind. In fact, Maruschak (2006, 1) reported that 2.6 percent of female state prisoners are HIV positive, compared with 1.8 percent of male prisoners.

One problem is unique to female inmates, however. Every year we have females coming into local, state, and federal correctional facilities who are pregnant, and pregnancies behind bars present special problems. Estimates are that 10 percent of the female jail and prison inmates admitted each year are pregnant and that correctional facilities must deal with about 14,000 births each year. In many instances, newborns as young as two days old are taken from their mothers and given to other family members. If a family placement is not possible, these children are sent to foster homes or placed for adoption. Some prisons, by contrast, offer comprehensive programs for infants and their mothers, and the babies can stay with their mother for several years (Fearn and Parker 2004).

Some correctional facilities have a general medical staff (doctors, nurses, nurse practitioners, and physicians' assistants) on duty on a regular basis. Others have them on call. Most facilities do not have medical specialists such as obstetricians or gynecologists on staff, thus their visits are on an as-needed basis and are much more sporadic. There are two key challenges in correctional health care for women. First, medical treatment for women is often based on models developed for male prisoners, and women require more care. Second, lack of proper preventative care contributes to long-term illness or the unnecessary transmission of disease to correctional and community populations.

The same also may be true of psychological or psychiatric services for women, a significant number of whom have suffered physical, mental, and sexual abuse prior to incarceration. In fact, in jail populations, 23 percent of the female inmates have an identifiable mental illness compared with 16 percent of the male inmates; and for prison populations, the numbers are 24 percent female and 16 percent male. Additionally, in the late 1990s, over two-thirds of female prison inmates reported receiving mental health services while incarcerated (Ditton 1999).

As we have mentioned, the War on Drugs in the United States has had a major impact on the general rates of incarceration. Additionally, as Mays and Winfree (2005, 335) noted, "the nation's antidrug policy has had a gender-specific impact, as proportionately more women offenders find their way into state and federal prisons for drug-related crimes than is the case for men." A number of these incarcerated females also have conspicuous drug- and alcohol-use histories (see, for example,

Greenfield and Snell 1999; James 2004; James and Glaze 2006; Mays and Winfree 2005). Many times females report a greater prevalence of substance abuse than their male counterparts (Mumola 1999). Therefore, incarcerated women will have medical, psychological, and rehabilitative treatment requirements at least as great as males and perhaps even greater. Some of this substance abuse may result from being involved in a deviant lifestyle along with males who also are heavily involved in drug and alcohol use. Some of it may be attributable to past problems with physical and sexual abuse and may be a form of self-medication to deal with trauma (Casey-Acevedo, Bakken, and Welton 2002). Whatever the causes, jails and prisons need to provide adequate treatment for both the men and women who are incarcerated.

What is our record on providing correctional treatment to state and federal inmates in the United States? The results show that women do receive drug and alcohol treatment, but as with most areas in corrections, the treatment programs are too few and greatly underfunded. In most states, this seems to be a policy choice whereby legislators and correctional administrators put the funding where the bulk the inmates are, namely in men's prisons.

Job training, particularly in prisons, is essential given the fact that many women will leave prison to resume their roles as primary caregivers and breadwinners for their dependent children. In the past, job training programs for women have been severely lacking, and where they did exist often they were stereotypical (Gray, Mays, and Stohr 1995; Pollock 2002). In other words, either because of tradition or because of the perception of appropriateness, women were taught domestic skills, such as cooking and sewing, and not the kinds of job skills that would allow them to be financially self-supporting for themselves and their children.

Family-related issues seem to be particularly critical for incarcerated females. We often ask in class, What happens to the children when Dad goes to prison? The answer typically is that Mom keeps the children. The follow-up question is, What happens to the children when Mom goes to prison? The answer is slightly more complicated. In some instances grandparents or other relatives take over childcare. Often the state steps in and places the children in foster care or some other type of temporary living arrangement. Only in rare instances does the father assume full custody and responsibility for minor children (see Johnston 1995; Mumola 2000).

Briefly, a number of family-related issues surface in any discussion of females who are incarcerated (Greene 2002). Among these issues are phone calls and letters to and from children, visits by the children, and generally maintaining relationships with their children while they are incarcerated. Phone calls seem to be especially problematic in some facilities. Many jails and prisons around the United States have installed collect-call only phone systems, and while these systems generate significant income to support some programming efforts, they also place a substantial financial burden on inmates' families. Over time, the calls may become less frequent as the costs escalate, and inmates may depend on letters and cards rather than phone contacts. Visits also may prove difficult when many states operate only one women's prison facility, and it may be located many miles from a particular inmate's home. Inmates also may express some degree of frustration with the visiting arrangements offered by the prisons and the lack of intimacy and privacy available with their children. In the end, incarceration makes the difficult job of parenting even more difficult for incarcerated mothers.[7]

One final note needs to be added concerning the stigma of women who have been in prison. We have mentioned that increasing numbers of women are going to prison in the United States for drug-related crimes. A conviction for such offenses has a lingering effect that goes beyond the mere stigma associated with having served time in prison. In 1996, the U.S. Congress passed legislation that makes people who have been convicted of felony drug crimes ineligible for "federal benefits, including food stamps, student loans, federal grants and fellowships, federal insured housing loans, commercial vehicle licenses, and small business loans" (Greene 2002, 1732). Thus, the obstacles that women leaving prison traditionally have faced got even greater. We address these barriers to community reentry more comprehensively in Chapter 10.

Women As Crime Victims

In addition to women being processed as offenders in the criminal justice system, it is also essential that we consider the role of women as victims processed by the system. Although most of the women victimized by crime do not become criminal offenders, some do. In this section, we briefly explore the victimization of women and the responses to that victimization by agents of the criminal justice system.

First, it is important to acknowledge that just as is the case with offenders, men are more frequently victims of crime than are women. Second, the types of victimizations that are encountered by women may be different in both type and magnitude from men's. We focus on physical, sexual, and emotional victimization and address the fact that for some women, victimization begins early in childhood and continues well into their adult lives. The technical terms **child endangerment** and **child maltreatment** often are used in regard to the phenomenon we commonly call child abuse. Child endangerment exists when parents or guardians place a child in jeopardy physically, emotionally, or sexually (Mays and Winfree 2006, 393). The Office of Juvenile Justice and Delinquency Prevention announced that "child maltreatment occur[s] when a caretaker (a parent or parent substitute, such as a day-care worker) is responsible for or permits the abuse or neglect of a child" (Snyder and Sickmund 1999, 40). At the least serious level, we have various forms of neglect, including physical neglect, emotional neglect, and educational neglect. At the more serious level, there is physical abuse, sexual abuse, and emotional abuse, for example. Box 8.1 provides brief definitions of each of these types of neglect and abuse. While not all cases are reported—and of the cases that are reported not all are investigated—we know that in 1996, there were about 3 million cases of child maltreatment reported in the United States (see Mays and Winfree 2006, 273–285). These numbers give us something of a measure of the scope of abuse and neglect of youngsters, and some of this abuse carries over into adulthood.

Box 8.1
Types of Neglect and Abuse

In the area of child maltreatment, one of the issues that plagues child welfare advocates, first responders, and medical personnel is the lack of consistent definitions of the various types of abuse and neglect (or even how many types of abuse and neglect there might be). Nevertheless, the following list provides the common elements contained in many of the definitions of the various types of child maltreatment:

- **Physical neglect**—this condition exists when a child is abandoned or thrown out of the home; physical neglect also occurs when the parents or guardians fail to provide the necessary food, clothing, shelter, or medical care needed by a child.

- **Emotional neglect**—this area often causes problems for those trying to provide a workable definition; in most instances, authorities say that emotional neglect happens when the parents or guardians fail to provide adequate levels of support, nurturance, or affection.

- **Educational neglect**—this often is detected through the habitual truancy of a child; the causes can be many, but in some circumstances a single parent may keep an older sibling out of school to care for younger siblings during work periods (dysfunctional families may be more likely to have frequent moves, which might also contribute to truancy).

- **Physical abuse**—Childhelp USA (2004) said that physical abuse of children results from them being hit, kicked, slapped, shaken, burned, pinched, bitten, choked, thrown, shoved, whipped, paddled, and having their hair pulled; often these situations arise out of what the caregiver perceives to be a situation requiring discipline, but the response is disproportionate to the behavior.

- **Sexual abuse**—sexual abuse of children comes about as a result of adults (or perhaps adolescents) utilizing children for the purpose of sexual gratification; females are three times more likely to be victims of sexual abuse than are males.

- **Emotional abuse**—like emotional neglect, circumstances involving emotional abuse may be very difficult to detect; no physical marks are left, but the victims suffer from extreme forms of verbal and emotional assault; the results of emotional abuse may not appear until years after the abuse has taken place.

- **Prenatal substance abuse**—many states are now recognizing the abuse of drugs and alcohol by pregnant women as prenatal substance abuse, and it may be defined as a crime; this type of abuse particularly has been highlighted nationally as a result of the birth of "crack babies" and through the occurrence of fetal alcohol syndrome (FAS). ✦

Sources: Adapted from: Snyder and Sickmund (1999), ten Bensel (1984).

Beyond the various forms of neglect and abuse that they suffer as children, females also are the victims of both traditional criminal victimization and **domestic violence** or **intimate partner abuse** as adults. In terms of general criminal victimization, about five million women per year are victims of some type of crime. This rate is substantially lower than that of men. The differences in victimization rates can be explained in several ways. First, women often take precautions that prevent victimization. Second, they act much more cautiously than men. Either by nature or by socialization, women tend to be more risk aversive than men. However, when they do take risks, they may significantly increase their likelihood of victimization. For example, a study of college students and date (or acquaintance) rape found that male offenders often viewed women who drank or consumed drugs as "suitable targets" (Schwartz et al. 2001, 647).

Third, since they do not engage in as much criminal activity as men, women limit their exposure (reduce their vulnerability) to many types of crimes. Furthermore, even in some risky lifestyles (such as gang activity), females tend to be the beneficiaries of less violent treatment (Peterson, Miller, and Esbensen 2001). Last, rates of victimization may differ because they are not reported to the police, and many acts of domestic violence, stalking, and rape—where the victims are overwhelmingly women—are often unreported. We examine some of the reasons for these differences in the following pages.

In addition to traditional or conventional criminal victimization, women uniquely are at risk for rape/sexual assault and intimate partner abuse. Dobbs (2002) speculated that the general fear of crime that women have really is a fear of sexual assault. As we have previously mentioned, some of these assaults occur before women turn 18 years of age (even at preschool ages), but a number also occur after age 18. In most instances, the offender is someone known to the female, since only 16 percent of rapes of women 18 and older are committed by strangers and 14 percent of those committed on females younger than 18 years are committed by strangers (Dobbs 2002, 1727).

There do not seem to be reliable figures on the number of rapes that are committed each year. Rape is among the least reported of the *UCR* Part I Index crimes, and there are a variety of explanations for the low reporting rates. A key factor is the level of embarrassment felt by the victim and the potential for unwanted publicity. Another issue is the relationship between the victim and the offender (see Johnson 2002; Schwartz et al. 2001) and potential for ongoing relationships or contacts. There also can be concerns over being believed, as well as the fear of retaliation by the offender if the rape is reported. Finally, many women are reluctant to go through the criminal justice process because of what faces them at a trial.

Often the question is raised about who actually is on trial in a rape case. For example, a recent article examined the idea of **intrafemale gender hostility** in rape cases. *Intrafemale gender hostility* is defined as "the propensity (or at least the hypothesis that the propensity exists) of female jurors to attribute more blame to the female victim than do male jurors" (Batchelder, Koski, and Byxbe 2004, 182). This study was conducted using mock juries who reviewed case scenarios and then engaged in simulated jury deliberations. The authors of this study concluded that female jurors especially focused on the victim's lifestyle and character and that they were more likely to return a not guilty verdict for a male perpetrator than were male jurors. While this type of hostility may not manifest itself in actual trials, it once again demonstrates the types of obstacles women face in obtaining justice when they are victims of crime.

Although we do not know how many people suffer from intimate partner abuse (or domestic violence), we do know this is a crime that in all likelihood is substantially underreported and that it is a crime with a high percentage of female victims. Sometimes the intimate partner abuse suffered by women is physical and sometimes it is sexual. However, no matter what form the abuse takes, the result is "harm to the victim, and [it is] a demonstration of control over the victim by the offender" (Dobbs 2002, 1727). The most extreme forms of intimate partner abuse result in death, and one third of female homicide victims are killed by intimates versus 4 percent of male homicide victims (Dobbs 2002).

Another crime where women are victimized at higher rates than males is stalking. According to Rugala, McNamara, and Wattendorf (2004, 9), this offense is characterized by a "pattern of harassing behaviors intended to frighten, intimidate, terrorize, or injure another person." While justice systems have been slow to gather statistics about the true rate of this offense (one estimate is that 1 in 12 of all women are stalked at some point in their life), we know that stalking reduces the quality of life for many women, it has serious long-term consequences for a number of victims, and ends in the murder of some women.

When examining male and female crime victims, three conclusions can be drawn. First, there are differential victimization patterns. For most crimes, women are significantly less likely to be victimized than men. However, for the crimes of rape and sexual assault, they are 20 times more likely to be victimized (Dobbs 2002, 1726). Second, women are much more likely than men to be victimized by someone they know. This especially is apparent in the area of intimate partner violence. In some instances, women who have been abused over a long period of time finally retaliate and kill their victimizer. Occasionally, some of the women charged with homicide have tried to employ a defense of "**battered woman syndrome.**" Lifschitz (2004, 153) observed how "every state court permits some form of expert testimony on battered woman syndrome when introduced by the defense on behalf of a woman charged with killing or injuring her abuser." Yet, there have been few long-term studies to show whether this is an effective defense and under what conditions this defense is most likely to be successful. Third, no matter what the likelihood of victimization actually is, women are much more fearful of crime than are men.

Another way to measure the scope of the victimization of women is to look at those offenders processed by the criminal justice system to gauge the level of victimization they have experienced. For example, Harlow (1999, 1) reported, "For women, abuse as children [is] more likely in correctional [populations] than [the] general population." In fact, she found that between 23 percent and 37 percent of female offenders (both inmates and probationers) said they had been physically or sexually abused before they turned age 18. This compares with general population estimates of 12–17 percent. One-third of these women said that they had been victims of rape at some time in their lives (Harlow 1999, 1). Greenfield and Snell (1999) reported even more startling numbers: They found that almost 6 of 10 state prison inmates said that they had been physically or sexually abused in the past (see also James and Glaze 2006).

So what do these numbers mean to us, and how do they impact the criminal justice system? Probably two concerns stand out. First, although most females who suffer some type of abuse do not commit crimes or enter the criminal justice system, some do. Second, female offenders in the system are significantly more likely to be regular drug users than are offenders who were not abused—89 percent to 65 percent (Harlow 1999, 1). Both of these considerations must be accounted for when we look at the female offender population in the United States and ways in which female (and male) criminality might be prevented.

It is important to note a final sense of victimization often encountered by women in the criminal process. Women who are victims of physical and sexual assaults, such as rape and domestic violence, often express an additional sense of victimization by the criminal justice system. Although states now have laws that prevent attorneys from questioning a woman's past sexual history, rape cases often hinge on the degree to which the victim may have "provoked" the crime. In terms of domestic violence, roughly 1 in 10 violent victimizations in the United States occur in the context of the family (Durose et al. 2005, 1), and women who have suffered from domestic violence for some period of time may be scrutinized closely by actors in the criminal justice system for not leaving an abusive situation sooner. They may be treated in an uncaring way by police officers and court workers, and there may be instances in which prosecutors refuse to take their cases. In all of these cases, female victims may feel that they are on trial and thus suffer a **double sense of victimization,** once by the offender and again by the criminal justice system. Box 8.2 illustrates this point.

Box 8.2
The Kobe Bryant Case: Accuser or the Accused?

One of the recent cases that exemplifies the situation female victims may find themselves in is that of professional basketball star Kobe Bryant. Bryant was charged with sexual assault of an 18-year-old woman who worked in a Colorado resort hotel in which he stayed. This case, which became very public, very quickly was played out in television, newspaper, and magazine reports almost daily until the situation was resolved.

Several factors complicated this case. First, Bryant admitted that he and the young woman engaged in sex, but that it was consensual. Second, prior to any adjudication, the legal system presumed Bryant innocent, though accused, of the charges (see the discussion of legal and factual guilt in Chapter 2). Third, although states now have what are known as "rape shield" laws that protect the identity of the victim, Bryant's accuser became publicly known as a result of statements made by his attorneys outside of court. Finally, the focus of the case eventually seemed to be the moral character of Kobe Bryant's accuser, who was said to have voluntarily accompanied him to his room and who was alleged to have had sex with several other men just days before her encounter with Bryant. Bryant's defense team engaged in what some legal and media observers called "victim trashing," and one reporter said that the case raised "some serious issues about the way the justice system treats rape complaints and defendants" (Young 2004, 22–23). Eventually, the case came to an end when the accuser refused to testify in court against Bryant. ✦

Source: Markels (2003); Saporito (2004); Young (2004).

The Work World of Women in Criminal Justice

A critical point of consideration is the role that women are playing as agents of criminal justice in the United States. For much of our nation's history, virtually all of the jobs in the criminal justice field were occupied by men. Now women can be found working in every segment and every type of agency in criminal justice. To what extent is their presence felt? What difference has it made? We attempt to answer these questions.

One of the most difficult areas to discuss sufficiently in relation to gender and justice is the level of female employment in the criminal justice system. In a very real sense, the data often simply are not available. However, we do know that women occupy a relatively small, but growing, percentage of the people employed by justice agencies in this nation, but there is some variance among jurisdictions. For instance, in 1987 women constituted 7.6 percent of the sworn officers in police departments in the United States. By 2003, this number had increased to 11.3 percent (Hickman and Reaves 2006, 7). In sheriff's offices, however, women represented 12.9 percent of all sworn deputies in 2003, yet this percentage was almost unchanged from 1987, when 12.6 percent of deputies were women (Reaves and Hickman 2006, 7). In both local police departments and sheriff's offices, the percentage of women officers goes up with the size of the jurisdiction, and smaller jurisdictions typically have a smaller percentage of sworn female officers or deputies.

In state law enforcement agencies, women generally are found in smaller numbers than in city or county policing, and in 2000, females represented anywhere from 1 percent (South Dakota) to 14 percent (Wisconsin) of the sworn state police officers (Reaves and Hickman 2004, 243). In 2002, 14.8 percent of the sworn law enforcement personnel working for federal agencies were women, but they tended to cluster in certain agencies. For example, 24.6 percent of the personnel in offices of inspector general were female, and they represented 28.0 percent of the sworn employees in the Internal Revenue Service.[8] By contrast, only 8.6 percent of the Drug Enforcement Administration's sworn officers were female, and the Veterans Health Administration, Federal Protective Service, Bureau of Diplomatic Security, and the U.S. Secret Service all reported fewer than 10 percent of their sworn personnel as being female (Reaves and Bauer 2003, 6–7).

In the field of corrections, the numbers on female employment are somewhat more illusive. We do know that of the nation's roughly 210,000 local jail employees, about one-third are female and 28 percent work in direct line positions (those that have direct, immediate contact with the inmate population) as detention officers (Mays and Winfree 2005, 347). When it comes to employment in prisons, women are more commonly found in exclusively women's prisons (almost half of all employees). However, females are employed in all sectors of institutional corrections, and the number of women employed in 2000 was 141,727, an increase of 41 percent from 1995. In 2000, females represented about one-third of all staff members in federal, state, and private corrections, and 64,095 (about one-fourth) of the custody staff members were women. This was a five-year increase of 53 percent (Stephan and Karberg 2003, vi).

Women also work in probation and parole and other community corrections agencies. While the employment numbers are not available in this area, we can assume that higher percentages of women work in the noninstitutional domain of corrections than in institutional facilities. Nevertheless, we are left with a lingering question: Why do women represent fairly small percentages of employees in most criminal justice agencies? Several answers have been suggested.

First, traditionally there have been hiring impediments—physical requirements such as height, weight, and tests of strength—in law enforcement agencies, which have created barriers to employment for many women. Second, related to the first impediment is the view held by male agency administrators that women may not be able to perform the work adequately (this especially seems to have been an issue in state police agencies). Donna Hale (2002, 1720) stated that especially in law enforcement, the numbers of females have remained low because of the "unwelcome reception women have received from the predominantly male members of the departments who believe women do not belong on patrol." Third, in many male-dominated work environments, both gender discrimination and sexual harassment (sometimes subtle and sometimes not so subtle) have been conspicuous problems (Belknap 2001; Hale 2002). Finally, while the pay and fringe benefits such as insurance and retirement are attractive, the nature of criminal justice employment may be undesirable to prospective female employees. For example, shift work and holiday work assignments are common in both law enforcement and corrections. These situations often combine with family obligations and childcare responsibilities to make many criminal justice positions unattractive to females. Therefore, what are the answers to the question we posed concerning female employment in criminal justice? As usual, some of all of these elements generally are at work.

Conclusions

Women occupy a number of roles relative to criminal justice processes in the United States. They are offenders, victims, and agents of criminal justice, and none of these roles can be ignored by the serious student of criminal justice.

In terms of their offending patterns, while there have been some changes over the years, women typically are charged with and convicted of property crimes, such as larceny, fraud, and embezzlement. The biggest change in the past decade has been the significant number of females appearing in jail and prison populations who have been charged with or convicted of drug-related offenses.

Perhaps the victimization of females—especially in rapes and domestic violence—is the area that attracts the most public attention. Clearly, women are victimized by property crimes just like men, but when they are victims of personal crimes, there seems to be an added component of vulnerability and victimization involved in their cases. Added to this, however, is a lack of sensitivity by agents of the justice system in responding to female crime victims. Women frequently express a sense of double victimization as a result of the way they are treated by justice system personnel (Florida Supreme Court 1990).

Finally, we see police, court, and correctional agencies as places of increasing employment opportunities for females. In fact, many of the workforce development surveys done in the past decade have indicated that if justice agencies expect to fill all of their positions in the future, they will increasingly have to look to women (and minorities) to locate enough candidates to staff all of their openings. If women find these jobs attractive, they may find increased earnings potential as well as the opportunity for career development and advancement.

Notes

1. This section largely is based on numbers from the most recent complete edition of the *Uniform Crime Reports* (FBI 2006).
2. The violent crimes are murder, forcible rape, robbery, and aggravated assault. The property crimes are burglary, larceny-theft, motor vehicle theft, and arson (FBI 2006).
3. Many women kill with chemicals, especially poisons.
4. The Bureau of Justice Statistics reports cited do not break down population figures by race and gender. Therefore, it is difficult to know what percentage of the female population is white, African American, or other.
5. For an extended discussion of this topic, see Rowe (2001).
6. It is very difficult and not methodologically correct to talk about the "average" prison inmate. This discussion draws from the demographic information available to outline the most prevalent categories in order to arrive at a "profile" for female inmates (see Greene 2002).
7. On issues such as this one that is facing women generally, see Belknap (2001) and Pollock (2002).
8. The offices of inspector general exist in a variety of agencies, and they "investigate criminal violations and prevent and detect fraud, waste, and abuse related to Federal programs, operations, and employees" (Reaves and Bauer 2003, 6).

Key Terms

battered woman syn-
  drome
child endangerment
child maltreatment
chivalry
domestic violence
double sense of victim-
  ization

educational neglect
emotional abuse
emotional neglect
intimate partner abuse
intrafemale gender hos-
  tility
paternalism
physical abuse

physical neglect
prenatal substance
  abuse
sexual abuse

Critical Review Questions

1. As a small-group project, discuss this general proposition: When it comes to violating the law, there should be no difference in the way men and women are treated.
2. Can you think of any criminological theories that could help explain why women do (or do not) commit crimes? Would these theories apply generally or just to certain crimes?
3. Why would the police be more likely or less likely to arrest female suspects? Would the age of the suspect make a difference?

4. Is there any evidence that a "new" female offender (more male-like in offense patterns) has emerged in the past 20 years? Have you seen stories in the newspaper or on television that seem to support this notion?

5. Could sexual orientation make a difference in how offenders are treated? In other words, are less feminine women treated more like male suspects? Explain your answer.

6. Are the small numbers of women in jails and prisons good news or bad news? To what extent are their programming needs being met? Explain.

7. The movement toward determinate sentences (especially with sentencing guidelines) seems to have narrowed the gap between male and female sentences. In handing down sentences, which value—*individualism* (tailoring the sentence to the person) or *equity* (gearing the sentence to the offense)—seems more important to you?

8. To what extent should "domestic violence" be allowed as a defense in murder cases? Should it be treated like self-defense, would it simply be a mitigating factor in decreasing the level of punishment, or should it be considered at all?

9. Some people take the view that "prisons are prisons are prisons." This would imply that what is good for men in prison is also good for women. Do you subscribe to this view or not?

10. Should we have separate prisons for men and women? Why or why not? How about jails?

11. Is crime victimization linked to female criminality? What evidence can you find one way or the other?

12. As an interesting exercise, divide into groups of male and female students and answer the following question, What factors make criminal justice employment attractive to females? Compare the answers developed by the males with those arrived at by the females.

References

Adler, Freda. (1975). *Sisters in Crime: The Rise of the New Female Criminal.* New York: McGraw-Hill.

Batchelder, John Stuart, Douglas D. Koski, and Ferris R. Byxbe. (2004). "Women's hostility toward women in rape trials: Testing the intra-female gender hostility thesis." *American Journal of Criminal Justice* 28 (2), 181–200.

Belknap, Joanne. (2001). *The Invisible Woman: Gender, Crime, and Justice,* second edition. Belmont, CA: Wadsworth.

Bonczar, Thomas P. (2003). *Prevalence of Imprisonment in the U.S. Population, 1974–2001.* Washington, DC: Bureau of Justice Statistics, U.S. Department of Justice.

Bottcher, Jean (2001). "Social practices of gender: How gender relates to delinquency in the everyday lives of high-risk youths." *Criminology* 39 (4), 893–932.

Casey-Acevedo, Karen, Timothy Bakken, and Mark Welton. (2002). "Women as offenders." Pp. 1722–1725 in *Encyclopedia of Crime and Punishment*, edited by David Levinson. Thousand Oaks, CA: Sage.

Chesney-Lind, Meda. (1991). "Patriarchy, prisons, and jails: A critical look at trends in women's incarceration." *Prison Journal* 71, 51–67.

Childhelp USA (2004). "Child abuse definitions." Retrieved on June 27, 2006 from: *http:// www.childhelp.org/resources/learning-center*.

Clowers, Marsha. (2002). "Women who kill." Pp. 1733–1735 in *Encyclopedia of Crime and Punishment*, edited by David Levinson. Thousand Oaks, CA: Sage.

Ditton, Paula M. (1999). *Mental Health and Treatment of Inmates and Probationers*. Washington, DC: U.S. Department of Justice, Bureau of Justice Statistics.

Dobbs, Rhonda R. (2002). "Women as victims." Pp. 1725–1729 in *Encyclopedia of Crime and Punishment*, edited by David Levinson. Thousand Oaks, CA: Sage.

Dugan, Laura, Daniel S. Nagin, and Richard Rosenfeld. (2003). "Do domestic violence services save lives?" *National Institute of Justice Journal* 250, 20–25.

Durose, Matthew R., Caroline Wolf Harlow, Patrick A. Langan, Mark Motivans, Ramona R. Rantala, and Erica L. Smith. (2005). *Family Violence Statistics*. Washington, DC: U.S. Department of Justice, Bureau of Justice Statistics.

Durose, Matthew R., and Patrick A. Langan. (2004). *Felony Sentences in State Courts, 2002*. Washington, DC: U.S. Department of Justice, Bureau of Justice Statistics.

Dworkin, Gerald. (2005). "Paternalism." *The Stanford Encyclopedia of Philosophy*, Retrieved July 24, 2006 from: *http://plato.stanford.edu*.

Fagan, Abigail A. (2002). "Gender." Pp. 764–768 in *Encyclopedia of Crime and Punishment*, edited by David Levinson. Thousand Oaks, CA: Sage.

Fearn, Noelle E., and Kelly Parker. (2004). "Washington state's residential parenting program: An integrated public health, education, and social service resource for pregnant inmates and prison mothers." *Californian Journal of Health Promotion* 2 (4), 34–48.

Federal Bureau of Investigation (FBI). (2006). *Crime in the United States: Uniform Crime Reports 2005*. Washington, DC: U.S. Department of Justice.

Florida Supreme Court. (1990). *Report of the Florida Supreme Court Gender Bias Study Commission*. Tallahassee, FL: Author.

Fox, James A., and Marianne W. Zawitz. (2006). *Homicide Trends in the United States*. Retrieved June 23, 2006 from: *http://www.ojp.usdoj.gov/bjs/homicide/homtrnd.htm*.

Glaze, Lauren E., and Thomas P. Bonczar. (2006). *Probation and Parole in the United States, 2005*. Washington, DC: U.S. Department of Justice, Bureau of Justice Statistics.

Gray, Tara, G. Larry Mays, and Mary K. Stohr. (1995). "Inmates needs and programming in exclusively women's jails." *Prison Journal* 75 (2), 186–202.

Greene, Susan. (2002). "Women in prison." Pp. 1729–1733 in *Encyclopedia of Crime and Punishment*, edited by David Levinson. Thousand Oaks, CA: Sage.

Greenfield, Lawrence A., and Tracy L. Snell. (1999). *Women Offenders*. Washington, DC: U.S. Department of Justice, Bureau of Justice Statistics.

Hale, Donna C. (2002). "Women and policing." Pp. 1718–1722 in *Encyclopedia of Crime and Punishment*, edited by David Levinson. Thousand Oaks, CA: Sage.

Harlow, Caroline Wolf. (1999). *Prior Abuse Reported by Inmates and Probationers*. Washington, DC: Bureau of Justice Statistics, U.S. Department of Justice.

Harrison, Paige M., and Allen J. Beck. (2006). *Prison and Jail Inmates at Midyear 2005*. Washington, DC: U.S. Department of Justice, Bureau of Justice Statistics.

Hickman, Matthew J., and Brian A. Reaves. (2006). *Local Police Departments, 2003*. Washington, DC: U.S. Department of Justice, Bureau of Justice Statistics.

James, Doris J. (2004). *Profile of Jail Inmates, 2002*. Washington, DC: U.S. Department of Justice, Bureau of Justice Statistics.

James, Doris J., and Lauren E. Glaze. (2006). *Mental Health Problems of Prison and Jail Inmates*. Washington, DC: U.S. Department of Justice, Bureau of Justice Statistics.

Johnson, Ida M. (2002). "Rape, date and marital." Pp. 1346–1352 in *Encyclopedia of Crime and Punishment*, edited by David Levinson. Thousand Oaks, CA: Sage.

Johnston, Denise. (1995). "Child custody issues of women prisoners: A preliminary report from the Chicas Project." *Prison Journal* 75 (2), 222–239.

Lifschitz, Jennifer. (2004). "Battered woman syndrome and prosecution of domestic abuse and rape cases." *Georgetown Journal of Gender and the Law* 5, 149–165.

Markels, Alex. (2003). "A seismic shift in sex-case law." *U.S. News & World Report* 135 (12), 45.

Maruschak, Laura M. (2006). *HIV in Prisons, 2004*. Washington, DC: Bureau of Justice Statistics, U.S. Department of Justice.

Mays, G. Larry, and L. Thomas Winfree, Jr. (2005). *Essentials of Corrections*, third edition. Belmont, CA: Wadsworth.

——. (2006). *Juvenile Justice*, second edition. Long Grove, IL: Waveland Press.

McGuire, M. Dyan. (2005). "The impact of prison rape on public health." *Californian Journal of Health Promotion* 3 (2), 72–83.

Miller, Jody, and Scott H. Decker. (2001). "Young women and gang violence: Gender, street offending, and violent victimization in gangs." *Justice Quarterly* 18 (1), 115–140.

Mumola, Christopher. (1999). *Substance Abuse and Treatment: State and Federal Prisoners, 1997*. Washington, DC: U.S. Department of Justice, Bureau of Justice Statistics.

——. (2000). *Incarcerated Parents and Their Children*. Washington, DC: U.S. Department of Justice, Bureau of Justice Statistics.

Peterson, Dana, Jody Miller, and Finn-Aage Esbensen. (2001). "The impact of sex composition on gangs and gang member delinquency." *Criminology* 39 (2), 411–440.

Pollock, Joycelyn M. (2002). *Women, Prison, and Crime*, second edition. Belmont, CA: Wadsworth.

Reaves, Brian A., and Lynn M. Bauer. (2003). *Federal Law Enforcement Officers, 2003*. Washington, DC: U.S. Department of Justice, Bureau of Justice Statistics.

Reaves, Brian A., and Matthew J. Hickman. (2004). *Law Enforcement Management and Administrative Statistics, 2000: Data for Individual State and Local Agencies With 100 or More Officers*. Washington, DC: Bureau of Justice Statistics, U.S. Department of Justice.

——. (2006). *Sheriff's Offices, 2003*. Washington, DC: Bureau of Justice Statistics, U.S. Department of Justice.

Rowe, David C. (2001). *Biology and Crime*. Los Angeles: Roxbury Publishing.

Rugala, Eugene, James McNamara, and George Wattendorf. (2004, November). "Expert testimony and risk assessment in stalking cases." *FBI Law Enforcement Bulletin*, pp. 8–17.

Saporito, Bill. (2004). "Kobe rebounds. Dismissal of rape charges against K. Bryant." *Time* 164 (11), 72–73.

Schlanger, Margo. (2003). "Inmate litigation: Results of a national survey." *National Institute of Corrections Large Jails Network Exchange*, 1–12.

Schwartz, Martin D., Walter S. DeKerseredy, David Tait, and Shahid Alvi. (2001). "Male peer support and a feminist routine activities theory: Understanding sexual assault on the college campus." *Justice Quarterly* 18 (3), 623–649.

Simon, Rita James. (1975). *Women and Crime*. Lexington, MA: Heath.

——. (2002). "Women and crime in a global perspective." Pp. 1715–1718 in *Encyclopedia of Crime and Punishment*, edited by David Levinson. Thousand Oaks, CA: Sage.

Smith, Michael R., Matthew Makarios, and Geoffrey P. Alpert. (2006). "Differential suspicion: Theory specification and gender effects in the traffic stop context." *Justice Quarterly* 23 (2), 271–295.

Snell, Tracy L. (2006). *Capital Punishment, 2005*. Washinton, DC: U.S. Department of Justice, Bureau of Justice Statistics.

Snyder, Howard N., and Melissa Sickmund. (1999). *Juvenile Offenders and Victims: 1999 National Report*. Washington, DC: U.S. Department of Justice, Office of Juvenile Justice and Delinquency Prevention.

Steffensmeier, Darrell. (1980). "Sex differences in patterns of adult crime, 1965–1977." *Social Forces* 58, 1080–1090.

Steffensmeier, Darrell, and M. J. Cobb. (1981). "Sex differences in urban arrest patterns, 1934–1979." *Social Forces* 29, 37–50.

Stephan, James J., and Jennifer C. Karberg. (2003). *Census of State and Federal Correctional Facilities, 2000.* Washington, DC: U.S. Department of Justice, Bureau of Justice Statistics.

ten Bensel, Robert W. (1984). "Definitions of child neglect and abuse." *Juvenile and Family Court Journal* 35 (4), 23–31.

Visher, Christy. (1983). "Gender, police arrest decisions, and notions of chivalry." *Criminology* 21 (1), 5–28.

Winfree, L. Thomas, Jr., and Howard Abadinsky. (2003). *Understanding Crime,* second edition. Belmont, CA: Wadsworth.

Young, Cathy. (2004). "Kobe's rights. Rape complaints and defendants." *Reason* 35 (8), 22–23.

Recommended Readings

Belknap, Joanne. (2001). *The Invisible Woman: Gender, Crime, and Justice,* second edition. Belmont, CA: Wadsworth. Belknap deals with the three statuses discussed in this chapter—women as offenders, victims, and criminal justice agents—in a very thorough manner. She deals with theories related to female delinquency and gives a critique of the various theories. She also delves into the world of females as victims of crime, particularly sexual crimes, battering, and stalking. Finally, she presents two chapters on women working in the criminal justice system and some of the legal, organizational, and operational barriers they face.

Merlo, Alida V., and Joycelyn M. Pollock. (2006). *Women, Law, and Social Control,* second edition. Boston: Allyn & Bacon. Merlo and Pollock's book is organized very much like this chapter. The book contains 15 readings by a variety of scholars, and these readings are organized into five major sections (plus a conclusion). The three primary themes covered in the book address the roles of women as criminal offenders, as practitioners in the criminal justice system, and as offenders. Any student interested in the topic of gender and justice would be well-advised to consult this timely book.

Pollock, Joycelyn M. (2002). *Women, Prison, and Crime,* second edition. Belmont, CA: Wadsworth. The primary focus of Pollock's book is on women in prison, and she provides an in-depth look at entry into the prison society and some of the means of adjusting to that society. She also addresses the thorny issue of special needs inmates and programming issues. Nevertheless, she does give the reader an overview of some of the theories of female criminality to provide an appropriate context for the book. Like the book by Belknap, Pollock addresses the topic of female staff members in the prison world. A unique chapter is the one that provides an international/comparative view of women in jails and prisons in other countries. ✦

Chapter 9

Wrongful Convictions

Introduction

Over the past two decades, we have heard how many offenders have been released from prison or death row as their convictions were found to be wrongful. These prisoners were not released on so-called technicalities but in most cases were completely exonerated, typically after DNA evidence established their innocence. Such cases are troubling for advocates of both the crime control and due process models. For those who believe in crime control, the fact that an innocent person has been imprisoned means that the guilty party is still in the community and could be committing further crimes. Persons who support the due process model, by contrast, are horrified by the prosecution, conviction, and sentencing of an innocent person. Members of either group probably would agree that these convictions shape our perceptions of justice, or injustice.

Overall, these errors have destructive effects on the innocent person who was wrongfully convicted, including the shame of being labeled as an offender and the damage that a criminal conviction has on one's relationships and employment. In many cases, individuals who were exonerated try to remedy the harm by launching lawsuits after their release; but even if they are successful, it is impossible to retrieve years or decades lost to imprisonment. The Innocence Project (2007) reported, for example, that the average length of imprisonment served by the 188 people exonerated (effective January 2007) was 11.5 years. While each of these miscarriages of justice represents an individual tragedy, these errors also cast disrepute on the entire criminal justice system, and they are a powerful symbol of failure. We examine how wrongful convictions occur, the effects of these incidents, and who is responsible. In addition, we outline how criminal justice systems can reduce these errors.

Wrongful convictions are not a new phenomenon: Edwin Borchard (1932) recognized this problem in the early 1900s, and Michael Radelet and his colleagues (1992) found that 416 Americans were exonerated on homicide charges from 1900 to 1991. However, wrongful convictions are not a challenge unique to the United States. In recent years, there have been a number of sensational cases in many common-law nations, including Australia, Canada, and Great Britain. Other countries, however, have been quicker to adopt safeguards to reduce the harm of these errors. Great Britain, for instance, created a government-operated investigative body, called the Criminal Case Review Commission, in 1995 to formally investigate alleged cases of wrongful conviction (American Bar Association [ABA] 2005).

Justice systems in the United States have not adopted similar safeguards, but there is some capacity for appellate courts to provide postconviction review. As noted in Chapter 2, some **indigent defendants** (people with no resources) have less effective access to the courts. As a result, a number of **Innocence Projects** have been established to investigate wrongful convictions and educate the public about the sources of these miscarriages of justice.[1] Typically, these projects are operated by law schools, and they rely upon professors and student volunteers to examine cases. Some journalism schools have also offered courses where students conduct similar investigations.

Samuel Gross and colleagues (2005) reported that the number of exonerations has increased significantly since 1989; and many of these persons have been released due to DNA evidence, although non-DNA exonerations have increased as well. Figure 1 depicts the trend in U.S. exonerations over time. A majority of these persons were convicted of murder and sentenced to death. In fact, as of January 1, 2007, 188 persons had been exonerated and released directly from prison or death row to the community (Innocence Project 2007). Such concerns lead Governor George Ryan of Illinois in January, 2003, to commute the sentences of all 167 Illinois death row inmates to life in prison because of a lack of confidence in the Illinois justice system.

Miscarriages of justice are thought to have a harmful effect on justice systems, reducing their legitimacy, and they actually may contribute to higher levels of crime. Tom Tyler (2006) proposed that the perception of a fair and unbiased justice system is important if citizens are expected to abide by the law. A cornerstone of procedural justice is that the activities of the police, courts, and corrections are seen by law-abider and lawbreaker alike as being just, fair, neutral, and free of bias. Tyler and Huo (2002, 1) observed that

> Public opinion polls suggest that Americans' trust in the police and the courts is low. These same polls also reveal a disturbing racial divide, with minorities expressing greater levels of distrust than whites. Practices such as racial profiling, zero-tolerance policing, the use of excessive force, and harsh punishment for minor drug crimes all contribute to low trust and confidence in the police and courts.

Perhaps the worst threat to the confidence in justice systems is when innocent defendants are convicted of or plead guilty to an offense they did not commit (due to fear of a harsher sanction if convicted at trial).

Figure 9.1
Exonerations by Year, 1989–2003

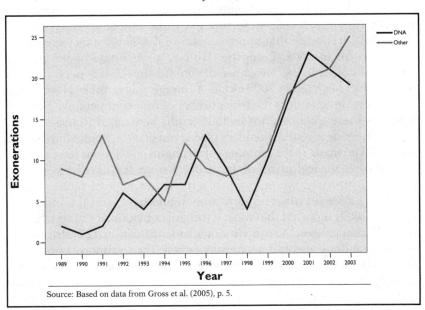

Source: Based on data from Gross et al. (2005), p. 5.

The effects on the individual who has been wrongfully convicted and sentenced are devastating. Adrian Grounds (2004) conducted a study of persons who were wrongfully convicted, sentenced to prison, and then exonerated. In many cases, costly trials forced these individuals and their families into bankruptcy. All of Grounds' sample were stigmatized by the prison experience, all underwent some elements of **prisonization** (where one takes on some of the institutional values of the penitentiary), others were physically victimized while incarcerated, and many experienced destructive effects on their marriages and family relationships. In many cases, the incarceration of a wage earner impoverishes a family.

Even release from prison does not result in happy endings; these exonerated ex-offenders generally suffered from a number of difficulties in adjusting to their new lives. Most of the persons investigated in this study had a high incidence of **posttraumatic stress disorder (PTSD)**—the emotional and psychological consequences of a stressful experience (Grounds 2004). In addition to the types of deprivation that anybody experiences during long-term incarceration, these exonerated ex-prisoners also harbored strong feelings of injustice. In most cases, persons who are exonerated may not qualify for community-based reintegration programs or other supportive counseling that would make the transition from prison to community more successful.

The total number of persons who are thought to have been wrongfully convicted is not trivial. In a groundbreaking study, Ronald Huff and his colleagues gathered the perceptions of justice-system officials—including prosecutors, 41 state attorneys general, sheriffs, police chiefs and judges—about wrongful convictions. Huff, Rattner, and Sagarin (1996) found that these officials estimated that 0.5 percent of all persons convicted in any given year were thought to be innocent. Harrison and Beck (2006) reported that approximately 697,000 persons were admitted to prison in 2005. Using the Huff et al. estimate of 0.5 percent wrongful convictions, we can extrapolate that 3,485 persons were wrongfully convicted in 2005 alone. Although this number is troubling, it probably undercounts the true number of innocent persons incarcerated—as these totals do not include adults sentenced to terms of jail confinement or juvenile offenders placed outside the home. Further, the officials who made these estimates of wrongful convictions have a significant stake in the legitimacy of the justice system. It is likely that a survey of defense attorneys would produce a higher estimate of such errors.

Mistakes are inevitable in any human endeavor, and the Innocence Project (2007) reported that most wrongful convictions can be traced to five different causes: (1) eyewitness misidentification, (2) false confessions, (3) jailhouse snitch testimony (where the testimony of other offenders is used to convict a defendant), (4) misleading forensic science (also called poor forensic science or junk science), and (5) prosecutorial misconduct. Underlying all of these causes is the ineffective assistance of counsel, since good lawyering can overcome many of these challenges. This chapter explores the problem of failures within justice systems and offers some suggestions about ways to respond to misconduct, error, and the challenge of wrongful convictions.

Eyewitness Misidentification

The testimony of a witness to a crime has long been regarded as one of the most reliable methods of establishing guilt or innocence. The use of DNA evidence in recent years has cast considerable doubt about the reliability of eyewitness evidence. The Innocence Project (2006) observed that of the first 130 cases of wrongful convictions that were overturned using DNA evidence, 101 of them were related to eyewitness misidentification. Radelet, Bedau, and Putnum (1992) reported similar results in their examination of wrongful homicide convictions. These findings are troubling, but when we examine the sources of such error, they are entirely understandable.

Huff, Rattner, and Sagarin (1996) also found that eyewitness misidentification was the leading cause of wrongful convictions. These scholars found that misidentification could be traced to the manner in which suspects are identified (for example, the way that photos or police lineups of suspects are conducted) and whether there is a reward at stake. Olson (2002, 76) observed that crimes are often traumatic events, and this sometimes distorts an individual's perceptions, especially as the length of time between the offense and witness identification lengthens. Moreover, eyewitnesses can be influenced by media publicity, the police, prosecutors, or even other witnesses (Turtle, Lindsay, and Wells 2005). Last, Olson (2002) noted that alcohol and drug use are often associated with many crimes, and witnesses may be under the influence, further reducing their ability to accurately remember events or to identify a suspect.

Few eyewitnesses to crimes act maliciously, but many have made errors in identifying the persons responsible for these offenses. In a commonly cited example, a Florida rape victim positively identified her assailant as Wilton Dedge at two trials. In both cases, the defendant was found guilty and sentenced to prison. DNA evidence later exonerated the man, but only after he had spent 22 years in prison (Sellers 2004). Despite the fact that analysis of DNA evidence in 2001 conclusively proved that he was innocent, Dedge remained in prison until 2004 (Innocence Project 2006). Upon release, the State of Florida offered Dedge $200,000 in compensation for his 22-year term of incarceration. Not surprisingly, Dedge filed a lawsuit for a substantially greater amount, and the legislature awarded him $2 million in December 2005; but it seems inconsistent with the aims of justice that compensation is not awarded automatically in most jurisdictions. At midyear 2005, only 20 states had established mechanisms to provide compensation for the wrongfully convicted (although other states are considering legislation that would automatically provide such compensation).

A number of strategies can reduce the types of mistakes that eyewitnesses make. First, the manner in which photographs are shown or police lineups are conducted has a significant effect on witness errors. Historically, police officers gave a witness a number of photographs, including one of the suspect. In some cases, the pictures would be so dissimilar that the witness could easily select the suspect (for instance, placing a picture of a African American suspect in a group of photos of white men, or using a different type or format of photograph for the suspect). One problem with using photographs or lineups is that the police might inadvertently or intentionally telegraph information to the witness, such as nodding if a witness hesitates over a suspect's photograph.

Psychologists suggest that a more effective way to conduct a photo lineup is to provide the witness only one picture at a time and present new photographs only if the suspect rejects a candidate. In some jurisdictions, police officers conducting a photo lineup will have no idea of the identity of the suspect, thus ensuring a blind review. Scheck (2006) argued that such blind reviews are the most scientifically accurate method of conducting lineups; they reduce misidentification without decreasing correct identification.

Lineups of suspects suffer from similar problems. In some egregious cases, only one suspect was shown to an eyewitness, virtually ensuring that he or she was selected. Like with using arrays of photos, the tradi-

tional way to conduct a lineup was to present the witness with a group
of persons, the way we are accustomed to seeing lineups portrayed on
television. Many jurisdictions are now allowing a witness to view only
one person at a time, again using a blind review process so that officers
will not unintentionally influence the witness.

The manner in which a photo array or suspect lineup is presented
has a great deal of influence on the way a witness will behave. When
given a choice among a number of photos or persons at the same time,
witnesses typically choose the person who *most closely* resembles the
suspect. But none of us would want to have that standard of identification applied if our future were at stake. By forcing a witness to evaluate
and reject candidates one at a time, however, eyewitness errors are reduced. In response to the number of wrongful convictions in Illinois,
Sullivan (2004a, 608) reported, "[police must tell witnesses] that the
suspect may not be in the array, that they are not obligated to make an
identification, and that they should not assume the administrator
knows which person is the suspect."

False Confessions

When somebody confesses involvement in a crime to an investigator,
it is compelling evidence of guilt. The problem is that people who confess to a crime, and are later convicted, are regularly released from
prison due to DNA or some other type of evidence that exonerates them
(Innocence Project 2006). Why would people confess to the police
about their involvement in a crime if they were innocent? The truth is
that statements sometimes are coerced from suspects, who later recant
these confessions. The Innocence Project (2006), for example, found
that slightly more than one-quarter of the first 130 persons exonerated
by DNA evidence had made false confessions. Unfortunately, the original confession has a powerful effect on a judge or jury, and these suspects are often convicted of serious offenses—primarily on the basis of
a recanted confession.

The problem of false confessions has long been recognized
(Borchard 1932). A generation ago, suspects were sometimes subjected
to the **third degree,** a police interrogation strategy that used intimidation, threats of violence, assaults, or other forms of coercion to obtain
confessions. Such practices have largely disappeared over time, and
due process protections, such as those guaranteed by the ***Escobedo v.
Illinois*** (1964) and ***Miranda v. Arizona*** (1966) decisions, gave suspects
the opportunity to seek the assistance of counsel when interrogated by
police, at least in theory.

Drizin and Leo (2004) conducted a comprehensive review of persons
who had been exonerated and found that innocent persons with mental
illness, juveniles, and children were more likely to confess to crimes than
other suspects. Such findings are not surprising as these groups are eas-

ier to intimidate, vulnerable to pressure, and may confess sometimes just to please the investigators. Forrest, Wadkins, and Miller (2002), by contrast, found that persons who scored lower on IQ tests were also more likely to confess to a crime that they did not commit. Such confessions have devastating consequences for the individual. In the sample of cases reviewed by Drizin and Leo (2004), 81 percent of these defendants were convicted despite the fact that they later recanted their confession.

A series of reports by the *Washington Post* exposed that suspects charged with serious crimes were often subjected to overzealous police interrogations that violated their constitutional protections (Witt 2001). Some of the suspects cited in this study were questioned by teams of investigators for 11 to 38 hours, and Witt (2001) reported that requests to see an attorney or family members were denied and that persons being interrogated were not allowed to sleep. All of these suspects eventually were vindicated of their involvement in crimes, although some were held in jail for months.

Investigators simply "wear down" some suspects, and individuals may confess in order to be left alone, stop the interrogation, to go to sleep, or because they have been promised that the consequences for the offense will be reduced if they confess. In fact, many people believe that as soon as they confess, the interrogation will stop and they will be allowed to go home. Forrest, Wadkins, and Miller (2002, 28) reported that "[p]hysiological factors such as intoxication, withdrawal and sleep deprivation also affect the likelihood that a suspect will make a false confession."

During these lengthy interrogations, the investigators generally have come to believe in their suspect's guilt. The police have considerable discretion in the manner by which they conduct an interrogation. For example, they can lie or manipulate suspects to obtain a confession. Officers might overstate the quality of their evidence (for example, "Your fingerprints are all over the gun" even though the fingerprints may not be a conclusive match). Officers also employ a number of other strategies to convince suspects to confess, including establishing rapport, encouraging confession to reduce guilty feelings, continually questioning the individual's version of an event (to exploit inconsistencies), and encouraging suspects to mitigate their responsibility in "their side of the story."

Drizen and Reich (2004, 624) observed that the problem with false confessions is that they typically result in the investigators being less likely to "seek out corroborating evidence because the confession alone, in most cases, is sufficiently persuasive evidence for a judge and jury to convict."

Once investigators are convinced of the guilt of the suspect, a condition called confirmatory bias is said to exist. **Confirmatory bias,** which is also called tunnel vision, occurs when the police or prosecutors believe so strongly in the suspect's guilt that they do not consider other options (or suspects). Sullivan (2004a, 167) observed that as investigators "conclude that a particular person is the culprit, we seek evidence to support that conclusion. And we tend to try to explain away evidence that leads away from that conclusion."

Scholars who examine the problem of false confessions overwhelmingly support the videotaping of the entire interrogation so that other investigators, as well as judge and jury, can verify the conduct and demeanor of both the suspect and police (Drizen and Reich 2004). A number of states, including Alaska and Minnesota, already videotape police interrogations, and the state of Illinois started taping the interrogation of homicide suspects in July 2005. To reduce abusive interrogations and confirmatory bias and to guarantee that the rights of the suspect are upheld, videotaping the interviews of suspects seems like an easy-to-implement, low-cost remedy to a significant problem.

Jailhouse Snitch Testimony

District attorneys often use the testimony of criminals to successfully prosecute a case. In return for their testimony, codefendants may be granted a reduction in the severity of their punishment (or immunity from prosecution). Another group of persons sometimes approaches the police or prosecutors with knowledge about an offense or offender. Often, their knowledge of a crime comes from involvement in the offense (directly or indirectly) or knowledge gleaned from the suspects or their associates. In other cases, testimony is based on direct statements made by the suspect, typically somebody who shares the same jail cell or lives in the same housing unit within a jail. These jailhouse confessions are the currency used by the **jailhouse snitch** to get out of trouble.

The testimony of jailhouse snitches has lead to numerous wrongful convictions. While there is a long tradition of using snitches on both sides of the Atlantic, most Americans feel slightly uncomfortable with the prospect of these offenders giving testimony (Elliot 2003). As Warden (2005, 2) noted, "when the criminal justice system offers witnesses incentives to lie, they will."

Harris (2000, 1) observed that the government can offer compensation, in the form of "immunity from prosecution, reduced charges, sentence reduction, or cash" in exchange for cooperation or testimony. Jailhouse snitches often testify that they overheard the defendant admit guilt. In return for their testimony, they receive a reduction in penalty. The problem is that their testimony is sometimes based on lies, and some individuals have testified against many defendants in return for reduced sentences. Two cases are especially outrageous—those of John Hall (who testified against five murder defendants in different cases) and Leslie Vernon White (who testified against three separate murder defendants and one burglary defendant after serving only 36 days in jail). Realistically, one might question how many murder suspects or defendants would actually "confess" to a cellmate about their involvement in an offense. Unfortunately, such egregious cases could not go forward without the tacit approval of the prosecutor.

The use of snitches, and concern over the type of testimony that they deliver, has increased significantly over the past decade. Yaroshefsky (2002) observed that a number of political and legal factors lead to these unreliable or biased witnesses giving testimony, including,

(1) expanded federal jurisdiction over crimes considered exclusively within the province of the state

(2) a significant shift in the types of crimes prosecuted in great measure because of significant funding of the "war on drugs"

(3) mandatory minimum sentences

(4) sentencing guidelines in state and federal courts; and

(5) in the federal system, a decrease in judicial discretion and the vesting of greater control over the ultimate sentence to prosecutors.

We learned in previous chapters that many offenders are increasingly at risk of lengthy prison sentences, and mandatory minimum sentences have some defendants facing the possibility of serving decades in prison. By constructing false testimony that incriminates another inmate, jailhouse snitches can greatly reduce their sentences.

The prosecutor's dilemma is that snitches are essential to gaining convictions in criminal conspiracies, such as gangs or organized crime. By contrast, some prosecutors might not be as discriminating about the legitimacy of the testimony as they should. Trott (1996, 1383–1385) provided a series of guidelines for use of this evidence but warned prosecutors that "[c]riminals are likely to say and do almost anything to get what they want, especially when what they want is to get out of trouble with the law." Likewise, the author observed that "[o]rdinary decent people are predisposed to dislike, distrust, and frequently despise criminals who 'sell out' and become prosecution witnesses."

Perhaps the greatest hazard of using the testimony of a snitch occurs in capital cases. Warden (2005) outlined how snitch witnesses were the foremost cause of wrongful convictions in capital cases since the 1970s. In some of these trials, the snitches were in a unique position to relate incriminating evidence, as they were actually responsible for the murders! Altogether, the use of snitches involves a significant challenge for ethical prosecutors, balancing their need to convict offenders without compromising justice.

Misleading Forensic Science

The popularity of forensic science depicted in television programs such as *CSI* has created optimism that wrongful convictions can be reduced. To a large extent, DNA evidence has reduced the likelihood of an offender being wrongfully convicted in cases where such evidence has been collected at a crime scene (see Purcell, Winfree, and Mays 1994). One limitation of entertainment television is that programs such as *CSI* may overstate the usefulness of scientific evidence. First, not all crime scenes produce usable evidence. Scheck (2006), for instance, observed that only 5–10 percent of serious felonies have usable biological evidence. Second, the technologies depicted in these popular programs do not always exist. Third, the speed at which television investigations are conducted is not often possible—facts that often confuse and disappoint the families of some victims who are accustomed to the speedy and successful resolution of cases on *CSI*.

In fact, depending on where the police department is located, it may take months for routine tests to be conducted. Big city departments, for instance, may have thousands of open murder investigations going back decades and thousands of current investigations of serious felonies. For example, Corwin (2003, 282–283) observed a Los Angeles Police Department (LAPD) detective requesting fingerprint information:

> He tells a technician he wants to compare a suspect's prints with those lifted at an apartment. McCartin is accustomed to the LAPD's bureaucratic inefficiency, but he is stunned anyway by the response: he will have to wait several months for the results.

Of course, waiting several months makes the complex job of investigating a crime even more difficult because of the lengthy time it would take to exclude a suspect. One wonders how many inmates have languished in jail for months awaiting DNA or other forensic test results.

Recently, there has been increasing criticism about the usefulness of obscure or unproven scientific evidence in criminal cases, the skills and professionalism of the persons hired to conduct analyses in such cases, and the funding that agencies receive to carry out these tests. While these factors may increase the possibility of wrongful convictions, the use of DNA evidence has contributed to hundreds of convictions being overturned, including a large number involving death row inmates (Innocence Project 2006). Thus, we have to acknowledge that science has aided law enforcement in apprehending offenders, but we also have to understand that employees of criminal justice agencies have sometimes misinterpreted or misrepresented scientific information.

Defense attorneys, scholars, and advocates for the due process model have become increasingly skeptical of forensic science and whether fingerprints, tool markings, or ballistics evidence are as conclusive as many of us believe. One of the problems is that physical evidence recovered from crime scenes may be difficult to interpret: Bullets are damaged when they hit bones (or other objects), fingerprints are frequently smudged (or only a partial fingerprint exists), and the marks from one chisel or hammer might not differ significantly from other tools. As a result, the effectiveness of scientific evidence to bring suspects to justice often depends on the skills of the persons who are analyzing and in-

> ## Box 9.1
> ## The Impact of CSI on Justice
>
> In January 2007 three CSI series and several other programs (*Bones, Crossing Jordan,* and *NCIS*) featured the analysis of forensic evidence. Such television programs are popular with viewers; however, because most of the crimes that these actors encounter are solved within an hour, this distorts expectations for the public and may also make it more difficult for prosecutors to try their cases. Podlas (2006) contended that these programs may create unrealistic expectations for jurors and that finding no evidence at a crime scene may be equivalent to reasonable doubt for some potential jurors. Podlas also suggested that viewers of these programs may form the belief that scientific evidence is infallible (although this may pose an advantage for both the prosecutor and the defense).
>
> Shows that feature scientific evidence have also increased interest in forensic science, and Podlas (2006) observed that applications to forensic science college programs have increased. Perhaps more important, Podlas notes that support for the funding for forensic science labs has increased as well. Given the chronic underfunding of these labs, maybe television can have a positive effect after all. ✦

terpreting the results. In some places, overworked, unethical, or incompetent scientists might overstate the conclusiveness of their evidence.

In other cases, evidence may be mishandled, misplaced, or stolen—a likely proposition as some evidence rooms or labs handle thousands of pieces of evidence each month. Crime labs in some jurisdictions may be less professional than in other places. The *Chicago Tribune* ran a series of articles in 2004 that highlighted the problems associated with crime labs, including incorrectly evaluated evidence (including fingerprints), false or misleading testimony by lab workers or scientists, hidden results (that might prove the innocence of a defendant), and inconsistent standards among crime labs (McRoberts, Mills, and Possley 2004). One recent scandal involved the operation of the Houston Police Department Crime Lab. Khanna and McVicker (2005) outlined how DNA, toxicology, ballistics, controlled substances, and blood-typing results from the Houston lab have all come under doubt, and there have been allegations of wrongdoing and falsification of test results.

Of course, sloppy laboratory or police procedures also enable offenders to escape justice. If laboratory tests are not conducted appropriately, there is the chance that the guilty person will go free. Police also lose evidence that might lead to the conviction of offenders. Corwin (2003) outlined a **cold case** (a case that is unsolved and may have been put aside for months or years), in which the police had unintentionally thrown out DNA evidence from a 1965 murder. Through the detectives had identified a possible suspect, the lack of evidence has made it impossible—short of a confession—to solve the case. Before criticizing hard-working and diligent laboratory staff and police officers, however, one has to acknowledge the complexity of their jobs and the difficulty

Box 9.2
Problems at the Houston Police Department Crime Lab

Between October 2003 and July 2006, *Houston Chronicle* reporters published over 100 articles about problems at the Crime Lab. These accounts have cast doubt on many convictions involving at least four defendants convicted of homicides, and such allegations have reduced the credibility of Houston's justice system. To restore the credibility of the lab, a group of stakeholders—including representatives from the justice system, academics, and community advocates—was formed; and the City of Houston funded an independent investigation of the activities at the lab. In May, 2006, Bromwich (2006, 5) reported that

> Thus far, our investigation has identified a total of 43 DNA cases and 50 serology cases analyzed by the Crime Lab that we have determined to have major issues, which we have defined to mean problems that raise significant doubt as to the reliability of the work performed, the validity of the analytical results, or the correctness of the analysts' conclusions.

Such findings cast doubt on whether our justice systems produce accurate findings, but the fact that the city has funded an independent investigation shows a commitment to restoring public confidence in the lab.

While the final reports have not been completed, the investigators found that many sections within the lab conducted accurate and thorough analyses of the evidence. This report suggested that many of the problems could be attributed to a small number of workers. One of the hazards of criminal justice operations is that the misconduct or incompetence of a few employees might cast disrepute upon an entire organization. That is one of the reasons why background checks for justice organizations and training for new employees are much more comprehensive than several decades ago. After all, if it was your evidence they were examining, and you were innocent, you would want the lab to employ the most honest, ethical, professional, and well-trained staff. ✦

of properly storing, inventorying, and sorting through hundreds of pieces of evidence in thousands of crimes that may have been committed before they were born.

DiFonzo (2005) and Scheck (2006) have both been critical that crime labs are closely tied to police departments or district attorneys' offices, and they argue that these labs should be independent. DiFonzo (2005) also made several recommendations that would strengthen the credibility of crime labs, such as requiring that these labs be nationally accredited and that evidence used in criminal cases be saved to conduct independent testing. Underlying all of these observations, however, is the fact that these labs are asked to do much with few resources.

In addition to operational problems within crime labs, there is concern over **junk science,** especially when scientists give testimony that has little or no basis in the scientific literature. Examples of junk science include the use of ear prints or lip prints being used to convict defendants, despite the fact that there is little scientific basis that such physical characteristics are unique (McRoberts and Possley 2006). Moreover, bite mark evidence has been used for years, despite the fact that there is some dispute whether interpretations of this evidence are accurate. Last, some have questioned whether marks left by tools or cartridge cases from firearms are as unique as we believe. It is possible that comparisons are often open to interpretation by the people conducting the analyses (Schwartz 2005). Altogether, some defendants risk being convicted each year on the basis of evidence that is not scientifically sound.

There also has been concern over the activities of individual scientists or other experts, some of whom may be incompetent, biased, or who conduct shoddy analyses. The case of Fred Zain, who directed the West Virginia State Police Crime Lab, is particularly egregious. Huff (2002b, 8) reported that "Zain's fraudulent lab reports and perjured testimony over a 16-year career contributed to many wrongful convictions." Not only did Zain's perjury result in wrongful convictions, but these innocent persons—who had spent years in prisons—successfully sued the State of West Virginia for millions of dollars.

Scientists who do shoddy analyses are not restricted to crime labs. A Tennessee pathologist was recently found to have done unprofessional work, such as "mishandling investigations into suspicious deaths, including some criminal cases" (Fly 2005). The problem is that juries of laypersons rely upon these experts to interpret the results of scientific analyses, and if their information is biased, incorrect, or unreliable, jurors cannot make meaningful decisions about the guilt or innocence of defendants. Moreover, the prosecutor or police may be misled into pursuing the wrong suspect if a technician, scientist, or analyst gives investigators the results "they want to hear" rather than the truth.

Prosecutorial Misconduct

The role of the prosecutor is to seek justice. A number of factors make this search more difficult, including the role of the prosecutor as an elected official. In a social climate characterized by fear of crime, there is little tolerance of failure to obtain a conviction—especially in the case of violent offenses. Unfortunately, this pressure sometimes drives prosecutors to win a particular case "at all costs," including engaging in "lying, distorting facts, engaging in cover-ups, paying for perjury, and setting up innocent people" (Moushey and Martinson 1998, 1).

We all have an interest in sentencing guilty offenders, but winning a case due to some type of misconduct actually reduces public safety by eroding confidence in the justice system (Tyler 2006). Until recently, we had little idea of the scope of this problem, and a number of difficulties keep us from understanding how often these acts occur. First, there were an estimated 26,520 prosecutors employed in 2,344 state and local prosecutors' offices in 2005 (Perry 2006, 2), and some 5,457 U.S. Attorneys in 2003 (Executive Office for U.S. Attorneys 2006, 3). The large number of attorneys, distributed throughout the nation, ensures that even if a relatively small percentage of prosecutors engage in unethical conduct, it will have a significant impact on the total number of wrongful convictions in a given year.

Second, the independent nature of the prosecutor's job makes it relatively easy to engage in misconduct. Prosecutors have considerable discretion, and their day-to-day activities, such as plea negotiations, have little public visibility. Some 95 percent of defendants enter a plea of guilty, and their cases never go to trial. Anecdotal accounts suggest that some defendants have pleaded guilty to a crime that they did not commit to avoid a trial that could be financially ruinous and result in a harsh sentence if found guilty. Cases that are heard at trial, by contrast, are transparent; the public can see what transpires, and there is an official record of the proceedings. The Center for Public Integrity (CFPI) tried to determine the scope of the problem and searched 11,452 legal opinions written between 1970 and 2002. The CFPI found that in 2,012 cases, indictments, convictions, or sentences were reversed due to prosecutorial misconduct (Weinberg 2003). While this is a large number, we also have to acknowledge that millions of criminal cases were heard during this era. In fact, Alexandra Dunahoe (2005) suggested that we have little idea of the true scope of this problem.

Prosecutors also enjoy absolute immunity from suit. Johns (2005, 120–135) argued that extending this immunity to prosecutors has a number of harms by denying victims a remedy, hindering the development of constitutional law, and obstructing the implementation of structural remedies to systemic problems. Johns (2005) found that immunity is unnecessary to protect honest prosecutors, and it introduces unnecessary complexity and confusion into the law. Perhaps most important, a greater number of layers of oversight, including access to civil remedies, may further discourage unethical or malicious behavior. Goldstein (2006), for instance, argued that victims of malicious prosecution should have recourse to Section 1983 lawsuits.

The Innocence Project (2006) outlined the major sources of prosecutorial misconduct (in order of importance), including suppression of **exculpatory evidence** (evidence that casts doubt on a defendant's guilt), fabricating evidence, allegations of coerced witness, and coerced confessions. Sometimes this misconduct may stem from an overzealous pursuit of justice, although Freedman (2002, 125–126) suggested that in some cases, this misconduct is motivated by career ambitions; that is, some prosecutors have an interest in increasing their public visibility prior to running for elected office or a career change to private practice.

The United States is the only nation that elects chief prosecutors or district attorneys.[2] There are some advantages to this approach, such as the ability of the electorate to remove incompetent prosecutors and to ensure that community standards of justice are upheld. Yet, there are some disadvantages as well. Because prosecutors are elected officials, some critics have suggested that they have much to lose by being "smart on crime" rather than being "tough on crime" (Miller 1996). Moreover, losing a high-profile case takes on a dimension of failure contrasted against the low-visibility of prosecutors in other nations where their jobs are not pathways to political careers.

While acknowledging that prosecutorial misconduct exists, we also have to recognize that the prosecutor has an inherently difficult job. In some cases, a district attorney may supervise hundreds of attorneys, and job turnover in many prosecutors' offices is often high, as experienced assistant district attorneys move to private practice after gaining a year or two of experience. Additionally, prosecutors must sift through sometimes conflicting information, confusing evidence, and faulty recollections of both victims and witnesses. They must base their decisions to prosecute on evidence that may be analyzed by incompetent technicians or rely upon information provided by police officers who might be engaging in some type of misconduct. Weinberg (2003) observed that even when ethical district attorneys follow all of the rules, they still might convict the wrong person.

Ineffective Assistance of Counsel

Many of the factors that lead to wrongful convictions are ultimately a consequence of ineffective representation of counsel. There is no shortage of accounts of attorneys who represented their clients while intoxicated, slept during capital trials, inadequately represented a client, or encouraged innocent defendants to plead guilty. Many of these situations are symptomatic of the lack of funding for indigent defense. The landmark **Gideon v. Wainwright** (1963) decision held that indigent defendants should receive state-funded counsel in noncapital felony cases. A number of prominent organizations, such as the American Bar Association (ABA) and the National Association of Criminal Defense Lawyers (NACDL) released reports on the fortieth anniversary of *Gideon*, expressing criticism that the promise of adequate representation for persons charged with serious crimes was unmet.

The ABA (2004) recently published one of the most comprehensive examinations of the status of indigent criminal defense. Although the ABA identified a number of problems with indigent defense, foremost is the fact that, in most places, funding for these defense programs is rationed: The number of attorneys and their budgets are fixed, but the number of defendants continues to grow. In many cases, public defenders will meet their clients only a few minutes before their court appearance, a necessary practice when average public defender caseloads number in the hundreds and approach 1,600 clients in New York alone (ABA 2004). Few defendants proceed to trial, and one reason is that public defenders do not have the resources to conduct a comprehensive examination of the case or the ability to hire experts or investigators to evaluate the state's evidence.

Few defendants can afford a "Dream Team" of attorneys, like O. J. Simpson had, and mounting a defense on a serious charge can bankrupt most people. As Ross and Richards (2002, 16) observed,

> The vast majority of people arrested on serious charges have no money to retain quality legal representation . . . They either hire some youngster fresh out of law school or are represented by a court-appointed public defender. Public defenders generally are sincere and concerned individuals, overworked, underpaid, and usually unable to give each case the attention it needs.

As a result, some defendants are encouraged by their public defenders to take plea bargains, even for crimes that they did not commit. Advocates of the due process model argue that providing adequate counsel is a serious challenge for American justice systems. Many offenders perceive that public defenders are incompetent, but in some cases, their participation in the local courtroom work group enables them to provide effective representation (Hanson and Ostrom 2004).

While not a comprehensive example of inadequate defense counsel behaviors, the outline of Berry (2003, 486) lists some problems specific to criminal defense:

(1) Failure to communicate with the client or communicating in a dismissive, callous, or hurried manner

(2) Perfunctory or no attempt at discovery

(3) Narrow, shallow, or no investigation

(4) Failure to retain needed experts and/or test physical evidence

(5) Minimal preparation, weak trial advocacy, and superficial or tentative cross-examination

When innocent defendants are encouraged to plead guilty, or even when a guilty person feels railroaded by the prosecution, the interests of justice are undermined.

It appears as though the most significant barriers to providing effective indigent counsel occur in poor counties, where these services must compete for scarce budget dollars with other community services. Overtaxed citizens and overburdened county commissioners have little sympathy for funding such programs. In one Mississippi case, for instance, the cost of a capital murder trial for two transients approached $1 million, threatening to bankrupt the entire county (ABA 2004). Such cases underscore the importance of providing indigent defense funded by the state, with its deeper pockets, rather than by individual counties.

Conclusions

We end this chapter with a review of the impact of wrongful convictions and some recommendations for changes. A recent case outlines the costs of miscarriages of justice, and it was the foundation for Illinois Governor George Ryan's decision to commute the sentences of 167 persons on death row to life imprisonment. Four defendants, who later came to be known as the Ford Heights Four, were convicted of rape and two counts of murder, in part because of exculpatory evidence that was not provided to the defense, and due to testimony that was coerced from a witness who was considered to be borderline mentally retarded. Fifteen years after sentences of imprisonment and death were imposed on the four men, students in a journalism course were able to identify the true murderers, based on a review of police reports that actually identified the four guilty persons. The students and their professor were able to obtain confessions from two of the four new suspects, and the Ford Heights Four were eventually released from prison.

Sullivan (2004b) outlined the direct and indirect costs of this one miscarriage of justice. In terms of direct costs, these four persons successfully sued Cook County for $36 million. In addition, the persons who had committed the murders continued to commit crimes in the community, and one of the actual killers ended up in prison for his involvement in another homicide. As a result, the wrongful convictions of four innocent men led to a reduction in public safety. Further, costly trials were held to convict the real offenders. Last, the state covered the cost to imprison each of the four wrongfully convicted persons for 15 years, including the higher costs of death row for two inmates. Thus, in addition to being a significant financial drain on the community and state, this one instance of wrongful conviction resulted in additional crimes, including at least one murder. Ultimately, the harm of the original crime was compounded by the state, and this ruined the lives of the four innocent men who were found guilty.

Yet, the indirect costs of wrongful convictions might be more significant in the long run. Sullivan (2004b, 191) observed a growing loss of public confidence in the criminal justice system, whereby "[p]olice, prosecutors, defense lawyers, and the courts all end up diminished in the public eye as a result of these exonerations, and tremendous distrust arises between criminal justice professionals and the public." Sullivan (2004b) also reported that such events have a powerful effect on the officials involved in these cases, which extends to witnesses (including the victim's families) who are required to testify at the trials of the actual murderers. A rush to judgment in this one offense, for example, had significant long-term repercussions throughout the entire state of Illinois.

When examining the problem of wrongful convictions, a number of scholars have observed that there is no single cause. Sometimes a number of factors interact to produce a miscarriage of justice. The effectiveness of snitch evidence, for instance, may be challenged by a prepared attorney. Further, sloppy forensic evidence might be overcome when a defense attorney arranges for a parallel series of forensic analyses to be conducted. While reducing prosecutorial misconduct may be more challenging, bringing individual cases of misconduct to the attention of state bar associations may result in a long-term change in the culture of a given office. In addition, since prosecutors are elected officials, publicizing the direct and indirect costs of wrongful convictions also may have an important influence on changing local prosecutorial practices.

Reducing the number of wrongful convictions is not a simple task. The state of Illinois, for example, brought forward 85 proposals to reduce the chance of these events occurring (Sullivan 2004b). A series of recommendations was also offered by Ronald Huff (2002a, 12–14), and we report them (in abbreviated form):

(1) States should enact measures to fairly compensate those who are wrongfully convicted.

(2) The death penalty should be abolished and replaced with sentences of 20 years, 30 years, or life imprisonment.

(3) Those convicted of crimes in which biological evidence is available for testing should be allowed to request such tests, and prosecutors should agree to such testing.

(4) In cases in which eyewitness identification is involved, the court should always permit the use of qualified expert witnesses and should issue precise cautionary instructions to juries informing them of the possibility of eyewitness misidentification.

(5) No identification procedure (pre- or postindictment) should be conducted in the absence of legal counsel for the suspect/accused.

(6) Police interrogations of suspects in the United States should be recorded in full.

(7) Law enforcement officers, criminalists, and prosecutors who engage in unethical, unprofessional, or illegal conduct contributing to wrongful conviction should be removed from their positions and subject to the most severe civil, professional, and (when appropriate) criminal penalties.

(8) Criminal case review commissions (or "innocence commissions") should be established at the national and state levels in the United States.

One item that is conspicuously absent in these proposals for reform is a closer examination of the political role of prosecutors in the United States. The United States has rates of wrongful convictions that seem greater than those in other democracies (Huff 2002b). It is possible that the role of chief prosecutor or district attorney as elected official may be associated with higher rates of wrongful convictions. In other first-world nations, there seems to be less emphasis on "winning at all costs," and civil service prosecutors might be more insulated from the public desire for punishment, which may make it easier for them to actively seek the truth and see that justice is done (George 2005; Miller 1996).

One of the important ways to minimize wrongful convictions is to utilize the best available scientific evidence in criminal cases. In support of this position, on June 12, 2006, the U.S. Supreme Court found that DNA evidence that became available after a defendant's conviction could be used in capital appeals (see *House v. Bell* 2006). Such a finding adds weight to the arguments that due process protections are important, although legislators have frequently challenged the ability of prisoners—especially ones on death row—from mounting a comprehensive postconviction defense. As noted in Chapter 2, the Antiterrorism and Effective Death Penalty Act (AEDPA) was intended to create obstacles for prisoners to make such appeals. Legislators have been trying to enact for several years the "Streamlined Procedures Act," which would further restrict appeals from condemned inmates.

While supporters of the due process model may be satisfied with Blackstone's decree that it is "better to let 10 guilty men go free than convict an innocent man," a public that is fearful of crime is unlikely to support proposals that might result in the release of any suspects who are thought to be guilty. Instead, we have to focus on providing a justice system that works as impartially as possible, provides effective counsel for criminal defendants, works quickly to redress the errors that are likely to occur in any human endeavor, and automatically compensates the person who is wrongfully convicted. Such measures would go a long way in restoring the faith and legitimacy of criminal justice systems in the United States.

Notes

1. Effective January 2007, there were innocence projects in every state except Hawaii, North Dakota, and South Dakota.
2. In some jurisdictions, prosecutors are appointed civil servants rather than elected officials, and the assistant district attorneys are usually city or county employees.

Key Terms

cold case
confirmatory bias
Escobedo v. Illinois
exculpatory evidence
Gideon v. Wainwright
House v. Bell

indigent defendants
innocence projects
jailhouse snitch
junk science
Miranda v. Arizona

posttraumatic stress
    disorder (PTSD)
prisonization
third degree

Critical Review Questions

1. How would supporters of the crime control model explain the problem of wrongful convictions?

2. Should a person who has been wrongfully convicted receive compensation for going to prison? If so, who should pay? How much should these people be compensated?

3. Tyler (2006) argued that people are more likely to follow the law if they perceive that it is legitimate and fair. Can you relate Tyler's theory with the problem of wrongful convictions?

4. What are some of the ways by which we might control prosecutorial misconduct?

5. How do television programs such as *CSI* influence our understanding of criminal investigations? Do you think that a potential jury member might be influenced by watching these programs?

6. The U.S. Supreme Court in the *Herrera v. Collins* (1993) decision found that the introduction of new exculpatory evidence was not a sufficient reason for the Court to stop a sentence of death. Do you agree with their position?

7. Jerome Miller (1996), in his book *Search and Destroy*, argued that prosecutors should not be elected but should be civil servants as they are in other nations. What are the advantages and disadvantages of each approach?

8. What are some of the ways by which we could reduce wrongful convictions? Which seem the easiest to implement? Which seem most effective?

References

American Bar Association (ABA). (2004). *Gideon's Broken Promise: America's Continuing Quest for Equal Justice.* Retrieved June 27, 2006 from *http://www.abanet.org/legalservices/sclaid/defender/brokenpromise/fullreport.pdf*.

——. (2005). *Report to the House of Delegates.* Retrieved June 27, 2006 from *http://www.abanet.org/yld/annual05/115A.pdf*.

Berry, Sheila Martin. (2003). *Bad Lawyering: How Defense Attorneys Help Convict the Innocent.* Retrieved June 27, 2006 from: *http://www.truthinjustice.org/Lawyering[1].doc*.

Borchard, Edwin M. (1932). *Convicting the Innocent: Errors of Criminal Justice.* New Haven, CT: Yale University Press.

Bromwich, Michael. (2006). *Fifth Report of the Independent Investigator for the Houston Police Department Crime Laboratory and Property Room.* Retrieved June 27, 2006 from: *http://www.hpdlabinvestigation.org*.

Corwin, Miles (2003). *Homicide Special: A Year With the LAPD's Elite Detective Unit.* New York: Owl Books.

DiFonzo, J. Herbie. (2005). "The crimes of crime labs." *Hofstra Law Review* 34 (1), 1–12.

Drizin, Steven A., and Richard A. Leo. (2004). "The problem of false confessions in the post-DNA world." *North Carolina Law Review* 82 (3), 891–1007.

Drizen, Steven A., and Marissa J. Reich. (2004). "Heeding the lessons of history: The need for mandatory recording of police interrogations to accurately assess the reliability and voluntariness of confessions." *Drake Law Review* 52 (4), 619–646.

Dunahoe, Alexandra W. (2005). "Revisiting the cost-benefit calculus of the misbehaving prosecutor: Deterrence economics and transitory prosecutors." *New York Survey of American Law* 61 (1), 45–110.

Elliot, C. Blaine. (2003) "Life's uncertainties: How to deal with cooperating witnesses and jailhouse snitches." *Capital Defense Journal* 16 (1), 1–17.

Escobedo v. Illinois, 378 U.S. 478 (1964).

Executive Office for U.S. Attorneys. (2006). U.S. Attorney's Annual Statistical Report, 2005. Washington, DC: U.S. Department of Justice.

Fly, Colin. (2005, April 21). "Medical board finds Harlan guilty on 18 misconduct counts." *Columbia Daily Herald.* Retrieved October 11, 2006, from: *http://www.columbiadailyherald.com*.

Forrest, Krista D., Theresa A. Wadkins, and Richard D. Miller. (2002). "The role of preexisting stress on false confessions: An empirical study." *The Journal of Credibility Assessment and Witness Psychology* 3 (1), 23–45.

Freedman, Monroe H. (2002). "Professional discipline of prosecutors: A response to Professor Zacharias." *Hofstra Law Review* 30 (1), 121–127.

George, Sandra C. (2005). "Prosecutorial discretion: What's politics got to do with it?" *Georgetown Journal of Legal Ethics* 18 (3), 739–758.

Gideon v. Wainwright, 372 U.S. 335 (1963).

Goldstein, Jacob P. (2006). "From the exclusionary rule to a constitutional tort for malicious prosecutions." *Columbia Law Review* 106 (3), 643–678.

Gross, Samuel R., Kristen Jacoby, Daniel J. Matheson, Nicholas Montgomery, and Sujata Patel. (2005). "Exonerations in the United States, 1989 through 2003." *Journal of Criminal Law and Criminology* 95 (2), 523–553.

Grounds, Adrian T. (2004). "Understanding the effects of wrongful imprisonment." *Crime and Justice: A Review of Research* 32, 1–58.

Hanson, Roger A., and Brian J. Ostrom. (2004). "Indigent defenders get the job done and done well." Pp. 227–250 in *The Criminal Justice System: Politics and Policies*, edited by George F. Cole, Marc G. Gertz, and Amy Bunger. Belmont, CA: Wadsworth.

Harris, George C. (2000). "Testimony for sale: The law and ethics of snitches and experts." *Pepperdine Law Review* 28 (1), 1–74.

Harrison, Paige M., and Allen J. Beck. (2006). *Prison and Jail Inmates at Midyear, 2005.* Washington, DC: U.S. Department of Justice, Bureau of Justice Statistics.

House v. Bell 547 U.S. ___; (2006).

Huff, C. Ronald. (2002a). "Wrongful conviction and public policy: The American Society of Criminology 2001 Presidential address." *Criminology* 40 (1), 1–18.

———. (2002b, September–October). "What can we learn from other nations about the problem of wrongful convictions?" *Judicature* 86, 91–97.

Huff, C. Ronald, Arye Rattner, and Edward Sagarin. (1996). *Convicted but Innocent: Wrongful Conviction and Public Policy.* Thousand Oaks, CA: Sage.

Innocence Project. (2007). *Police and Prosecutorial Misconduct.* Retrieved January 1, 2007 from: *http://www.innocenceproject.org/causes/policemisconduct.php.*

Johns, Margaret Z. (2005). "Reconsidering absolute prosecutorial immunity." *Brigham Young University Law Review* 2005 (1), 53–149.

Khanna, Roma, and Steve McVicker. (2005, June 1). "Crime lab faked results in 4 cases probe finds." *Houston Chronicle.* Retrieved October 11, 2006, from: *http://www.chicagotribune.com/news/specials/chi-forensics-specialpackage,1,3283040.special?coll=chi-newsspecials-hed.*

McRoberts, Flynn, Steve Mills, and Maurice Possley. (2004, October 17). "Forensics under the microscope: Unproven techniques sway courts, erode justice." *Chicago Tribune.* Retrieved October 11, 2006, from: *http://www.chron.com/disp/story.mpl/special/crimelab/3206130.html.*

McRoberts, Flynn, and Maurice Possley. (2006, March 10). "Judge doubts lip print, Orders retrial in murder. *Chicago Tribune.* Retrieved October 11, 2006 from: *http://*

www.chicagotribune.com/news/specials/chi-0603100181mar10,1,310258 *.story?coll=chi-newsspecials-hed&ctrack=1&cset=true.*

Miller, Jerome. (1996). *Search and Destroy: African-American Males in the Criminal Justice System.* New York: Cambridge University Press.

Miranda v. Arizona, 384 U.S. 436 (1966).

Moushey, Bill, and Bob Martinson. (1998). "Win at all costs." *Pittsburgh Post Gazette.* Retrieved July 20, 2006 from: *http://www.post-gazette.com/win/.*

Olson, Robert K. (2002, July–August). "Miscarriage of justice: A cop's view." *Judicature,* 86 pp. 74–77.

Perry, Steven W. (2006). *Prosecutors in State Courts, 2005.* Washington, DC: U.S. Department of Justice, Bureau of Justice Statistics.

Podlas, Kimberlianne. (2006). "The *CSI* effect: Exposing the media myth." *Fordham Intellectual Property, Media & Entertainment Law Journal* 16 (2), 429–465.

Purcell, Noreen, L. Thomas Winfree, Jr., and G. Larry Mays. (1994). "DNA (deoxyribonucleic acid) evidence and criminal trials: An exploratory survey of factors associated with the use of 'genetic fingerprinting' in felony prosecutions." *Journal of Criminal Justice* 22 (2), 145–157.

Radelet, Michael L., Hugo Bedau, and Constance E. Putnam. (1992). *In Spite of Innocence: Erroneous Convictions in Capital Punishment Cases.* Boston: Northeastern University Press.

Ross, Jeffrey I., and Stephen C. Richards. (2002). *Behind Bars: Surviving Prison.* Indianapolis: Alpha Books.

Scheck, Barry C. (2006). "Barry Scheck lectures on wrongful convictions." *Drake Law Review* 54 (3), 597–620.

Schwartz, Adina. (2005). "A systematic challenge to the reliability and admissibility of firearms and toolmark identification." *Columbia Science and Technology Law* Review 6 (1), 1–42.

Sellers, Laurin. (2004, August 12). "After 22 years in prison, wrongfully convicted Wilton Dedge will be released, possibly today." *Orlando Sentinel,* p. A1.

Sullivan, Thomas P. (2004a, January–February). "Close encounters of the first kind." *Judicature* 87, pp. 166–167, 191.

——. (2004b). "Preventing wrongful convictions—A current report from Illinois." *Drake Law Review* 52 (4), 605–617.

Trott, Stephen S. (1996). "Words of warning for prosecutors using criminals as witnesses." *Hastings Law Journal* 47 (4), 1381–1432.

Turtle, John, Roderick C. Lindsay, and Gary L. Wells. (2005). "Best practice recommendations for eyewitness evidence procedures: New ideas for the oldest way to solve a case." *Canadian Journal of Police and Security Services* 1 (1), 5–18.

Tyler, Tom R. (2006). *Why People Obey the Law.* Princeton, NJ: Princeton University Press.

Tyler, Tom R., and Yuen J. Huo. (2002). *Trust in the Law.* Retrieved June 27, 2006, from *http:/ /www.psych.nyu.edu/tyler/lab/trust-in-the-law-abstract.doc.*

Warden, Rob. (2005). *The Snitch System.* Retrieved June 27, 2006 from *http://www.law .northwestern.edu/wrongfulconvictions/documents/SnitchSystemBooklet.pdf.*

Weinberg, Steve. (2003). *Playing by the Rules: Even When a Prosecutor Tries to Do Everything Right, the Wrong Person May Still Be Convicted.* Retrieved June 27, 2006 from: *http://www.publicintegrity.org/pm/default.aspx?sID=sidebarsa&aID=30.*

Witt, April. (2001, June 3). "Allegations of abuses mar murder cases." *Washington Post,* p. A01.

Yaroshefsky, Ellen. (2002). "The cooperating witness conundrum: Is justice obtainable?" *Cardozo Law Review* 23 (3), 747–758.

Recommended Readings

Drizin, Steven A., and Richard A. Leo. (2004). "The problem of false confessions in the post-DNA world." *North Carolina Law Review* 82 (3), 891–1007. This article examines the problem of false confessions, and the authors present research that persons who are mentally ill, juveniles, and children are at highest risk of making a false confession. Moreover, they find that once a false confession is made, juries convict 81 percent of these defendants.

Huff, Ronald, Arye Rattner, and Edward Sagarin. (1996). *Convicted But Innocent: Wrongful Conviction and Public Policy.* Thousand Oaks, CA: Sage. This classic work provides an overview of the problems of wrongful conviction. It highlights the survey that Huff and colleagues conducted on criminal justice officials about the prevalence of wrongful conviction.

Scheck, Barry, Peter Neufeld, and Jim Dwyer. (2000). *Actual Innocence: Five Days to Execution and Other Dispatches From the Wrongfully Convicted.* New York: Doubleday. This book follows the lives of a number of persons who were wrongfully convicted, the circumstances that led to their convictions, and how they were ultimately exonerated. ✦

Chapter 10

What Are the Alternatives?

Introduction

We are locking up more offenders and for longer periods of time. If there are practical limits to the number of persons that we can imprison (such as state budgets), can we keep offenders in the community, and does this, or how does this, affect public safety? For instance, voters in California overwhelmingly supported the **diversion** of nonviolent drug offenders from jail or prison to community-based programs, and other states have adopted similar programs in recent years. But what do we do with more serious offenders? Furthermore, are we doing a good job supervising the probationary sentences of minor offenders?

At yearend 2005, over 4.1 million people in the United States were on probation, and 50 percent of these were felons (Glaze and Bonczar 2006). Of these probationers, at least 19 percent had been charged with violent offenses. Many citizens have criticized the way that community sentences are supervised because many probationers commit crimes, do not abide by their conditions of probation, or simply disappear (Manhattan Institute 1999). How can we make probationers take their sentences seriously?

Some jurisdictions are responding to special needs probationers by developing specialized or problem-solving courts that have a rehabilitative orientation. Starting in the late 1980s, specialized courts were developed to handle challenging offenders or specific crimes. Some examples include drug, gun, or mental health courts. Intended primarily for nonviolent misdemeanor defendants, these courts typically are characterized by a specialized docket, one judge who hears all such matters, and a diversionary orientation (Boothroyd et al. 2003). These courts use the criminal justice system's coercive power to increase the likelihood that persons with drug problems or mental illness will comply with their treatment conditions (Griffin, Steadman, and Petrila 2002).

We have also gotten tough with probationers; and since the 1980s, we have developed **intermediate sanctions** that straddle the gap between ordinary probation and jail or prison. Intermediate sanctions include boot camps, day reporting centers, electronic monitoring or house arrest, and intensive supervised probation. Each of these approaches has placed more accountability on offenders, enhanced levels of community supervision, and provided community-based alternatives to serious or repeat offenders who would otherwise go to jail or prison.

Like other criminal justice interventions reported throughout this book, intermediate sanctions have led to several unanticipated outcomes. For instance, boot camps seem to have been a short-term fad, and publicly operated adult camps are almost extinct (Parent 2003). By contrast, some critics have suggested that offenders placed in intensive supervised probation are the same persons who would have been placed on regular probation in earlier times and that we really have not reduced jail or prison incarceration as much as we intended (Petersilia 1998).

Another challenge also faces American communities: Each year, 630,000 prison inmates return to the community. Some of these persons have served their entire sentence, and we have no control over their behavior. Other inmates are paroled. Jeremy Travis (2005) observed that the **Iron Law of Incarceration** dictates that with the exception of a small percentage of inmates who will die in prison, the other 98 percent will be released to the community. In some places, parolees have a poor record of community success, and many new prison admissions are for **technical violations** of parole, such as failing to report to the parole officer, violating curfew, or using alcohol or drugs. Other parolees are involved in serious or violent offenses, and this creates considerable public safety concerns. The challenge of parole is twofold: We do not adequately prepare prison inmates for release, and we do not provide enough community support for them.

Overall, community programs for probationers and parolees encounter significant challenges. While there is widespread agreement that we need to do more for these offenders, there is less agreement on who will pay for the rehabilitative or vocational programs that these people require. Nevertheless, there is also considerable optimism that investing in these interventions will pay significant public safety dividends.

Specialized Courts

Courts always have had to deal with special needs offenders who pose challenges for local justice systems.[1] Starting in the late 1980s, several courts were established that handled just one type of offender. The rationale behind this approach was that members of the courtroom work group would become experts in dealing with these defendants, including understanding their special needs and community resources. Drug and mental health courts were the first specialized courts, and they are also known as **problem-solving courts** (Huddleston et al. 2005).

Over time, other specialized courts emerged in different jurisdictions to deal with gamblers or the homeless and specific offenses such as child support, domestic violence, driving while intoxicated, and prostitution. In addition, some Indian tribes have established Tribal Healing or

Wellness Courts that rely upon principles of **restorative justice.** Such courts focus on the impact of the offense on the victims and repairing the victim-offender relationship. Some 2,558 problem-solving courts existed within the United States at the end of December 2004, and the vast majority of these were drug courts (Huddleston et al. 2005).

In addition to working with a narrowly-defined group of offenders or offenses, specialized courts blend treatment and the court's coercive power to ensure that offenders comply with their probation conditions. The goal is to craft interventions for an offender that reduce the likelihood of relapse (in the case of drug or alcohol use) or recidivism. Shaffer (2004, 988) described the limitations with traditional courts: "It is pointless and an inefficient use of resources to simply send addicts, the mentally ill, and others with ongoing behavioral issues through a revolving door of incarceration and release."

Probationers typically are required to make frequent court appearances so that judges can monitor compliance with probation conditions. Offenders have a powerful incentive to participate as these courts can arrange to erase or expunge conviction records if they successfully complete the treatment requirements. A cornerstone of specialized courts is the coordinated nature of services and a unified or consistent message from the participating agencies that participants will be held accountable.

Research generally has provided positive support for domestic violence (Gover, MacDonald, and Alpert 2003), drug (Gottfredson, Najaka, and Kearley 2003), and mental health courts (Boothroyd et al. 2003). While specialized courts have demonstrated some success, there appear to be some cautions. First, the success of these programs, such as mental health courts, rests on community resource availability (Weisman, Lamberti, and Price 2004) and probation or court staff ability to monitor the defendant's progress. Second, legal scholars have criticized the lack of due process protections for defendants in these courts. Clarke and Neuhard (2004, 29) outlined several concerns about problem-solving courts, including the possibility of **net widening,** where defendants who might have received ordinary probation are now subject to additional interventions that might last a year or longer if they are participating in a specialized court.

Attorneys, activists, and scholars who are concerned with the due process protections of offenders are approaching specialized courts with a mixture of optimism and skepticism because they fear both net widening and the erosion of offenders' rights. While these offenders receive treatment, some critics have argued that this treatment is coerced and question whether it would have the same impact as voluntary treatment. It is unlikely that the supporters of the crime control approach would share the same concerns about coerced treatment, as many people engaged in addictive behaviors, for instance, might not otherwise participate.

As the number of problem-solving courts expands, there is a possibility that their rehabilitative philosophy might be co-opted. In some cases, criminal justice programs or interventions lose their rehabilitative focus and become more punitive, and a notable example is the juvenile court—a topic we address more comprehensively in Chapter 13. Nolan (2003, 1563) observed, "As with the formerly dominant rehabilitative ideal, the distinction between punishment and treatment withers away." Consequently, despite the tentative empirical support for the effectiveness of specialized courts, the long-term effectiveness of these interventions remains unknown.

Drug Diversion Programs

One consequence of the increased drug offender population in U.S. jails and prisons has been an interest in programs that divert drug offenders if they participate in treatment. This community-based approach responds to several significant challenges. First, approximately 20 percent of all state prison inmates are incarcerated on drug-related offenses (Bureau of Justice Statistics 2007), while 53.7 percent of all federal prisoners were drug offenders in November 2006 (Federal Bureau of Prisons 2007). Furthermore, approximately one-quarter of all sentenced jail inmates were held on drug possession or trafficking crimes. Last, Glaze and Palla (2005) reported that 26 percent of probationers in 2004 were convicted of drug law violations.

The number of persons under some form of correctional supervision for drug offenses is significant. Extrapolating the total jail and prison population from the statistics above, we estimate that approximately 561,366 Americans are incarcerated on drug-related offenses in jails or prisons, with another million on probation. The problem is that many of these offenders do not get any treatment. As we reported in Chapter 6, a recent Bureau of Justice Statistics study by Christopher Mumola and Jennifer Karberg (2006) found that only 15 percent of state prisoners and 17 percent of federal inmates had received drug treatment since their prison admission (although percentages were higher for 'other' addictions related programs). Ironically, about the same percentage of jail inmates will receive some form of alcohol or drug treatment. In her national study of jail inmates, James (2004, 1) reported that 15 percent received some type of treatment.

Many policymakers have challenged the wisdom of imprisoning so many drug offenders and then providing hardly any treatment opportunities. One alternative is to divert drug offenders from jail or prison and place them in community-based treatment programs that address their addiction problems. Many jurisdictions support these interventions as community-based treatment is considerably cheaper than institutional correctional treatment, and it allows probationers to continue working or attending school.

Perhaps one of the largest diversionary programs for drug offenders was created after the **Proposition 36** ballot initiative in California's

2000 state election (otherwise known as the Substance Abuse and Crime Prevention Act). Passed by 61 percent of the voters, Proposition 36 gives nonviolent offenders convicted of drug offenses the option of community-based treatment rather than incarceration. Appel, Backes, and Robbins (2004, 586) noted how similar programs were enacted in Hawaii (2002), Kansas (2003), Texas (2003), and Maryland (2004), and this approach has been proposed in other places as well.

While the introduction of community-based drug programs in California were not as smooth or problem-free as anticipated, the program has been successful. An evaluation done by Farabee and colleagues (2004) revealed that arrests were down for offenders who participated in the program. A 2005 analysis of Proposition 36 showed a significant cost savings (in reduced prison placements) as the outpatient drug treatment cost in 2004 was $3,333 compared with $30,929 to house a California prison inmate (Longshore et al. 2005). Moreover, this study revealed that participants had higher success rates than drug court offenders, demonstrating the intervention's effectiveness.

An analysis of the participants' characteristics reveals the challenges confronting these programs. When thinking of diversionary programs, we assume that populations are young marijuana users. However, of the referrals for treatment, the primary group consisted of methamphetamine users who were in their mid-30s and had used that drug for 11 years (Longshore et al. 2005). Long-term users have high treatment needs, but these methamphetamine users demonstrated greater success than other drug offenders (Longshore et. al. 2005).

Appel, Backes, and Robbins (2004) outlined some problems with the implementation of Proposition 36, including the fact that we do not have much knowledge about what actually occurs in the treatment programs, how they operate, and the lack of permanent funding for drug treatment programs. By contrast, practitioners are concerned that parolees are eligible to participate and that officers are unable to incarcerate participants until they have twice violated their drug treatment conditions. Regardless of the implementation problems, some 34,000 persons were referred for treatment the first year, and referrals have increased. The fact that California's Proposition 36 has demonstrated cost-savings and treatment effectiveness will undoubtedly inspire programs in other states.

Intermediate Sanctions

Critics suggest that we have trouble adequately supervising the probationers already living in the community (Manhattan Institute 1999). Intermediate sanctions attempt to bridge the gap between jail or prison and regular probation and make probation stricter. Several approaches were introduced since the 1980s to increase community supervision levels, including intensive supervised probation, home arrest (typically coupled with electronic monitoring, or EM), day reporting centers, and boot camps. These programs provide more formal control or supervision, but some have questioned whether these interventions had the desired results in reduced recidivism and increased long-term public safety (Petersilia 1998).

Probation has undergone a profound transformation in recent decades. Historically, probation officers were trained in social work, and their role was to help probationers. Over time, however, the philosophy of most probation departments shifted from rehabilitation to public safety or risk management. Miller (1996, 128) outlined how probation "has deteriorated to the point where the average probation officer is indistinguishable from a policeman." Perhaps Miller is correct: Probation officers in some jurisdictions wear body armor, they are armed (Fuller 2002) and many closely coordinate their activities with the police. It may be difficult for probationers to understand how an armed probation officer wearing a flak jacket standing at their front door is supposed to help them. In contrast, some probationers may be more likely to abide by the conditions of their probation when confronted by these tough interventions.

One way that probation departments "ratcheted up" levels of control and supervision for offenders was to develop specialized caseloads that enabled officers to closely supervise probationers. A higher level of supervision and control is the cornerstone of **intensive supervised probation (ISP).** A probation officer might supervise several hundred offenders on a generalized caseload. ISP caseloads, by contrast, are characterized by their smaller size, and a single officer might supervise only 25 to 50 offenders. Some examples of specialized caseloads associated with ISP include instances of domestic violence and sex offenses.

A cornerstone of probation is that the offender has to comply with a number of conditions to remain in the community. Standard conditions generally include the need to report to the probation officer or court when requested, to keep the peace and be of good behavior, and refrain from drug or alcohol use (or being in places where alcohol is sold). Other special conditions include restrictions on associates (for example, gang members or co-accused), the offender's place of residence, or curfews. Some offenders are ordered to make restitution to victims to repay the damages or losses. In addition, a number of probationers are required to attend specialized rehabilitative or treatment programs. Some scholars suggest that the level of compliance with probation conditions is low (Manhattan Institute 1999). As a result, when these probationers are closely monitored, rates of technical violations or arrests are high (Miller 1996).

Research about ISP programs reveals that these programs do not guarantee lower recidivism rates, but participants are more likely to engage in counseling and find employment (MacKenzie and Brame 2001). It is speculated that formal coercion may force probationers to engage in prosocial activities, and these positive activities reduce recidivism. However, without appropriate support levels, probationers are more likely to fail. A further dilemma for policymakers is whether officers should closely monitor probationers knowing that some will thrive and others will be jailed.

Other intermediate sanctions closely akin to ISP are electronic monitoring (EM) and house arrest programs. Often these sanctions are coupled. Probationers sentenced to house arrest must stay at home, unless attending school or working. Furthermore, electronic monitoring programs are intended to keep offenders in the community who would otherwise go to jail or prison. These probationers wear a device that transmits a signal to a monitoring center if they stray too far from a base (generally a device attached to their home phone). In many cases, the probationer attends school or works while in EM programs.

Probationers typically pay monitoring costs, approximately $15 per day. Obviously, the poor and homeless normally do not get to participate in EM programs. Another challenge is that while we know probationers are at home, we do not have much control over their activities: Home arrestees could be selling drugs out their front door. Moreover, if offenders have permission to leave home, we do not know their whereabouts. As a result, newly designed EM devices enable monitoring staff to locate the probationer using global positioning satellite (GPS) technology.

Most research about these programs reveals that participants are more successful if they receive some form of treatment. Finn and Muirhead-Steves (2002) conducted a study of parolees participating in EM programs and found that high-risk offenders, and in particular sex offenders, were more successful than lower-risk offenders, although a consistent predicator of failure was inmates with serious drug problems.

A recent comprehensive study of over 75,000 offenders on EM programs in Florida produced some noteworthy findings. First, these offenders were less likely to re-offend, abscond, or have a technical violation (Padgett, Bales, and Blomberg, 2006). The second finding was that most of these offenders were serious offenders (over one-third were violent offenders), and most would not have been placed on "normal" probation. This finding refutes the position that EM leads to an expansion in social control, something that we call net widening. People who believe in net widening would argue that if EM did not exist, many of these offenders would have been placed on regular probation.

One challenge to probation departments, and particularly to ISP and EM, is that some participants have no meaningful activities to occupy their time. Some large jurisdictions have established **day reporting centers (DRCs)** that offer probationers vocational, educational, and life-skills programs during the day.[2] This approach is intended to enhance public safety by providing high levels of daytime supervision combined with rehabilitative opportunities. These centers were first introduced in the 1980s, and they were based on British programs that offered DRCs as alternatives to prison.

Day reporting programs are intended for chronic, nonviolent, and drug offenders. In some places, such as Illinois, day reporting centers are also used for parolees (see La Vigne et al. 2003). Brunet (2002, 138–139) offered three reasons for implementing DRCs: (1) intensive surveillance will deter criminal behavior, (2) rehabilitative services will prevent offender recidivism, and (3) intermediate sanctions are a cost-effective alternative to incarceration. Most DRCs provide high supervision levels, and participants generally have to abide by curfews, are subject to drug tests, and have frequent (even daily) contact with their probation officers.

Parent and colleagues (1995) estimated the total number of DRCs within the United States at 114 operations. Results of studies that evaluated the success of these programs are mixed. Marciniak (1999) reported high failure rates (in the range of two-thirds) but speculated that one reason for these failures was that inappropriate (for example, high-risk) candidates were referred to the programs. Brunet (2002, 151) reported that prior empirical studies showed high-success rates for DRCs, but he found that only 18 percent and 36 percent of offenders completed DRC programs at two North Carolina facilities.

Similar to other criminal justice services, the interventions offered within a program, the leadership or staff involved in the operation, and the resources directed into the agency seem to have a significant impact upon effectiveness. Few programs are evaluated, and this can create significant problems, as anecdotal accounts of "what works" might be considerably different than research that examines the short- and long-term success of different programs and the characteristics of offenders who succeed or fail. One difficulty with DRCs is that relatively few are operational, and there are a variety of different approaches, which makes comparisons difficult. There seems to be little academic interest in DRCs, unlike another alternative to incarceration, the boot camp.

Boot camps (also known as **shock incarceration**) emerged as intermediate correctional programs in Oklahoma and Georgia in the early 1980s (MacKenzie 1993; Wright and Mays 1998). The first boot camps were modeled on military training and emphasized drill, strict rules, and physically demanding challenges that occupied the participants from dawn to dusk. Boot camps were enthusiastically received by policymakers and the public, especially given television images of tough drill instructors whose uncompromising expectations were reinforced with yelling and screaming (Simon 1995). Typically, candidates were young, male, first-time drug- or property-offenders who were sentenced to short terms in a boot camp—generally 10–16 weeks followed by a period of community supervision on probation—rather than longer jail or prison sentences. Boot camp administrators generally screened their candidates, and participation in these programs was voluntary.

Like their military counterparts, boot camp participants normally live in dormitory settings with little privacy. Often these programs start with intense military drill and physical activities for the first weeks. There are many restrictions placed on these inmates at the program outset, but they can earn more privileges, such as access to telephone calls, television, or family visits, if their behavior meets the expectations of the staff. The concept of boot camps was very popular, and they quickly expanded in many jurisdictions; they also were used with both juvenile and adult populations. These programs were not without controversy. Excessive physical activity and poor staff supervision in several camps contributed to some inmate deaths. In addition, women in some jurisdictions sued so that they could participate in their own boot camps, giving them also the opportunity to reduce their sentences.

However, perhaps the biggest problem with these sanctions is that they did not seem to be effective. While not declaring boot camps an outright failure, current research has demonstrated that these operations typically do not reduce jail (or prison) populations, save taxpayers money, or reduce recidivism (Parent 2003). By contrast, jurisdictions that invested heavily in **aftercare**—rehabilitative services provided to participants once they are discharged—tended to have lower rates of recidivism.

Today's boot camps offer inmates stronger rehabilitative components, including substance abuse treatment, educational or vocational programs, and comprehensive aftercare services. However, a recent census of federal and state prison facilities revealed that only 95 adult boot camps existed, 84 that were confinement-based, and 11 that were community-based (Stephan and Karberg 2003). Consequently, like other fads described throughout this book, boot camps largely have been a "flash in the pan" in terms of correctional programs. Despite the fact that boot camp programs failed to live up to their initial expectations, they persist. Nevertheless, research demonstrates that inmates who successfully complete shock incarceration generally feel positive about the experience (Styve et al. 2000). Yet, these studies rarely examine those who drop out of boot camps and end up serving the balance of their sentence in jail or prison.

Community-Based Jail Programs

Harrison and Beck (2006, 1) reported 819,434 jail inmates as of midyear 2005, although 8.7 percent of these offenders, or some 71,905 persons, were serving their sentences in the community. Because jail populations have grown so much, different jurisdictions have developed alternatives to reduce overcrowding and save money.[3] Harrison and Beck (2006, 7) noted that the population of jail offenders in the community increased by 100 percent between 1995 and 2005, and Table 10.1 shows the most common programs.

Table 10.1
Jail Inmates Supervised Outside the Facility, 2005

Weekender programs	19.6%
Electronic monitoring	15.9%
Home detention	2.1%
Day reporting	6.6%
Community service	21.6%
Pretrial supervision	21.5%
Other work programs	8.1%
Treatment programs	2.7%
Other	2.0%

Source: Harrison and Beck (2006).

Of these groups, one of the largest is pretrial supervision. These programs reduce jail overcrowding by releasing detainees who have positive social supports and are likely to show for their court dates. Jail employees working in these units gather information about defendants (including criminal history information from other jurisdictions) and determine whether there are family or community resources not considered by the judge (such as a stable residence). A foundation of most pretrial programs is that objective risk assessments are undertaken to determine whether the defendant is a good candidate for release.

One alternative sentencing option is the **weekender** or intermittent jail program. Designed for offenders who work or go to school during the week, these programs incarcerate offenders during the weekends, typically admitting inmates Friday afternoons and releasing them Monday mornings—until their sentences are complete. These programs are popular with inmates, but they pose challenges for jails because of the frequent admissions and discharges and the difficulty of placing these inmates in appropriate housing units each weekend. Weekender incarceration is an example of a "win-win" approach, where offenders keep their jobs and are held accountable for their behavior.

In some cases, weekender programs are targeted at specific offenses, such as driving under the influence (DUI). Glaze and Bonczar (2006) observed that about 15 percent of all persons on probation were sentenced for drinking and driving. Many jurisdictions have created weekend intervention programs where DUI offenders are required to participate in an intensive educational program that provides information about drinking, alcohol abuse, and the hazards of DUI. These interventions can occur within a jail setting or in the community. Such interventions target the core problem of alcohol abuse and are intended to reduce the demands on the local jail.

Some sheriff's departments offer community service programs, where unemployed inmates spend the day doing community service (such as road maintenance, county chores, or collecting litter) and go home every evening. These programs operate much like a DRC, but they lack a rehabilitative component. Inmates who do require comprehensive treatment may be given a **furlough** (also known as a temporary release) from the jail to participate in residential drug or alcohol treatment.

Jails have responded to the challenge of overcrowding or handling special needs inmates by developing alternatives to incarceration. These programs are often operated out of necessity, the alternative being a costly jail expansion.[4] Another significant challenge confronting law enforcement is the release of prison inmates into the community. Each year, approximately 630,000 offenders are released from federal or state prisons into the community. The following pages outline the problems that some parolees face and interventions that try to reduce their recidivism rates.

Parole

In 2006, California's average prison sentence was 46.7 months, and the average time served before release on parole was 24.1 months (California Department of Corrections and Rehabilitation 2007). This figure closely approximates the national average: Durose and Langan (2004) estimated that state prisoners released in 2002 served about 51 percent of their sentences (serving slightly less than 30 months if sentenced to the mean maximum sentence of 58 months). The fact that offenders are released before serving their entire prison term is distressing to advocates of the crime control model. Many believe that offenders should serve every day of their sentence, and this belief has become more popular since the U.S. Government ended parole for federal prisoners in 1984 with the Sentencing Reform Act (U.S. Sentencing Commission 2004).

Paroling offenders to the community gives correctional authorities a certain amount of control over inmates while they are in prison and after they are released to the community. Earning parole gives prison inmates a positive goal to work toward, and correctional officers have more control over the inmates' behavior, as good conduct will earn them an earlier release. Once in the community, parole increases the ability of the police and parole officers to supervise offenders. By contrast, when prisoners are released with no time remaining on their sentences, we have no ability to supervise their community conduct.

A parolee's terms or conditions of parole typically outline where the parolee lives, works, and is allowed to move about (in some cases, offenders have curfews or are restricted from being in certain places, such as taverns). Moreover, parolees are expected to observe several conditions, such as abstinence from alcohol or drugs, the people with whom they associate, and weapons possession. Parole officers can strictly enforce these conditions as parolees have no expectation of Fourth Amendment protections in regard to searches. If parolees violate the conditions of their parole (also called a technical violation) or commit a crime while on parole, the parole officer has the option of placing them in jail until a hearing is held.

Therefore, one of parole's strengths is that it increases formal control while offenders reenter society. This is a difficult time, given that many long-term prisoners suffer from **institutionalization** or **prisonization.** They have become so conditioned to the prison's formal and informal rules that they find it difficult to reenter society. Moreover, the skills that inmates develop to survive a prison term often do not translate successfully into the community upon release. The fact that some prisoners would rather serve every day of their sentence prior to release, because they view it too difficult to succeed on parole, speaks volumes about the temptations that offenders face.

One weakness of the parole system is that we have done a notoriously poor job of preparing prisoners for the transition back to the community. We often discharge inmates to the community with little more than a bus ticket and several hundred dollars (or less) to reestablish their lives. If offenders have a place to stay, a job to keep them busy, and a positive support mechanism at home, they are more likely to succeed. But this is seldom the case. Most often, offenders return to the same neighborhoods, the same peers with whom they associated prior to their incarceration, and a lack of legitimate opportunities. Many of these offenders become trapped in the same destructive behaviors and relationships that led them to prison in the first place. To make this clear, Langan and Levin (2002) provided these dismal statistics: 67.5 percent of inmates released from state prisons in 1994 were rearrested within three years.

There is increasing interest in prisoner reentry and the difficulties that inmates face. Even something as simple as having credentials upon release—such as a Social Security card or government identification, current driver's license, and bank card—can increase successful community reentry. In recognition of these challenges, President Bush in his State of the Union address (2004) said

> Tonight I ask you to consider another group of Americans in need of help. This year, some 600,000 inmates will be released from prison back into society. We know from long experience that if they can't find work, or a home, or help, they are much more likely to commit crime and return to prison. . . . America is the land of the second chance, and when the gates of the prison open, the path ahead should lead to a better life.

Supporters of both the crime control and the due process philosophies actively support, at least in theory, better methods of prisoner reentry.

Crime control model advocates value public safety, and there is an intuitive appeal to the notion that one's community will be safer if ex-prisoners have a smooth transition from prison and are given enough resources so that they do not engage in illicit activities to finance their reentry. By contrast, supporters of the due process perspective are generally in agreement that planned transitions from prison to the community provide a better outcome for ex-inmates, their families, and the community. While everybody seems to support smooth prisoner reentry, there is seldom enough funding for programs that provide vocational opportunities, social skills development, and subsidized housing. Although such interventions are not cheap, they represent a fraction of incarceration costs; and if they prevent parolees from committing crimes, they are a good investment in public safety.

Not all community reentry programs, however, are successful. Wilson and Davis (2006) outlined how participants in a prison-based prerelease program in New York State, called "Greenlight," fared worse than inmates who were assigned to normal parole. This intervention was criticized because it promised much but delivered little, and the policymakers who designed and implemented the program failed to fully understand offender motivation and behaviors. Marlowe (2006, 344) observed that "[m]ost offenders are characteristically irresponsible and have considerable difficulty satisfying basic obligations. It defies logic to expect that increasing the dosage of ineffective treatments would improve their outcomes."

Examining the same study, Rhine, Mawhorr, and Parks (2006) suggested that this reentry program failed because of a disconnect between the type of program that was supposed to be delivered and what actually occurred. Again, we return to the problem of program design, implementation, and follow-up; and we have to acknowledge that sometimes even the best plans go awry when they are confronted with the people who have to deliver the program and the actual participants (in this case, offenders).

One alternative to releasing prisoners directly into unsupervised settings is community-based residential programs. These programs go by different labels, including halfway houses, community residential facilities, residential treatment centers, or community-based correctional facilities. Consistent with DRCs, these facilities are community-based and offer educational, life-skills, or vocational programming, as well as a 24-hour residential component. Such programs are seen as bridges to the community, and they provide supportive environments for inmates' transition back to society.

A recent study reported that higher-risk parolees may have the most success in community-based facilities. Lowenkamp and Latessa (2005, 284) found that "almost 70 percent of the programs demonstrated effectiveness with moderate- and high-risk offenders" and that "low-risk offenders should be excluded, as a general rule, from residential programs." In addition to tailoring interventions based on risk, other demographic characteristics should be examined, including age and gender. The National Institute of Justice (2005) found that prisoner reentry programs that work well with men are not necessarily effective with women. Moreover, Lowenkamp and Latessa (2005) found that intervention programs that were intended for young, first-time offenders actually were more successful with older offenders.

These findings illustrate the importance of using evidence-based correctional interventions. MacKenzie (2005, 249) observed that "many policy makers and correctional administrators follow the latest fad or what feels appropriate in their guts." Unfortunately, correctional administrators sometimes implement programs without evaluating their effectiveness, relying instead on anecdotal accounts of success. Petersilia (2005) observed how comprehensive evaluations have been conducted on fewer than two dozen reentry programs, despite the fact that thousands have been operating for decades. Thus, in order to develop better probationary or reentry programs, we need to know "what works" and "what works best" with different offender populations.

Conclusions

There is a practical limit to how many people we can imprison. In the United States, we already incarcerate more inmates than any other nation, and incarceration rates are five or six times greater than in other first-world democratic nations (Ruddell and Fearn 2005). Many jurisdictions cannot afford to maintain mass imprisonment policies. We already supervise almost 5 million offenders in the community, but in many cases we do a poor job. We spent an average of $22,650 to imprison offenders in 2001, but we released them to the community with few resources, little preparation, and our best hope that they would not get in trouble. Moreover, current budget crises have reduced staffing of prison-based vocational or rehabilitative programs (Wilhelm and Turner 2002).

Some community-based correctional programs are fads: A jurisdiction develops an intervention that seems to be effective, and the program is copied elsewhere. In many cases, there is no theoretical foundation for the intervention, and evaluations are seldom undertaken; a program seems to work, and other places adopt it. These programs eventually draw the attention of scholars, a series of articles is written about the intervention, and eventually evaluations are conducted. By the time that these evaluations are finished, programs are sometimes found to be ineffective or fail to produce the desired results. In the meantime, jurisdictions have invested time, energy, and funding in ineffective approaches, and promising programs slowly disappear as enthusiasm wanes.

It is plausible that in some cases, programs fail because the initial elements were not copied correctly or success may be linked to political support, inspired leadership, funding, or even the presence of community agencies and stakeholders that supported the intervention. Goldkamp (2003, 200) observed that sustainability of interventions depends heavily on funding, leadership, and enthusiasm. Perhaps local community characteristics are also responsible for successes that cannot be replicated in other places.

Clearly we need more effective community correctional interventions, although policymakers have been reluctant to fund such approaches, often preferring to spend on prison expansion. A review of the literature indicates a number of shortfalls with existing community corrections. First, specialized courts and probation programs require strong community-based resources to support probationers. Second, there is a need for integrated prison-community programs for inmates to increase their parole success. Treatment should start in prison and extend into the community (Little Hoover Commission 2003). Third, community-based interventions for probationers and parolees must be integrated through the efforts of the police, courts, and corrections as well as community stakeholders. Fourth, interventions must be based on what the research demonstrates about the effectiveness of a particular program, rather than fads. Last, we should dismantle legal barriers to community reintegration.

There are a number of obstacles faced by ex-prisoners or persons with criminal records that make it more difficult for them to return to society or pursue legitimate opportunities. The label of **collateral consequences** has been applied to laws or policies that make it more difficult for ex-inmates or convicted felons to restore their lives (Mauer and Chesney-Lind 2002). Collateral consequences are intended to deter potential criminals from engaging in crime, but some scholars observe that they also restrict some ex-offenders' ability to pursue legitimate opportunities (National Center for Institutions and Alternatives 2000). Some collateral consequences make perfect sense, such as making sex offenders ineligible to work with children, but employers in 37 states can deny jobs to persons who were arrested for an offense but were never convicted (Legal Action Center 2004). Additional restrictions place barriers to employment on service occupations, such as barbers and hairdressers, professions that hardly represent a significant public risk. Harris and Keller (2005) outline how ex-offenders' criminal records already pose a considerable barrier to employment.

Reducing these barriers to community reintegration, when consistent with public safety, seems an important step in enhancing the likelihood of successfully obtaining jobs, accessing school, and securing short-term housing (through welfare programs). There has been significant interest in community reentry, not only from the liberals who have advocated increased rehabilitation but also from conservatives who understand that failure in the community means increased crime. Petersilia (2005, 8) observed that we need to take advantage of this current support for community corrections, because "crime policy is a fickle business and today's interest in re-entry will likely be replaced in a few years by another corrections hot topic."

Notes

1. The first specialized court was the juvenile court, first established in Cook County, Illinois, in 1899. There are also many teen courts within the United States and some truancy courts, although here we focus on adult courts.

2. In some jurisdictions, DRCs are also available for pretrial release defendants, and the programs might be run in conjunction with a DRC for probationers. In either case, the goal is to reduce demand on institutional corrections, either jails or prisons.

3. Jail incarceration rates have increased from 100 inmates per 100,000 residents in the population in 1983 to 252 inmates in 2005.

4. The unfortunate reality of correctional administration is that once a jurisdiction increases its capacity, those beds are almost immediately filled, and some have observed "If you build it, they will come."

Key Terms

aftercare
collateral consequences
day reporting centers (DRC)
diversion
furlough
institutionalization

intensive supervised probation (ISP)
intermediate sanctions
Iron Law of Incarceration
net widening
prisonization

problem-solving courts
Proposition 36
restorative justice
shock incarceration
technical violations
weekender (incarceration programs)

Critical Review Questions

1. You are given the task of reducing your state's correctional population by 10 percent by diverting offenders away from prison or releasing prison inmates to parole. What approach would you take? Provide a rationale for your choice. What community services would help your offenders?

2. Provide examples of "fads" in the field of criminal justice, including corrections. Why do justice systems seem prone to fads?

3. What is net widening? How does this relate to intermediate sanctions, such as electronic monitoring?

4. How do voluntary and coerced forms of treatment differ? Are there offenders for whom coerced treatment might be more successful?

5. Provide some reasons why boot camps failed to decrease recidivism, reduce jail or prison populations, or save taxpayer dollars.

6. Petersilia (1998) argued that intermediate sanctions have had a more symbolic than substantive impact. Is it important for justice systems to have symbolic success?

7. Provide examples of collateral consequences. Some of these consequences are controversial. For example, how does restricting an ex-felon from voting enhance public safety?

References

Appel, Judith, Glenn Backes, and Jeremy Robbins. (2004). "California's Proposition 36: A success ripe for refinement and replication." *Criminology & Public Policy* 3 (4), 585–592.

Boothroyd, Roger A., Norman G. Poythress, Annette McGaha, and John Petrila. (2003). "The Broward Mental Health Court: Process, outcomes, and service utilization." *International Journal of Law and Psychiatry* 26 (1), 55–71.

Brunet, James R. (2002). "Day reporting centers in North Carolina: Implementation lessons for policymakers." *Justice System Journal* 23 (2), 135–156.

Bureau of Justice Statistics. (2007). *Prison Statistics.* Retrieved January 1, 2007 from: *http://www.ojp.usdoj.gov/bjs/prisons.htm.*

Bush, George W. (2004). "State of the Union Address." Retrieved July 11, 2006 from: *http://www.whitehouse.gov/news/releases/2004/01/20040120-7.html.*

California Department of Corrections and Rehabilitation. (2005). *Prison Census Data as of December 31, 2004.* Sacramento: Author.

——. (2007). *Second Quarter 2006 Facts and Figures.* Retrieved January 1, 2007 from: *http://www.cya.ca.gov/DivisionBoards/AOAP/FactsFigures.html.*

Clarke, Cait, and James Neuhard. (2004). "Who's in control as problem solving and client-centered sentencing take center stage?" *New York University Review of Law & Social Change* 29 (1), 11–56.

Durose, Matthew R., and Patrick A. Langan. (2004). *Felony Sentences in State Courts, 2002.* Washington, DC: U.S. Department of Justice, Bureau of Justice Statistics.

Farabee, David, Yih-Ing Hser, M. Douglas Anglin, and David Huang. (2004). "Recidivism among an early cohort of California's Proposition 36 offenders." *Criminology & Public Policy* 3 (4), 563–584.

Federal Bureau of Prisons. (2007). *Quick Facts.* Retrieved January 1, 2007 from: *http://www.bop.gov/about/facts.jsp.*

Finn, Mary A., and Suzanne Muirhead-Steves. (2002). "The effectiveness of electronic monitoring with violent male parolees." *Justice Quarterly* 19 (2), 293–312.

Fuller, Karen. (2002). *American Probation and Parole Association's Adult and Juvenile Probation and Parole National Firearms Survey, 2001–2002.* Lexington, KY: American Probation and Parole Association.

Glaze, Lauren E., and Thomas P. Bonczar. (2006). *Probation and Parole in the United States, 2005.* Washington, DC: U.S. Department of Justice, Bureau of Justice Statistics.

Goldkamp, John S. (2003) "The impact of drug courts." *Criminology & Public Policy* 2 (2), 197–206.

Gottfredson, Denise C., Stacy S. Najaka, and Brook Kearley. (2003). "Effectiveness of drug treatment courts: Evidence from a randomized trial." *Criminology & Public Policy* 2 (2), 171–196.

Gover, Angela R., John M. MacDonald, and Geoffrey P. Alpert. (2003). "Combating domestic violence: Findings from an evaluation of a local domestic violence court." *Criminology & Public Policy* 3 (1), 109–132.

Griffin, Patricia A., Henry J. Steadman, and John Petrila. (2002). "The use of criminal charges and sanctions in mental health courts." *Psychiatric Services* 53 (10), 1285–1289.

Harris, Patricia M., and Kimberly S. Keller. (2005). "Ex-offenders need not apply: The criminal background check in hiring decisions." *Journal of Contemporary Criminal Justice* 21 (1), 6–30.

Harrison, Paige M., and Allen J. Beck. (2006). *Prison and Jail Inmates at Midyear 2005.* Washington, DC: U.S. Department of Justice, Bureau of Justice Statistics.

Huddleston, C. West, Karen Freeman-Wilson, Douglas B. Marlowe, and Aaron Roussell. (2005). *Painting the Current Picture: A National Report Card on Drug Courts and Other Problem-Solving Programs in the United States.* Washington, DC: Bureau of Justice Assistance.

James, Doris J. (2004). *Profile of Jail Inmates, 2002.* Washington, DC: U.S. Department of Justice, Bureau of Justice Statistics.

La Vigne, Nancy G., Cynthia A. Mamalian, Jeremy Travis, and Christy Visher. (2003). *A Portrait of Prisoner Reentry in Illinois.* Washington, DC: Urban Institute.

Langan, Patrick A., and David J. Levin (2002). *Recidivism of Prisoners Released in 1994.* Washington, DC: U.S. Department of Justice, Bureau of Justice Statistics.

Legal Action Center. (2004). "After prison: Roadblocks to reentry." Retrieved July 11, 2006 from, *http://www.lac.org/lac/upload/lacreport/LAC_PrintReport.pdf#search='legal%20action%20center%20after%20prison'.*

Little Hoover Commission (2003). *Back to the Community—Safe and Sound Parole Policies.* Sacramento, CA: Author.

Longshore, Douglas, Darren Urada, Elizabeth Evans, Yih-Ing Hser, Michael Pendergast, and Angela Hawkin. (2005). *Evaluation of the Substance Abuse and Crime Prevention Act 2004 Report.* Los Angeles: UCLA Integrated Substance Abuse Programs.

Lowenkamp, Christopher T., and Edward J. Latessa. (2005). "Increasing the effectiveness of correctional programming through the risk principle: Identifying offenders for residential placement." *Criminology & Public Policy* 4 (2), 263–290.

MacKenzie, Doris L. (1993). *Boot camp prisons, 1993.* Washington, DC: National Institute of Justice.

——. (2005). "The importance of using scientific evidence to make decisions about correctional programming." *Criminology & Public Policy* 4 (2), 249–258.

MacKenzie, Doris L., and Robert Brame. (2001). "Community supervision, prosocial activities, and recidivism." *Justice Quarterly* 18 (2), 429–448.

Manhattan Institute. (1999). *'Broken Windows' Probation: The Next Step in Fighting Crime.* New York: Author.

Marciniak, Liz Marie (1999). "The use of day reporting as an intermediate sanction: A study of offender targeting and program termination." *Prison Journal* 79 (2), 205–222.

Marlowe, Douglas B. (2006). "When 'What Works' never did: Dodging the 'Scarlet M' in correctional rehabilitation." *Criminology & Public Policy* 5 (2), 339–346.

Mauer, Marc, and Meda Chesney-Lind. (2002). *Invisible Punishment: The Collateral Consequences of Mass Imprisonment.* New York: New Press.

Miller, Jerome. (1996). *Search and Destroy: African-American Males in the Criminal Justice System.* New York: Cambridge University Press.

Mumola, Christopher J. (1999). *Substance Abuse and Treatment, State and Federal Prisoners, 1997.* Washington, DC: U.S. Department of Justice, Bureau of Justice Statistics.

National Center for Institutions and Alternatives. (2000). *The Collateral Consequences of an Individual Arrested or Convicted in the United States.* Baltimore, MD: Author.

National Institute of Justice. (2005, July). "Reentry programs for women offenders." *NIJ Journal* 252, 2–7.

Nolan, James L. (2003, Fall). "Redefining criminal courts: Problem solving and the meaning of justice." *American Criminal Law Review* 40, 1541–1565.

Padgett, Kathy G., William D. Bales, and Thomas G. Blomberg. (2006). "Under surveillance: An empirical test of the effectiveness and consequences of electronic monitoring." *Criminology & Public Policy* 5 (1), 61–92.

Parent, Dale G. (2003). *Correctional Boot Camps: Lessons From a Decade of Research.* Washington, DC: National Institute of Justice.

Parent, Dale G., James Byrne, Vered Tsarfaty, Laura Valada, and Julie Esselman. (1995). *Day Reporting Centers* (Vol. 2). Washington, DC: U.S. Department of Justice.

Petersilia, Joan. (1998). "A decade of experimenting with intermediate sanctions: What have we learned?" *Federal Probation* 62 (2), 3–9.

——. (2005). "What works in prisoner reentry? Reviewing and questioning the evidence." *Federal Probation* 68 (2), 4–8.

Rhine, Edward E., Tina L. Mawhorr, and Evalyn C. Parks. (2006). "Implementation: The bane of effective correctional programs." *Criminology & Public Policy* 5 (2), 347–358.

Ruddell, Rick, and Noelle E. Fearn. (2005). "The stability of punishment hypothesis revisited: A cross-national analysis." *International Journal of Comparative Criminology* 5 (1), 1–28.

Shaffer, Catherine. (2004). "Therapeutic domestic violence courts: An efficient approach to adjudication?" *Seattle University Law Review* 27 (4), 981–997.

Simon, J. (1995). "They died with their boots on: The boot camp and the limits of modern penalty." *Social Justice* 22 (1), 25–48.

Stephan, James J., and Jennifer C. Karberg. (2003). *Census of State and Federal Correctional Facilities, 2000.* Washington, DC: Bureau of Justice Statistics.

Styve, Gaylene, J., Doris L. MacKenzie, Angela R. Gover, and Ojmarrh J. Mitchell. (2000). "Perceived conditions of confinement: A national evaluation of juvenile boot camps and traditional facilities." *Law and Human Behavior* 24 (3), 297–308.

Travis, Jeremy. (2005). "Prisoner reentry: The iron law of imprisonment." Pp. 64–71 in *Key Correctional Issues*, Rosyln Muraskin, editor. Upper Saddle River, NJ: Pearson Prentice Hall.

U.S. Sentencing Commission. (2004). "Fifteen years of guideline sentencing." Washington, DC: Author. Retrieved October 11, 2006 from: *http://www.ussc.gov/15_year/15year.htm.*

Weisman, Robert L., Steven J. Lamberti, and Nancy Price. (2004). "Integrating criminal justice, community healthcare, and support services for adults with severe mental disorders." *Psychiatric Quarterly* 75 (1), 71–85.

Wilhelm, Daniel F., and Nicholas R. Turner. (2002). *Is the Budget Crisis Changing the Way We Look at Sentencing and Incarceration?* New York: Vera Institute of Justice.

Wilson, James A., and Robert C. Davis. (2006). "Good intentions meet hard realities: An evaluation of the project Green Light reentry program." *Criminology & Public Policy* 5 (2), 303–338.

Wright, Dionne T., and G. Larry Mays. (1998). "Correctional boot camps, attitudes, and recidivism: The Oklahoma experience." *Journal of Offender Rehabilitation* 28 (1&2), 71–87.

Recommended Readings

Maruna, Shadd. (2000). *Making Good: How Ex-Convicts Reform and Rebuild Their Lives.* Washington, DC: American Psychological Association. This book departs from traditional academic parole studies by focusing on the life experiences of parolees who are "making good" or desisting from crime. Readers will be interested in the individual stories that describe the factors that made this sample of British parolees stop committing crimes.

Petersilia, Joan. (2003). *When Prisoners Come Home: Parole and Prisoner Reentry.* New York: Oxford University Press. Petersilia is a widely-acknowledged expert when it comes to community corrections. In this book, she outlines the shortcomings in parole systems and how the cycle of inmates returning to their communities, parole failure, and readmission to prison is a function of few rehabilitative or vocational programs in prison, along with barriers that we create for these inmates upon reentry. Petersilia makes a number of recommendations for change in prison systems, parole, and parole supervision.

Travis, Jeremy. (2005). *Prisoner Reentry and Crime in America.* New York: Cambridge University Press. This edited book tackles key questions about parole and prisoner reentry. The authors outline the characteristics of parolees and ex-prisoners, document their contributions to current crime rates, and critically examine parole supervision, the impact of imprisonment on employment, neighborhood crime rates, and families. Altogether, the authors provide fresh perspectives on the challenges of returning 630,000 offenders back to their communities with little preparation or support. ✦

Chapter 11

Build More Prisons?

Introduction

Previous chapters outlined how Americans supported tough-on-crime policies: sentencing offenders to longer terms of incarceration, developing tough community-based probation programs, and strictly enforcing the conditions of parole of ex-prisoners who returned to the community. The sheer number of probationers and parolees, and the limited supervision in some jurisdictions, has led some supporters of the crime control model to advocate tougher sanctions for the almost 5 million persons on probation or parole at yearend 2005 (Glaze and Bonczar 2006). Moreover, according to the Federal Bureau of Investigation (FBI), there were approximately 10.2 million arrests in 2005 (FBI 2006). What are the answers to problems of continuing crime: Should we build more jails and prisons? Or are these facilities too costly given budget shortfalls? In other words, should justice be limited by budgets? And what are the short- and long-term costs and benefits of prison expansion on individuals, families, and communities? In this chapter, we examine these questions, including the **opportunity costs** of prison expenditures (how governments could spend the funds not invested in corrections or punishing offenders).

Although the costs of imprisoning offenders are high, there is broad consensus that some offenders must be incarcerated to protect the public because they are too dangerous to remain in the community. The challenge is that tax dollars are limited, which affects the number of offenders that we can incarcerate. Anecdotal accounts of prison staff from the 1980s suggest that in some places we discharged homicide offenders and other violent criminals to make room in prisons for drug offenders. Most voters would not support these practices, as they do not make common sense. We have demonstrated throughout this book, however, that many of our criminal justice policies are ill-conceived, ineffective, or destructive in the long term.

Like other issues in this book, the prison expansion problem is a dilemma, the choice between two equally unappealing outcomes. At midyear 2005, we housed 1.43 million offenders in federal or state prisons and almost 750,000 persons in local jails (Harrison and Beck 2006). Correctional populations have grown fourfold since the mid-1970s, and they are still increasing. Harrison and Beck (2006, 1) reported that state prison populations increased 1.2 percent between 2004 and 2005; federal imprisonment increased 2.9 percent, while local jail incarceration grew 4.7 percent during that same time. While U.S. jail populations are increasing at the highest rate, the Federal Bureau of Prisons' population growth has outpaced the states by a substantial margin since 1995.

Yet, support for increased imprisonment seems to be eroding. Even conservative organizations—such as the Heritage Foundation (which supports incarcerating violent offenders and the death penalty)—argue that the federal government should reduce the regulation of social and economic conduct (Heritage Foundation 2006). Others have observed that many prison admissions are actually parolees who are readmitted, and there is significant interest aimed at improving community reintegration (Little Hoover Commission 2003). To better understand the problem, we examine the issue from several perspectives. First, we examine the relationships between imprisonment and crime: If we lock up more offenders, for example, how much will crime decrease? We also examine the rising costs of corrections and how state governments have responded to these challenges.

Imprisonment and Crime Control

Imprisonment is an important component of criminal justice systems. While there is widespread agreement that some imprisonment is necessary, the problem arises when we debate how many people should be incarcerated. Historically, states tried to balance public safety and fiscal responsibility. We know that there are budget limits to incarceration, but the problem becomes more complex when debating the types of offenders we should imprison, how much time they must serve, and the rehabilitative programs (if any) they might receive. Although it is difficult to reach consensus on these issues, public policy analysts recently have tried to evaluate the short- and long-term consequences of these policies (Lynch and Sabol 2004). Some scholars, for example, have questioned whether mass imprisonment actually will increase long-term neighborhood crime rates (Piehl 2004; Rose and Clear 1998).

Throughout the last few decades, researchers have attempted to measure imprisonment's costs and benefits. Perhaps one of the most controversial studies was by Edwin Zedlewski (1987), who reported that for every $1 taxpayers invested in prisons, they saved $17.20 in costs related to crimes. Zedlewski based his analysis on the proposition that incarcerated offenders would each commit 187 crimes per year if they lived in the community. However, do all offenders commit over three crimes a week, and what are the actual economic costs of these offenses? Piehl, Useem, and DiIulio (1999) criticized the fact that Zedlewski estimated the cost of each crime committed at $2,300, which is high considering that a majority of reported crimes are minor offenses, such as larceny. Further, how do you place an economic value on public order offenses or drug sales?

Zimring and Hawkins (1995) also took issue with Zedlewski's (1987) statistics, using California crime and imprisonment data. They reported that if Zedlewski was correct, California's increased use of imprisonment starting in the mid-1970s should have eliminated crime altogether by the 1990s. Thus, Zedlewski's estimates of incarceration benefits are overly optimistic. The problem is that once published, these discredited studies develop a life of their own, and politicians, scholars, and practitioners still use these data to advocate policy changes based on faulty assumptions.

There can be little dispute that incarcerating 1.41 million offenders in federal and state prisons results in decreased community crime. The important question is whether crime would have had a similar decrease if we locked up only one million offenders. Alternatively, if we admitted more offenders but subjected them to shorter prison terms, would the deterrent effect of prison increase (Block 1997)? Thus, to conduct an effective cost-benefit analysis of imprisonment, we have to understand prison population dynamics (the annual number of admissions and the sentence length served), as well as the indirect costs and benefits.

Spelman (2000) provided a summary of different studies that estimated incarceration's costs and benefits. He found that it is fairly easy to estimate the direct costs of punishment (annual cost to hold someone in prison), but it is very difficult to predict how many offenses (if any) a prisoner would have committed in a given year if released. First-time, violent offenders might never commit another offense in their lifetime, while heroin-addicted burglars might commit 100 residential burglaries a year.

Spelman (2000) examined the long-term relationships of the imprisonment rate on crime. He found that the 300 percent increase in federal and state imprisonment rates resulted in a 27 percent decease in U.S. crime rates between 1972 and 1996. This translates into a reduction of approximately 1 percent for every 10 percent increase in imprisonment: Is this a good return for our investment? Spelman's analysis, however, did not differentiate between violent, property, and drug offenders. A 27 percent decrease in violent crime is a much better outcome than an identical reduction in public order offenses.

Steve Aos (2003) conducted an economic assessment of correctional spending and came up with statistics that reveal a greater incarceration benefit than Spelman. He estimated that a 10 percent increase in imprisonment will decrease crime between 2 percent and 4 percent. An important consideration is the type of offender who is incarcerated. Aos (2003, 22) demonstrated that incapacitating violent and property offenders is economically feasible and that for every dollar spent on incarcerating a violent offender, there is a crime-reduction benefit of approximately $2.74; this increases to $2.84 for property offenders. Incarcerating drug offenders, by contrast, provides only a $0.37 return on each incarceration dollar invested. Such findings may lead us to question the economic benefits of imprisoning drug offenders.[1]

Cost-benefit studies are economic analyses, and Aos (2003) argued that business approaches that clearly outline the costs and benefits of different alternatives be undertaken for all social policies, including the use of imprisonment. If we are going to consider building or closing prisons, it is important that policymakers and the public have access to the social and economic implications of their decisions, including whether there is a crime-reduction benefit. Aos (2003) also outlined one important concept, often overlooked in criminal justice research: the question of **diminishing returns.** According to diminishing marginal returns, the more incarceration is increased, the less the benefit. Thus, there was a greater benefit in crime reduction at the start of the imprisonment boom, but this decreased as the worst offenders were incapacitated. Altogether, taking an economic view of sentencing and corrections makes sense during times of budget crises.

Block (1997) contended that one measure is often overlooked in cost-benefit analyses: **incarceration probability.** Block argued that admitting a greater number of offenders to shorter prison terms in a given year is an effective crime-control strategy because increasing the likelihood of incarceration has a greater deterrent effect. Using this approach, we would sentence more offenders to shorter terms, an approach used in some European nations. Block also suggested that targeting violent offenders provides the greatest economic returns.

Recent studies have demonstrated a diminishing return on imprisoning offenders, using county-level (Kovandzic and Vieraitis 2006) and national-level analyses (Liedka, Piehl, and Useem 2006). Yet, a criticism of any economic analysis of crime and punishment is the difficulty of accurately evaluating all of the costs and benefits. For example, it is relatively easy to estimate the direct economic cost of a gunshot wound: the hospitalization costs, police investigation, and court-related costs if a culprit is apprehended. But, do we also consider the victim's pain and suffering, the days of lost work (or productivity), the psychological stress that such injuries place on individuals and their families, and ultimately the public fear these offenses create? It is equally difficult to explain accurately the benefits of crime control strategies.

Another problem of these studies is methodological: Most analyses are based on a limited number of variables, and dozens of other factors may contribute to crime that are not considered. Like with the gun control data described in Chapter 5, researchers sometimes use the same data and come up with different conclusions. As a result, one needs to be a careful consumer of research.

In an insightful statement about prisons and public policy, Greenberg (2006, 207) suggested that cost-benefit analyses may not be as important as an approach based on **proportionality** (punishment is proportional to the seriousness of the crime) and **uniformity,** in other words, "what criminals deserve when they are convicted of a crime." While this approach works well philosophically, it is less successful when we attempt to determine sentencing solely on these principles. Our discussion of guided sentences in Chapter 6 outlined how judges often depart from prescribed sentences because of mitigating factors. When we increase the discretion of judges, we increase disparities (often along racial lines). Yet, when we base sentences on strict guidelines, we sometimes impose lengthy sentences on otherwise law-abiding persons who are sometimes caught up in crime for the first time in their lives.

The Rising Cost of Corrections

Prisons have always had to compete against other state programs for scarce budget dollars. While criminal justice students overwhelmingly support this spending because it may affect their future livelihoods, taxpayers are not so easily convinced, especially when given the choice between spending on prisons or funding health care, better roads, law enforcement, parks and recreation, and education. From the 1980s to the mid-1990s, state budgets were able to absorb higher corrections spending. However, by the late 1990s, there were budget crises in most states, and Crutchfield (2004, 266) observed that

> states are experiencing dampened incomes as a result of the lagging (in many states still depressed) economies, diminished tax base (resulting from the spreading anti-tax movement), and demographic changes (aging populations and in some states declining populations).

Maintaining high correctional populations, once thought necessary, was increasingly questioned as extravagant.

As correctional populations increased, so did operating costs of correctional facilities. In 2003, the total outlay for federal, state, and local corrections was almost $68 billion (Hughes 2006). It cost an average of $22,650 to hold an inmate for a year in prison in 2001 (Stephan 2004). Most people are outraged that it costs as much to incarcerate an inmate as it does to enroll a student in a private college. The trouble is that only about 26 percent of the actual price tag goes for direct inmate care, such as medical care, food, and utilities (Stephan 2004). In addition, most of the inmate care expenditure is a result of constitutional guarantees to provide appropriate housing and health care. Of the remaining outlays, most are for staffing, and it is difficult to reduce these costs. A foundation of effective correctional programs is having a well-educated, professional, and competent workforce (Latessa 2003). By decreasing salaries, it is harder to recruit and retain higher-skilled employees.

The figures we outline here represent the direct government expenditure for imprisonment. Governments operate within fixed budgets; and by spending money on corrections, those funds cannot be used for

Box 11.1
The Crime Control Perspective and Incarceration

While the overall cost of incarceration is some $68 billion, the individual taxpayer contributed about $209 per year to incarcerate offenders in 2003 (Hughes 2006). Many would argue that this is a good investment in public safety, and some would gladly contribute more. An offender who is incarcerated is unable to commit crimes in the community, and this increases our safety while the prisoner is behind bars.

Supporters of the crime control model argue that first-time offenders rarely go to prison (unless they have committed a serious offense), and many prisoners have been before the courts numerous times prior to the offense that led to their incarceration. If these offenders are not learning from minor punishments, such as probation or short periods of jail incarceration, they argue, perhaps a term of imprisonment will convince the offender that the community has "had enough."

While many supporters of the due process model point to places such as Australia, Canada, and Europe as models for criminal sentencing that is less severe, people in many of these nations are angry when serious and violent offenders are sentenced to relatively short periods of incarceration. In 2002, for instance, the average sentence for a violent offender in the United States was 62 months (Durose and Langan 2004), while in England, the average sentence was 17.6 months (Home Office 2005).[2] Severe penalties for serious crimes may also have some deterrent effect as crime rates in many rich first-world nations are increasing, while they have decreased and been stable in the United States. ✦

other programs, the principle of opportunity cost. Greene and Schiraldi (2002, 8) cited a New York City corrections official:

> Every dollar spent on imprisonment is a dollar not available for a different public investment. We cannot speak about increased investment in corrections today without allowing that those dollars have to come from policing, teen pregnancy prevention programs, pre-natal and peri-natal programs, and increasingly, public education.

Hagan and Dinovitzer (1999) observed that policymakers have done a very poor job of considering alternatives to correctional spending. It has been suggested that if we made a greater investment in community spending, we might be able to prevent persons from violating the law in the first place, resulting in greater public safety and decreased correctional spending (Ruddell 2004). The problem is that it is difficult to convince skeptical and increasingly disgruntled taxpayers of these long-term benefits.

We direct a relatively small portion of state prison budgets to offender rehabilitation, and it has been argued that by investing in effective correctional interventions (Latessa 2003) and community reentry or reintegration programs, we reduce recidivism. This offers both increased public safety and decreased correctional spending (Little Hoover Commission 2003). To save on corrections over the long term, we temporarily have to increase spending on rehabilitation or cut existing government programs (such as decreasing correctional populations), an unattractive policy dilemma.

Indirect Costs of Incarceration

One cannot debate the proposition of increasing correctional populations without fully understanding the impacts of imprisonment on individuals, families, and communities (Meares 2004). Ruddell (2004) argued that the criminal justice system has been used to respond to long-term problems, such as addictions, large populations of persons with mental illness, and entrenched poverty. In some cases, criminal justice interventions have destructive effects on the persons involved with these systems. Consider that once people have been placed in prison, they often face considerable challenges in making a successful reentry into society.

Ex-prisoners, especially during times of high unemployment, may be effectively removed from legitimate job opportunities. Few employers are willing to hire persons with a criminal record, and even fewer will hire an ex-inmate (Harris and Keller 2005). If parolees cannot get legitimate jobs, their chances of success are very limited. One of the cornerstones of success in job markets is **social capital,** the relationships and trust we build through positive social networks (Coleman 1990). A lack of social capital restricts the individual's ability to find employment. It is difficult for prisoners to accumulate social capital when they are incarcerated, and this is one rationale for transitioning offenders into community halfway houses. Such placements allow prisoners to build legitimate employment, educational, and social networks, although this approach does not work with every offender (see Latessa 2004).

We learned in Chapter 10 that prisoners are often optimistic about their chances for legitimate employment prior to their release. Unfortunately, their previous criminal convictions, drug use, and imprisonment make it difficult for them to reintegrate successfully into society (Lotke and Ziedenberg 2005). Thus, while incarceration does have a positive effect on reducing crime, we also have to understand that punishment reduces a person's access to legitimate opportunites. The more barriers that we construct, the more likely the individual will return to jail or prison.

Other individual-level incarceration costs must also be considered. The FBI reported approximately 10.2 million arrests in 2005 (FBI 2006). Most arrestees pass through jails or juvenile halls, and these populations have high rates of communicable diseases, such as HIV/AIDS, tuberculosis, or hepatitis. Close confinement within these correctional facilities also results in higher transmission rates of these communicable diseases. One problem that many jurisdictions are confronting is that correctional medical services did not increase with the rising number of inmates, and this has led to rationed health care

(Murphy 2005). As a result, health-related problems that originate in corrections are sometimes spread to the community (Ruddell and Tomita 2005).

Other inmates are physically or sexually victimized while incarcerated and return to the community suffering from physical injuries and posttraumatic stress disorder (PTSD) (McGuire 2005). While we understand that prisoners are not sympathetic populations, we also have to acknowledge that victimization that occurs within a correctional facility may have a long-term effect on the individual. We speculate that the more inmates are victimized, the more angry and unsettled they will be when they return to the community, which may further jeopardize our safety. Hochstetler, Murphy, and Simons (2004) found that many of the prisoners who had been victimized were likely to exhibit symptoms of PTSD and depression. These investigators speculated that prison violence may have a powerful impact on individuals as they are forced to live with their attackers. Altogether, many people return to the community from jail or prison with more physical and psychological problems than when they were admitted.

Imprisonment's effects extend beyond the individual and have significant costs to families, neighborhoods, and communities. Imprisoning a person has a destructive effect on family relationships. A short term of incarceration, for instance, often strains family finances as collect calls, visits to prisons (often located in rural areas away from the inner cities, which are home to many offenders), and providing even modest financial support to somebody incarcerated can cause significant financial stress. Some families have mortgaged their homes to pay for legal fees when their loved ones face serious charges.

A number of scholars have tried to estimate indirect imprisonment costs. Grinstead and colleagues (2001) found that the female spouses of prison inmates spent an average $292 per month to support their relationships. These costs included travel to visits, postage, providing money directly to the inmate's account, and telephone charges (most inmates can only make expensive collect calls). Meares (2004, 297) outlined how one family, with an annual income of less than $20,000, spent $12,680 supporting a relative in prison. The problem is that money spent to keep a prison relationship viable is not going to the family, and it is funneled away from the community.

By supporting imprisoned family members, a family places itself at greater risk of poverty. While this may appear to be a short-sighted practice, it also represents their hope of a better future for the family. Maintaining the relationship reduces recidivism once the inmate is released (Hairston 1991). As a result, a family's investment in supporting a prison inmate is also an investment in long-term public safety.

In addition to the direct economic effect of incarceration, there are other costs that are harder to estimate. Some scholars, for instance, argue that the imprisonment of a parent decreases the ability of the remaining parent to supervise children. Miller (2003) observed that since half the men incarcerated are fathers, their children receive less male closeness, involvement, or contact. Loss of the male **role model** may also contribute to higher rates of acting out (Gabel 2003). Moreover, if the remaining parent works, he or she has less time to participate in school or community activities. Imprisonment sometimes leads to social isolation when parents are so busy working and caring for their family that they detach themselves from economic, religious, and social supports (Meares 2004). Braman (2002) also observed that children of imprisoned parents lose important role models.

Imprisonment of women has a devastating impact on families. Prison systems are holding larger numbers of females, who are primarily nonviolent offenders. Harrison and Beck (2006, 5) outlined how the total numbers of males imprisoned increased 30 percent between 1995 and 2004, but female imprisonment grew 47 percent during the same time. Since there are fewer women's institutions (some smaller states have only one), females are often imprisoned far away from their families, increasing the costs of visits and reducing their frequency. Fewer visits reduce family integration, an important matter when approximately three-quarters of the women imprisoned are mothers (Richie 2002).

Yet, one might look at some of these claims skeptically and carefully weigh whether an offender is a positive role model or actually invests much time in child rearing. We know that rates of drug and alcohol use are high in offender populations. It might be possible that a term of incarceration will "interrupt" the criminal career of offenders and make them realize the costs of their addictions or lifestyle choices. As a result, while there may be indirect individual or family costs of incarceration, imprisoning an out-of-control offender may actually help the family in the long term if the individual learns from the experience. Many persons do not willingly change their behaviors unless confronted with some form of crisis (such as legal trouble).

Individual and family-level effects of incarceration are also transferred to the community. Imprisonment is not distributed randomly through a city, and high incarceration levels overwhelmingly impact a small number of neighborhoods (Lotke and Ziedenberg 2005). In an influential statement, Rose and Clear (1998) demonstrated that communities affected by high imprisonment practices actually suffer from decreased **informal social control.** Informal social control represents the efforts of families, neighbors, or community members to reduce unacceptable behavior through persuasion, encouragement, or other means. When families, neighbors, and communities can respond to crime informally, the police or other authorities do not become involved. However, when families and communities are disrupted and unstable, it is harder for them to exert informal social control. We noted earlier that people in disadvantaged neighborhoods were more likely to call the police, and a breakdown in informal social control may be a cause of this reliance on the police. Yet, every time the police become involved in a situation, it increases the likelihood of an arrest.

Piehl, Useem, and DiIulio (1999, 14) argued that the overuse of imprisonment reduces its deterrent value when it is seen as commonplace. Consistent with our earlier observations, overinvolvement of the justice system in some communities also may undermine the legitimacy of government and law. Taking a similar perspective, Lynch and Sabol (2004, 267) outlined the relationships between high incarceration rates and community functioning. They found that "[m]ass incarceration disrupts patterns of social interaction, weakens community social organization, and decreases the stigma of imprisonment its longer-run effects may be to reduce its effectiveness."

These scholars raise interesting questions about the true costs of mass imprisonment policies. We also have to consider how the stigma of imprisonment prevents ex-prisoners from pursuing legitimate opportunities, the relationships between prison and community health, and the harmful effects of placing family members in prison. Not everybody agrees about the extent of these costs, but it is important to acknowledge the (1) human costs in lost opportunities; (2) the indirect economic costs of high imprisonment policies; and, (3) that mass imprisonment may erode trust and legitimacy of criminal justice systems.

Punishing More Effectively

While correctional rehabilitation has been on the back burner of penal policies for several decades, there are indications that public support for rehabilitation has increased. Recent surveys reveal that the public may support rehabilitation more than policymakers might believe (Cullen and Gendreau 2000). The concept of rehabilitation should be an "easy sell." Advocates of the crime control model, for instance, support lower recidivism rates because they translate into greater public safety. However, there is less confidence in the actual delivery of correctional treatment, despite the fact that in the past decade, considerable empirical work has begun to outline the cornerstones of effective rehabilitative programs. In addition, adopting these policies in eras of fiscal crisis is problematic: Where will the money come from?

In Chapter 10, we discussed how community-based programs have been driven by simplistic notions that we can make significant changes in people's attitudes, values, or goals in a short time by somehow breaking them down in a boot camp or scared straight program, and then building them up again. Institutional correctional programs have been somewhat less vulnerable to these fads, but prisons are also guilty of developing programs with little or no theoretical foundation. In fact, the cornerstones of effective correctional programs are straightforward, and Latessa (2003, 33–35) outlined these elements:

(1) Assess offenders' needs and risks.

(2) Use treatment models that are proven effective.

(3) Employ the "3 Cs" of effective corrections (credentialed employees, credentialed programs/agencies, and credentialed knowledge).

(4) Understand the principles of effective intervention.

According to this model, an important first step is to evaluate the prisoner's needs. One way to do this is to use objective risk and needs assessment instruments. These instruments enable **classification officers** (people who make decisions about offenders' security risk and are responsible for their placement within the institution) and **case managers** (people in charge of an inmate's treatment program) to make more objective decisions.

Classification is a foundation of effective corrections, and it has been speculated that implementing effective classification schemes has greatly reduced violence in correctional facilities (Austin 2003). Classification is a process, usually done at admission to a jail or prison (often at a prison system's reception center), that tries to determine the most appropriate institutional setting and unit assignment for an inmate. Classification instruments, much like a juvenile **risk assessment,** are based on a score that considers the individual's current and prior offenses, past institutional behavior (if any), age at first arrest, and his or her length of sentence. Generally speaking, the higher the score, the greater the need for security, although most classification officers have the ability to "override" the score. In most places, these scores will decrease if a period of stable conduct takes place within the institution.

Chapter 10 outlined a number of effective community and correctional programs. Generally these programs promote family cohesion, social skills development, or target criminal (criminogenic) thinking. The best programs provide an integrated approach that targets the attitudes, behaviors, and lack of knowledge or skills that led to the person's incarceration.

One problem is that we have a pretty good idea of "what works," but it is sometimes difficult to translate these good intentions into effective treatment programs (Lin 2000). That is why Latessa (2003, 34) highlighted the importance of the three "Cs"—"employing credentialed staff members, ensuring that the agency . . . is credentialed . . . founded on the principles of fairness and improvement of lives, and basing treatment decisions on credentialed knowledge . . . high quality, research-based information." An implementation challenge in correctional institutions is that changing the culture to one that supports rehabilitation needs front-line correctional officers' support, the positive leadership of correctional managers, appropriate funding, as well as the support of community stakeholders, such as employers and inmate families.

Further, the inmates have to be convinced that these interventions are going to result in meaningful change. Altogether, this is a complex proposition, and programs often fail if one or more of these elements are missing.

Last, effective correctional interventions rest on eight principles that range from creating a positive correctional environment to evaluating program success or failure. According to Latessa (2003), these principles include recruiting high-quality staff, basing interventions on "what works," an understanding of offender needs, and interacting with community stakeholders. In general, such an approach requires professional managers and staff who base interventions on a thorough understanding of the research about correctional rehabilitation and constant communication and evaluation to ensure that the desired goals are being met. These goals may be difficult to reach in a closed environment with scarce resources, staff who might actively undermine the intervention, and working within civil service guidelines that typically reward seniority over enthusiasm, education, and commitment to offender rehabilitation.

Lin (2000) outlined a number of challenges associated with implementing prison rehabilitative programs. One significant obstacle is that every institution has its own culture, and this is based on the organization's history, the people who work within the agency, and even the inmates' goals (for example, whether they are amenable to rehabilitation). Lin (2000, 5) found that unsuccessful implementation is the norm in many prisons, and these failures are attributed to "garish mismanagement . . . warfare between staff, outright subversion of programs by prisoners or administrators, untrained staff directed to run a program, or trained staff who are not given the latitude to act." Essentially, Lin's approach is that prisoners and staff have to see benefits in a program, and each must support the other, a tricky proposition in institutions sometimes filled with mutual distrust, skepticism, and histories of failure.

While there are many barriers to developing effective rehabilitative programs, the end product is essentially "win-win." Every year, some 630,000 inmates return to the community, and it is in everybody's interest if they move into our neighborhoods less damaged than when they were admitted to prison. The United States' recidivism rates are at relatively high levels (see Langan and Levin 2002), but effective correctional interventions can provide significant long-term cost benefits (Aos 2003). Last, it is plausible that correctional officer cynicism is reduced when inmates are discharged and are not readmitted. There is much to be gained and little to lose by introducing evidence-based correctional treatment; however, like other criminal justice challenges, political and financial support are needed for these interventions. The following pages outline suggestions for another policy alternative: cutting correctional populations without compromising public safety.

Cutting Correctly

Wilhelm and Turner (2002) examined the relationships between state fiscal crises and correctional spending. They found that in times of budget crises, lawmakers considered it important to put the brakes on correctional spending. State correctional systems have implemented several approaches to save money, but three deserve special attention. First, 13 states closed prisons and many jurisdictions took this opportunity to shut antiquated facilities that were expensive to operate (Wilhelm and Turner 2002). Second, prison systems reduced their staff, either through layoffs or by not replacing employees who retire or quit. Last, programs deemed "nonessential," such as education, substance-abuse treatment, or vocational programs, were cut.

As we have learned throughout our examination of crime and justice, each policy action is likely to result in unanticipated consequences. For instance, in the case of limiting correctional officer hiring, some agencies found themselves without enough staff to operate institutions, leading to high overtime rates. Since it is much more expensive to hire senior staff members to cover a shift at 150 percent of their pay than for new officers to do this, failure to recruit new staff can be costly. Cutting rehabilitative programs may also increase recidivism, which has a significant long-term cost in public safety and higher correctional populations. Last, closing institutions can be disruptive to the morale of a correctional system if employees who lost their jobs are allowed to "bump" less senior staff from their positions in other prisons.

Wilhelm and Turner (2002, 4) also found that states modified their diversionary, sentencing, or parole schemes to reduce inmate populations. For example, prison populations were reduced in some states by diverting drug offenders to community-based treatment, while other jurisdictions offered more drug treatment. Nineteen states and the District of Columbia modified their sentencing models by repealing mandatory minimum sentences, easing habitual offender laws, or eliminating truth in sentencing programs (Wilhelm and Turner 2002). Some jurisdictions eased parole eligibility requirements. Last, in three states, sentencing commissions were asked to develop recommendations for change within entire prison systems.

In some places, fiscal crises resulted in the wholesale release of prison inmates. Butterfield (2002) has reported how Kentucky initiated an emergency prisoner release in December 2002 in response to a $500 million budget shortfall. One hazard of such approaches is that prisoners probably do not have well-thought-out community reintegration plans, and this places prisoners at a higher risk of failing and threatens public safety.[3] Butterfield (2002) cited the Kentucky Attorney General saying, "The amount of time a criminal serves in prison should be based on the crime committed, not on the balance of the state treasury." While these sentiments make good press, correctional systems lived within their capacities for decades. It was not until the mid-1970s that correctional populations were allowed to grow (Caplow and Simon 1999).

Given these realities, some scholars and advocacy groups have made recommendations about "cutting correctly" so that prison populations are reduced while protecting public safety. Greene and Schiraldi (2002, 9) recommended that the following strategies be used:

(1) Return of discretion to judges and reduction of nonviolent prisoner populations

(2) Drug policy reform

(3) Comprehensive sentencing reform

(4) Parole reform

(5) Policy reforms

A cornerstone of this approach is that low-risk prisoners can be released, mandatory sentencing schemes are scrapped in favor of a return to judicial discretion, prison sentences for drug offenders are restricted, parole is reinstated especially for low-risk prisoners, and parole violations are reduced by reforming release procedures and strengthening community services. Although any suggestion to reduce prison populations is controversial, these strategies are based on releasing people with the lowest risk and supporting them in the community.

There are also special needs populations within prisons that are very costly to house, and strategies to release these offenders with appropriate community supervision make good fiscal sense. For example, female prisoners with children pose a double cost when we incarcerate the mother and place her children in foster care. Moreover, elderly inmates—typically defined as persons over 55 years of age—can cost three times more than other inmates due to health care costs (see Aday 2003). Further, persons with mental illness pose considerable challenges to correctional systems. When these special needs populations have been imprisoned for drug or property offenses, it seems reasonable to develop parole strategies that provide appropriate supervision levels.

Elderly prisoners represent a special case. The increasing use of mandatory minimum sentences and three-strikes or habitual offender sentencing enhancements has resulted in high populations of elderly inmates in some prison systems. For instance, in California, 4.7 percent of the prison population, or 7,550 persons, over the age of 55 were in prison on December 31, 2004 (California Department of Corrections and Rehabilitation 2005). Our knowledge of offender behavior suggests that this group is at comparatively lower recidivism risk than their younger counterparts. While not advocating a wholesale inmate release based on age, it seems feasible to release elderly inmates convicted of nonviolent crimes if suitable community alternatives exist.

In response to fiscal crises, some jurisdictions closed prisons, terminated staff, released inmates, changed sentencing practices, restored parole, or returned discretion to judges. While each of these steps may save the state money, such responses should not be a knee-jerk response to an emergency. Instead, any changes should be based upon well-thought-out plans that are intended to ensure public safety (Greene and Schiraldi 2002), as well as based upon our knowledge of offender behavior (Latessa 2004). Some correctional systems have developed long-term prison population plans based upon computer simulations (Wilhelm and Turner 2002). Managing correctional populations through advanced planning, forecasting, and simulation models represents a significant step forward in correctional administration.

Privatization

One of the few things that critics and supporters of high imprisonment policies agree upon is that incarceration within the United States is a big industry. Increasing prison populations by a factor of four has raised the total bill for local, state, and federal incarceration in 2003 to $68 billion (Hughes 2006). As old prisons became crowded, new industries emerged that supplied fixtures to refurbish them. Further, private corporations that specialized in the planning, construction, and leasing of new prisons were able to make lucrative, long-term arrangements with cash-strapped counties and states to finance and construct jails and prisons.

One way that some jurisdictions reduced their incarceration costs was to privatize some or all of their correctional programs. There was considerable scholarly argument about correctional privatization a decade ago. Like with many other criminal justice innovations, there was much excitement, and researchers wrote numerous books and articles about privatization's pros and cons (see Mays and Gray 1996). Despite this interest, at midyear 2005, only 101,228 inmates lived in privately operated facilities, representing 6.7 percent of all U.S. federal and state inmates; and these mostly were located in the south and west (Harrison and Beck 2006). This total had increased by about 11,000 inmates since yearend 2000, but most of this increase was due to the incarceration of federal inmates. When looking at the total percentage of all federal and state prisoners who were held in private facilities, it has remained almost constant between 1995 and 2005.

Privatization's appeal is that corporations can operate detention centers, jails, or prisons more effectively and efficiently than can governments. Private operators also promised that they could decrease recidivism (Gaes 2005). One of the problems with this approach, however, is that state prisons already operate relatively efficiently, and there are only a few ways to save money using private operators. First, as staffing is a major correctional cost, private operators can hire less-qualified staff, not contribute to pensions, or run institutions with fewer staff (that is, by building **new generation jails** that use fewer staff to supervise and control inmates) and by utilizing closed-circuit surveillance instead of correctional officers. Second, these operators sometimes can negotiate to hold low-risk inmates, such as prisoners with no history of violence or escapes. By "creaming" (taking only the least problematic inmates), private operators can reduce costs because there should be fewer incidents.

Box 11.2
New Generation Design and Philosophy

Much of our exposure to corrections comes from television and movies, and most of these films or programs depict prisoners living in cells made of iron bars. These cells are often stacked in tiers in long corridors. Correctional officers in these facilities have a limited ability to observe the inmates in their cells (intermittent supervision) because of the layout of the facility. While jails and prisons that feature this construction are still in use, most of the facilities constructed in the last few decades have utilized the new generation or podular design. The new generation design places inmate cells around the perimeter of a living unit (also called a pod). The center of the living unit is used for recreation, dining, or watching television, and one staff member can continuously supervise all of the inmates.

In addition to enabling better supervision of prisoners, these designs were intended to facilitate better communication between officers and inmates. The goal of this philosophy was to help inmates increase their problem-solving skills and allow officers to adopt a more proactive approach to supervision that reduces disruptive behavior or violence. Many facilities failed, however, to implement all aspects of the **new generation philosophy.** Despite the fact that much of the philosophy was not implemented, jails and prisons that use this design are generally safer for inmates and staff. ✦

The fact that local and state jurisdictions have not expanded the percentage of populations in private facilities speaks volumes about the effectiveness of private operations. They can do some things more effectively—from quick responses to jail or prison crowding (including construction and the transfer of inmates to different jurisdictions) to providing food service or health care within a publicly operated jail or prison. According to Segal (2006) a Director of Government Reform for the Reason Foundation (an organization that supports the privatization of public services), many firms are delivering these services more effectively than government agencies. One of the challenges of these comparative analyses, however, is that it is sometimes difficult to accurately evaluate the costs and benefits of private and public services because of differences in accounting. Segal (2006) argues that government bodies sometimes deliberately underestimate the costs of delivering their services, making these comparisons even more difficult.

Firms that are providing basic supervision to short-term inmates, such as illegal aliens held pending their deportation, seem to be doing an acceptable job (for a contrary perspective, see Welch 2002). While few in-depth studies consider these detainee populations, they would seem to be ideal for a private firm: generally noncriminal persons who are held for only a few days or weeks. When private firms operate prisons, they are responsible for the supervision of more sophisticated offenders, and the services that these prisoners require is much greater than jail inmates or immigration detainees. However, program evaluations typically find that recidivism rates in these institutions are about the same as in government-operated facilities (Thomas 2005). Segal (2006), however, is critical of the comparisons between private and publicly operated prisons and suggests that sometimes state correctional administrators actually manipulate data to show that their facilities operate more efficiently. Similar to other controversies in criminal justice, the issue of privatization suffers from limited credible research and cost-benefit analyses.

Some jurisdictions may be able to avoid jail or prison construction by utilizing private corporations to transfer inmates to facilities in other jurisdictions and, in some cases, other states. While saving on construction costs, these approaches are destructive to family contacts: and in some places, the treatment of transferred inmates has been abusive (Schlosser, 1998). Some of the most vocal objections to privatization come from correctional officer associations or unions. In some cases, these interest groups are powerful: The California Correctional Peace Officers Association gained political power by donating several million dollars to gubernatorial campaigns, which translated into lucrative raises for their members.

Conclusions

Prison reformers have much to be optimistic about in the twenty-first century. The decreased crime rate has caused us to reconsider whether we have reached the upper boundaries of punishment. Despite the fact that imprisonment rates continue to grow, states are adding inmates at a slower rate than in previous decades (Harrison and Beck 2006). In addition, there has been a noticeable lack of unrest in American prisons. Riots rarely occur and homicide and suicide rates within both jails and prisons have decreased significantly over the past two decades. For instance, the prison homicide rate dropped 93 percent between 1980 and 2000 (Mumola 2005).

Useem and Piehl (2006) examined the sources of stability within American corrections. This is an important topic because many had speculated that the increased prison populations would bring more misconduct, especially if inmates felt that they were being incarcerated unjustly. Although a number of different explanations have been developed to explain this reduction (for example, reduced number of violent offenders imprisoned, building more new generation jails, and the increased use of supermax prisons), Useem and Piehl (2006) believe that the primary reason for stability is greater managerial control over prison operations.

Noticeably absent in debates about increased imprisonment, however, has been a voice for prison inmates. As the wars on crime and drugs increased prison populations, we saw the increase of advocacy groups, such as Families Against Mandatory Minimums, the Vera Institute of Justice, the Center on Juvenile and Criminal Justice, and the Sentencing Project. In addition, scholars such as James Austin, Michael Irwin, Michael Tonry, and Franklin Zimring have been critical of punitive criminal justice policies. These individuals and groups support more humane and rehabilitative correctional systems and the abolition of mandatory-minimum sentences and lengthy sentences for nonviolent offenders. In addition, independent government bodies, such as the Little Hoover Commission (2003), have drawn attention to the problems in providing adequate community resources for parolees.

As of midyear 2005, the numbers of persons held in jails and prisons continued to grow for the third decade, and there is increasing concern about whether we are headed in the right direction and whether we can afford high imprisonment policies. While some politicians and policy analysts still advocate high levels of prison use, there is a growing support for correctional rehabilitation and a recognition that by preparing inmates for the community we not only save taxpayer dollars (in lower recidivism) but also increase public safety. The question is not whether we should build more prisons but whether we should help prison inmates make positive changes that will increase our long-term safety and taxpayer dollars, while holding them accountable for the crimes that they committed in the community.

Notes

1. Shepherd's (2006) analyses of prison sentences for drug offenders suggested that imprisoning drug offenders may actually contribute to higher rates of crime.

2. One has to be careful in the comparison of cross-national statistics; and higher rates of murder in the United States, and lengthy sentences for these crimes, may increase the U.S. average sentence for violent crimes.

3. Harrison and Beck (2005, 2006) reported that Kentucky's imprisonment rate at midyear 2005 had grown by 6.4 percent since midyear 2004 and 8.5 percent in the previous 12 months, suggesting that their plans to reduce correctional populations were short-lived.

Key Terms

case managers	incarceration probability	proportionality
classification	informal social control	risk assessment
classification officers	new generation jails	role model
cost-benefit studies	(and philosophy)	social capital
diminishing returns	opportunity cost	uniformity

Critical Review Questions

1. Discuss the impact of a five-year term of imprisonment on a mother, a gang member, a middle-class wage earner, and an elderly man. Does a term of imprisonment have the same effect on these different persons?

2. What are imprisonment's effects on families and communities? Do you believe the argument that taking offenders from a community actually decreases the informal social control in those neighborhoods?

3. What are the opportunity costs of imprisonment? If you were directed to cut your state's correctional budget by one-half and invest these funds in programs to reduce prison admissions, what types of programs would you prioritize?

4. Piehl, Useem, and DiIulio (1999, 14) observed that "[p]rison may lose its value as a penalty if it is seen as commonplace." Do you agree or disagree with this statement?

5. Should budget limits be a factor in determining how much incarceration should be used?

6. One way to measure privatization's effectiveness is to examine the numbers of persons held in these facilities. Another method is to review the stock market performance of corporations that hold inmates. What are the long-term earnings and stock value of the Corrections Corporation of America and Wackenhut?

7. It has been speculated that the increased use of imprisonment resulted in a significant benefit in crime control, but this effect decreased as imprisonment increased. Discuss the concept of diminishing returns as it relates to imprisonment.

8. Compare the severity of punishment in the United States and England (these data are available on the Bureau of Justice Statistics and Home Office Web sites).

References

Aday, Ronald H. (2003). *Aging Prisoners: Crisis in American Corrections*. Westport, CT: Praeger.

Aos, Steve. (2003). "Using taxpayer dollars wisely: The costs and benefits of incarceration and other crime control policies." Pp. 19–29 in *Corrections Policy: Can States Cut Costs and Still Curb Crime?* edited by Elizabeth Gross, Betina Friese, and Karen Bogen-Schneider. Madison: University of Wisconsin Center for Excellence in Family Studies.

Austin, James. (2003). *Findings in Prison Classification and Risk Assessment*. Longmont, CO: National Institute of Corrections.

Block, Michael K. (1997). "Supply side imprisonment policy." Pp. 9–29 in *Two Views on Imprisonment Policies: Presentations from the 1996 Annual Research and Evaluation Conference*, edited by National Institute of Justice. Washington, DC: National Institute of Justice. Retrieved October 29, 2006 from: *http://www.ncjrs.gov/pdffiles/165702.pdf.*

Braman, Donald. (2002). "Families and incarceration." Pp. 117–135 in *Invisible Punishment: The Collateral Consequences of Mass Imprisonment*, edited by Marc Mauer and Meda Chesney-Lind. New York: New Press.

Butterfield, Fox. (2002, December 18). "Inmates go free to reduce deficits." *New York Times*, p. A1.

California Department of Corrections and Rehabilitation (2005). *Prison Census Data as of December 31, 2004*. Sacramento: Author.

Caplow, Theodore, and Jonathan Simon. (1999). "Understanding prison policy and population trends." Pp. 63–120 in *Crime and Justice: A Review of Research*, edited by Michael Tonry and Joan Petersilia. Chicago: University of Chicago Press.

Coleman, James S. (1990). *Foundations of Social Theory*. Boston: Harvard University Press.

Crutchfield, Robert D. (2004). "Editorial introduction (Commentary: Mass incarceration)." *Criminology & Public Policy* 3 (2), 265–266.

Cullen, Francis T., and Paul Gendreau. (2000). "Assessing correctional rehabilitation: Policy, practice, and prospects." Pp. 109–175 in *Criminal Justice 2000: Policies, Processes, and Decisions of the Criminal Justice System*, edited by Julie Horney. Washington, DC: National Institute of Justice.

Durose, Matthew R., and Patrick A. Langan. (2004). *Felony Sentences in State Courts, 2002*. Washington, DC: U.S. Department of Justice, Bureau of Justice Statistics.

Federal Bureau of Investigation (FBI). (2006). *Crime in the United States, 2005*. Washington, DC: Author.

Gabel, Stewart. (2003). "Behavioral problems in sons of incarcerated or otherwise absent fathers: The issue of separation." Pp. 105–120 in *Impacts of Incarceration on the African American Family*, edited by Othello Harris and R. Robin Miller. New Brunswick, NJ: Transaction.

Gaes, Gerald G. (2005). "Prison privatization in Florida: Promise, premise, and performance." *Criminology & Public Policy* 4 (1), 83–88.

Glaze, Lauren E., and Thomas P. Bonczar. (2006). *Probation and Parole in the United States, 2005*. Washington, DC: U.S. Department of Justice, Bureau of Justice Statistics.

Greenberg, David F. (2006). "Editorial introduction: Crime and imprisonment." *Criminology & Public Policy* 5 (2), 203–212.

Greene, Judith, and Vincent Schiraldi. (2002). *Cutting Correctly: New Prison Policies for Times of Fiscal Crisis*. Washington, DC: Justice Policy Institute.

Grinstead, Olga, Bonnie Faigeles, Carrie Bancroft, and Barry Zack. (2001). "The financial cost of maintaining relationships with incarcerated African American men: Results from a survey of women prison visitors." *Journal of African American Men* 6 (1), 59–69.

Hagan, John, and Ronit Dinovitzer. (1999). "Collateral consequences of imprisonment for children, communities, and prisoners." Pp. 121–162 in *Crime and Justice: A Review of Research*, edited by Michael Tonry and Joan Petersilia. Chicago: University of Chicago Press.

Hairston, Creasie F. (1991). "Family ties during imprisonment: Important to whom and for what?" *Journal of Sociology and Social Welfare* 18 (1), 87–104.

Harris, Patricia M., and Kimberly S. Keller. (2005). "Ex-offenders need not apply: The criminal background check in hiring decisions." *Journal of Contemporary Criminal Justice* 21 (1), 6–30.

Harrison, Paige M., and Allen J. Beck. (2005). *Prisoners in 2004*. Washington, DC: U.S. Department of Justice, Bureau of Justice Statistics.

——. (2006). *Prison and Jail Inmates at Midyear 2005*. Washington, DC: U.S. Department of Justice, Bureau of Justice Statistics.

Heritage Foundation. (2006). *Issues, 2006: Crime*. Retrieved July 14, 2006 from: *http://www.heritage.org/research/features/issues/issuearea/Crime.cfm*.

Hochstetler, Andy, Daniel S. Murphy, and Ronald L. Simons. (2004). "Damaged goods: Exploring predictors of stress in prison inmates." *Crime & Delinquency* 50 (3), 436–457.

Home Office. (2005). *Sentencing Statistics, 2004*. Retrieved July 15, 2006 from: *http://www.homeoffice.gov.uk/rds/pdfs05/hosb1505.pdf*.

Hughes, Kristen A. (2006). *Justice Expenditure and Employment in the United States, 2003.* Washington DC: U.S. Department of Justice, Bureau of Justice Statistics.

Kovandzic, Tomislav V., and Lynn M. Vieraitis. (2006). "The effect of county-level prison population growth on crime rates." *Criminology & Public Policy* 5 (2), 213–244.

Langan, Patrick A., and David J. Levin. (2002). *Recidivism of Prisoners Released in 1994.* Washington, DC: Bureau of Justice Statistics, U.S. Department of Justice.

Latessa, Edward J. (2003). "Promoting public safety through effective correctional interventions: What works and what doesn't?" Pp. 31–36 in *Corrections Policy: Can States Cut Costs and Still Curb Crime?*, edited by Elizabeth Gross, Betina Friese, and Karen Bogen-schneider. Madison: University of Wisconsin Center for Excellence in Family Studies.

——. (2004). "The challenge of change: Correctional programs and evidence-based practices." *Criminology & Public Policy* 3 (4), 547–560.

Liedka, Raymond V., Anne M. Piehl, and Burt Useem. (2006). "The crime-control effect of incarceration: Does scale matter?" *Criminology & Public Policy* 5 (2), 245–276.

Lin, Ann Chih. (2000). *Reform in the Making: The Implementation of Social Policy in Prison.* Princeton, NJ: Princeton University Press.

Little Hoover Commission. (2003). *Back to the Community: Safe and Sound Parole Policies.* Sacramento, CA: Author.

Lotke, Eric, and Jason Ziedenberg. (2005). *Tipping Point: Maryland's Overuse of Incarceration and the Impact on Community Safety.* Washington, DC: Justice Policy Institute.

Lynch, James P., and William J. Sabol. (2004). "Assessing the effects of mass incarceration on informal social control in communities." *Criminology & Public Policy* 3 (2), 267–294.

Mays, G. Larry, and Tara Gray, editors. (1996). *Privatization and the Provision of Correctional Services.* Cincinnati, OH: Anderson.

McGuire, M. Dyan. (2005). "The impact of prison rape on public health." *Californian Journal of Health Promotion* 3 (2), 72–83.

Meares, Tracey L. (2004). "Mass incarceration: Who pays the price for criminal offending?" *Criminology & Public Policy* 3 (2), 295–302.

Miller, R. Robin. (2003). "Various implications of the "race to incarcerate" on incarcerated African Americans men and their families." Pp. 3–17 in *Impacts of Incarceration on the African American Family*, edited by Othello Harris and R. Robin Miller. New Brunswick, NJ: Transaction.

Mumola, Christopher J. (2005). *Suicide and Homicide in State Prisons and Local Jails.* Washington, DC: U.S. Department of Justice, Bureau of Justice Statistics.

Murphy, Daniel S. (2005). "Health care in the Federal Bureau of Prisons: Fact or fiction?" *Californian Journal of Health Promotion* 3 (2), 23–37.

Piehl, Anne M. (2004). "The challenge of mass incarceration." *Criminology & Public Policy* 3 (2), 303–308.

Piehl, Anne M., Bert Useem, and John J. DiIulio. (1999). *Right-Sizing Justice: A Cost-Benefit Analysis of Imprisonment in Three States.* New York: Center for Civic Innovation at the Manhattan Institute.

Richie, Beth. (2002). "The social impact of mass incarceration on women." Pp. 136–149 in *Invisible Punishment: The Collateral Consequences of Mass Imprisonment*, edited by Marc Mauer and Meda Chesney-Lind. New York: New Press.

Rose, Dina, and Todd Clear. (1998). "Incarceration, social capital, and crime: Implications for social disorganization theory." *Criminology* 36 (3), 441–480.

Ruddell, Rick. (2004). *America Behind Bars: Trends in Imprisonment, 1950–2000.* New York: LFB Scholarly Press.

Ruddell, Rick, and Mark Tomita. (2005). "Opportunities for change in correctional and community health." *Californian Journal of Health Promotion* 3 (2), iv–x.

Schlosser, Eric. (1998, December). "Prison industrial complex." The *Atlantic Monthly* 282 (6), 51–77.

Segal, Geoffrey F. (2006). *Comparing the Performance of Private and Public Prisons: If You Can't Win, Change the Rules.* Retrieved July 14, 2006 from: *http://www.reason.org/commentaries/segal_20060404.shtml.*

Shepherd, Joanna. (2006). "The imprisonment puzzle: Understanding how prison growth affects crime." *Criminology & Public Policy* 5 (2), 285–298.

Spelman, William. (2000). "The limited importance of prison expansion." Pp. 97–129 in *The Crime Drop in America,* edited by Alfred Blumstein and Joel Wallman. New York: Cambridge University Press.

Stephan, James J. (2004). *State Prison Expenditures, 2001.* Washington, DC: U.S. Department of Justice, Bureau of Justice Statistics.

Thomas, Charles W. (2005). "Recidivism of public and private state prison inmates in Florida: Issues and unanswered questions." *Criminology & Public Policy* 4 (1), 89–100.

Useem, Burt, and Anne M. Piehl. (2006). "Prison buildup and disorder." *Punishment & Society* 8 (1), 87–115.

Welch, Michael. (2002). *Detained: Immigration Laws and the Expanding I.N.S. Jail Complex.* Philadelphia: Temple University Press.

Wilhelm, Daniel F., and Nicholas R. Turner. (2002). *Is the Budget Crisis Changing the Way We Look at Sentencing and Incarceration?* New York: Vera Institute of Justice.

Zedlewski, Edwin. (1987). *Making Confinement Decisions.* Washington, DC: National Institute of Justice.

Zimring, Franklin E., and Gordon Hawkins. (1995). *Incapacitation: Penal Confinement and the Restraint of Crime.* New York: Oxford University Press.

Recommended Readings

Johnson, Robert. (2002). *Hard Time: Understanding and Reforming the Prison.* Belmont, CA: Thomson/Wadsworth. This book provides a comprehensive examination of the American prison and how history has shaped the prisons that we have today. Johnson outlines the challenges of living and working within prisons and how inmate and guard cultures influence life behind bars.

Reiman, Jeffrey. (2004). *The Rich Get Richer and the Poor Get Prison.* Boston: Allyn & Bacon. This controversial book outlines how the poor always have been disadvantaged when it comes to their interactions with criminal justice systems. Reiman argues that crime is functional and that occupational, workplace, and environmental crimes go unpunished despite the fact that they result in as many fatalities as street crime.

Schlosser, Eric. (1998, December). "The prison industrial complex." *Atlantic Monthly,* 282 (6), 51–77. Schlosser presents a compelling argument about the increasing ties between punishment and private industries. Central to this article is the question of whether anybody should profit from the delivery of punishment and whether economic factors influence the use of incarceration. Furthermore, Schlosser is critical of politicians who support punishment policies while understanding their destructive effects on individuals, families, and communities. ✦

Chapter 12 .

The Death Penalty

Introduction

One of the most controversial sanctions for offenders is the death penalty. Once widely used, capital punishment is gradually falling out of favor. Amnesty International (2007) reported that 128 countries have abolished the death penalty either by statute or in practice, while 69 nations still execute offenders. The United States is one of the few industrialized countries where judges still sentence offenders to death for ordinary crimes.[1] Yet, even within the United States, there is considerable diversity in the use of this sanction. Twelve states and the District of Columbia have abolished capital punishment. In fact, Wisconsin abolished the death penalty in 1853, and Hawaii has never carried out an execution (Shepherd 2004a).

Of the remaining 37 states where executions still occur, Texas was responsible for almost one-third of all deaths in 2005 (Snell 2006). Some states may sentence an offender to death, but the sanction is rarely used. Seven of the 37 states have not had an execution since capital punishment resumed after the *Gregg v. Georgia* (1976) decision. The federal government also has the ability to sentence offenders to death, and the execution of Timothy McVeigh in 2001 was the first time a federal prisoner had been killed since 1961.

Ultimately, the death sentence is rarely imposed and even less likely to be carried out. Liebman and colleagues (2000) reported that fewer than 6 percent of all persons sentenced to death are actually executed. In many cases, inmates live on death row for decades before their execution. With few inmates being executed, death row populations have swelled, although the number of persons condemned to death have been decreasing, in sharp contrast to the growing jail and penitentiary populations. Snell (2006, 1) reported that "[t]he 128 inmates received under sentence of death during 2005 represent the smallest number of admissions since 1973." In 2006, 53 prisoners were executed, which is a substantial decrease from a high of 99 offenders who were executed in 1999 (Death Penalty Information Center 2007). Moreover, the number of persons in jeopardy of the death penalty is also shrinking. Historically, defendants were sentenced to death for offenses such as rape, or crimes against the state, although in practice this has not occurred for decades.[2] In addition, the Supreme Court decisions of *Atkins v. Virginia* (2002) and *Roper v. Simmons* (2005) have excluded mentally retarded or juvenile offenders from the death penalty.

Supporters and opponents of the death penalty passionately tend to defend their own positions. Not surprisingly, persons who believe in the death penalty tend to support the crime control model, and they propose that due process protections, such as appellate review of death penalty cases, be restricted and the process streamlined. Executions, they argue, are an effective method of deterring crime, and they point to studies finding that one execution can result in lives saved as potential murderers are more reluctant to kill (Zimmerman 2004). Furthermore, an execution is the ultimate form of incapacitation, as it effectively removes the offender from ever returning to society as well as saving lives in prison. The death penalty, supporters argue, is also a powerful symbol of crime denunciation.

Opponents of the death penalty argue that the sanction is more expensive than life imprisonment (once the cost of death penalty trials, death row housing, and appeals are considered) and that the sentences have been imposed on minorities in a disproportionate manner. Moreover, they suggest that the penalty is applied arbitrarily because some serial killers are not executed, but murderers who commit less serious crimes are sentenced to death. Further, the killing of an innocent person is seen as the ultimate failure of justice systems. Opponents also refer to social science research that demonstrates no deterrent value in the death penalty. In fact, as we will see, some scholars suggest that legal executions might actually increase homicides.

Because emotions are so highly involved in arguments over the death penalty, it is sometimes difficult to separate facts and myths about capital punishment. To help us better understand the death penalty, this chapter explores the historical context of capital punishment within the United States, legal and illegal executions, recent controversies about the application of the sanction, and the social and political factors that have led to changes in the use of the death penalty. Finally, we offer a number of possible scenarios about the death penalty's future. Like Walker (2006), we avoid the emotionally charged issues of whether the death penalty is morally correct and instead focus on the question of whether it is an effective criminal justice policy.

Capital Punishment in America

Colonial Times

Prior to the development of the penitentiary in the early 1800s, the range of punitive sanctions for offenders was limited. Offenders convicted of most felonies could be sentenced to death, but historians ob-

serve that legally sanctioned executions were rare. In a historical review of early colonial law in Virginia, for instance, King (2003, 949)
pointed to many practical and procedural barriers to actually executing
an offender. She observed that, "[g]iven the opportunities for derail-
ment along the way, only an unusual case ended in execution." While
advocates of the crime control model lament the fact that persons sentenced to death have many protections today, a greater number of legal
and extralegal barriers existed two centuries ago.

King (2003) observed that the transportation required for witnesses
to travel long distances to a district court (where serious offenses were
heard) and the difficulty in selecting an impartial jury were practical
barriers to justice in the colonies. Escapes from the rudimentary jails of
the day also were common and may have been encouraged by jailers
(especially if suspects were indigent and authorities had no way to ex-
tract revenue from them). Convictions for serious felonies in that era
are thought to have been rare. As death was one of the few punishments, juries were reluctant to find someone guilty if this finding would
place the accused at jeopardy of the death penalty. Even if a person
were convicted and sentenced to death, there was no certainty that the
actual execution would occur.

King (2003, 947–949) outlined how three procedural protections
limited use of the death penalty in colonial Virginia. First, persons convicted and given the death penalty could have a higher court review
their case. The reluctance to use the death penalty is evidenced by the
high number of convictions that were "set aside" for various technical
reasons. Second, convicts sentenced to death were able to ask for **benefit of clergy** which was basically a reprieve. Historically, clergy members who were accused of crimes could ask to be tried by religious authorities. Over time, this benefit was extended to many first-time offenders, and their sentences were often commuted. Persons granted
benefit of clergy were branded on the hand so they could not ask for
forgiveness twice. King (2003, 948) cited historians who "estimate that
up to a third of all felons in Virginia . . . were granted clergy." In addition, persons sentenced to death had the ability to seek pardons. Unlike
executive clemency today, when political officials, such as the President or a state governor, can pardon offenders or **commute** their sentence (which means to reduce the severity of the sanction), gubernatorial pardons were commonly granted. Thus, there were various legal
barriers to executions.

As a result, only the worst offenders ever reached court, and few
were actually punished. It has been suggested that the penitentiary's development was a result of the fact that juries were unlikely to convict an
offender if the only sanction was death (Banner 2002). Moreover, some
scholars have speculated that executions decreased because of the
changing values of human life (Elias 1939/2000). Despite these social
and legal changes, capital punishment did not always occur as a result

of official sanctions; and from the time of the colonial era, extending to the mid-twentieth century, it was not unusual for extralegal or vigilante executions to occur.

Legal and Extralegal Executions

Our views about the death penalty are shaped by its use throughout history and, more recently, by the media. Capital punishment was imported from Britain, and it was a type of entertainment in England and some European nations. Legal executions in the United States were public spectacles, where the community gathered to see the sentence carried out (Banner 2002). These executions included denunciation and repentance and had a strong educative function about public laws and norms. Over time, public participation in punishment gradually decreased, although practices differed throughout the nation. Norbert Elias (1939/2000) attributed this reluctance to use punishment as a public spectacle as a product of civilization.

One type of extralegal execution that remained a public spectacle was lynching, and this practice was prevalent in early America and persisted in the South until the 1940s. Several thousand accused were taken from jails or police custody by mobs and hanged or shot in close proximity to the jails where they had been held. Oftentimes, lynching had a racial component; and on the frontier, "justice" was administered to suspects before town constables or the sheriff arrived. In some cases, law enforcement officials were powerless to stop such mobs. In other instances, the police gave tacit approval for these executions. While African Americans were often the victims of such executions in the South, other minority groups, such as Chinese laborers, were also victimized on the West Coast. In many cases, the guilt of these persons was not established. In all cases, these illegal executions tarnished the history of American justice systems.

Historical Trends in Capital Punishment

Throughout the twentieth century, the number of persons legally executed significantly decreased over time. Figure 12.1 reveals that legal executions have a "U" shaped distribution. They decreased over time and then stopped altogether during the 1970s (due to the *Furman v. Georgia* case). After the death penalty was restored in 1976, more executions were carried out. The peak occurred in 1999 with 98 executions, but they have decreased since that time.

The Supreme Court in the 1972 *Furman v. Georgia* decision found that executions were being applied in an arbitrary and capricious manner and directed states to develop procedures to reduce the discretion of judges and juries in recommending the death penalty. Until states had corrected these procedures, there was a halt to executions for several years. In the *Gregg v. Georgia* decision in 1976, the Court found that

Figure 12.1
Annual Executions in the United States, 1930 to 2005

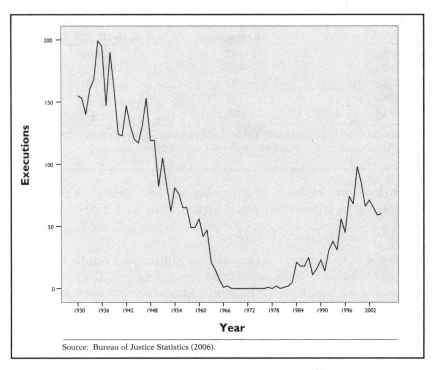

Source: Bureau of Justice Statistics (2006).

states had developed mechanisms to ensure that capital punishment was not implemented in a capricious manner. These changes included (1) considering a range of mitigating and aggravating circumstances and (2) instituting a two-level (**bifurcated**) trial process with a determination of guilt or not guilty and a subsequent penalty phase. Also, in most states, there is an automatic appellate review of capital cases.

Shepherd (2004b, 4) calculated the average annual number of executions for each decade, and they decreased from 167 in the 1930s to 48 in the 1990s. We also calculated the annual number of executions from 2000 to 2005, using Bureau of Justice Statistics execution data, and the average increased somewhat from the 1990s. Because the U.S. population increased greatly throughout this era, we translated this statistic into a rate per 100,000 residents in the population to better understand the use of capital punishment over time.

Table 12.1 reveals the change in the execution rate since the 1930s. The trend shows a substantial decrease, as levels of executions in the 1990s were one-thirteenth their 1930s average. Although the average annual number of executions in the 2000s is higher than in previous decades, the use of capital punishment decreased in 2004 and 2005. While

Table 12.1
Executions in the United States, 1930–2005

Era	Average Annual Executions	Annual Execution Rate/100,000 Residents
1930s	167	0.13
1940s	130	0.09
1950s	75	0.04
1990s	48	0.01
2000s (2000–2005)	68	.02

Source: Adapted from Shepherd (2004a) and Bureau of Justice Statistics (2006). Execution rates calculated using Census Bureau population data.

it is too soon to evaluate whether this will be a long-term trend, the death sentence is more frequently applied than are actual executions.

Support for the Death Penalty

Advocates for and against capital punishment use results from survey research that provide support for their positions. The Gallup Poll has measured American public opinion about the death penalty since 1936. Figure 12.2 demonstrates the long-term trend in support for the death penalty. Although support shifts over time, it had fluctuated around the 70 percent range, especially in the past three decades. Interestingly, the support for the death penalty was lowest when trust in government was the highest, in the 1950s.

Moore (2004, 1), a Gallup Poll researcher, observed that survey responses about support for capital punishment depend on the manner in which the question is asked, and a "large majority supports the death penalty if no alternative is specified." By contrast, if a respondent is given the choice between the death penalty and **life in prison without the possibility of parole (LWOP),** support for executing offenders decreases to approximately 50 percent. Moore (2004, 4–5) also found that approximately one-third of respondents feel that the death penalty is morally wrong, that approximately 40 percent believe that the death penalty is applied unfairly, and that most respondents believe that capital punishment deters homicides. Public support for the execution of offenders is also dependent upon highly visible or particularly heinous crimes—or egregious cases of wrongful conviction—and after these occur, there can be a significant change in public perceptions about this sanction.

The Death Penalty Today

At the end of 2005, 3,254 state and federal inmates had been sentenced to death, and most of these offenders were being held in five states: California, Texas, Florida, Pennsylvania, and Ohio (Snell 2006).

Figure 12.2
Support for the Death Penalty—1936 to 2006

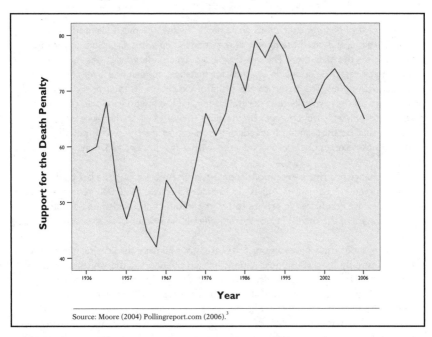

Source: Moore (2004) Pollingreport.com (2006).[3]

Two other statistics are noteworthy: the number of offenders who are condemned to death and their length of stay in prison prior to the sentence being carried out. Together, these facts shed some light on our willingness to use the death penalty.

The number of condemned offenders has increased significantly over the past few decades: from 131 in 1953 to 3,254 at yearend 2005 (Bureau of Justice Statistics 2006). The biggest increase of offenders sentenced to death occurred at about the same time the imprisonment rate increased from 107 to 488 inmates per 100,000 residents. One reason is the length of time inmates will spend incarcerated prior to their actual execution. For persons executed in 2005, for instance, a condemned inmate served approximately 147 months on death row prior to the sentence being carried out (Snell 2006). In some jurisdictions, the length of time is even greater. In California, for instance, the six inmates executed between 2000 and 2006 each served an average of 260 months (21.66 years) prior to their sentence being carried out, according to the California Department of Corrections and Rehabilitation (CDCR) (2006a). In fact, the CDCR (2006b) reported that of all the inmates on death row who have died since 1978, only 14 were executed (one of these was actually executed in Missouri), while 50 others died due to other reasons (33 of natural causes, 12 committed suicide, and 5 of "other causes").

Box 12.1
Making Executions More Civilized

For most of history, executions were public events, the methods used were sometimes barbaric, and often the bodies of the condemned were displayed, sometimes for months after the execution. The most significant change, however, was the move from public to private executions. In England, for instance, condemned offenders would be paraded from Newgate Prison to the place of execution at Tyburn, some two miles away. This journey typically took several hours, and the prisoners would often be given alcohol to bolster their courage. By the time they arrived at the place of execution, there would be thousands of spectators (sometimes nearly 30,000 people). By the 1870s, these executions were conducted within the prison, and they were private events.

The change to private executions took longer in America, and the last public execution occurred in Kentucky in August 1936 before a crowd of 20,000 people. Although executions are conducted in private today, the victim's and condemned inmate's families, members of the media, justice system officials, and other observers attend executions.

The methods used in executions today are more humane than capital punishment in earlier times. By the 1700s, most nations hanged offenders, although the French used the guillotine to cut off the condemned person's head. The problem with hanging was that it sometimes took almost a half hour for some persons to die (and sometimes longer), so the electric chair was introduced in some U.S. jurisdictions in the late 1800s as a more humane method of execution (although it was not foolproof and some offenders had to be electrocuted a number of times before they died). Bonczar and Snell (2005) noted that in the United States today, there are five approved methods of execution: lethal injection (37 states), electrocution (9 states), lethal gas (4 states), hanging (3 states), and firing squads (3 states).

Lethal injection was intended to be the most humane way of killing an offender, although some prisoners have challenged that the drugs used in the procedure (there are three different drugs) to anesthetize them might not always be effective. For example, some inmates are awake but incapacitated (unable to move or speak) when the other medications are injected that actually paralyze the inmate's breathing or that stop the heart. These issues were raised in the British Medical Journal *The Lancet* in October 2005. At midyear 2006, executions in several states have been halted until questions about the constitutionality of the punishment (whether it would be cruel and unusual) are addressed. On June 30, 2006, the President of the American Society of Anesthesiologists advised members of that organization that they should "steer clear" of executions (Guidry 2006). ✦

Many persons wonder why it takes so long to carry out the execution once an offender has been sentenced. This is a complex question, and it relates to the time that it takes for these cases to be scrutinized by higher courts. All states except South Carolina have an automatic review of their death sentences, and the case will be reviewed by an appellate court. In South Carolina, inmates can choose to waive the appeal if they are deemed competent. These reviews are intended to ensure that a person has not been wrongfully convicted, which is an important consideration given that 123 death row inmates have been exonerated from 1973 to midyear 2006 (DPIC 2006). In any case, these appeals are typically lengthy, drawn-out processes, especially if the condemned inmate opposes the sentence.

No discussion of the death penalty would be complete without an examination of the demographic characteristics of the condemned inmates. Snell (2006, 1) noted that 56 percent of the prisoners sentenced to death were white, 42 percent were African American, and the remaining 2 percent were of other or unknown races. In terms of ethnicity, 13 percent of the inmates were Latino. Consistent with our discussion of the racial disparities in Chapter 7, African Americans are overrepresented on American death rows. In terms of ethnicity, however, Latinos are represented at approximately the same level as their prevalence in the population.

Women condemned to death are underrepresented, with 52 women or about 1.6 percent of the total death row population at yearend 2005 (Snell 2006), but the Federal Bureau of Investigation (FBI) reported that women were responsible for 11 percent of murders in 2005 (of the known offenders; see FBI 2006). However, women are overrepresented on California's death row. Although the state has approximately 10 percent of the national population, it has almost 29 percent of the female death row inmates. Only seven states have more than one woman on death row, demonstrating that the sentence is unlikely to be imposed in most jurisdictions. The racial characteristics of female death row inmates are similar to the male rate statistics, with 63.7 percent white, 26.9 percent African American, and the rest of other or unknown race (statistics were rounded).

Recent scholarship suggests that the decision to impose the death penalty is not associated with the offender's race, but the victim's race. Pierce and Radelet (2005) examined California death sentences between 1973 and 2003 and found that the death penalty was more likely to be imposed when the victim was white, after controlling for aggravating factors (such as multiple victims). These findings should motivate scholars to more closely examine the victim-offender relationship in punishment decisions.

Capital Punishment Policy

While the number of condemned inmates has increased along with the length of time between sentence and execution, over the past few years the number of felons actually receiving death sentences has decreased. In 1994, for instance, 327 persons were sentenced to death, and by 2005, this total had decreased to 128 persons (down from 188 the previous year). Furthermore, many death row residents have been released, either due to wrongful convictions or commutation of sentences (typically to life imprisonment). In 2003, for example, Illinois

Governor George Ryan commuted the sentences of 155 offenders and pardoned 4 others (Bonczar and Snell 2005).

The one jurisdiction that seems to be increasing the number of persons sentenced to death is the federal government. As Bonczar and Snell (2005, 8) noted, "The 10 offenders who entered the Federal prison system in 2004 was twice the previous largest number of annual admissions" to death row. Mannheimer (2006, 819) outlined

> Recent changes to the way the U.S. Department of Justice decides whether to pursue capital charges have made it more likely that the federal death penalty will be sought in cases in which the criminal conduct occurred in states that do not authorize capital punishment for any crime.

Thus, Mannheimer argued that persons condemned to death in these states actually receive a more severe sentence than proscribed by state statutes and questions whether this is constitutionally appropriate.

There are some plausible reasons why the application of the death penalty has decreased. The Death Penalty Information Center (2006, 3–7) attributed the decline to several reasons, including (1) the number of innocent death row inmates released in the past few decades; (2) racial bias; (3) arbitrariness; (4) costs; (5) the sanction's effectiveness; (6) Supreme Court decisions, such as *Roper v. Simmons;* (7) new voices opposing the penalty, including police officials, prosecutors, and judges; and (8) international developments. The following paragraphs outline these issues.

In many places, the public has lost confidence in the ability of justice systems to impose the death penalty on the correct person. Unnever and Cullen (2005) found that many respondents to national polls believe that innocent persons have been executed and that has led to less support for capital punishment. In Chapter 9, we outlined some causes of wrongful convictions, and these miscarriages of justice have occurred throughout the nation. Regardless of one's position on the death penalty, it must be acknowledged that 188 prison inmates have been exonerated (Innocence Project 2007) and that, as the Death Penalty Information Center stated, 123 of these prisoners had been on death row (DPIC 2006).[4]

A second reason for the decreased use of the death penalty is the belief that there is racial bias in these sentences. African Americans are overrepresented on death row, and recent studies have demonstrated that the victim's race has a significant impact on the sentence imposed. Moreover, attorneys, scholars, and advocacy organizations suggest that there is a great deal of arbitrariness in the death penalty's imposition. The Death Penalty Information Center (2006, 5) noted that "defendants guilty of multiple murders were spared a death sentence, while mentally ill defendants and those guilty of far less egregious offenses were executed."

It is nearly impossible to find accurate or unbiased data about the true costs of imposing the death penalty versus keeping people in prison for the rest of their lives. The American Civil Liberties Union (ACLU) outlined the costs of both options and found that it was less expensive to hold inmates in prison for life (ACLU 2003). Similar findings were reported by Richard Dieter (2005), the executive director of the DPIC, an abolitionist organization. The problem is that it is difficult to trust organizations or public interest groups that have a stated agenda because their analyses may be biased.

One challenge is the difficulty of correctly estimating the costs either of executing offenders or of keeping them incarcerated for the rest of their natural lives. Accurate comparisons must include court costs (which are far greater in capital murder cases), the costs of postconviction appeals, and housing the inmates—either on death row prior to incarceration or serving their natural lives imprisoned. Few studies take into account the impact of inflation or life expectancy of prison inmates in their estimates. Research commissioned by the Tennessee comptroller suggested that it is more expensive to execute offenders than to keep them incarcerated for their natural lives (Wilson, Doss, and Phillips 2004). Regardless of one's support for the death penalty or LWOP, both options are costly propositions for the state.

One troublesome challenge about the death penalty is gauging the sanction's effectiveness. A number of punishment philosophies provide theoretical justification for use of the death penalty. Those who believe in **retribution** (an "eye for an eye"), **deterrence,** and **incapacitation** generally support use of the death penalty. Everyone would agree that a death sentence achieves the goal of retribution. But what about the alternative option of LWOP? This sanction effectively incapacitates an offender forever as escapes from maximum security prisons are rare. Opponents of capital punishment argue that in the event of a wrongful conviction, the inmate is still alive.

Another justification for the death penalty is that it deters other citizens from killing. This has been the subject of many scholarly studies, and the investigators typically report contradictory results. One of the earliest studies that used econometric methods was conducted by Issac Ehrlich (1975), and he found that each legal execution deterred eight other murders. Ehrlich's study was strongly criticized in the criminological literature, mostly due to the limitations of his research methods. Despite these criticisms, the study is widely cited, and advocates of the crime control model are quick to use such studies as support for executions.

Ehrlich's (1975) research led to several dozen follow-up studies, and the results are difficult to summarize. Findings in these studies are very contradictory: (1) some show that capital punishment deters future murders, or (2) after a governor commutes a death penalty, murders will increase (see Sunstein and Vermeule 2005, or Zimmerman 2004). Furthermore, other studies revealed a **brutalization effect,** where increases in legal executions resulted in higher numbers of murders. Cochran and Chamlin (2000) found that after the state executes someone, nonstranger homicides increase, while stranger or felony homicides decrease. By contrast, Shepherd (2004b) found that legal executions in some states produced a brutalization effect, but in other jurisdictions, there was a deterrent effect. Most of the studies used time-series statistical models, and these models are somewhat sensitive to the variables that are included, the lags that the researcher chooses, and the years examined (see Ruddell 2004).

Fagan (2005) provided an analysis of the capital punishment-deterrence research, and argued that most research examining this relationship is flawed. He contended that there is no scientifically sound evidence that supports the claim that executions deter homicides. It is difficult to fully explain any complex human behavior, such as the deterrent effect of capital punishment using statistical tests, and Fagan (2005, 18) argues that "omissions and errors are so egregious that this work falls well within the unfortunate category of junk science." One of the difficulties in deterrence research is that there are almost unlimited causal factors associated with a given behavior (such as murder), and statistical procedures enable us to include only a few explanatory variables. Interestingly, homicide rates are highest in the southern states, where the death penalty is more likely to be used than in northern states, suggesting that there may be a brutalization effect.

Donohue and Wolfers (2005) conducted an analysis of death penalty studies and found that the death penalty is applied so rarely that most studies of brutalization or deterrence have produced results that are basically meaningless to inform any policy debate. The hazard of such research is that the findings may be repeated by politicians and policymakers for years afterwards. Donohue and Wolfers (2005) cited Dezhbakhsh (1999) as saying, "The academic survival of a flawed study may not be of much consequence. But unfortunately, the ill-effects of a bad policy, influenced by flawed research, may hurt generations."

Inconsistent research results confuse the issues and complicate decisions for policymakers. Thinking back to other criminal justice interventions reviewed in this book, these results are entirely predictable. Interventions in one place might be successful as they are consistent with a state's cultural, historical, political, social, or economic characteristics. In addition, interventions that might have been effective in the 1980s might have an entirely different impact two decades later. The hazard with the capital punishment debate is that advocates or opponents will often use the data and results that support only their position, regardless of one study's limitations. Some of these research findings, however, may have influenced legal decisions about who is executed.

Recent Supreme Court decisions have reduced the number of defendants in jeopardy of the death penalty. In 2002, for example, the Supreme Court's *Atkins v. Virginia* decision made it unlawful to execute the mentally retarded. Furthermore, in 2005, the *Roper v. Simmons* decision extended these protections to persons under the age of 18 at the time of the offense. The justification for these restrictions is that these offenders are not entirely responsible, mature, or sophisticated enough to be held fully accountable. It is plausible that death penalty abolitionists are attempting to whittle down the number of persons who may be put to death. By contrast, this might be a good criminal justice policy because executing persons who are immature or unsophisticated is likely to decrease support for the death penalty.

While organizations such as the ACLU have always opposed the death penalty, there is an increasing opposition to the death penalty from some surprising sources. The DPIC (2006) outlined how judges, police officers, and prosecutors are increasingly apt to oppose capital punishment. Most significant are statements from former Supreme Court Justice Sandra Day O'Connor, who suggested that the penalty has been imposed on innocent persons.[5] There is some question whether these officials are leading or following public opinion, but such statements reflect doubt about the sanction.

The Future of the Death Penalty

Capital punishment is disappearing in most first-world nations. In recent years, the number of persons executed within the United States has declined as well. It is likely that the number of persons sentenced to death in the near future will continue to decrease. The Supreme Court in the *Atkins* and *Roper* decisions has limited the types of offenders in jeopardy of the death penalty. Moreover, while public support for the death penalty in the United States remains at approximately 70 percent, there is broad opposition to capital punishment, especially in light of publicity about wrongful convictions during the past decade.

One issue that deserves special attention is the increased international opposition to capital punishment. One example of the globalization of social control is the coupling of punishment practices and membership in international federations, trading relationships, or treaties. If the European Community can restrict membership to nations that have abolished capital punishment, could similar arrangements also be extended to trading partners? The influence of international practices was recently cited by American jurists in the *Roper v. Simmons* decision.

Delivering the *Roper v. Simmons* (2005) opinion, Supreme Court Justice Anthony Kennedy made several references to international opinion and observed how

> [t]he overwhelming weight of international opinion against the juvenile death penalty is not controlling here, but provides respected and significant confirmation for the Court's determination that the penalty is disproportionate.

The fact that Kennedy cited international considerations was upsetting to the Court's conservative members, and the dissents of both Justices O'Connor and Scalia questioned whether the United States should heed the crime-control practices of other nations.

Box 12.2
Should International Practices Influence the U.S. Justice Policies?

Statements in the *Roper v. Simmons* 543 U.S. 551 (2005) decision caused considerable debate about whether the policies or practices of other nations should shape U.S. criminal justice policies. In his dissent of the decision, Justice Antonin Scalia noted,

More fundamentally, however, the basic premise of the Court's argument—that American law should conform to the laws of the rest of the world—ought to be rejected out of hand. . . . To invoke alien law when it agrees with one's own thinking, and ignore it otherwise, is not reasoned decision-making, but sophistry. (543 U.S. 551 (2005), Dissent, Scalia, J., p. 18)

This is an important observation as Justice Scalia framed his dissent by the fact that we often reject the legal practices of other nations if those practices do not conform to U.S. legal customs. Scalia specifically cited two examples of constitutional protections that most other nations do not have: the exclusionary rule and the protection against double jeopardy. If we want to be consistent with the legal systems of other nations, should we retain these due process protections?

Tushnet (2006) examined the issue of the adoption of legal practices and norms from other nations. He noted (2006, 1267) that

In foreign law you can find anything you want. If you don't find it in the decisions of France or Italy, it's in the decisions of Somalia or Japan or Indonesia or wherever. . . . It allows the judge to incorporate his or her own personal preferences, cloak them with the authority of precedent . . . and use that to determine the meaning of the Constitution.

Many supporters of the crime control model share similar sentiments. Should a nation be autonomous in its criminal justice policy? Given these observations, should we in the United States be concerned about the types of criminal justice system interventions that exist in other nations? ✦

While almost one-third of executions occurred in just Texas in 2005 (see Snell 2006)—there is variation even within this state. Steiker (2002, 8) noted that

> Dallas County (Dallas) and Harris County (Houston), two counties with strikingly similar demographics and crime rates, have very different death sentencing rates, with Dallas County returning 11 death verdicts per 1000 homicides, while Harris County returns 19 death verdicts per 1000 homicides.

Steiker (2002) reported similar findings in other states as well, suggesting that political factors influence the county-level use of the death penalty.

Jacobs and Carmichael (2004) examined the use of capital punishment and found that states with greater membership levels in conservative churches and higher crime rates were more likely to impose the death penalty. Moreover, these scholars found that Republican Party strength and state minority populations also influenced the number of death sentences. These findings suggest that prosecutors and politicians use the death penalty to demonstrate being "tough on crime." One of the most blatant examples of a politician using a death sentence to lure voters was then-Governor Bill Clinton of Arkansas who did not commute the death sentence of Ricky Ray Rector, a brain-damaged offender,[6] out of fear of being labeled "soft on crime" during his Presidential campaign. The fact that politicians would use the deaths of others to win elections, however, increases cynicism of both punishments as well as politicians.

Conclusions

Capital punishment will continue to be a controversial sanction for crime control. Support for capital punishment has remained more or less constant for over six decades, although it has fluctuated greatly in recent years. Like public opinion about other criminal justice policies, a racial element exists in support of the death penalty. White survey respondents generally support the penalty, while African Americans tend to be abolitionists (Unnever and Cullen 2005). This issue also shows a considerable gap between academic scholars, who almost always are abolitionists, and the general public, who overwhelmingly support the death penalty.

Should policies about the operations of criminal justice systems, including punishment, be based on public opinion, or should objective bureaucrats make these decisions based on what the research demonstrates about crime and justice? Marshall (2000) argued that Canadians and Europeans (who have abolished the death penalty) crave punishments as much as Americans, but their governments do not support capital punishment. Similar to the analysis presented in Chapter 6, the results of current research show that the United States is more punitive, in part because state governments are less insulated from punitive public values or opinions (see Savelsberg 1994).

One of the limitations of the death penalty debate is that policymakers lack a comprehensive body of research about capital punishment to inform decision making. For instance, we do not have a very good idea about the actual costs and benefits of executing offenders. Moreover, we have little understanding about the deterrence effect (if any) of a single execution. Sunstein and Vermeule (2005) argued that policymakers are remiss if executions have a life-saving deterrent effect and they fail to take action. Yet, if executions do have a brutalization effect, then capital punishment actually reduces public safety. As with almost all controversial criminal justice issues, it is often difficult to separate the facts from the myths.

It is nearly impossible to predict future criminal justice policy. However, given the events of the past decade, we suggest that the use of the death penalty will continue to decrease: Fewer offenders will be sentenced to death, and relatively few will be executed. This trend hinges upon a number of factors, including homicide and violent crime rates. Murder rates are currently at a five-decade low. If they continue to be stable, there will probably be less public demand for harsh penalties. Moreover, public opinion in the United States can have a significant effect on criminal justice policy. If public support for the death penalty slips, there will less political support for capital punishment.

Barkan and Cohn (2005) observed that high levels of support for the death penalty are a function of the attitudes of white respondents, and they are pessimistic that there will be any significant change in these punitive values. However, changes in public mood are sensitive to many factors. One outrageous crime or terrorist act, such as the 9/11 tragedy, can have the ability to transform or sway public opinion, political priorities, and criminal justice policy at the same time.

Notes

1. Some nations have retained capital punishment for crimes against the state (such as treason) or crimes against humanity (such as genocide).
2. Other serious or violent crimes may also result in the death penalty in some states, such as the rape of a child in Louisiana. Also, the federal government can execute persons involved in treason or espionage, and some 15 military offenses can result in the death penalty, although some of these are limited to wartime. There have been no executions of persons for offenses other than homicide since the 1960s.
3. With the exception of the 2005 data obtained from *Fox News,* all other public opinion data were from the Gallup Organization.
4. These statistics were obtained in January 2007.
5. O'Connor said to a group of women attorneys in Minneapolis in July 2001, "[i]f statistics are any indication, the system may well be allowing some innocent defendants to be executed" (Editorial 2001).
6. Although this example is frequently used by death penalty abolitionists, it is important to note that Rector's brain injury occurred in a suicide attempt that happened after his involvement in a double-homicide.

Key Terms

benefit of clergy	deterrence	life without the possiblity
bifurcated	executive clemency	of parole (LWOP)
brutalization effect	incapacitation	retribution
commute		

Critical Review Questions

1. Given your knowledge of criminal behavior, and the factors that lead to murders, do you think that a state execution has a deterrent or brutalization effect?

2. If executions deter murders, explain why the average homicide rate in Wisconsin for the period 1999 to 2001 was 3.68 per 100,000 residents, while the homicide rate for Texas was 6.50 per 100,000 residents for the same years, given that Wisconsin abolished capital punishment in 1853 and Texas has had the nation's highest execution rate?

3. Do you think that public officials have used executions to enhance their political status? If so, is this ethical or unethical? Why?

4. What is your prediction about the future of capital punishment in the United States? Is it likely to increase or decrease? Support your answer with statistics from the latest Bureau of Justice Statistics capital punishment data.

5. Is the disproportionate use of capital punishment on African Americans cause for concern, especially in light of the Pierce and Radelet (2005) study, which showed that California offenders convicted of killing whites are more likely to be sentenced to death than those killing Latinos or African Americans?

6. Should the federal government impose a sentence of death on an offender in a state that has abolished capital punishment? Why, or why not?

References

American Civil Liberties Union (ACLU). (2003). "The high cost of the death penalty." Retrieved July 16, 2006 from: *http://www.moratoriumcampaign.org/facts/highcost.DOC*.

Amnesty International. (2007). "Abolitionist and retentionist countries." Retrieved January 1, 2007 from: *http://web.amnesty.org/pages/deathpenalty-countries-eng*.

Atkins v. Virginia, 536 U.S. 304 (2002).

Banner, Stuart. (2002). *The Death Penalty: An American History*. Cambridge, MA: Harvard University Press.

Barkan, Steven E., and Steven F. Cohn. (2005). "On reducing white support for the death penalty: A pessimistic appraisal." *Criminology & Public Policy* 4 (1), 39–44.

Bonczar, Thomas P. (2005). *Capital Punishment, 2004*. Washington, DC: U.S. Department of Justice, Bureau of Justice Statistics.

Bureau of Justice Statistics. (2006). *Capital Punishment Statistics*. Retrieved July 16, 2006 from: *http://www.ojp.usdoj.gov/bjs/cp.htm*.

California Department of Corrections and Rehabilitation (CDCR). (2006a). "Inmates executed, 1978 to the present." Retrieved July 16, 2006 from: *http://www.cdcr.ca.gov/ReportsResearch/InmatesExecuted.html*.

——. (2006b). "Condemned inmates who have died from 1978 to the present." Retrieved July 16, 2006 from: *http://www.cdcr.ca.gov/ReportsResearch/docs/CIWHD.pdf*.

Cochran, John K., and Mitchell B. Chamlin. (2000). "Deterrence and brutalization: The dual effects of executions." *Justice Quarterly* 17 (4), 685–706.

Death Penalty Information Center (DPIC). (2006). "Facts about the death penalty," June 30, 2006. Retrieved July 16, 2006 from: *http://www.deathpenaltyinfo.org/FactSheet.pdf*.

——. (2007). *The Death Penalty in 2006: Year End Report.* Retrieved January 1, 2007 from: *http://www.deathpenaltyinfo.org/2006YearEnd.pdf*.

Dezhbakhsh, Hashem. (1999). "First person: More guns, less crime? Hashem Dezhbakhsh disagrees." *Emory Report,* 52 (6) Retrieved October 11, 2006 from: *http://www.emory .edu/EMORY_REPORT/erarchive/1999/September/erseptember.27/9_27_ 99dezhbakhsh.html*.

Dieter, Richard C. (2005, January 25). *Cost of the Death Penalty and Related Issues.* Presentation made to the New York State Assembly: Standing Committees on Codes, Judiciary, and Correction.

Donohue, John J., and Justin Wolfers (2005). "The ethics and empirics of capital punishment: Uses and abuses of empirical evidence in the death penalty debate." *Stanford Law Review* 58 (3), 791–846.

Editorial. (2001, July 4). "Second thoughts." *Washington Post,* p. A18.

Ehrlich, Issac. (1975). "The deterrent effect of capital punishment: A question of life and death." *American Economic Review* 65 (3), 397–417.

Elias, Norbert. (1939/2000). *The Civilizing Process: Sociogenetic and Psychogenetic Investigations.* New York: Blackwell.

Fagan, Jeffrey. (2005, July 14). *Public Policy Choices on Deterrence and the Death Penalty: A Critical Review of New Evidence.* Testimony before the Joint Committee on the Judiciary of the Massachusetts Legislature on House Bill 3834, "An Act Reinstating Capital Punishment in the Commonwealth."

Federal Bureau of Investigation (FBI). (2006). *Crime in the United States, 2005.* Washington, DC: Author.

Furman v. Georgia, 408 U.S. 238 (1972).

Gregg v. Georgia, 428 U.S. 153 (1976).

Guidry, Orin F. (2006). "Observations regarding lethal injection." Retrieved July 17, 2006 from: *http://www.asahq.org/news/asanews063006.htm*.

Innocence Project. (2007). "Police and prosecutorial misconduct." Retrieved January 1, 2007 from: *http://www.innocenceproject.org/case/display_cases.php?sort=year_exoneration*.

Jacobs, David, and Jason T. Carmichael. (2004, September). "Ideology, social threat, and death sentences: Capital sentencing across time and space." *Social Forces* 83, 249–278.

King, Nancy J. (2003). "The origins of felony jury sentencing in the United States." *Chicago Kent Law Review* 74 (3), 937–993.

Liebman, James S., Jeffrey Fagan, Valerie West, and Jonathan Lloyd. (2000). "Capital attrition: Error rates in capital cases, 1973–1995." *Texas Law Review* 78 (7), 1839–1865.

Mannheimer, Michael J. Z. (2006). "When the federal death penalty is cruel and unusual." *Cincinnati Law Review* 74 (1), 819–885.

Marshall, Joshua M. (2000, July 31). "Death in Venice." *New Republic,* 12, 14. Retrieved October 29, 2006 from: *http://www.tnr.com*.

Moore, David W. (2004). "Public divided between death penalty and life imprisonment without parole." Retrieved September 21, 2005 from: *http://www.deathpenaltyinfo .org/ article.php?scid=23&did=1029*.

Pierce, Glenn L., and Michael L. Radelet. (2005). "The impact of legally inappropriate factors on death sentencing for California homicides, 1990–1999." *Santa Clara Law Review* 46 (1), 1–47.

Pollingreport.com. (2006). "Crime/law enforcement." Retrieved July 16, 2006 from: *http:// www.pollingreport.com/crime.htm*.

Roper v. Simmons, 543 U.S., 125 S.Ct.1183 (2005).

Ruddell, Rick. (2004). *America Behind Bars: Trends in Imprisonment, 1950–2000.* New York: LFB Scholarly Press.

Savelsberg, Joachim J. (1994). "Knowledge, domination, and criminal punishment." *American Journal of Sociology* 99 (4), 911–943.

Shepherd, Joanna M. (2004a). "Murders of passion, execution delays, and the deterrence of capital punishment." *Journal of Legal Studies* 33 (2), 283–322.

——. (2004b). "Deterrence versus brutalization: Capital punishment's differing impacts among states." *Emory Legal Scholarship Working Paper Series.* Retrieved October 24, 2005 from: *http://law.bepress.com/cgi/viewcontent.cgi?article=1000&context=emorylwps.*

Snell, Tracy L. (2006). *Capital Punishment, 2005.* Washington, DC: U.S. Department of Justice, Bureau of Justice Statistics.

Steiker, Carol S. (2002, July 19). "Capital Punishment and American Exceptionalism." Paper presented at the International Law, Human Rights and the Death Penalty Conference, Geneva, Switzerland.

Sunstein, Cass R., and Adrian Vermeule. (2005). "Is capital punishment morally required? The Relevance of life-life tradeoffs." Retrieved October 10, 2005 from: *http://papers.ssrn.com/sol3/papers.cfm?abstract_id=691447.*

Tushnet, Mark. (2006). "When is knowing less better than knowing more? Unpacking the controversy over Supreme Court reference to non-U.S. law." *Minnesota Law Review* 90 (5), 1275–1302.

Unnever, James D., and Francis T. Cullen. (2005). "Executing the innocent and support for capital punishment: Implications for public policy." *Criminology & Public Policy* 4 (1), 3–38.

Walker, Samuel. (2006). *Sense and Nonsense About Crime and Drugs,* sixth edition. Belmont, CA: Wadsworth.

Wilson, Emily, Brian Doss, and Sonya Phillips. (2004). *Tennessee's Death Penalty: Costs and Consequences.* Retrieved July 16, 2006 from: *http://www.comptroller.state.tn.us/orea/reports/deathpenalty.pdf#search='Tennessee%27s%20Death'.*

Zimmerman, Paul R. (2004). "State executions, deterrence, and the incidence of murder." *Journal of Applied Economics* 7 (1), 163–193.

Recommended Readings

Bedau, Hugo A., and Paul G. Cassell. (2004). *Debating the Death Penalty: Should America Have Capital Punishment? The Experts on Both Sides Make Their Best Case.* New York: Oxford University Press. This edited book presents seven contributors who argue for and against the death penalty. The contributors deal with a number of issues including race, the morality of the death penalty, and the problem of convicting innocent defendants.

Johnson, Robert. (1997). *Death Work: A Study of the Modern Execution Process.* Belmont, CA: Wadsworth. This book is based on Johnson's research on death rows, including interviews and observations of condemned inmates who live within these units, as well as the correctional officers who supervise them. Johnson paints modern death row life as inhumane; but regardless of your position of the death penalty, you will gain considerable insight into how death row inmates live after reading this book.

Zimring, Franklin E. (2004). *The Contradictions of American Capital Punishment.* New York: Oxford University Press. Zimring provides a comprehensive and thoughtful analysis of American death penalty policy. Zimring traces the source of American capital punishment as a consequence of traditions of vigilantism, especially how this relates to removing due process protections, such as appeals, from persons sentenced to death. ✦

Chapter 13

Juvenile Crime and Violence

Introduction

Juveniles tend to be overrepresented in their crime involvement compared with other age groups.[1] Most of their offenses are minor property or **public order offenses,** such as vandalism or disorderly conduct. Throughout the 1980s and early 1990s, however, a disturbing number of serious and violent juvenile offenses had legislators in every state advocating for increasing the sanctions for juvenile offenders. Academic researchers and some policy analysts looked at demographic statistics indicating that the juvenile population in the early years of the twenty-first century would be at the highest levels ever. These scholars predicted that if only a small percentage of these juveniles were involved in serious offenses, there would be a "bloodbath" perpetrated by "the young and the ruthless" (Fox 1992) or "superpredators" (Bennett, DiIulio, and Walters 1996).

Such predictions were featured prominently in newspapers or in television reports; and given our knowledge about gang-involved juveniles, school shootings, and some high-profile violent cases, we were all too willing to believe the worst. At the time that Fox (1992) made his predictions, juvenile crime had increased dramatically, and he had reason to be pessimistic. In 1993, at the height of the juvenile violence epidemic, there were 3,790 juvenile arrests for homicide (Snyder 2005, 1). But juvenile arrests for violence dropped the following year and have decreased ever since. The 1,103 juveniles who were arrested for murder in 2003 represented a decrease of 68 percent in a decade (Snyder, 2005). The latest Federal Bureau of Investigation (FBI) data show that 929 persons under 18 years of age were arrested for murder in 2005 (FBI 2006, Table 38).[2] In terms of serious crimes committed by juveniles, we seem to be experiencing a respite, which is great news after the high rates of violence of the 1980s and early 1990s. But patterns of violence can change along with increases in gang membership, involvement in other crimes (such as drug sales), and whether crime-involved youths have illegal access to firearms.

This chapter examines juvenile involvement in crime and finds that serious juvenile crime has decreased. We also provide some possible reasons why this has occurred. Further, we examine the different ways that policymakers frame juvenile justice problems—which often shapes the interventions that will be developed. While acknowledging that many juveniles engage in crime, we find that most of it is minor and that few juveniles are ever involved in serious or violent offenses.

Juvenile Crime Trends

In a recent Office of Juvenile Justice and Delinquency Prevention (OJJDP) study of juvenile arrests, Snyder (2005) reported that approximately 2.2 million persons under the age of 18 years were arrested in 2003. While this total number is high, it must be placed in context. For instance, some youths are arrested more than once in a given year, so this total reflects a smaller number of actual delinquents. Further, the number of children under the age of 18 years during that same year was estimated to be 73.1 million (Federal Interagency Forum on Child and Family Statistics 2006). However, youngsters are rarely arrested, and youths between the ages of 12 and 17 are at the highest risk for delinquency. In 2006, there were an estimated 21.3 million youths between those ages, a number exceeding the post-World War II baby boomer population.

Arrests represent one measure of crime involvement, but we need to use more than one approach to examine a social problem. Some youths who are arrested are later found to be innocent. Furthermore, juvenile crime tends to occur in groups, and a single offense can result in the arrest of a number of youths. As a result, arrest data reflect an imprecise measure; however, since these data have been collected for several decades, they provide an important benchmark of juvenile crime involvement, especially when they are contrasted against victimization data or crime statistics.

Juvenile arrests reflect involvement in a broad range of offenses. Most of the offenses that youths commit are relatively minor crimes, such as larceny and public order offenses (Snyder 2005; Snyder and Sickmund 2006). Self-report studies that ask youths about their involvement in delinquent activities generally find that most adolescents engage in some of these acts at some point (Farrington et al. 2003). Of the 2.2 million juvenile arrests in 2003, over 1.66 million were for non-index offenses. These are the acts that we would typically expect juveniles to engage in—troublesome, destructive or senseless, expensive to the community (such as vandalism), and often associated with some type of risky behavior, yet not overly threatening to public safety.

Despite the fact that most youths engage in minor offenses, our perceptions about juvenile crime generally come from television. In the past decade, there has been considerable focus on school shootings, such as the Columbine tragedy and other high-profile cases that captured media interest. However, students are safer at school today than they were a decade ago. In terms of murder, for instance, in the 2001–2002 school year, 17 homicides occurred on school property, on the way to or from school, or at school events (National Center for Education Statistics 2005). While even one murder is too many, these school homicides represent less than 1 percent of all murders of youths aged 5–19 years.

Reductions in the number of school shootings are parallel with other declines in youth violence: Juvenile arrests for all types of violent crime have decreased. Of all 2.2 million juvenile arrests in 2003, some 92,300 were for violent offenses, such as homicide, aggravated assault, rape, and robbery (Snyder 2005). These are the crimes that most concern us because they pose the greatest threat to public safety. Furthermore, these offenses are most likely to be reported in the media since, as Kerbel (2000) observed, "if it bleeds, it leads." The problem is that television news reports greatly increase citizen fear of crime, even in places where violent crime is rare. In fact, Weitzer and Kubrin (2004) found that fear of crime is directly related to watching local television newscasts.

Because serious offenses pose the greatest threats to community safety, we take a closer look at these crimes. There were an estimated 16,500 murders reported in 2003, for instance (see Fox and Zawitz 2006), and 1,130 juveniles were arrested for involvement in these offenses. One encouraging fact is that the total numbers of arrests for homicide have decreased 68 percent over the past decade (Snyder 2005). The most recent data available about trends in youth violence are from the FBI (2006) and their trends generally mirror those of Snyder (2005) and Snyder and Sickmund (2006). One distinction is that while overall juvenile homicide arrests dropped from 1995 to 2004, they dropped at a higher rate for males than females.

Juvenile involvement in other serious offenses dropped as well. Snyder (2005, 4) reported that arrests for forcible rape, robbery, and aggravated assaults also dropped significantly between 1994 and 2003, although rates of these acts decreased less than rates for homicide. These decreases were not trivial, and they ranged from 25 percent for rape to 43 percent for robbery. The fact that arrests for serious violent crimes are decreasing in a pattern similar to that of homicide is encouraging. Clearly something seems to be working, but what?

Juveniles always have been overrepresented in their involvement in crime. Yet, in the 1980s, levels of youth crime increased dramatically, and many jurisdictions reported significant increases in the number of aggravated assaults, firearms crimes, robberies, and homicides. These offenses occurred primarily in urban areas, and there were a number of reasons for these increases. Changing drug markets, for instance, made cocaine and crack cocaine widely available. Many users of these drugs turned to violent crimes, such as robbery, to fund their addictions (Baumer et al. 1998). There is a direct relationship between robbery and homicide, however, and FBI (2006) crime data reveal that over 6 percent of murders in 2005 were associated with robberies.

Gang activity increased throughout the 1980s, although youth gangs did not have a significant impact on violence in all places. Rather, gang violence tended to be concentrated in inner-city America. McCorkle and Miethe (2003) argued that the gang problem was overstated in some places. But one cannot discount the increases in violence when adolescent aggression, firearms availability, rivalry within drug markets, and gangs intersect (Lizotte et al. 2000). For instance, in 2003 the FBI (2006) attributed 804 murders to juvenile gang activity.

Gang activities and involvement vary throughout the nation. The media have reported the increasing gang violence in Los Angeles, including higher numbers of gang-related murders in recent years (*Los Angeles Daily News* 2004). Yet, in rural areas, law enforcement surveys indicate that the presence of youth gangs is stable or decreasing (Egley and Ritz 2006). Such findings reinforce the importance of the local context and local solutions for criminal justice problems. Some communities have crime outbreaks, and this underscores the need to implement local solutions that take into account the community's economic, social, or demographic characteristics, as well as the strengths and limitations of the police, courts, and corrections in those places. Youth violence peaked between 1992 and 1994 and then decreased substantially, but it is difficult to attribute this drop to any one intervention or cause.

A number of scholars have tried to identify the reasons for the overall crime drop that occurred in the 1990s. In a book edited by Blumstein and Wallman (2000), the contributing authors offered a number of hypotheses, but there was little agreement on the exact reasons for the substantial decrease in violent crime. However, there are two issues upon which most observers agree. First, many law enforcement officials have reported that their interventions were responsible for the crime decrease. Most policy analysts, however, discount this claim because crime dropped at approximately the same rate in places that employed a variety of different intervention strategies. Violent crime decreased in New York City with its emphasis on strict "quality of life policing" at pretty much the same rate as it did in Los Angeles with its *lassiez faire* policing approach. As a result, most criminologists suggest that while some law enforcement interventions had important effects in some places, they were not responsible for the entire crime decline (Eck and Maguire 2000).

Second, violent juvenile crime did not drop at the same time or at the same rate as adult violence rates. Thus, it is important to disaggregate crime data or, as Rosenfeld (2004) observed, to "take apart the trends" to better understand the contributions of both adults and juveniles. Violent juvenile crime started decreasing after adult rates had already started dropping (Butts and Travis 2002). Rosenfeld (2004) speculated that one reason for this difference was that adult incarceration for trafficking in crack cocaine lured juveniles into the drug trade, keeping violence rates high. Yet, the arrest data from Snyder (2005) and Snyder and Sickmund (2006) show that once juvenile arrests for homicide started dropping, the decrease was greater than that for adult murder arrests.

There are also racial and gender differences in the distribution of serious juvenile crimes. Arrests for common or simple assault, for example, increased 103 percent for males between 1980 and 2003, but female arrests grew 269 percent during the same period (Snyder 2005). Some of this increase may be a consequence of zero tolerance enforcement programs in schools and communities. Yet, Snyder (2005) also observed that female juvenile involvement in DUI, disorderly conduct, and drug-abuse violations also increased significantly between 1994 and 2003. The latest FBI (2006) arrest data also indicate a rise in prostitution, sex offenses, and disorderly conduct. As we noted in Chapter 8, our view of young women seems to have changed over time, and criminal justice systems today are less likely to engage in chivalrous behavior toward female offenders of any age.

There are also racial differences in juvenile arrest rates. Snyder (2005, 9) reported that there were minor fluctuations of murder arrests for whites between 1980 and 2003, while rates for African American juveniles increased significantly, peaked in 1993, and then decreased. By 2003, African American homicide arrests were approximately one-half of the 1980 total. Robbery shows a similar pattern, and although arrests have decreased, 63 percent of all juveniles arrested for robbery in 2003 were African American (Snyder 2005).

Thus, while crime has dropped, it has not dropped at the same rate in all places, and different races and genders contribute to arrest statistics in dissimilar ways. These facts make it hard to make sweeping generalizations about juvenile crime. Butts and Travis (2002, 3) attributed this decrease to the

> influence of a strong economy during the late 1990s, growing cultural intolerance for violent behavior, changes in the market for illegal drugs, new policies to regulate access to firearms, expanded imprisonment, the growth of community policing, and other criminal justice interventions.

This observation clearly outlines the complexity of explaining social problems and further reinforces our position that responses to crime or delinquency defy simple "single focus" interventions. Thus, even if we have a strong economy, it may not contribute to reduced violence if gangs have increased their involvement in illegal drug markets.

Violence-reduction strategies must also rely upon a number of different approaches that are based on our knowledge of youths, violent crime, and the effectiveness of different interventions. Snyder and Sickmund (2006) maintain that after-school programs might have a greater impact on juvenile violence than curfew programs, as more crimes are committed by juveniles from 3 to 7 p.m. They found that aggravated assaults and sexual assaults, for instance, occurred at the highest rate during the weekday afternoons (juvenile sexual assaults also peaked at 8 a.m. on weekdays). This weekday pattern of involvement in crime was the same for males and females, as well as for African Americans and whites.

Box 13.1
A Short History of the Juvenile Court

A number of legal and social forces led to the development of the juvenile court. Historically, youngsters who broke the law were treated much like adults; they appeared in adult courts after they were arrested, and they were held in adult jails. They also were subject to the same punishments as adults, and some youngsters were executed. In fact, Streib (2005) reported that at least 366 juveniles have been executed in the United States since 1642, but it is possible that the number is higher because this represents information only from formal records.

Social activists at the turn of the twentieth century believed that juveniles should not be punished as severely as adults because they lacked maturity and adult decision-making skills. A second factor that led to the development of the juvenile court is that the severity of adult sentences made it unlikely that juveniles would be convicted of offenses because juries of the era were hesitant to find them guilty and judges were reluctant to mete out harsh sentences. Legal reformers were looking for a way of holding youths accountable for their offenses, but they also recognized that sanctions should be tempered because youngsters are less mature than adults.

Certain social conditions also led to the development of the juvenile court. Displacement of families after the Civil War, the increasing movement of people from rural to urban areas (where there was less informal social control), and growing numbers of new immigrants resulted in large numbers of unsupervised youths, especially in cities that were struggling with rapid growth. Few of these juveniles attended schools, and they sometimes formed gangs and caused trouble in their neighborhoods. While other interventions, such as **houses of refuge** (residential placements that emphasized schooling and work), had been used to respond to neglect and delinquency, many of these places were disreputable and some families had successfully challenged the right of the state to place youths in these institutions.

The first U.S. juvenile court emerged in Cook County, Illinois (Chicago), in 1899, and it was intended to respond to youths who were neglected and dependent, as well as those who were delinquent. The court was based on the concept of ***parens patriae*** *(the state as parent), a notion borrowed from English courts that acted on behalf of orphaned or dependent children. The juvenile court promised to rehabilitate youths and it was intended to help—rather than punish—delinquents. But it had few due process protections (such as the right to be represented by an attorney). Looking back, we now realize that the interventions of these courts often resulted in injustices for juveniles. Young women who were experimenting with their sexuality were sometimes treated more harshly than males who had committed violent offenses. In addition, even reformers of the day realized that many of the juveniles who appeared before the court were poor or immigrant youths (Mack 1909).*

Supporters of the due process model were critical that most youths appearing before the juvenile court had no constitutionally guaranteed rights. Appellate courts typically had a "hands off" orientation to the juvenile court until the 1960s. They also were critical that juvenile courts did not offer the types of rehabilitation that many youths required. Proponents of the crime control model, by contrast, maintained that juvenile courts often failed to hold youths accountable for their offenses. Sometimes youths who committed heinous crimes would receive very little punishment if they were perceived as amenable to rehabilitation. Feld (1999, 4), a long-time critic of juvenile courts, has called them "a conceptually and administratively bankrupt institution with neither a rationale nor a justification." Most observers, however, would support the position that many of the people employed within juvenile justice systems have been well intentioned and have worked toward the best interest of the child. ✦

Cycles of Juvenile Justice

It is important to acknowledge that societies always have been plagued with a certain amount of juvenile crime. The public and legislators who represent us, however, often are conflicted about whether we should punish youngsters harshly (especially those involved in violent crimes) or whether we should recognize juveniles' ability to make significant rehabilitative changes. There is significant tension between the "**best interests of the child**" and public safety or crime control in the treatment of juveniles. Starting in the 1980s, however, this balance shifted toward public safety, and the sanctions for juveniles involved in crimes increased throughout the United States.

In an important statement about juvenile crime, Bernard (1992, 21–22) observed five important facts about juveniles and youth crime that have remained constant. First, juveniles, especially young males, commit more crime per capita than other age groups. The fact that young males are involved in crime is partly a function of adolescent development, role experimentation, and risk taking that naturally occur. During this developmental era—from the ages of 12–17—adolescents test different roles, experiment with adult behaviors, and engage in thrill-seeking or risky behaviors (Ruddell and Mays 2004). Furthermore, many juveniles perceive themselves to be indestructible or invincible. Altogether, this youthful experimentation, a rush to assume adult roles, and the perception of invincibility can lead to countless negative consequences: from teenage pregnancies, running away from home, and drug and alcohol use to involvement in unintentional injuries and, sometimes, violent crime.

The one thing that has changed over the past two centuries is that juveniles historically assumed adult roles and responsibilities at earlier ages. According to Felson (1994), juveniles successfully were able to channel their energies into starting families and physically demanding, full-time employment. Often males were married at 16 or 17 years of age, and they quickly became parents. Between full-time work and raising families, juveniles had fewer opportunities for destructive, risky, or delinquent behaviors.

Today, the transition time to full adult responsibilities seems to have been extended. In addition, urban life does not offer the same opportunities for tiring chores that kept young people occupied 50 years ago. At the same time, the temptations available to juveniles occur at younger ages. Social and technological changes such as the Internet, video games, and adult television programs on cable networks or films have exposed youngsters to violent behavior and sexuality. This exposure may increase juveniles' interests in testing these adult roles.

Early exposure to sexuality, pornography, or violence occurs during a developmental era when juveniles are less likely to make thoughtful decisions. Research suggests that there may be a biological basis to destructive or delinquent behaviors. For example, brain development is not complete until an individual is approximately 21 years of age (ABA 2004). More important, the part of the brain that governs the most advanced thinking skills, such as decision making, is the last to develop (ABA 2004). These factors were carefully considered in the *Roper v. Simmons* (2005) decision of the Supreme Court, which found the juvenile death penalty unconstitutional. Adolescents are different than adults, in part because their brains have not fully developed.

A second important observation about juvenile crime is that there are laws that only juveniles must obey (Bernard 1992). **Status offenses** include acts that are unlawful depending on one's age, such as disobeying curfew laws, smoking, gambling, drinking, engaging in sexual activities, and running away from home. Such laws are intended to protect juveniles from behaviors that are inconsistent with their best interests.

Historically, status offenders who came to the juvenile court's attention sometimes received consequences that today appear very onerous. Advocates for juveniles were concerned about these youngsters' treatment. Prior to the mid-1960s, for instance, there were no constitutional guarantees of due process protections for juveniles. Thus, some youths were incarcerated in training schools or reformatories for months or even years for their involvement in status offenses. Yet, juveniles who had been involved in serious or violent offenses may have served less time (Schwartz 1989).

A series of Supreme Court decisions in the 1960s and 1970s extended a number of constitutional protections to juvenile defendants.[3] Altogether, these decisions have been labeled a "due process revolution" in the juvenile court (Feld 1999). At the core of these decisions was the recognition that youths were being treated in conditions closely akin to punishment, and they needed the representation of counsel to ensure fairness. Feld (1999 and 2003) questioned whether the due process revolution actually delivered as many rights to juveniles as promised, especially since youths still appear in court without counsel and because juvenile defense services are rationed in many places (ABA 2004; Pudlow 2005).

Bernard (1992) also observed that juveniles are punished less severely than adults who commit the same crimes. We always have acknowledged that juveniles have less ability to consider the consequences of their behaviors, and this is one reason why we restrict them from engaging in adult behaviors. Their ability is further impaired if they are under the influence or drugs or alcohol. Juveniles also may resort to earlier functioning levels (such as temper tantrums or running away) when encountering stressful situations, such as being confronted or challenged. As a result, mitigation of consequences for juveniles always has been an important principle of juvenile justice.

The fourth component of Bernard's (1992, 21) analysis was the observation that the public believes that the "current group of juveniles commit more frequent and serious crime than juveniles in the past." In some cases, these assessments have been correct: The juvenile crime wave from the mid-1980s to 1993 is a good example. At that time, the juvenile crime rates of the 1970s were looked upon favorably, just as Americans in the 1950s longingly looked back to the previous decades. Taking this retrospective view of crime, however, distorts our perceptions about the current crime problem: Some juveniles in the 1950s were involved in horrible crimes, just as some youths will be involved in serious offenses this year.

Bernard's (1992) last observation about juvenile crime was that the public believes that juvenile justice practices are responsible for juvenile crime increases. When juveniles were treated as harshly as adults, some believed that these penalties were a source of juvenile crime. In eras when rehabilitative goals formed the basis of juvenile justice systems, the public believed that juveniles were likely to re-offend if sanctions were not severe enough. Bernard (1992) identified three eras where policies shifted from tough on crime interventions to rehabilitation. The one constant aspect of juvenile justice is that these cycles of transformation and change are repeated.

As we have seen throughout this book, policymakers are drawn to politically popular solutions that either failed to work in the past or effectiveness was never evaluated. To better understand complex problems, we often distill these issues into simple catch phrases, such as "three-strikes-and-you-are-out." Crime control model supporters argue that juveniles who offend "shouldn't do the crime if they can't do the time." Consistent with the get-tough movement for adults outlined in Chapter 6, we have increased the sanction severity for youthful offenders.

Different assumptions about juveniles and their involvement in crime underlie the rehabilitative and punitive approaches to youth justice. If policymakers perceive juvenile crime as an entirely predictable outcome of adolescent development, interventions are likely to be based on rehabilitation, providing youths with education, life skills, or counseling so they will not repeat their mistakes. Politicians who believe that juveniles are sophisticated offenders are likely to advocate tough sanctions, including lengthy incarceration terms to incapacitate or deter these youths.

Models for Controlling Crime

Many of the debates about juvenile justice speak to the delicate balance between the child's best interests and whether the court's interventions ensure public safety. At the broadest level, these two positions or models form endpoints of a continuum that extends from **nonintervention** (doing nothing) to life imprisonment in state prisons for some juveniles. Most jurisdictions have adopted elements of each model, and while most policymakers would agree that both options are necessary, there often is considerable disagreement when juvenile justice systems confront the problem of youths who commit serious or violent offenses. Should juvenile court judges, state legislatures, or prosecutors decide the punishments that serious offenders should receive? Moreover, if we decide to rehabilitate a youth, do we have the capacity within our juvenile justice systems to provide a meaningful rehabilitative program that will meet the needs of the juvenile? Further, if we decide to severely punish a youth who is a good candidate for rehabilitation, we have forever harmed that person's chances for a meaningful life. Is the punishment, in some cases, worse than the crime?

The following pages summarize some of the key trends within the noninterventionist, rehabilitative, and crime control models. Each of these perspectives is guided by a punishment philosophy or goal, and these guide policymakers' decisions about juvenile justice. While juvenile codes have elements of each model, it is important that our interventions are consistent, just, and fair. Extralegal differences, such as race, gender, or geography, should not influence juvenile dispositions.

Noninterventionist Model

The noninterventionist model is based on the premise that labeling youths as offenders reinforces their perceptions of themselves as delinquents, and this label may influence their future behavior. Labeling theory was very popular in the 1950s and 1960s (see Lemert 1951), and this approach still guides juvenile justice interventions in some places. There is an intuitive appeal to the notion that contact with justice systems may change young peoples' impressions of themselves, especially after being taken into custody, and their interactions with probation officials or juvenile court judges. An impressionable youth who has been classified as a delinquent, outsider, or offender might adopt that label. Such definitions are enhanced when fellow students, peers, and even family members treat the young person in a different manner. Ultimately, labeling theories propose that the end result of this process is that juveniles start behaving like delinquents.

Despite the fact that this noninterventionist model has had limited empirical support—it is very difficult to test many of these propositions—it still remains popular. The principle underlying this approach is to do nothing and trust that, over the long term, the young person will assume law-abiding behaviors. However, it is notoriously difficult to do nothing when confronted with a crime, or any other problem. Our natural inclination is to act. In addition, despite our best intentions, a small percentage of youths will continue to engage in delinquent behavior.

One program that emerged from the noninterventionist model is **juvenile diversion.** Diversion programs keep youths from penetrating into juvenile justice systems. Designed primarily for minor offenders, diversion programs are operated by a wide variety of agencies, and they usually involve informal probation where the youths are expected to engage in counseling, perform community service work, and abide by other conditions. In some jurisdictions, the police operate such programs. Most often, diversion programs are operated by juvenile probation agencies or nonprofit community-based organizations.

The **deinstitutionalization of status offenders** (DSO) also has been associated with the noninterventionist model. In most jurisdictions, status offenders are seen as children in need of assistance or guidance, and they are referred to community agencies to get this help. Only South Dakota still places status offenders in juvenile halls (secure detention). The challenge of both diversion programs and working with status offenders is that some youths are not successful in abiding by program conditions, and these cases end up in juvenile courts for violating their informal probation conditions.

While not a noninterventionist program in its truest sense, one approach that defines juvenile crime as a community problem, rather than a failure of the individual, is **restorative justice.** First used in Australia and New Zealand, restorative justice practices reject the criminal justice philosophy of blame and focus on the offense. Bazemore and Umbreit (1997) observed that conventional responses to crime have not worked because they are based on abstract principles that do not make sense to youths. Their court appearances often do not have a lasting impact on youngsters, do not give the victim a voice, and do not really hold juveniles accountable, especially for minor offenses that result in a probationary disposition (Bazemore and Umbreit 1997). According to this perspective, most important is juveniles' willingness to accept responsibility for their offenses and to take some meaningful steps to repair the harm that they caused.

Restorative justice is based on bringing victims and offenders together, and the victims are given the opportunity to confront offenders in a safe and supportive environment. A number of different approaches have been developed, and they go by different names, such as family group conferencing or community justice forums. In addition to victims and offenders, other community members may attend, including persons who have an interest in the case and lay volunteers (see Karp and Drakulich 2004). In some cases, teachers, therapists, or other professionals may be involved, but often family members or other persons who are significant in the lives of the youths attend. Police officers frequently are involved in these interventions and often are the biggest program supporters.

While restorative justice interventions can be used for all offenders, they characteristically involve young persons. An analysis of the success of these programs suggests that they reduce recidivism (Latimer, Downden, and Muise 2001). However, it is plausible that the early success in some jurisdictions may be a result of **creaming:** selecting offenders who have positive parental and social supports, limited prior criminal records, and a record of relatively minor crimes. Ultimately, these are the youths who might be successful without any intervention.

Rehabilitation Model

As Bernard (1992) noted, the original juvenile court was built on a rehabilitative model. Although states took different approaches, all operated in the best interests of the child. The rehabilitation of the child was the main objective of the court, and public safety was a secondary concern. Because youths were seen as being treated and not punished, early juvenile court supporters believed that there was no need for due process protections, and juveniles rarely had the assistance of attorneys. The nonconfrontational, informal, and confidential nature of these courts led to abuses and injustices, especially given the large percentage of status offenders held in juvenile institutions (see Schwartz 1989).

In Chapter 6, we discussed how policymakers lost confidence in the rehabilitation of adult offenders. Yet, there is still optimism that troubled youths can be reformed because they are considered amenable to change. Some jurisdictions have invested heavily in juvenile rehabilitation and their efforts seem to have borne fruit. To provide more rehabilitative environments, for example, some states have abandoned large juvenile institutions in favor of smaller, more "home-like" facilities for youths in the state's care. Missouri is leading the nation in terms of innovative juvenile justice programs. Their emphasis on "small is beautiful" has resulted in significant positive results, as recidivism rates within Missouri are much less than in other states (Mendel 2003).

Juvenile programs often have been ruled by optimism, or what Bernard (1992) called the "good intentions" of reformers. Often there is a significant difference between reformers' intentions and the actual performance of juvenile justice systems. Programs developed for youths seem to fail when agencies are operated by unskilled or unmotivated staff, or when they do not receive the financial or political support required.

There are indications that juvenile justice systems are becoming more accountable to the youths they hold as well as the public. In California, for instance, the *Farrell v. Allen* (2004) lawsuit has brought about a significant change in the way that youth justice is delivered. In this case, juvenile justice advocates found substantial deficiencies in the way that youths were treated, and had specific concerns about mental health care, the rehabilitative treatment that was provided to sex offenders, the medical care delivered to youths, the education that they received, and the lack of appropriate treatment for wards with disabilities. The California Youth Authority (now renamed the Division of Juvenile Justice, [DJJ]) entered into a consent decree with the Prison Law Office (which represented the plaintiff) that specified a number of remedial actions that the DJJ must take to deliver rehabilitative programs that better prepare their wards to re-enter society. Such broad reform is based on a rehabilitative model that balances community protection, offender accountability, and improving offender competency (Youth and Adult Correctional Agency 2005).

Litigation such as the *Farrell v. Allen* case has sought to improve the conditions of confinement for juveniles. Youth correctional programming is expensive, and taxpayers ought to be concerned when they are making a $115,129 investment to incarcerate a juvenile for a year in California; and there are high rates of recidivism once these offenders are released (Murray et al. 2006). As we have learned in other chapters, litigation has forced the police, courts, and correctional agencies to change their policies, procedures, and conduct (see Schlanger 2003).

Crime Control Model

The juvenile crime wave that began in the 1980s forced legislators and policymakers to confront the fact that relying upon rehabilitation did not always serve public safety and that some juveniles need to be incapacitated. One of the subtle changes that has occurred over time is how public safety became the primary goal of many juvenile justice systems. In California, for instance, the term *public safety* is repeated twice in the first sentence of that state's juvenile code. Getting tough on juvenile offenders had a popular appeal, especially when gang activity increased, youths became involved in the distribution of crack cocaine and other drugs, and gun-involved juvenile assaults and murders increased. Yet politicians struck gold when they discovered that offenders had few supporters and the electorate supported their campaigns based on getting tough on criminals.

Juvenile justice systems that rely upon one extreme of the rehabilitation-punishment continuum inevitably will make mistakes. In states that emphasize public safety, youths who would otherwise be good candidates for rehabilitation may serve lengthy prison terms. By contrast, in states where juvenile codes emphasize treatment or rehabilitative interventions, there are bound to be failures; and public safety is compromised when a youth who was given a second chance commits a violent offense. In the end, many jurisdictions are unwilling to trust in rehabilitation (probably due to high failure rates in the youths with the highest risk), and most have chosen to err on the side of public safety, which is the safest goal politically.

There is no dispute that legislators enacted a series of laws that resulted in tougher sanctions for juvenile offenders. First, every jurisdiction made it easier to transfer juveniles to adult court (Feld 2003). Second, there was a shift from rehabilitative juvenile correctional programming to more punitive sanctions. Third, we introduced a series of sanctions such as boot camps and intensive supervised probation that emphasized getting tough on juvenile crime. Altogether, these interventions enhanced the ability of juvenile justice systems to punish youthful offenders.

Transfers to adult court are intended to place juveniles at risk of more serious sanctions. In most states, juvenile justice systems cannot hold youths past their twenty-first birthday, even for the most serious offenses. Thus, if youngsters with lengthy juvenile records are 17 years old when they are charged with a violent offense, it may be appropriate to sentence them in an adult court that has the ability to levy sentences that will end after their twenty-first birthdays. Moreover, given the short period of time to rehabilitate a serious juvenile offender who has a lengthy prior record, prosecutors may be reluctant to file charges in juvenile court.

Every state eased its ability to transfer youths to adult court, and this resulted in a 70 percent increase of persons transferred between 1985 and 1994 (Puzzanchera et al. 2004). As rates of youth violence decreased, so did the number of cases transferred. Puzzanchera and colleagues noted that by the year 2000, however, the number of transfers had dropped by over half. Consequently, the use of transfers seems to have followed a pattern similar to that of youth violence in the 1980s and 1990s, and they decreased as rates of youth violence declined.

Consistent with our understanding of **waivers** (transfers to adult court), the 2000 juvenile court statistics reveal that older youths and males are more likely to be transferred (Puzzanchera et al. 2004). One troubling statistic is that African American juveniles are placed in institutions and transferred to adult court at a greater rate than other youths. They also are more likely to serve time in an adult prison, compared with their white counterparts (Hsia, Bridges, and McHale 2004). Many juvenile justice observers argue that such patterns reflect racism or differential treatment of minority youths (Feld 1999 and 2003).

There may be several reasons for the finding of disproportionate minority confinement and transfers to adult court. Such outcomes may reflect a differential involvement in crime, discrimination on the part of juvenile justice systems, or lack of access to public defenders who advocate against such transfers. More troubling is that the possibility that the treatment of juveniles parallels the discriminatory treatment of mi-

---

Box 13.2
The Crime Control Model and Juvenile Offenders

One of the problems with juvenile justice systems is that some youths fall outside our expectations of "normal delinquents." These youths have either committed horrible crimes, have engaged in a number of serious felonies, or have been given opportunities to reform themselves but still engage in crime. Gang-involved juveniles represent a special challenge as their allegiance to the gang is much stronger than adhering to conventional goals, and gangs are increasingly violent. One difficult-to-manage group of offenders has been labeled **state-raised youth** (Irwin 1970). State-raised youths are persons who have been shuffled from foster care to group homes and juvenile detention facilities. By the time they are adolescents, they have little regard for conventional lifestyles or life in the "free world." Many will spend most of their lives in a series of juvenile prisons, jails, and adult prisons.

Every nation has to confront these troubling cases; and in many countries where the crime control is less prevalent, these youths receive sentences that most Americans would perceive as lenient and unjust. On June 22, 2006, the Supreme Court of Canada found that the principle of deterrence had no place in sentencing young offenders. They upheld the short sentences of two youths who had committed serious offenses. In the first case, a teenager killed a 21-year-old man in a fight and was sentenced to a 15-month sentence for manslaughter (the offender was ordered to serve one day in custody, and the rest in community supervision). In the second case, a teenage drug dealer beat and stabbed a drug addict over a debt (after threatening him with a gun several days earlier), and was given a 9-month sentence, of which at least one third would be spent on community supervision (*Regina v. B.W.P.; Regina v. B.V.N.* 2006).

Such cases emerge in many nations that have placed rehabilitation over public safety. Scotland, for instance, is a nation that boasts a strong rehabilitative model of youth justice. Yet, Allardyce (2006) reported, "Last year two teenage killers were jailed for a total of six years and four months for assaulting and robbing a 63-year-old widower from Cumbernauld, who later died." But even when strong sentences are imposed, they are often "discounted" and inmates serve only a short portion of their sentence. An editorial in London's *Sunday Times* ("Lenient Judges" 2006), for instance, noted how 53 adults sentenced to terms of life imprisonment in 2000 were on the streets by 2006.

Ultimately, if "soft on crime" strategies worked, citizens would be confident in their justice systems. But in England, the Home Office (an agency similar to the U.S. Department of Justice, Bureau of Justice Statistics) reported that 32 percent of respondents in 2005 felt that "teenagers hanging around on the streets" was a significant problem. In addition, while respondents in that same study felt that the system respected the rights of offenders, only 26 percent of respondents were fairly or very confident that the justice system was "dealing with young people accused of crime" (Bangs and Kara 2006). Perhaps one of the reasons that people in the United Kingdom are not confident in their youth justice system is that the public feels that juveniles are not held accountable for their crimes. ✦

---

nority adults. A Pennsylvania Supreme Court working group (2004, 509), for instance, found that there was evidence of racial discrimination within juvenile justice systems and that when case characteristics were compared, African American or minority youths were more likely to be transferred than their white counterparts.

A number of different methods can be used to transfer juveniles to adult courts. Historically, juvenile court judges made the decision whether the case would remain in juvenile court or be waived to adult criminal courts (Champion and Mays 1991). Prosecutors were also given the discretion to file juvenile cases directly in adult courts in many states. In other places, violent or serious offenses committed by juveniles are automatically excluded from juvenile courts, and these cases are heard in adult courts. Altogether, these changes removed discretion from the juvenile court judge and transferred this decision making to prosecutors and the legislature. Again, we have placed the discretionary power in the hands of the officials who have the most at stake by being tough on crime.

Conclusions

Juvenile courts were founded at the end of the nineteenth century to respond to youth crime. A central goal of the reformers who established the court was to provide interventions that were in the child's best interests. By the centennial of the juvenile court in 1999, however, most states had invested heavily in interventions that were punitive, focusing on public safety rather than rehabilitation. Youth justice advocates have long awaited a return to more forgiving social attitudes toward juveniles, and there are some indications that policymakers are moving toward more thoughtful juvenile justice practices. This optimism is a product of the reduction in youth violence over the past decade and lack of high-profile youth outbreaks of violence, such as the Columbine tragedy.

Juvenile justice practitioners have observed that two decades ago they worked with "children from troubled families" and operated with higher levels of community support than are present today. Today, they work with "youthful criminals" although the juveniles are the same populations, have the same problems, generally have committed similar offenses, and sometimes have the same last names. While most believe that juveniles should be held accountable for their delinquent behaviors, there seems to be more optimism about our ability to provide meaningful interventions that will reduce delinquency. Restorative justice programs, a renewed focus on rehabilitation within juvenile facilities, and a move to smaller juvenile programs that provide intensive treatment all signal an optimistic view of juveniles that has been missing for several decades. It is possible that we are moving toward a new cycle of juvenile justice.

The future of juvenile justice is not without some significant challenges. One of the biggest challenges confronting juvenile justice in the twenty-first century is disproportionate minority contact (DMC). To remove racial bias from juvenile justice systems, many jurisdictions have introduced **risk assessment instruments** to guide decision making. A typical risk assessment sums the scores of factors associated with delinquency, such as the youths' age at their first appearance before the juvenile court, the number of prior arrests, whether the parents provide support and guidance, and the presence of an alcohol or drug problem. Higher scores generally are associated with a greater delinquency risk. In some places, the risk is matched with the seriousness of the current offense, much like a sentencing grid that specifies a potential range of sanctions.

Interestingly, some jurisdictions have found that after implementing these objective tools, the demographic characteristics of juveniles transferred to adult court, as well as the youths placed outside the home, changed. In Missouri, for instance, researchers found that the number of white youths as well as girls placed outside the home or waived to adult courts increased (see Kempf-Leonard 1999). Other researchers have found significant differences in the severity of sentences between urban, suburban, and rural counties, which have been labeled **justice by geography** (Feld 1991). In rural counties where delinquency is rare, for example, some juveniles receive lengthy dispositions compared with city youths who are guilty of the same offenses and receive less severe sanctions. One of the reasons for using objective instruments is that they may be able to reduce differences in the treatment of youths with similar circumstances and offenses, thus ensuring consistency and fairness. A continual theme throughout this book is that working toward just and fair outcomes in justice systems will pay long-term dividends in reduced crime.

Using objective measures to develop a "score" reduces a youth to a series of numbers, and these measures do not always take into account the individual's actual strengths and weaknesses or aggravating and mitigating factors. Thus, it is important that juvenile court judges use their discretion to override such sentencing schemes when it is in the child's best interests and when consistent with public safety. Yet, increased judicial discretion also brings a greater likelihood of a return to patterns of differential treatment based on race, gender, or the court's location.

One federal government initiative that relates to both the crime control model and the use of objective assessment instruments is the concept of **graduated sanctions,** the incremental response of justice systems to juvenile crime. Graduated sanctions are based on a model of measured, consistent, and proportional punishments for delinquent behavior (Zavlek 2005). While objective classification systems are one positive step, some critics have argued that we are a long way from juvenile justice systems that are just and fair (see Pudlow 2005). Many youths waive their right to counsel, and others appear before courts represented by overburdened public defenders who have large caseloads and can invest relatively little time in a given case (ABA 2004). Burruss and Kempf-Leonard (2002) also observed that most attorneys would rather not practice in juvenile courts and that many judges may harbor the same feelings.

The influence of the federal government in juvenile justice cannot be overlooked. In the three decades since the Juvenile Justice and Delinquency Prevention Act was introduced, the **Office of Juvenile Justice and Delinquency Prevention (OJJDP)** has acted as a clearinghouse for research and has provided funding for projects that support its goals. The rehabilitative model proposed by California's Division of Juvenile Justice in 2006, which balances community protection, offender accountability, and improving offender competency, is based on a federal initiative. Again, as we have seen throughout this book, federal funding often guides justice practices, and Juvenile Accountability Block Grants have supported the development of information systems, research on DMC, and the introduction of graduated sanctions in state-operated juvenile justice systems.

Perhaps what has been missing for the last several decades is an optimism that it is worthwhile to invest in youths. Crime dropped at the same time that birth rates to teenagers and HIV infections have decreased, along with self-reported drug use (see Walker 2006). In addition, television reports have recently focused on the positive activities of youths, including their involvement in family, faith-based, educational, and community activities. American youths are certainly doing their part, and politicians should strengthen opportunities within the workforce for long-term employment, health coverage, education, and access to support, guidance, and assistance when youngsters make mistakes, as we all have.

Notes

1. In our discussion, we define juveniles as persons less than 18 years of age, although not all states use this age limit.
2. Not all law enforcement agencies report their data to the FBI, but the 10-year trend from 1995 to 2004 shows a 63.3 percent decrease, which is similar to the Office of Juvenile Justice and Delinquency Prevention (OJJDP) data. It is important to note, however, that arrests for homicides committed by juveniles increased 19.9 percent between 2004 and 2005.
3. The main cases were *Kent v. United States, In re Gault, In re Winship, McKeiver v. Pennsylvania, Breed v. Jones*, and *Schall v. Martin*. The rights extended to juveniles included the right to a transfer hearing, assistance of counsel during police interrogations, the ability to review transfer documents, representation by counsel at juvenile court hearings, notices of charges, the ability to confront and cross-examine witnesses, and protections against self-incrimination. Subsequent cases found that when youths' freedom was in jeopardy, they were entitled to a standard of proof beyond a reasonable doubt, and prohibiting double jeopardy if youngsters were adjudicated delinquent in a juvenile court. Youths may also be subject to preventative detention, but the right to a jury trial was not extended to juveniles.

Key Terms

best interests of the
  child
creaming
deinstitutionalization of
  status offenders
graduated sanctions
houses of refuge

justice by geography
juvenile diversion
nonintervention
Office of Juvenile Jus-
  tice and Delinquency
  Prevention (OJJDP)
parens patriae

public order offenses
restorative justice
risk assessment instru-
  ments
state-raised youth
status offenses
waivers (transfers)

Critical Review Questions

1. Barry Feld (1999) argues that the juvenile court should be abolished and replaced with an adult court that mitigates punishments for minors. Is this a step forward or a step back in time? Who would benefit from such a change? Who would oppose it?
2. In the *Roper v. Simmons* (2005) case, the juvenile death penalty was found to be unconstitutional. Do you agree with this decision? Do you think that the death penalty deters adolescents from engaging in capital crimes? Why or why not?
3. Despite the fact that homicides on school property have decreased, there still remains considerable fear of school shootings. Why do these fears persist during times of decreasing crime? How do the media influence the way we think about justice or juveniles?
4. What is the most appropriate type of sanction for a juvenile homicide offender? Should we sentence 15-year-old juveniles, who are neither mature nor responsible enough to drive a car, to a term of life imprisonment because their crimes are mature or sophisticated?
5. Single egregious offenses committed by juveniles have resulted in sweeping changes in the New York and Missouri juvenile justice systems. Why would policymakers be so easily swayed by a single case, however tragic, to change legislation for all juvenile offenders?

References

Allardyce, Jason. (2006, April 30). "Ministers force judges' hands over tough sentences." *Sunday Times.* Retrieved October 11, 2006 from: *http://www.timesonline.co.uk/article/0,,2090-2158518,00.html.*

American Bar Association (ABA). (2004). *Adolescence, Brain Development, and Legal Culpability.* Washington, DC: Author.

Bangs, Mark, and Maya Kara. (2006). *Crime in England and Wales: Quarterly Update to December 2005.* London, U.K.: Home Office.

Baumer, Eric P., Janet Lauritsen, Richard Rosenfeld, and Richard Wright. (1998). "The influence of crack cocaine on robbery, burglary, and homicide rates: A cross-city, longitudinal analysis." *Journal of Research in Crime and Delinquency* 33 (3), 316–340.

Bazemore, Gordon, and Mark Umbreit. (1997). *Balanced and Restorative Justice for Juveniles.* Washington, DC: Office of Juvenile Justice and Delinquency Prevention.

Bennett, William J., John J. DiIulio, and John P. Walters. (1996). *Body Count: Moral Poverty and How to Win America's War Against Crime and Drugs.* New York: Simon and Schuster.

Bernard, Thomas. (1992). *The Cycle of Juvenile Justice.* New York: Oxford University Press.

Blumstein, Alfred, and Joel Wallman. (2000). *The Crime Drop in America.* New York: Cambridge University Press.

Burruss, George W., and Kimberly Kempf-Leonard. (2002). "The questionable advantage of defense counsel in juvenile court." *Justice Quarterly* 19 (1), 37–68.

Butts, Jeffrey, and Jeremy Travis. (2002). *The Rise and Fall of American Youth Violence, 1980–2000.* Washington, DC: Urban Institute.

Champion, Dean J., and G. Larry Mays. (1991). *Transferring Juveniles to Adult Courts: Trends and Implications for Criminal Justice.* Westport, CT: Praeger.

Eck, John E., and Edward R. Maguire. (2000). "Have changes in policing reduced violent crime? An assessment of the evidence." Pp. 207–265 in *The Crime Drop in America,* edited by Alfred Blumstein and Joel Wallman. New York: Cambridge University Press.

Egley, Arlen, and Christina E. Ritz. (2006). *Highlights of the 2004 National Youth Gang Survey.* Washington, DC: Office of Juvenile Justice and Delinquency Prevention.

Farrell v. Allen, California Consent Decree RG 03079344 (2004).

Farrington, David P., Darrick Jolliffe, J. David Hawkins, Richard F. Catalano, Karl G. Hill, and Rick Kosterman. (2003). "Comparing delinquency careers in court records and self-reports." *Criminology* 41 (3), 933–958.

Federal Bureau of Investigation (FBI). (2006). *Crime in the United States, 2005.* Washington, DC: Author.

Federal Interagency Forum on Child and Family Statistics. (2006). *America's Children: Key National Indicators of Children's Well-Being, 2005.* Retrieved July 18, 2006 from: *http://www.childstats.gov/.*

Feld, Barry C. (1991). "Justice by geography: Urban, suburban, and rural variations in juvenile justice administration." *Journal of Criminal Law & Criminology* 82 (1), 156–210.

——. (1999). *Bad Kids: Race and the Transformation of the Juvenile Court.* New York: Oxford University Press.

——. (2003). "The politics of race and juvenile justice: The 'due process revolution' and the conservative reaction." *Justice Quarterly* 20 (4), 765–800.

Felson, Marcus. (1994). *Crime and Everyday Life: Insight and Implications for Everyday Life.* Thousand Oaks, CA: Pine Forge Press.

Fox, James A. (1992, June 10). "The young and the ruthless." *Chicago Tribune,* p. 23.

Fox, James A., and Marianne Zawitz. (2006). *Homicide Trends in the United States.* Retrieved July 18, 2006 from: *http://www.ojp.usdoj.gov/bjs/homicide/homtrnd.htm.*

Hsia, Heidi M., George S. Bridges, and Rosalie McHale. (2004). *Disproportionate Minority Confinement, 2002 Update.* Washington, DC: Office of Juvenile Justice and Delinquency Prevention.

Irwin, John.(1970). *The Felon.* Englewood Cliffs, NJ: Prentice Hall.

Karp, David R., and Kevin M. Drakulich. (2004). "Minor crime in a quaint setting: Practices, outcomes, and limits of Vermont reparative probation boards." *Criminology & Public Policy* 3 (4), 655–686.

Kempf-Leonard, Kimberly. (1999). *Assessing the Impact of 1995 Changes to the Missouri Juvenile Code.* Jefferson City: Missouri Department of Public Safety and the Governor's Juvenile Justice Advisory Group.

Kerbel, Matthew R. (2000). *If It Bleeds, It Leads: An Anatomy of Television News.* Boulder, CO: Westview.

Latimer, Jeff, Craid Dowden, and Danielle Muise. (2001). *The Effectiveness of Restorative Justice Practices: A Meta-Analysis*. Ottawa, Canada: Department of Justice Canada.

Lemert, Edwin. (1951). *Social Pathology*. New York: McGraw Hill.

"Lenient judges: Guilty as charged." (2006, June 13). *Sunday Times*. Retrieved October 11, 2006 from: *http://business.timesonline.co.uk/article/0,,2092-2230398,00.html*.

Lizotte, Alan J., Marvin D. Krohn, James C. Howell, Kimberly Tobin, and Gregory J. Howard. (2000). "Factors influencing gun carrying among young urban males over the adolescent-young adult life course." *Criminology* 38 (4), 811–834.

Los Angeles Daily News. (2004). *Terror in Our Streets: A Special Report on Gang Violence in Southern California*. Retrieved July 18, 2006 from *http://lang.dailynews.com/gangs/*.

Mack, Julian. (1909). "The juvenile court." *Harvard Law Review* 23 (1), 109–122.

McCorkle, Richard C., and Terance D. Miethe. (2003). *Panic: The Social Construction of the Street Gang Problem*. Belmont, CA: Wadsworth.

Mendel, Dick. (2003). *Small Is Beautiful: The Missouri Division of Juvenile Justice*. Retrieved July 18, 2006 from *http://www.aecf.org/publications/advocasey/spring2003/pdf/small.pdf*.

Murray, Christopher, Chris Baird, Ned Loughran, Fred Mills, and John Platt. (2006). *Safety and Welfare Plan*. Sacramento: California Department of Corrections and Rehabilitation, Division of Juvenile Justice.

National Center for Education Statistics. (2005). *Indicators of School Crime and Safety, 2005*. Washington, DC: National Center for Education Statistics.

Pennsylvania Supreme Court. (2004). *Final Report of the Pennsylvania Supreme Court Committee on Racial and Gender Bias in the Justice System*. Retrieved July 18, 2006 from: *http://origin-www.courts.state.pa.us/Index/Supreme/biasreport.htm*.

Pudlow, Jan. (2005, February 15). "Funding woes stifle call for juvenile representation." *The Florida Bar News*. Retrieved from: *http://www.floridabar.org/*.

Puzzanchera, Charles, Anne L. Stahl, Terrance A. Finnegan, Nancy Tierney, and Howard S. Snyder. (2004). *Juvenile Court Statistics, 2000*. Washington, DC: Office of Juvenile Justice and Delinquency Prevention.

Regina v. B.W.P.; Regina v. B.V.N., SCC 27 (2006).

Roper v. Simmons, 543 U.S., 125 S.Ct.1183 (2005).

Rosenfeld, Richard. (2004, February). "The case of the unsolved crime decline." *Scientific American* 290 (2), 82–89.

Ruddell, Rick, and G. Larry Mays. (2004). "Risky behavior, guns, firearms legislation and unintentional firearms fatalities." *Youth Violence and Juvenile Justice* 2 (4), 342–358.

Schlanger, Margo. (2003). "Inmate litigation." *Harvard Law Review* 116 (6), 1557–1701.

Schwartz, Ira M. (1989). *(In)justice for Juveniles: Rethinking the Best Interests of the Child*. Lanham, MD: Lexington.

Snyder, Howard N. (2005). *Juvenile Arrests, 2003*. Washington, DC: Office of Juvenile Justice and Delinquency Prevention.

Snyder, Howard N., and Melissa Sickmund. (2006). *Juvenile Offenders and Victims: 2006 National Report*. Washington, DC: Office of Juvenile Justice and Delinquency Prevention.

Streib, Victor. (2005). *The Juvenile Death Penalty Today: Death Sentences and Executions for Juvenile Crimes, January 1, 1973 to February 28, 2005*. Retrieved July 18, 2006 from: *http://www.law.onu.edu/faculty/streib/documents/juvdeath.pdf*.

Walker, Samuel. (2006). *Sense and Nonsense About Crime and Drugs*, sixth edition. Belmont, CA: Wadsworth.

Weitzer, Ronald, and Charis E. Kubrin. (2004). "Breaking news: How local TV news and real-world conditions affect fear of crime." *Justice Quarterly* 21 (3), 497–520.

Youth and Adult Correctional Agency. (2005). *California Youth Authority Defines New Model*. Sacramento, CA: Youth and Adult Correctional Agency.

Zavlek, Shelley. (2005). *Planning Community-Based Facilities for Violent Juvenile Offenders as Part of a System of Graduated Sanctions*. Washington, DC: Office of Juvenile Justice and Delinquency Prevention.

Recommended Readings

Bernard, Thomas. (1992). *The Cycle of Juvenile Justice*. New York: Oxford University Press. Bernard outlines how juvenile justice in America has repeated a number of cycles—from the punitive treatment of juveniles to widespread support for rehabilitation. He traces the sources of these changes and provides an analysis of how the good intentions of reformers often fail. Bernard provides an alternative method of sanctioning juveniles based on youths he has labeled as the "naïve risk-taker" and the "rational calculator."

Feld, Barry. (1999). *Bad Kids: Race and the Transformation of the Juvenile Court*. New York: Oxford University Press. Feld provides a comprehensive examination of the social construction of adolescence as a developmental stage and how this led to the creation of the juvenile court. Moreover, Feld critiques how the juvenile court is a compromise between a social welfare agency and a criminal court, and that it fulfills neither the goal of rehabilitating youths nor punishing serious youthful offenders. This book ends with the controversial proposal to abolish the juvenile court.

Zimring, Franklin. (1999). *American Youth Violence*. New York: Oxford University Press. Zimring examines the issue of youth violence in America and identifies three major social policy challenges: The access and use of firearms by juveniles, the use of transfer to adult court for juvenile offenders, and the problem of what to do with adolescents who are involved in homicides. In the 1990s, Zimring was a voice of reason who countered the claims of a wave of teenaged superpredators. ✦

Chapter 14

Living in a Post-9/11 World

Introduction

On the morning of September 11, 2001, the notion of *public safety* for the United States suddenly was shattered. It changed for those of us living in this country and, to a significant extent, it changed for our global neighbors as well. This chapter will touch on issues relating to domestic terrorism, global terrorism, threats to our daily lives, and the question of how much freedom we are willing to trade to feel safer. We consider a number of major pieces of federal legislation spanning the past 30 years, as well as the emerging notion of homeland security. As a part of homeland security, we discuss the major policy initiatives related to the reorganization of federal law enforcement and intelligence functions that have occurred. Finally, we examine the thorny issue of balancing due process and crime control, especially in regard to the civil liberties greatly treasured by Americans versus the changes that may be necessitated to ensure public safety and security. Of all of the chapters in this book, this one most clearly demonstrates the contemporary clash between the due process and crime control models and even the ways in which we define these concepts. Furthermore, it is the most speculative. It is likely to leave you with more questions than answers.

Federal Legislation

In some ways, when we examine criminal justice in a post-9/11 world, the temptation is to begin with passage of the **USA PATRIOT Act** (hereafter the PATRIOT Act). However, there are two major pieces of federal legislation that pre-date the PATRIOT Act and in many ways set the stage for this legislation.

The Foreign Intelligence Surveillance Act

As a result of covert activities by governmental agents and agencies in the 1960s and 1970s, including spying on dissident political groups,

Congress passed the 1978 **Foreign Intelligence Surveillance Act (FISA)** that enabled federal investigators to conduct intelligence operations under the supervision of a secret federal tribunal known as the Foreign Intelligence Surveillance Court" (Baker and Gregware 2004, 484).

This legislation "prescribes procedures for requesting judicial authorization for electronic surveillance and physical search of persons engaged in espionage or international terrorism against the United States on behalf of a foreign government" (Federation of American Scientists 2006). In simplest terms, the FISA defined the circumstances under which people and organizations who were suspected of espionage against the government of the United States or who were engaged in terrorist activities in, or directed against, the United States (Bazan 2004) could be investigated.

For a person to be investigated under the FISA, that person (or group) had to be suspected of espionage or terrorism against the United States. As Bell (2006) noted,

> Initially, FISA required that foreign intelligence information gathering be the sole or "primary purpose" of electronic surveillance. The Patriot Act expanded the application of FISA situations where foreign intelligence gathering is only a "significant" purpose of the investigation. Significant is not defined and is subject to interpretation by the FISC.

In the years subsequent to passage of the FISA, it has become apparent that the provisions contained in the Act also can be used in cases involving what are known as "predicate offenses." Therefore, electronic surveillance is allowed for a long list of offenses, including treason, riots, malicious mischief, bribery of public officials, violations of trade secret protections, and money laundering (Doyle 2002a).

As previously mentioned, one of the major provisions of the FISA—and one almost unknown by the general public—was the creation of the U.S. **Foreign Intelligence Surveillance Court (FISC).** This court reviews, but cannot deny, requests for surveillance warrants by federal law enforcement agencies such as the FBI directed at foreign intelligence agents suspected of operating in the United States. When an agency files a request for a surveillance warrant, a FISC judge must establish that the target of the investigation is a foreign power or an agent of a foreign power and that the location is one that is likely to be used by the target of the surveillance. The warrants issued by the FISC are not public records, and the subject of the search need not be notified until after the search is completed. These often are called **"sneak and peek" searches** (see ACLU 2005a; Doyle 2002b). Sneak and peek searches allow law enforcement authorities to search a home or office while the occupants are absent without notifying the people that they are a target of a search. The premise of these searches is that authorities may uncover evidence of terrorist activities, and they do not want the suspects to know that they are under investigation. Sneak and peek searches differ from traditional criminal law enforcement searches in that the element of notice is absent.

Given the existence of the Foreign Intelligence Surveillance Act, a legitimate question to ask is why intelligence and law enforcement officials were not able to act preemptively in regard to the 9/11 attacks. At least two answers can be given to this question. First, although the FISA seemed to give federal agencies a great deal of authority to investigate individuals and groups thought to be engaged in espionage and terrorism, the definition of terrorism provided by the Act was so narrow that the activities of the men who engaged in the 9/11 attacks on the World Trade Center and the Pentagon could not be investigated by the Central Intelligence Agency (CIA) or FBI. The attackers were receiving aid from a group (**al Qaeda**), but not a foreign government.

Second, this is another case where a policy was in place, but the implementation was lacking. The Congressional investigations that were held in the wake of the attacks on New York and Washington found that information on the attackers had been intercepted, but that federal law enforcement agencies were totally unprepared to process, analyze, and act upon the information. There especially seemed to be a gap between the functions of the CIA and the FBI.

The Antiterrorism and Effective Death Penalty Act

In Chapter 2, we discussed the impact of the **Antiterrorism and Effective Death Penalty Act (AEDPA)** (Public Law 104-132) on *habeas corpus* appeals for prisoners. This act was passed in the wake of the 1995 bombing of the Murrah Federal Building in Oklahoma City and the World Trade Tower bombing in 1993. It had been introduced in Congress five weeks prior to the Oklahoma City bombing (as the Omnibus Counterterrorism Act of 1995). Beall (1998) noted that one week after the Oklahoma bombing, the act was again presented to the Senate, but a Republican-backed bill was introduced a day later, and was affirmed, but stalled in the House of Representatives. The AEDPA eventually passed one year after the Oklahoma City attack.

One of the cornerstones of the legislation was to give the federal government the ability to disrupt funding to terrorist nations and organizations (Peed 2005). The AEPDA also restricted U.S. aid to nations that provided support or funding to terrorist organizations. Peed (2005) also noted how the Act made it possible for U.S. citizens who were harmed by terrorist acts to sue for compensation. Finally, the Act enabled the government to deport legal residents of the United States—even those who had committed no crimes—with classified information that the defendants were not able to review (Beall 1998).

Despite the fact that the Act addressed issues related to terrorism, in reality, the greatest impact of the AEDPA was on imposition of the death penalty and setting limits on the time in which prisoners under capital sentences could file habeas corpus appeals in federal courts (Scalia 2002). The result of this legislation has been a drastic reduction in the number civil rights claims and an increase in the number of habeas corpus petitions by prison inmates.

The USA PATRIOT Act

In response to the September 11, 2001, attacks on the World Trade Center and the Pentagon, on October 26, 2001, Congress passed and President George W. Bush signed the Uniting and Strengthening America by Providing Appropriate Tools Required to Intercept and Obstruct Terrorism Act of 2001 (Public Law 107-56). This bill, with such an unwieldy title, simply is referred to as the very patriotic sounding USA PATRIOT Act.

Almost from the beginning, questions have been raised about what the PATRIOT Act was intended to do. For example, although the bill passed by votes of 99-1 in the Senate and 357-66 in the House of Representatives, most of the members of Congress admitted that they had not read all of the 342 page document (ACLU, 2005b). In this section, we examine the impact the PATRIOT Act has had on criminal justice processes and civil liberties in the United States.

First, the PATRIOT Act broadened the definition of terrorism that had been operative since passage of the Foreign Intelligence Surveillance Act. Under the PATRIOT Act, Sections 411 and 808 modified and expanded the definitions of terrorism that already existed in federal statutes. In particular, Section 411 identified terrorist activities as those acts designed

> (I) to commit or incite to commit, under circumstances indicating an intention to cause death or serious bodily injury, a terrorist activity;
>
> (II) to prepare or plan a terrorist activity;
>
> (III) to gather information on potential targets for terrorist activity;
>
> (IV) to solicit funds or other things of value for (aa) a terrorist activity; (bb) a terrorist organization.

In order for law enforcement and intelligence agencies to carry out their mandates under the PATRIOT Act, Section 214 of the bill provided expanded authority under the FISA to engage in electronic surveillance, including the use of pen registers and trap and trace devices. Federal law defined a **pen register** as "a device or process which records or decodes dialing, routing, addressing, or signaling information transmitted by an instrument or facility from which a wire or electronic communication is transmitted" (18 U.S.C. Sect. 3127 (3)). Champion (2005, 187) added that a pen register is a "dialed number recorder; a manual system of recording numbers dialed from a particular telephone." Likewise, a **trap and trace device** means a device or process which captures the incoming electronic or other impulses which identify the originating number or other dialing, routing, addressing, and signaling information reasonably likely to identify the source of a wire or electronic communication. (18 U.S.C. Sect. 3127 (4))

Pen registers and trap and trace devices originally were instruments used to detect the numbers called to or from telephones. Now, however, equipment is available that lets law enforcement authorities capture the URLs or Web addresses accessed by computers from the World Wide Web (ACLU 2005a). The PATRIOT Act also permitted the Federal Bureau of Investigation to require "doctors, libraries, bookstores, universities, and [I]nternet service providers" to surrender information on their customers and clients at government request (ACLU 2005a). Additionally, Section 206 of the Act permitted "roving surveillance." These are "court orders omitting the identification of the particular instrument, facilities, or place where the surveillance is to occur when the court finds the target is likely to thwart identification with particularity" (Doyle 2002b, 3).

Second, Section 802 of the PATRIOT Act for the first time created the federal crime of **domestic terrorism.** The definition for this new crime provided that domestic terrorism means activities that:

(A) involve acts dangerous to human life that are a violation of the criminal laws of the United States or of any State;

(B) appear to be intended—

    (i) to intimidate or coerce a civilian population;

    (ii) to influence the policy of government by intimidation or coercion; or

    (iii) to affect the conduct of government by mass destruction, assassination, or kidnapping; and

(C) occur primarily within the territorial jurisdiction of the United States.

In addition to these changes, the PATRIOT Act created a group of new federal crimes, such as

terror attacks on mass transportation facilities, for biological weapons offenses, for harboring terrorists, for affording terrorists material support, for misconduct associated with money laundering, for conducting the affairs of an enterprise which affects interstate or foreign commerce through the patterned commission of terrorist offenses, and for fraudulent charitable solicitation. (Doyle 2002b, 5)

In reality, most of these offenses existed in one form or another, but the PATRIOT Act supplemented the federal laws that already existed, and generally it expanded the penalties for these offenses (Doyle 2002b).

Third, two particular provisions of the PATRIOT Act seem crucial to criminal justice operations (Doyle 2002b). One of these apects was an increased emphasis on cooperation between those agencies whose responsibilities primarily were law enforcement and those agencies devoted to the intelligence gathering and analysis processes. Legal, operational, and traditional barriers had been erected between federal law enforcement and intelligence agencies, and between federal agencies, on the one hand, and state and local agencies, on the other hand. This made information sharing problematic, and the intelligence failures related to the 9/11 attacks painfully illustrated the disjointed nature of law enforcement and intelligence related to terrorism. The other provision of note arising out of the PATRIOT Act was the one relating to **money laundering,** both as it relates to terrorism and to traditional criminal activities. A key assumption was that to trace the activity, agencies had to have the capacity to "follow the money." Doyle (2002b, 3) noted, "In federal law, money laundering is the flow of cash or other valuable derived from, or intended to facilitate, the commission of a criminal offense. It is the movement of the fruits and instruments of crime."

One hypothesis was that groups within the United States were receiving funds from multinational organizations such as al Qaeda and potentially from foreign governments such as Iraq, Iran, and Libya to carry out acts of terrorism against the United States. The PATRIOT Act gave the Secretary of the Treasury the regulatory authority to ensure that financial institutions in the United States were not being utilized for the purpose of laundering money that might be used by domestic and international terrorists. It is crucial to note that this provision of the PATRIOT Act goes beyond the realm of terrorism, and this is an issue to which we will return later in the chapter.

Finally, out of the passage of the PATRIOT Act came a sense that defense of the territory of the United States was essential, and the current structural arrangements within the federal government (and among the federal, state, and local agencies) was totally inadequate. Therefore, President George W. Bush proposed the creation of a cabinet-level **Department of Homeland Security (DHS)** with a secretary who would report directly to the President. This proposal became a reality on November 25, 2002, when President George W. Bush signed the Homeland Security Act, which created the Department of Homeland Security. The result was not only a heightened focus on homeland security but also a massive reorganization of criminal justice agencies at the federal level.

Homeland Security

There are varying definitions of **homeland security** and, as with many social science concepts, the definition often springs from the person or group doing the defining. White (2006, 270) said that "Homeland security simply means keeping the country safe." It is important to recognize that this notion has impacted the criminal justice system in the United States in two very distinct ways. First, as a policy matter, there has been a general diversion of funds from crime-fighting efforts at all levels of government to provide additional funding to fight the global "war on terror" and to provide increases in **national security.** For example, recent budget figures show that the federal government has allocated billions of dollars in funding to state and local agencies for homeland security functions (including grants, training, and technical assistance), and the 2005 federal budget provided for a 780 percent increase for the training and support of first responders (fire, police, and emergency medical technicians) compared with the budget prior to 9/11 (DHS 2005).

Furthermore, $5.6 billion has been devoted to medical responses to biological, chemical, nuclear, and radiological threats, $7 billion has been directed at bio-defense strategies, and another $4.4 billion has been provided to deal with potential public health crises. Finally, about $9 billion has been directed at border and transportation security, and an additional $15 billion has been allocated to strengthen airline security (DHS 2005). Some of this money represents new dollars made available by Congress, but much of it has been diverted from other domestic priorities or is the result of deficit spending.

Similar to our discussion about funding criminal justice operations in previous chapters, there is a limited amount of money for government spending, and increases for one program must be made at the expense of others. This is the principle of opportunity cost: in other words, a dollar spent by the government on one program is not being spent to fund some other program. But do Americans support Homeland Security spending? A Harris poll conducted in October 2005 found that 62 percent of Americans supported the Department of Homeland security a "great deal/fair amount" (Harris Interactive 2005). That same study found that of the 14 federal government services that were listed, Homeland Security ranked number 10 in terms of public support.

Second, the principle of homeland security has been translated into a federal policy that has created a Department of Homeland Security. This department was not established as an entirely new entity. Instead, there were major shifts in agency locations and structures to staff the new department. The following discussion will highlight some of these changes.[1]

One of the first changes that occurred as a result of the Homeland Security Act was the creation of an Office of Inspector General (these exist in virtually every federal government agency) and the transfer of parts or all of 22 other existing agencies and 180,000 employees into the Department of Homeland Security (DHS). For example, one of the most often transferred agencies in the federal government—the U.S. Coast Guard—and the Transportation Security Administration were shifted from the Transportation Department to Homeland Security.[2]

Additionally, the Secret Service, the Federal Law Enforcement Training Centers, and most of the Customs Service were moved from the Treasury Department to Homeland Security. The Bureau of Alcohol, Tobacco, and Firearms (now called the Bureau of Alcohol, Tobacco, Firearms, and Explosives) had its law enforcement responsibilities transferred from the Treasury Department to Homeland Security also. The Immigration and Naturalization Service ceased to be as such, and its functions were moved from the Justice Department to Homeland Security and divided into the Bureau of Immigration and Customs Enforcement (BICE) and the Bureau of Citizenship and Immigration Services (BCIS). Finally, the Federal Protective Services, which had the security responsibilities for many federal buildings, was relocated to Homeland Security from the General Services Administration. These changes made the Department of Homeland Security the largest federal employer of armed and sworn officers with arrest powers (at 38 percent), slightly ahead of the Justice Department (with 37 percent).

One nonlaw enforcement agency that was transferred into the DHS was the Federal Emergency Management Agency (FEMA). The slow response to the Hurricane Katrina disaster in New Orleans in August 2005 has been blamed, in part, on the placement of this agency in the DHS; and because it was not an independent agency, it was less responsive to emergencies. When a reporter from the Public Broadcasting Service (PBS) (2006) asked FEMA Director Michael Chertoff about the relationship between FEMA and DHS in February 2006, he remarked,

> Had FEMA not been part of DHS, things would have been worse. . . . So I think the answer here is not to pull apart what has been put together but is to complete the job of integration that will give us the department that the Congress expected.

So, should FEMA be located in the Department of Homeland Security, another cabinet-level agency, or exist as an independent entity? In the end, whether situating FEMA in DHS is a good strategy or not, it is important to acknowledge that unintended consequences sometimes occur when even the best laid-out plans are implemented.

The massive restructuring of federal agencies has clear implications for criminal justice students. There are increased employment opportunities with certain agencies (notably those in Homeland Security), and some of the agencies that students traditionally would have sought employment with (such as BATF and INS) now have been moved or had their missions redefined.

Security Versus Liberty

In a very practical way, what have the policy changes following September 11, 2001, meant in terms of increased public security for people (both citizens and non-citizens) living in the United States, and what have been the costs in terms of civil liberties to provide increased security? These are significant questions, and in this section, we will grapple with them. We already have some sense of how security and liberty are being balanced.

Several groups and organizations have been especially critical of the USA PATRIOT Act. One of these organizations (the American Library Association) might be a surprise to some of you (see Box 14.2). The other—the **American Civil Liberties Union** or ACLU—probably is not a surprise. The ACLU has been very disturbed by the broad sweep of the PATRIOT Act. On its Web site, the ACLU provides a one-page document, entitled "The USA PATRIOT Act and Government Actions That Threaten Our Civil Liberties." In this statement of the ACLU's official stance, the organization says that the PATRIOT Act threatens rights under the

- *First Amendment*—especially rights related to freedom of religion, speech, assembly, and the press;
- *Fourth Amendment*—protections against unreasonable searches and seizures abridged by the surveillance procedures allowed under the PATRIOT Act;
- *Fifth Amendment*—violations of the due process clause relating to life, liberty, and property;
- *Sixth Amendment*—provisions concerning speedy public trials by impartial juries, notice of the accusations, confrontation and cross-examination of accusers, and assistance of counsel (especially in regard to people held as suspected terrorists and those labeled "**enemy combatants**");[3]
- *Eighth Amendment*—protections against excessive bail (or, more properly, refusal to set bail) and cruel and unusual punishment; and
- *Fourteenth Amendment*—due process and equal protection provisions for citizens and non-citizens alike under U.S. law.

Specifically, concerns under the First Amendment have been expressed that the PATRIOT Act will be used to target individuals who belong to certain religious groups (Muslims) and that individuals who assemble and speak out against unpopular government policies, such as the war in Iraq, risk being labeled somehow as threats to national security. Fourth Amendment concerns particularly have been raised as a result of expanded federal powers to obtain warrants with less than probable cause (through the Federal Intelligence Surveillance Court), and as a result of expanded surveillance powers related to communications and other personal transactions, such as library and medical records. The Sixth and Eighth Amendment protections seem of concern to groups such as the ACLU, and that is especially evident in the cases involving both U.S. citizens and those detained under the "enemy combatant" status. Box 14.1 discusses some of the cases that have highlighted constitutional concerns by the ACLU and other organizations.

Box 14.1
The Legal War on Terrorism

There is no end to the legal controversies surrounding the avowed "war on global terrorism" declared by President George W. Bush after the attacks of September 11, 2001. This war has resulted in a number of challenges to the administration's policies regarding the response of the United States, and we briefly address four of the prominent cases that are related to this issue.

Clearly, the case against Saddam Hussein is of interest to many in the United States and around the world. On November 5, 2006, Hussein was sentenced to death for his role in the murder of 148 Iraquis. His execution, on December 30, 2006, has drawn condemnations from human rights organizations, such as Amnesty International and Human Rights Watch.

The second case of significance involves José Padilla, a U.S. citizen arrested in Chicago as a suspect in a plot involving a so-called radioactive dirty bomb. Padilla was brought to New York for detention as a result of a grand jury investigation into al Qaeda activities related to the 9/11 attacks. The criminal case against Padilla seemed marginal, at best, and prior to the case proceeding further, President Bush issued an order to then Secretary of Defense Rumsfeld that Padilla be declared an enemy combatant and that he be transferred to military custody. This case eventually reached the United States Supreme Court where, by a vote of 5 to 4, the justices upheld Padilla's rejected *habeas corpus* assertion that Secretary Rumsfeld was his nominal custodial and asserted that the petition must be filed against the actual custodian, who was the military brig commander in South Carolina. At the present time, the essential point of the President's power as Commander in Chief to designate someone as an enemy combatant has not been over-ruled or redefined (***Rumsfeld v. Padilla*** 2004).

A third case that made national and international headlines for months involved Zacarias Moussaoui, the so-called twentieth highjacker related to the 9/11 attacks. In Moussaoui's case, unlike some others related to the legal war on terrorism, the United States government filed criminal charges and brought Moussaoui to trial in the federal district court for the Eastern District of Virginia (Alexandria, just outside of Washington, D.C.). There was some question concerning Moussaoui's mental state and his fitness to stand trial, but the government was able to convince the court of Moussaoui's competency. The U.S. Attorney sought the death penalty for Moussaoui's role in planning the September 11 attacks, and he eventually pleaded guilty to conspiracy (1) to commit acts of terrorism, (2) to use weapons of mass destruction (commercial airliners), (3) to destroy aircraft, (4) to aircraft piracy, (5) to murder federal government employees, and (6) to the destruction of property. Each of the first four charges carried the potential of the death penalty. In the first phase of the sentencing portion of Moussaoui's case, the jury decided that he was eligible for the death penalty. However, in the second phase of sentencing, jury members decided not to impose death but rather a lengthy prison sentence ("Q & A: Moussaoui trial" 2006).

In some ways, Moussaoui's trial is interesting because he was the only person charged in the United States with the September 11, 2001, airplane attacks (a number of Germans were charged and imprisoned in 2003 for their roles in assisting the plot). Furthermore, his case was processed within the normal arena of federal criminal law, unlike others designated enemy combatants. ✦

The third group of cases involves the group of individuals detained at the U.S. military base at Guantánamo Bay, Cuba. These cases present the most interesting dimension of the legal war on terror because all of the individuals involved were taken into custody on foreign soil (most in Afghanistan), turned over to U.S. military and intelligence officials, and declared enemy combatants but not prisoners of war. If the prisoner of war designation had been used, then international rules, such as the Geneva Convention, would apply. As it now stands, most of this group of people—approximately 400 detainees in January, 2007—have not been charged with anything, and they are not being accorded the normal constitutional protections that would be provided to criminal defendants (such as Zacarias Moussaoui).

Perhaps the case that best illustrates the plight of the Guantánamo Bay detainees is that of Salim Ahmed Hamdan. Hamdan was captured by U.S. forces in the invasion of Afghanistan and has admitted to having served as Osama bin Laden's driver for a time. He was finally charged with conspiracy to commit terrorism, and his case was to be heard before a special military tribunal constituted to hear the enemy combatant cases. On June 29, 2006, Hamdan's case reached the U.S. Supreme Court, which by a 5-to-3 decision (Chief Justice Roberts did not participate) ruled that the Bush administration did not have the authority it claimed to have and that the military tribunals established to hear these cases were not legal under existing military law (the Uniform Code of Military Justice) or the Geneva Convention (*Hamdan v. Rumsfeld* 2006). While some conservatives have seen this decision as a setback, civil libertarians suggest that this ruling will force President Bush to go to Congress to legalize military tribunals for these captives—in essence, this could be a "democracy-forcing decision" (Balkin 2006).

To date, while President Bush has tried to pursue a broad-scale war on global terrorism, some of the administration's policies have not withstood legal scrutiny. The next decade will show whether legal tactics will be effective against terrorism the way they have been used against traditional organized crime.

The ACLU maintains that the PATRIOT Act was passed in haste with little discussion and debate and with most members of Congress never having read the bill (ACLU 2005a). In the view of the ACLU, there has been a dangerous rejoining of international intelligence gathering with domestic law enforcement duties. In effect, the PATRIOT Act has given almost unchecked authority to the Executive Branch of government to do what it thinks is necessary to provide domestic security. The ACLU said,

> In short, not only has the Bush Administration undermined judicial oversight of government spying on citizens by pushing the Patriot Act into law, but it is also undermining another crucial check and balance on surveillance powers: accountability to Congress and the public. (ACLU 2005a, 4)

Box 14.2
The American Library Association's Position on Privacy

Largely in response to the federal government's efforts to combat terrorism through legislation, and especially in regard to the gathering of various types of information on private citizens, the American Library Association (ALA) passed the following resolution in 2003:

WHEREAS, The American Library Association's Policy on Governmental Intimidation opposes any use of governmental prerogatives that lead to the intimidation of the individual or the citizenry from the exercise of free expression; and

WHEREAS, the ALA Interpretation on Privacy describes the impact of freedom of inquiry on privacy or when privacy is compromised; and

WHEREAS, In matters of national security and the preservation of our nation, the concept of Terrorism Information Awareness (formerly called Total Information Awareness) as defined by the Defense Advanced Research Projects Administration (DARPA), may be used in making key national security decisions; and

WHEREAS, It is the responsibility of the federal government to protect its citizens from government sanctioned invasion of privacy; and

WHEREAS, Personally identifiable information compiled in a database by a government agency should be governed by the Privacy Act; and

WHEREAS, The Terrorism Information Awareness Program (TIAP) has the potential to build a large database of personally identifiable information; now, therefore, be it

RESOLVED, That the American Library Association urges the Congress of the United States to take action to terminate the Terrorism Information Awareness Program; and, be it further

RESOLVED, That the American Library Association urges the Defense Advanced Research Projects Administration (DARPA) to comply with all provisions of the Privacy Act; and, be it further

RESOLVED, That copies of this resolution be transmitted to the President of the United States, the Vice President of the United States, the appropriate committees of the United States Congress, the Secretary of Defense, and other entities as appropriate. ✦

Source: ALA (2003).

Many of these concerns came to a head when Congress reauthorized the PATRIOT Act on March 9, 2006. The Act was originally supposed to sunset on December 31, 2005, but the legislation was extended for several months to allow for more debate. Civil libertarians questioned four controversial elements of the Act (the government's ability to access business records, roving wiretaps, "sneak and peek" warrants, and national security letters). Opposition to the Act came from an unlikely alliance of Democrats, civil libertarians, right-wing groups (that generally oppose more government), and legal scholars. There was a broad opposition to the government's expanded powers, and hundreds of town councils, counties, and cities denounced the Act.

Critics believe that the PATRIOT Act has provided too much governmental authority in the quest for public safety. Although the Attorney General has assured Congress that the federal government has never used the powers granted it to obtain private information from bookstores, libraries, and medical records, nevertheless "liberals and libertarian-oriented conservatives have pressed for changes, citing privacy and civil liberties concerns" (Taylor 2005). Supporters of the Act, such as Comey (2006, 404) argued that "much of what is in the Act is so smart, so ordinary, so constitutional, so lawful that nobody would oppose it."

From a policy perspective, the one noteworthy feature is that as time has passed, legislators seem less pressured to enact or reauthorize legislation. On the one hand, the AEDPA was introduced only one week after the Oklahoma City bombing (Beall 1998). On the other hand, the PATRIOT Act was enacted only a few weeks after the 9/11 tragedy. But with several years to consider the full impact of the legislation, politicians were more hesitant to reauthorize the Act. As a result, adding sunset clauses to hastily enacted legislation might be a powerful tool to ensure more thoughtful debate when there is less urgency. The PATRIOT Act is now scheduled to sunset on December 31, 2009, and it will be interesting to see whether it will be reauthorized in its current form.

Will the USA PATRIOT Act and other pieces of federal legislation undermine the fundamental civil liberties of American citizens and others living in this country? Perhaps a more basic question to ask is: What are we willing to trade in exchange for our safety? (See Box 14.3 for two other dimensions of the privacy-security debate.) While these questions largely remain unanswered for the time being, some of the answers are being played out in the courts. The following section examines a few of the legal issues and the court cases that may provide us with greater understanding and insights in the future.

The Changing Legal Environment

Some observers (see, for example, Baker and Gregware 2004) believe that the nature of the courts and the legal process in the United States have changed in the past decade. Traditionally, the struggle for control over the courts has been between citizens and the professionals who work in the courts. However, beginning with the attacks on U.S. targets on September 11, 2001, the executive branch of the federal government has moved decisively to expand its powers over court processes in the name of the war on terror. Baker and Gregware (2004, 484) said, "This expanded executive authority comes at the expense of the citizen's ability to oversee the process and the court professionals' ability to control the courts."

As we outlined before in the chapter, the mechanisms have existed for some time that allow the government to conduct surveillance of citizens for intelligence purposes. However, two particular aspects of the legal environment have changed. First, there is an increased level of secrecy not only in the gathering of intelligence data but also in adjudicating legal claims relating to the intelligence function. The United States now has the Foreign Intelligence Surveillance Court (FISC) to

Box 14.3
Technology and the Debate Over Privacy

Video Surveillance

After the bombings on the London Underground (subway) and on a double-decker bus in July of 2005, police agencies all over England moved quickly to identify the suicide bombers directly involved and to apprehend any others who might have supported them. When the bombers were identified within days and a group of individuals was taken into custody after the incident, many in the United States asked how the police in England could move so quickly. The answer is closed circuit video surveillance cameras. Visitors to London often are stuck by the pervasiveness of video surveillance in the city, especially related to the transportation network. Now, "the extensive use by Scotland Yard of images taken by the thousands of cameras in the London Underground stations has encouraged a number of governments to install this type of surveillance" ("Video and telephone surveillance" 2005). In fact, governments all over Europe are set to follow London's example.

How about the United States? To many in the United States, constant video surveillance smacks of the concept of "Big Brother," first offered in George Orwell's book, *1984*. Civil liberties groups are particularly concerned about snooping by the government of average citizens going about their normal routines. Despite these concerns, CCTV cameras are currently being used by most of the largest U.S. police departments. Ratcliffe (2006) reported that CCTV is widely used in patrol vehicles and within police department buildings. CCTV operated by police departments has also been used to provide surveillance of public areas in many U.S. communities. What do you think? Would you be willing to have less privacy in order to have greater security?

Another significant question that relates to CCTV surveillance is that there is very little oversight of the private companies that monitor customers in their stores, hotels, malls, casinos, restaurants, or banks. CCTV cameras are often so pervasive that we do not notice them, but most of us are "on camera" several times a day. However, we do not know whether the persons who work for these companies are using the cameras in a professional manner, or what happens to images of us that are collected by these operators.

The Matrix

One of the technological applications that has been offered to fight terrorism in the United States and to provide greater homeland security is that of the **MATRIX (Multistate Anti-Terrorism Information Exchange)**. The MATRIX involves a network of databases in various states. The Departments of Homeland Security and Justice had supported the creation of the system, which allowed law enforcement and domestic intelligence agencies to search across state lines for files of criminal histories, driver's license information (including photos), telephone numbers, vehicle registrations, and other personal information. In 2005, the federal funding for this experiment ran out. Many states discontinued the program, but Connecticut, Florida, Ohio, and Pennsylvania have continued to employ the MATRIX software. Like video surveillance, many civil libertarians and privacy advocates are concerned that such a powerful tool allows the government to engage in all types of mischief along with its quest for homeland security. The next step in this progression may occur with the introduction of the "Real ID" or national identification card. ✦

hear requests for surveillance warrants. Additionally, there also is a secret federal appeals court to hear cases that are in dispute within the FISC. All of this operates out of the public view based on the executive branch's assertion that "in order to protect us from terrorists, it must have secrecy so that potential terrorists will not know what it knows" (Baker and Gregware 2004, 494).

The second change in the legal environment that is related to the war on terrorism is the lowering of standards related to search and seizure. Federal authorities now can obtain search warrants on less than probable cause if they can convince the Foreign Intelligence Surveillance Court that a target of an investigation is suspected of terrorist activities or connections. The PATRIOT Act and other federal legislation give authorities access to a wide variety of personal information as well. Finally, search and seizure principles such as notice are abridged by the "sneak and peek" searches that now have been authorized.

Third, the PATRIOT Act now allows for (and even encourages) the commingling of functions that traditionally existed separately as criminal and intelligence investigations (Baker and Gregware 2004). There has always been something of a legal or operational wall between criminal investigations and intelligence gathering, but federal law enforcement officials have recognized that the authority they now possess is a powerful tool in the fight against conventional crime. Therefore, the distinction between what is a purely criminal issue and what relates to the intelligence function is getting harder to discern. Should law enforcement be using extraordinary powers to pursue "ordinary criminals"?

In a recent Nevada case, FBI agents used provisions of the PATRIOT Act to monitor the activities of a strip club owner who was allegedly involved in political corruption. Hudson (2003) reported that there have been more than 250 criminal charges that have resulted from using the PATRIOT Act, but few of these suspects appear to be terrorist-related. It would seem that this is not its intended use, and another reason why civil libertarians are concerned about the reach of the Act.

Finally, the designation of a group of people as enemy combatants has taken the United States into largely uncharted legal waters. As the federal courts continue to address the issues surrounding enemy combatants (such as in the *Hamdan v. Rumsfeld* case), we will begin to get better definitions concerning the executive branch's powers to carry out its duties in responding to threats, both foreign and domestic. For the time being, however, concerns have been expressed—particularly by due process advocates—over the degree to which the Constitution applies in the war on terror.

Conclusions

It is not an exaggeration to say that the balance between safety and liberty may present the greatest challenge to American government today. The criminal justice system is one arena where this dynamic tension is manifested. State and local law enforcement agencies are being asked to shoulder significant responsibilities for providing homeland security. Training and federal dollars are being directed at these agencies as first responders to any type of terrorist attack (or even a natural disaster).

Members of the various New York City Police departments and the New York City Fire Department found themselves on the frontlines of disaster response on Tuesday, September 11, 2001. Other agencies around the country have had to respond to actual events, but more often to heightened security alerts that put agency personnel in a defensive posture for days at a time. Furthermore, a number of the nation's criminal justice personnel who belong to the National Guard and Reserves have been called to active duty to serve in Afghanistan and Iraq, as well as stateside assignments. These responses have put increasing stresses on the nation's domestic law enforcement agencies and this, in turn, creates stresses within the entire criminal justice system. The final question facing us, then, is how long these agencies and their personnel can stand under such stresses.

Notes

1. Much of this material is based on Reaves and Bauer (2003). Additional materials and current information also can be located on the Department of Homeland Security Web site (DHS 2007).
2. At different times in our nation's history, the Coast Guard has been in the Treasury, Defense (Navy), and Transportation Departments (U.S. Coast Guard 2007).
3. The term enemy combatant traditionally has been applied to members of the armed forces of one nation against which another is at war. ("Detention of Enemy Combatants Act" 109th Congress, 1st Session, H.R. 1076, March 3, 2005)

Key Terms

al Qaeda
American Civil Liberties Union (ACLU)
Antiterrorism and Effective Death Penalty Act (AEDPA)
Department of Homeland Security (DHS)
domestic terrorism
enemy combatants
Foreign Intelligence Surveillance Act (FISA)
Foreign Intelligence Surveillance Court (FISC)
Hamdan v. Rumsfeld
homeland security
money laundering
Multistate Anti-Terrorism Information Exchange (MATRIX)
national security
pen register
Rumsfeld v. Padilla
"sneak and peek" searches
trap and trace device
USA PATRIOT Act

Critical Review Questions

1. Is the global war on terrorism related to criminal justice processes in the United States? If so, how?

2. Do an Internet search for the Foreign Intelligence Surveillance Act and the USA PATRIOT Act. How many "hits" did you get for each? What does that tell you about the interest in and concerns with these pieces of legislation?

3. Divide up into groups of 3 to 4 students and discuss the following proposition: "The USA PATRIOT Act has (or has not) made the U.S. public safer."

4. What do we mean by "sneak and peek" searches? How do these searches alter the fundamental elements traditionally associated with the Fourth Amendment?

5. What is meant by the notion "domestic terrorism," and is it related in any way to the war on global terrorism? Can you think of (or find) the names of any organizations that might be classified as "domestic terrorism" groups?

6. Are some groups potentially labeled as domestic terrorists merely exercising their First Amendment rights? Can you think of any groups in our nation's history that might have been given this label? Explain your answer and the position you have taken.

7. Are youth street gangs "domestic terrorists" as you understand this notion? Could they be called this? Why or why not?

8. Look at some of the agencies reorganized under the Department of Homeland Security. Why was the FBI not included? Are there organizational problems associated with moving these agencies around? In other words, has the massive federal reorganization made us safer? (Hint: Look back at Chapter 1 on politics and policy.)

9. What are some of the significant legal changes that have occurred as a result of our war on terrorism? Do these changes present threats to the privacy and security of the average citizen of the United States, or are they only directed at international terrorists? How can we know for sure?

10. Is it possible that we will have to surrender some freedoms in order to be safer? Are there any examples already in place that you can think of? And after such surrender, how can we check to see if we really are safer? (At this point, reexamine Critical Review Question 3 in Chapter 1.)

References

American Civil Liberties Union (ACLU). (2005a). "Surveillance and the USA PATRIOT Act." Retrieved from: *http://www.aclu.org/SafeandFree/SafeandFree.cfm?ID=12263&c=206*.

———. (2005b). "The USA PATRIOT act and government actions that threaten our civil liberties." Retrieved from: *http://www.aclu.org*.

American Library Association (ALA). (2003). "Resolution on the Terrorism Information Awareness Program." *Newsletter on Intellectual Freedom* 52 (5), 213–214.

Baker, Nancy V., and Peter Gregware. (2004). "Citizens, professionals, or the executive: Who owns the courts?" Pp. 483–497 in *Courts and Justice*, third edition, edited by G. Larry Mays and Peter R. Gregware. Long Grove, IL: Waveland.

Balkin, Jack. (2006, June 29). Hamdan *as a Democracy-Forcing Decision*. Retrieved July 1, 2006 from: *http://balkin.blogspot.com/2006_06_25_balkin-archive.html*.

Bazan, Elizabeth B. (2004). "The Foreign Intelligence Surveillance Act: An overview of the statutory framework and recent judicial decisions." [Order code RL30465]. Washington, DC: Congressional Research Service.

Beall, Jennifer. (1998). "Are we only burning witches? The Antiterrorism and Effective Death Penalty Act of 1996's answer to terrorism." *Indiana Law Journal* 73 (2), 693–708.

Bell, Anne. (2006). "Domestic security: The homefront and the war on terrorism." *PBS Online Newshour*. Retrieved from: *http://www.pbs.org/newshour/bb/terrorism/homeland/fisa.html*.

Bergen, Peter L. (2001). *Holy War, Inc.: Inside the Secret World of Osama bin Laden*. New York: Free Press.

Champion, Dean John. (2005). *The American Dictionary of Criminal Justice*, third edition. Los Angeles: Roxbury Publishing.

Comey, James B. (2006). "Fighting terrorism and preserving civil liberties." *University of Richmond Law Review* 40 (2), 403–518.

Department of Homeland Security (DHS). (2007). "Homeland Security Homepage" at *http://www.whitehouse.gov/infocus/homeland/*.

Doyle, Charles. (2002a). "The USE PATRIOT Act: A Legal Analysis." Washington, DC: Congressional Research Service [Order code RL31377, April 15].

———. (2002b). "The USA PATRIOT Act: A sketch." Washington, DC: Congressional Research Service [Order code RS21203, April 18].

Federation of American Scientists. (2006). "Foreign Intelligence Surveillance Act." Retrieved from: *http://www.fas.org/irp/agency/doj/fisa/*.

Hamdan v. Rumsfeld, 548 U.S. ___ (2006).

Harris Interactive (2005, December 21). "National parks, crime-fighting, Medicare, and Social Security top the list of government services which have strongest public support. Retrieved July 1, 2006 from: *http://www.harrisinteractive.com/harris_poll/index.asp?PID=620*.

Hudson, Audrey. (2003, November 12). "Patriot Act said misused in Vegas." *Washington Times*. Retrieved October 12, 2006 from: *http://www.washingtontimes.com*.

"Information databases aid investigators." (2003). *Information Management Journal* 37 (6), 10.

O'Harrow, Robert, Jr. (2003, August 6). "U.S. backs Florida's new counterterrorism database." *Washington Post*, p. A01.

Peed, Matthew J. (2005). "Blacklisting as foreign policy: The politics and law of listing terror states." *Duke Law Journal* 54 (5), 1321–1352.

Public Broadcasting System (PBS). (2006, February 15). "Chertoff speaks." *NewsHour With Jim Lehrer* transcript. Retrieved July 1, 2006 from *http://www.pbs.org/newshour/bb/fedagencies/jan-june06/chertoff_2-15.html*.

"Q & A: Moussaoui trial." (2006, May 3). *BBC News*, Wednesday. *http://newsvote.bbc.co.uk/mpapps/pagetools/print/news.bbc.co.uk/1/hi/world/americans/4471019.stm*.

Ranum, Marcus. (2004). *The Myth of Homeland Security*. Indianapolis: Wiley.

Ratcliffe, Jerry. (2006). *Video Surveillance of Public Places*. Washington, DC: U.S. Department of Justice. Office of Community Oriented Policing Services.

Reaves, Brian A., and Lynn M. Bauer. (2003). *Federal Law Enforcement Officers, 2002*. Washington, DC: U.S. Department of Justice, Bureau of Justice Statistics.

Royse, David. (2005). "Police still using MATRIX-type database." Retrieved from: *http:// www.lasvegassun.com/sunbin/stories/text/2005/jul/10/97100642.html*.

Rumsfeld v. Padilla, 542 U.S. 426 (2004).

Scalia, John. (2002). *Prisoner Petitions Filed in U.S. District Courts, 2000*. Washington, DC: U.S. Department of Justice, Bureau of Justice Statistics.

Smith, Lisa. (2005). "RFID report." *Humanist* 65 (3), 37–38.

Taylor, Andrew. (2005). "Patriot act critics laud vote to limit use." Associated Press news release, retrieved July 16, 2005 from: *http://www.news.yahoo.com/s/ap/20050616/ ap_ on_go_co/patriot_act_libraries_15*.

United States Coast Guard. (2007). Retrieved January 1, 2007 from: *http://www.uscg.mil/ hq/g-cp/history/faqs/when.html*.

"Video and telephone surveillance to be upgraded in the face of terrorist threat." (2005). Agence France Press. Retrieved July 16, 2005 from: *http://www.lasvegassun.com/ sunbin/stories/bw-cong/2005/jun/16/061607365*.

White, Jonathan R. (2006). *Terrorism and Homeland Security*, fifth edition. Belmont, CA: Wadsworth.

Recommended Readings

Bergen, Peter L. (2001). *Holy War, Inc.: Inside the Secret World of Osama bin Laden*. New York: Free Press. Bergen's book is different than many of the recommended readings presented in this text. It is written by a journalist (Bergen is a correspondent with CNN), not an academic. Nevertheless, Bergen presents a fascinating account of the historical, religious, and political origins of al-Qaeda and its shadowy leader, Osama bin Laden. Bergen helps the Western mind grasp the political/religious notion of holy war (or jihad) in order to provide a greater understanding of why a group would choose to attack the United States and why people would be willing to die in pursuit of a cause.

Ranum, Marcus. (2004). *The Myth of Homeland Security*. Indianapolis: Wiley. You may feel better or worse, depending on your orientation toward this topic, after reading this book. Ranum's work is not a college textbook but one written for a general audience. He spends a great deal of time talking about what is wrong with the federal government's efforts in addressing homeland security and deals with the mythology and politics that surround this area. The bottom line for Ranum is that, unfortunately, some areas of our lives cannot be made much more secure (without altering our ways of life) and that much of what passes for the government's homeland security efforts is really an illusion.

White, Jonathan R. (2006). *Terrorism and Homeland Security*, fifth edition. Belmont, CA: Wadsworth. This book represents an effort to deal in a comprehensive way (18 chapters) with the evolving face of terrorism. White begins by addressing definitional issues and some of the religious, historical, and political factors related to terrorism. He next deals with terrorism as an international problem. Finally, he turns to America's problem of homegrown or domestic terrorism and the struggle we face as a nation in providing homeland defense. ✦

Chapter 15

Making Sense of Criminal Justice

Introduction

Delivering criminal justice interventions that are just and fair, as well as effective and efficient, poses numerous challenges, a fact that you are more likely to appreciate after reading through 14 chapters. The tasks are made more difficult given the incredible complexities of the justice systems that operate at all levels in the United States. For example, almost one million law enforcement officers work within almost 18,000 federal, state, and local agencies, and almost 10,000 judges sit in over 3,000 courts, interpreting the laws of 50 states (and multitudes of local entities) and the federal government, as well as processing criminal cases filed by some 27,000 prosecutors. Each actor within each justice system is likely to have his or her own priorities and to possess slightly different views about justice and the reasons why criminals commit offenses. Each will confront these offenders (and the public) in ways that were shaped, at least in part, by the history of their organization, the training and supervision that they received, the culture of the community, and their own values and beliefs. With all of these variables, there is relatively little uniformity.

At times, the system might seem likely to collapse under its own weight. Every year there are at least 60 million 9-1-1 calls and some 14 million arrestees being processed through juvenile halls and local jails, and these suspects appear before increasingly busy judges to have "their day in court." Almost 2.2 million Americans can be found in a jail or prison while you are reading this paragraph, either awaiting an appearance before a judge or having been sentenced—and about 4,000 of these inmates will die in jail or prison (most of natural causes) this year. Almost five million other offenders are serving sentences of probation or parole in the community. To accommodate these crushing workloads, each organization has developed its own approach to dispensing justice, with varying degrees of fairness, professionalism, and respect for the Constitution.

We started this book with two chapters that outlined a number of ways of looking at justice systems, and here we will provide a short review. First, it is impossible to disentangle politics from the operations of criminal justice systems as all law enforcement agencies, courts, and correctional systems depend on governments and political acts and actors for most of their revenues. Second, the activities of each element of our justice systems (police, courts, and corrections) are shaped by constitutional requirements; federal, state, and local laws; and organizational policies. We have outlined numerous examples in which interventions that make a lot of "common sense" failed after they were introduced. In some cases, elected or appointed officials attempt to "reform" the operations of different agencies, and these efforts generally result in mixed results as the people who work within organizations typically are resistant to change.

Second, we also have to acknowledge how different stakeholders influence the operations of justice systems. Politicians levy taxes to fund police, court, and correctional agencies; but citizen advisory panels, local business owners, employee associations (or unions) of officers or deputies, federal or state inspectors, and other regulatory bodies all influence the managers of agencies. Moreover, a number of public interest groups have a powerful influence on the way that justice is dispensed. The National Rifle Association (NRA), for instance, actively supports and funds politicians who advance the NRA's political agenda. The American Civil Liberties Union, by contrast, is able to muster significant legal resources to challenge legislation or policies that they perceive as unjust. Because some of these interest groups have lots of money and millions of members, they have powerful voices.

The media also have a role in shaping justice policies. If you doubt their influence, see what occurs when the local newspaper writes over one hundred articles about problems within an organization (as happened at the Houston Police Department Crime Lab), or every television network in America continuously replays a film clip of a late-night traffic stop where the driver of the vehicle is beaten by police (as occurred with the Rodney King incident). But even entertainment television is responsible for influencing the way that we perceive the world. Eschholz (2002) found that people who watched more television were more fearful of crime, a finding that supports prior research.

Perhaps more important, litigation has also fashioned the way that justice is dispensed in America. The Supreme Court has a key role in determining the boundaries of individual rights that suspects, arrestees, and prisoners enjoy. While few police officers actually fear any of the nine Supreme Court Justices, they dread the possibility of letting a murderer walk free because they did not conduct a proper interrogation or search. Workers within justice systems are equally apprehensive that they will lose their home in a lawsuit because they acted with deliberate indifference, and supervisors are fearful of being held accountable when their subordinates were not properly trained to conduct their duties or because of a split-second decision that they made under pressure, having had little time to weigh different options.

While all of these challenges create immeasurable stress for agency administrators, they also act to constrain the unethical or illegal activities of people working within criminal justice organizations, which is important to protect us from overzealous law enforcement officers, prosecutorial misconduct, incompetent or biased judges, or correctional officers who engage in some form of wrongdoing.

Sometimes college professors and members of advocacy organizations are critical of people who work within criminal justice agencies. We have to acknowledge, however, that most criminal justice jobs are stressful, unpleasant, and dangerous. In addition, police officers or deputies, court staff members, and correctional officers often confront situations that have little possibility of a "win-win" outcome. We do not always give these employees the tools they need to conduct their duties—in Chapter 9, we related an account of LAPD detectives who had to wait months for fingerprint evidence to exclude a possible suspect in an investigation, for example. We expect much of these employees, and the pay is frequently meager. Paying higher salaries and recruiting better prepared employees in the past few decades has gone a long way in improving the quality of the police and correctional officers, and we speculate that this trend will continue.

Given these realities, one way that we can better understand the functioning of criminal justice operations was introduced in Chapter 2, that is, Packer's due process and crime control models. We noted that neither of these models exists in a true form and that the operations of justice organizations will fall somewhere between these two ends of a continuum. The most conservative of agencies, for instance, has to respect the due process protections provided by the Constitution to suspects or offenders. By contrast, even the most liberal organization and vocal civil libertarian would acknowledge that the harsh intervention of the justice system is needed at some times and for some offenders to protect the safety of the public.

Understanding Criminal Justice Policy

We have avoided the term *theory* throughout this book, but in essence, theories of criminal justice operations have underscored all of our discussions about responding to crime; differential treatment by justice systems based on race, class, or gender; policy development; the influence of politicians in the operations of criminal justice agencies; the contribution of culture to our understanding of justice systems; and how organizations strive to get the best results from their operations (either in crime control or reducing recidivism). Most of the theories that you have discussed in your classes try to explain crime or criminal behavior, but we are going to examine briefly some approaches that help us better understand how justice systems operate, and we relate these to examples from prior chapters. While we have generally focused on the crime control and due process models developed by Packer (1968), other scholars have explained the factors that influence criminal justice policies. We examine these different approaches using classifications outlined by Kraska (2006, 177–178), and we focus on the influence of partisan politics, critical theories, social construction, and late modernity on criminal justice policy.

First, a consistent theme throughout this book is that partisan politics has influenced changes in criminal justice systems, especially law enforcement and corrections. This approach contends that politicians often have exploited the problem of crime for their own purposes. By being "tough on crime," they are more likely to win elections, and offenders are convenient scapegoats as they elicit little public sympathy. But does this approach have any support?

Recall from Chapter 2 how Richard Nixon used crime as a major political issue in his 1968 presidential campaign. Prior to this election, crime was seen primarily as a local problem. While we observed that other Republican Presidents have used the issue of crime control to win elections, President Bill Clinton also introduced a number of policies to be tough on crime, including federal funding for 100,000 police officers, the enactment of the AEDPA, and the Prison Litigation Reform Act. In addition, during the Clinton Presidency (from 1993 to 2001), the number of persons held in jail or prison increased from 1.36 to 1.96 million. Federal politicians have also used their financial clout to shape the ways that criminal justice policies are formed in the states, such as the highway funding given to states that lowered the definition of intoxication to blood alcohol levels of .08, or money for prison construction in states that enacted truth in sentencing laws.

Yet, local and state politicians also have a powerful influence on the operations of justice systems. Local governments, for instance, pay the largest share of criminal justice expenditures (Hughes 2006). Even the role of prosecutor is highly political in most jurisdictions. It is clearly evident that federal, state, and local politicians do influence justice policies, and this has both positive and negative consequences. Because the United States has a decentralized government, politicians are not insulated from the wishes of the people like they are in Europe. As a result, when the public wants tough on crime policies, they get them, even though such policies may have unanticipated long-term costs (such as creating mistrust in the "system" and the problem of what to do with the 650,000 prisoners we release back into society each year).

A second theoretical model examines the relationships between different social groups (typically race, class, and gender) and is based on **critical criminology.** This approach is associated with feminist and Marxist theories, and the cornerstone of these models is founded on the relationships among different social groups: Those groups with political or economic clout (the "haves") exploit the groups without political or economic power (the "have-nots").

We explored these issues in our examination of race and gender in Chapters 7 and 8 and in our discussions of the management of prisoners as "dangerous classes." Nobody, in good conscience, can deny that criminal justice systems historically have been used to control persons based on race, class, and gender. Prior to the 1970s, many young women were imprisoned for experimenting with their sexuality, and throughout history we have prosecuted women for prostitution but have been reluctant to arrest the men who purchase their services. We also addressed how the issues of paternalism and chivalry influenced the way that women were treated by justice systems: Were we doing these women a favor, or did this preferential treatment reinforce stereotypes of women as "inferior"?

No discussion about justice in America can avoid the issue of race. All levels of governments have used justice systems to enforce unfair laws or social practices. The close relationship between justice systems and slave owners in the antebellum South, for instance, ensured that slaves who ran away were hunted down and returned to their owners. Justice systems after the Civil War were also punitive to African Americans, as they encountered **black codes** or **Jim Crow laws** (laws that were discriminatory toward African Americans, or laws that applied only to African Americans). For southern African Americans who ran afoul of these laws—and were sentenced to a term of incarceration—many were leased out to private entrepreneurs in conditions worse than slavery (if inmates who were leased from the state died, the operators would simply get others to replace them—as a result there was no incentive to keep these leased prisoners healthy).

African Americans were not the only ones mistreated by governments, and we often forget how American Indians were forced off their lands onto reservations. Although U.S. Army personnel were responsible for these operations, they were aided by Indian agents and law enforcers of the era. Japanese Americans were also rounded up and placed in internment camps during World War II, despite the fact that many of these people were born in the United States (Norgren and Nanda 2006).

The boundaries of race and justice will also be tested in the twenty-first century as the Latino population grows. With increasing immigration—both legal and illegal—the total percentage of Latinos in the United States has overtaken the African American population as the largest minority group in America. Several advocacy groups, such as the National Council of La Raza (NCLR), have observed that Latinos are overrepresented in prison populations, but they point out that many of these prisoners are incarcerated on relatively minor, nonviolent offenses (NCLR 2004). In addition, they have reported that Latinos in the criminal justice system are less likely than any other racial or ethnic group to receive treatment (such as programs for addictions or other rehabilitative services). As the size of this group increases, it will continue to flex its political muscle.

Do modern justice systems oppress women and members of minority groups? And what effect does that have on perceptions of justice systems? We addressed the issues of "driving while black," disproportionate minority confinement of juveniles, and the likelihood of imprisonment for different minority groups. Statistics on vehicle stops, arrests, criminal justice processing, the use of imprisonment, and the death penalty seem to suggest that things are improving—that the disparities between different groups are decreasing. However, these are complex issues and ultimately rest upon differential involvement in crime and calls-for-service, the deployment of the police, family and neighborhood dynamics, rates of social disorganization, and various cultural values and beliefs, including racism and stereotypes.

Perhaps the best way of measuring whether people feel excluded or oppressed is to ask them about their perceptions of justice systems. According to Gallup Polls taken in 2004, approximately one-third of African Americans, approximately 28 percent of other nonwhites, and one-fifth of whites had very little confidence in criminal justice systems (reported in Maguire and Pastore 2005, 113). High levels of mistrust may be attributed to the historical treatment of minority populations by justice systems or current law enforcement practices. Regardless of the cause, however, justice systems need to do a much better job in improving public confidence in their operations. We have repeated many times in the previous chapters that when justice systems are seen as more legitimate, people are more likely to follow the law (Tyler 2006). Yet, identifying a problem is much easier than solving it.

Interestingly, the 2004 Gallup poll results (reported in Maguire and Pastore 2005, 113) found that the attitudes of women and men concerning the criminal justice system are almost identical, both 34 percent of men and women reported that they had a great deal of confidence in the system. The percentage of women who reported having very little confidence in justice systems, by contrast, was only slightly less (22 percent) than their male counterparts (23 percent). Given these findings, it appears as though women have about the same amount of faith (or lack of faith) in justice systems as their male counterparts.

As we have mentioned, theoretical models that focus on race, class, and gender relationships are based in feminist, Marxist, and critical criminology. These approaches are probably much more popular with professors than students, but they do offer a meaningful way of analyzing the relationships between different social groups. When a criminal justice policy is proposed, for instance, it is important to ask who wins and who loses. What is the language of a policy debate: Is it based on helping, controlling, or punishing? If a policy discussion focuses on punishment, does the language scapegoat or stereotype the offenders?

Finally, does our desire to punish increase when the state is undergoing some sort of economic, political, or legitimacy crisis? Whether or not one believes in such theories, these are important questions that should underscore every debate about criminal justice policy. In fact, the questions that we should ask about criminal justice are often formed by the way that we interpret the world, a cornerstone of the **constructionist perspective,** which relates to theories of **social construction.**

Social construction is a theoretical approach that tries to explain our understanding of the world. We have outlined how justice policies and the media often seem intertwined. On the one hand, the news industry reports extensively on crime and justice, and as a society we have an almost morbid interest in these matters. The entertainment industry, on the other hand, also shapes our notions about offenders and justice. These accounts may have a powerful influence on the way that we feel about persons who commit crimes. If offenders are portrayed as beyond all help, that will shape the types of criminal justice interventions we will support. Lilly, Cullen, and Ball (2001, 5–7) maintained that "ideas have consequences." For example, if we believe that offenders are animals, then the best place for them is in a cage. To the contrary, if we suppose that offenders are people who have made mistakes, then we will probably support interventions that are intended to correct their mistakes.

One of the problems we face is that the distinction between news and fictional accounts of crime and justice are often blurred. Programs such as *Law and Order* frequently base their story lines on crimes that actually occurred. This may make it difficult for some viewers to distinguish between fiction and reality. The entertainment media also fashion our understanding of the operations of the police, courts, and corrections. But, many of the duties carried out by the police within courts and in jails or prisons are routine, so only the most outrageous, unusual, or egregious cases are depicted. To obtain an hour's worth of television for a "reality" detective program—about 45 minutes of actual content—Seagal (1993) reported that producers had to screen through 6,000 to 12,000 minutes of footage.

Because the entertainment media are not accountable for mistakes, the television programs and films that we watch may distort or greatly oversimplify the administration of justice. We outlined in Chapter 9 how television programs that depict the analysis of evidence using forensic science not only are popular but have also disappointed victims and their families when evidence cannot be retrieved from a crime scene or, if found, cannot be analyzed, is inconclusive, and it may take months to get results. Seldom are offenses neatly wrapped up in an hour.

The constructionist approach is based on our understanding of the world, and we interpret the world through our observations, our interactions with other people, and from external sources (such as the media). In some cases, political stakeholders have a vested interest in manipulating these definitions. As Beckett and Sasson (2000, 6) observed,

"Our understanding of the significance of crime as a social problem and our views on its causes and cures depend largely on the way in which the issue is represented." We briefly addressed the issue of moral panics in Chapter 6 where we pointed out that the media are sometimes responsible for creating public fear of a particular subculture (or a group that represents some form of threat).

How do the news and entertainment media influence our ideas about persons who commit crimes? Most of us know very little about sex offenders, except that they are a group that has little public sympathy or support. Most college students are openly hostile toward these offenders and feel that they are not capable of reform, will always pose a danger to the public, and should receive lengthy prison sentences, or worse. To increase our public safety, we have enhanced sentences for sex offenders, developed sex offender registries, and have created specialized probation and parole caseloads. We have also introduced **civil commitment,** where sex offenders who are thought to pose a risk to the public can be kept beyond their release date from prison.

Yet, most sex offenders are not "strangers" but are family members (somewhere around two-thirds of rapes are committed by spouses, relatives, friends, paramours, or parents). In addition, adolescent sex offenders are very amenable to rehabilitation (Schwartz 2005). Even adult sex offenders, once released, have very low rates of recidivism, and only rarely are they convicted of further sex offenses (see Langan and Levin 2002). Some scholars have even questioned whether sex offenders are dangerous (Sample and Bray 2003). Of course, one single repeat offender who commits dozens of these crimes—especially toward vulnerable victims such as children—makes us want to punish all of these offenders so these crimes will not occur again. But, is that rational criminal justice policy?

Last, a number of scholars have explained our current criminal justice policies—especially high levels of enforcement and incarceration—are a function of **late modernity.** Some scholars have defined a number of stages of society and observe that we are currently in a period of late modernity (the modern period having started in the early 1900s). David Garland (2001) contended that our punitive attitudes toward offenders come from the social structures of this era that feature an aversion to risk and insecurities. One element of changing social structures is our increasing **social isolation,** when individuals are not attached to others in the community (Putnam 2000). Historically, we believed that we could reduce risk and fear by controlling dangerous populations through social welfare systems, but in the past few decades, we have shifted our focus to justice systems.

Some of the concepts that we introduced in our discussions of corrections, such as the new penology, are related to theories of late modernity. Feeley and Simon (1992) argued that we have abandoned individualized justice in favor of actuarial justice and safety. Because we feel isolated and insecure, the public wants more people locked up in order to feel safe. As a result, instead of locking up only the most dangerous of offenders, we should incarcerate all members of threatening groups. The fact that one-third of all African Americans born in 2001 will go to prison in their lifetime, if imprisonment rates stay at their current trends, suggests that Feeley and Simon (1992) may have been correct. These practices, however, may be impossible to sustain, and that might force us to confront our fears and insecurities.

Another element of this approach is an increasingly managerial response to crime and punishment. We are taking a much more analytical look at the problems of crime and are increasingly sophisticated in our responses to crime: The police are using COMPSTAT in most large jurisdictions, probation agencies are starting to use global positioning systems (GPS) technology to track the whereabouts of individual offenders, and radio frequency identification (RFID) technology is currently being tested for the positive identification of inmates, case files, and evidence. Computerized software is now available for tracking shift and training assignments for police departments and correctional facilities, and courts also have been using software that tracks offenders, offenses, fines, and dockets. A cornerstone of late modernity is to take advantage of technology and managerial efficiency to maximize the efforts of justice systems.

One of the challenges of this increasing sophistication, at least in the eyes of late-modernity scholars, is that due process protections may be threatened. One response to the risk of terrorism that we addressed in the previous chapter was the increased use of all types of surveillance. Even something as nonthreatening as closed circuit television systems to oversee crowded or crime-prone public spaces poses a threat to our privacy. The question we asked in our examination of terrorism and safety was, How much freedom should we surrender to be safer? Scholars who view the world through the lens of late modernity might suggest that our good intentions (the quest for a safer society) may produce unexpected or unanticipated results.

We have added four additional approaches to our examination of Packer (1968), although we could have listed several more. Students interested in reading a bit more about theories of criminal justice processing (as opposed to theories of criminology) should review the work of Kraska (2004 and 2006). Theory is important because it directs the types of research questions that we have to ask to determine whether our interventions are effective; and if they are failing, which if any of the elements are working. Also, other important questions include whether we need to introduce a given policy and why such a policy is needed now. Although most readers will likely equate research with theory in terms of interest (in other words, many will not be especially interested), research has to guide policy, a cornerstone of the evidence-based practice.

Box 15.1
McJustice in the New Millennium?

Criminologists and criminal justice theorists are coming up with new ways of looking at crime control. Several have proposed that parallels exist between criminal justice systems and fast-food and entertainment giants McDonald's and Disney (Bohm 2006; Robinson 2003). A cornerstone of these approaches is "sameness" and a move away from the individual: Do these approaches decrease individualized justice?

Bohm (2006) built on the work of several other scholars who proposed that the McDonald's Corporation has had a significant influence on the way that modern corporations and governments operate. The features that made McDonald's so successful—efficiency, predictability, and high levels of control (fixating on the details of an operation)—are becoming increasingly present in the way that criminal justice operations function. Bohm (2006) suggested that plea bargaining, guided sentencing (he refers to this as "justice by computer"), and additional control technologies (often nonhuman, such as CCTV or GPS technology) are in some ways parallel to the way that McDonald's does business—what he has labeled McJustice.

Yet, other large corporations also provide services that are characterized by "sameness," and Robinson (2003, 79) said that as

> Americans come to expect quick, easy solutions to food (McDonaldization), entertainment (Disneyization), and even shopping (WalMartization), this likely affects their expectations for achieving other goals as well, including the reduction of crime.

Do you think that Robinson's approach is correct? Do these metaphors help you better understand the work of contemporary justice systems? ✦

Research and Criminal Justice Policy

In an ideal world, we would introduce criminal justice policies based on what the research demonstrates has been successful at either preventing or responding to crime. And once these new practices or policies were in place, we would rigorously evaluate them to ensure that they were effective (and that taxpayers were getting the best return on their investment in criminal justice). Unfortunately, this is seldom the case. One of the most important works in criminal justice in the past decade was the release of the study conducted by Lawrence Sherman and his colleagues (1998) about "what works" in criminal justice, in other words, programs that have been effective in preventing crime. The findings were discouraging because many of the programs that we thought were effective—such as Drug Abuse Resistance Education (DARE), neighborhood watch programs, arrest of unemployed persons for domestic violence, correctional boot camps, shock probation (programs that add short jail terms to probationary sentences), house arrest with electronic monitoring, and summer jobs for at-risk youths—were not effective crime control strategies.

The key finding of Sherman and his colleagues (1998) was that most criminal justice programs receive funding to deliver a program, but we often do not fund the evaluations of these interventions. Thus, we do not know whether many of these programs are truly effective or, if they are effective, why they are. As a result, we continue to fund programs that "seem good on paper" but do not actually deliver any meaningful results. The problem goes beyond wasted taxpayer dollars: A more serious implication of this finding is that we may be delivering ineffective programs to offenders for years or decades. If these offenders commit further offenses, then our own safety is threatened.

Sherman et al. (1998, 1) did find a number of programs that were effective in preventing crime, and these include home visits for infants from at-risk families, preschool classes with weekly home visits, school-based programs, vocational training for older ex-offenders, extra police patrols for crime "hot spots," therapeutic community programs for drug offenders, and rehabilitation programs that target specific risks for convicted offenders. It is important to note that many of these programs are oriented for infants or youngsters, and it is possible that these early interventions may represent the lowest-cost interventions over the long term. It may be far less expensive to spend a few thousand dollars providing in-home nurse visits to at-risk children than holding someone in prison at nearly $30,000 a year.

Over the past few years, increasing attention has been paid to evidence-based criminal justice programs. Several academic journals that relate to policy analysis and evaluation have recently been introduced (for example, *Criminology & Public Policy* and the *European Journal on Criminal Policy and Research*). In addition, the National Institute of Justice has sponsored an annual conference where policymakers, researchers, and practitioners meet and discuss program effectiveness, evaluation, and the relationship of research to policy. Such changes outline the momentum that policy-based research and program evaluation are gaining in the delivery of criminal justice programs.

Langan and Levin (2002) found that over two-thirds of all prisoners were rearrested or reconvicted within three years of their release. Clearly our correctional institutions are "failing to correct." We are only starting to understand which programs are effective, why, and whether there are specific types of prisoners who might have a greater success (such as first offenders). Some program participants might be successful without any help, while our best efforts may be unsuccessful with an offender who is not fully committed to change. One challenge of this type of research is that we often have to wait years before we know whether an intervention has been successful.

Much of our knowledge about crime control is based on our beliefs about offenders and their motivations (typically to get the best and fastest return with as little risk as possible). Yet, Kleiman (2005, 14) suggested that we have sometimes based crime control on "brute force" (such as harsh penalties) and that we might be more successful if we based our interventions on "predictability, swiftness, concentration, and communication." He argued for targeted interventions that increase the deterrent effect and communicate to offenders the increased risks and costs of engaging in crime. Although much of Kleiman's analyses are economic, his work makes us reflect on being "smart on crime."

In the previous chapters, we outlined a number of policy interventions that did not seem to transfer well to other jurisdictions. The quest to find programs that are effective is frustrated by the fact that in some places policy implementation is relatively successful. This may be due to a number of factors, including the leaders who champion the reform or intervention (some leaders may be more credible or dynamic), the support for the program (staffing and funding), the history of the organization (for example, if the organization goes through frequent "reforms" it is likely that staff will tire of the changes), and the support of community stakeholders. Thus, a program that works in one place may be completely ineffective in another. In some cases, new programs are given only "lip service" (a program is initiated, but there is no funding for new staff positions or support), and nobody is really surprised if the intervention fails. As a result, there is increasing interest in policy-oriented and evaluation research.

In an influential statement, Thomas Winfree and Howard Abadinsky (2003) outlined how theory, research, practice, and policy should be applied to our understanding of crime and the ways each element should guide and inform the others. While many academics, scholars, practitioners, and policy analysts are devoting their attention to one element of this relationship, few are committed to the total integration of this knowledge. The movement toward policy evaluation, best practices, using evidence-based interventions, and linking theory to criminal justice interventions will have a significant impact on criminal justice policies over the next few decades.

It is possible that some of the influences on criminal justice systems will come from outside the United States. Ideas about policing, courts, and corrections are transmitted rather quickly, and practitioners are likely to adopt policies or practices that "make sense." Morris and Maxwell (1998) observed that family group conferences (also known as community accountability conferences or conferencing), for instance, were introduced in New Zealand in 1989, and their use spread quickly throughout English-speaking common law nations. This restorative justice initiative brings together victims and offenders and was seen as a new way of "doing justice." Yet, while popular in many nations, it has not really caught on in the United States, perhaps because it is perceived as being soft on crime. Therefore, we should ask: Would these practices be more popular if research demonstrated their effectiveness?

Muncie (2005) suggested that globalization has influenced justice systems in the same manner that it has influenced other spheres of our lives. In many ways, the United States is an exporter of criminal justice ideas rather than an importer. Further, these ideas are usually diffused from the large urban areas to the rest of the nation. Klinger (2003), for example, traced the development of Special Weapons and Tactics (SWAT) teams in the United States. While there are many factors that contribute to the spread of a new practice—such as SWAT teams—one of the cornerstones is success: If an approach is perceived to be effective, it likely will be quickly adopted. Of course, some criminal justice policies, such as boot camps or chain gangs, were fads. They were popular for a short period of time but quickly disappeared.

Criminal justice policies are also linked to membership in cross-national organizations or as a condition of receiving economic support. Ruddell (2005) outlined how the abolition of the death penalty in European nations was a condition of membership in the European Union (EU). To gain entry to the EU, for instance, the former Soviet Republics had to end the practice of capital punishment. The United States also fashions the way that the justice systems in some smaller nations will respond to crime, as U.S. economic aid or support may be conditional on a nation developing drug policies consistent with U.S. interests. While nations in these scenarios are free to reject these new policies or practices, nations that want truly independent criminal justice systems may have to live with the economic consequences.

Criminal Justice in the Twenty-First Century

Police, courts, and corrections will have to adapt to a number of significant changes in the future. These adjustments will be a result of social and demographic changes, such as growing numbers of aging Americans who are showing up in jails and prisons (in addition to those who are growing old in these facilities) and shifts in the racial and ethnic composition of the population. There are also external forces that law enforcement must confront, such as the possibility of terrorism, natural disasters (such as Hurricane Katrina, which devastated the Gulf Coast in 2005), or public health disasters, such as the possibility of a **pandemic** (an epidemic that extends beyond the borders of one nation, such as the 1918 influenza pandemic that killed somewhere between 50 and 100 million people). The breakdown in social order witnessed in New Orleans might be multiplied in any of the scenarios above. Of all these challenges, however, to date technology has been the most significant force in shaping the way that justice systems operate.

The one constant in the administration of justice is change—although sometimes these changes are **old wine in new bottles.** This means that while the packaging has changed, there might not be a significant shift in the way that things are done. Community-oriented policing, for instance, is a return to styles of policing that were popular more than 100 years ago and that featured officers who had a comprehensive knowledge of their communities, the people who lived there, and the problems that some of these individuals caused. However, technology has made a significant impact on the activities of justice professionals.

Crime mapping, for instance, was used in New York City as early as 1900, and police used pins in city maps to depict crimes (Harries 1999). The computerized COMPSTAT information systems are technically much more advanced, but the principles of mapping crimes remain the same. Technology has influenced almost every other dimension of criminal justice. Prior to the invention of the telephone—and radios in patrol cars— police officers rarely went to someone's residence. Now, it seems as though everybody has a cellular phone and can be in almost instant communication with the police. In fact, about one-third of all calls for assistance to the police are from portable phones (GAO 2003). This change has reduced the time it takes for a victim or witness to call for assistance.

Anybody who has recently done a ride-alone with the police in a large agency probably has a good understanding of the influence of technology on law enforcement. Most patrol cars have "on-board" computers that enable the officers to do driver's license or criminal records checks, and some have a running tally of calls for service for the shift, visually show the dispatcher's communication with other units, and display whether other agencies are "in the field" and available to provide aid. Such communication enables dispatchers and officers to make far better decisions about resources, but better forms of communication will not replace the ability of officers to de-escalate a volatile situation or use their presence to calm a distraught person. Thus, police departments will still rely upon getting the best people for the job, but the officers will require more training as the complexity of their jobs increases.

Future police administrators and civil libertarians will have to carefully weigh the costs and benefits of introducing new technologies that are intended to make us safer. In the last chapter, we addressed how we have to balance our freedoms and safety when law enforcers have access to more sophisticated methods to listen to our conversations, monitor our e-mail, or observe us from long distances. As our ability to use more sophisticated methods of conducting surveillance increases, there possibly may be unforeseen and negative consequences, such as hackers stealing these technologies and using them to invade the privacy of others (Ventura, Miller, and Deflem 2005).

While nobody looks forward to the security screening at airports, new backscatter x-ray technology allows security staffs to remotely scan the ticketholder for prohibited items. Critics of the technology, however, contend that these x-rays depict such a clear image that airport screeners virtually strip search the passengers (the images are nude). Meckler (2005) suggested that these were early models and new technology obscures "private parts." Less controversial applications of technology may include less intrusive methods of testing for narcotics, explosives, and radiation. Such testing instruments will increase safety, and because of the potential government demand for these devices, it is likely that corporations will develop them.

Additionally, as computers become less expensive and more powerful, the applications for law enforcement will increase, especially as they relate to record-keeping, detection, and analysis of information. For instance, some scholars have outlined how scanners will be able to recognize faces and better identify persons through iris scans. While prototypes of these instruments already exist, they are cost-prohibitive, and as prices fall they will likely be used more widely.

We discussed in Chapter 4 how less-lethal weapons such as the Taser are being used by many police departments, and the use is spreading in jails and prisons. These tools add some "distance" to stopping unlawful or disruptive behavior, and officers do not have to use their batons to disarm or disable an uncooperative suspect (which may result in more severe injuries). Scientists are currently working on other nonlethal and less-lethal methods to incapacitate offenders, and there has been speculation for years that devices that transmit microwaves that make people ill may be effective for crowd control. Not all of this technology is directed at stopping humans: Scientists are attempting to develop a tool that emits a burst of electronic pulse that disables a car's engine to stop vehicle pursuits.

Offenders also respond to changing technological and economic conditions, just as law enforcement adapts. While technology has increased the ability of law enforcement to respond to offenses, criminals are also using the Internet to defraud victims and sell stolen goods on Internet auction sites. By selling stolen goods online, they bypass "fences" and reap bigger profits. Other offenders are switching from high-risk and low-return offenses such as bank robbery to high-return and low-risk crimes such as identity theft: Identity theft is much more lucrative, and even if the offender is caught, the penalties are not as severe as violent crimes such as bank robbery. In a federal study of identity thefts committed in 2004, Baum (2006, 1) found that "3.6 million households, representing 3 percent of households in the United States, discovered that at least one member of the household had been the victim of identity theft in the previous six months."

Changes in the drug markets might also influence the types of crimes that offenders are likely to commit. Offenders in need of "quick cash" to buy drugs such as crack cocaine are likely to engage in higher rates of robbery, and this influences rates of violence (Baumer et al. 1998). One significant change that law enforcement has had to confront is the spread of methamphetamine in the West and Midwest to other regions of the country. In addition to changes in the rates of crime and violence in some rural areas, this illegal drug use also has an impact on community social services, including family service agencies, addiction treatment services, and schools (as these agencies have to respond to the

problems of addiction). It is also likely that newer forms of illegal or de-
signer drugs will emerge in the next few decades.

Criminal justice system responses to crime will also have to account
for the changes in the demographic characteristics of the U.S. population. Not only are Americans growing older, but the population is more
diverse. There is increasing attention, for instance, relating to the ways
patterns of immigration have influenced street gangs. It has been proposed that if immigrant populations feel marginalized or otherwise cut
off from legitimate sources of employment, they may be more likely to
engage in street crime and join gangs. In some cases, such as with the
MS-13 gang, members are gang-affiliated before they come to the
United States. This is not just a contemporary problem, since gangs
have traditionally formed along racial or ethnic lines. European police
departments are also contending with emerging gang problems and the
importation of gangs through immigration, similar to the challenges
confronted by American law enforcement agencies.

One significant change that we often fail to acknowledge is the growing size of private justice agencies. Although technically not a formal
part of the criminal justice system, private police, security officers, and
corporate investigators support the activities of public law enforcement agencies. The total number of persons employed in these organizations is larger than the number of sworn public law enforcement officers (Singh 2005). To reduce their losses to organized offenders—and
to keep consumer prices low—some of these corporations actively engage in surveillance of persons living in the community, and they share
their information with law enforcement agencies. While these efforts
multiply the ability of law enforcement to respond to serious offenders,
these persons are less formally accountable than those who work in

---

Box 15.2
The Future: Challenges and Possibilities

The fact that the Federal Bureau of Investigation has a "Futurist in Residence" and
that there is a group of academics and police executives called the Police Futurists suggest that organizations are taking an active role in trying to forecast the future of law enforcement. Who would have predicted prior to September 2001, for instance, that
there would be a major terrorist attack on the United States and the implications that
attack would have on the entire nation? In addition, who could have foreseen the social
breakdown in New Orleans only days after Hurricane Katrina ravaged the Gulf Coast in
August 2005? In either case, law enforcement was required to take a leadership role in
confronting these challenges.

Changes in technology, the demographic and social characteristics of the population, the
health of our economic system, and the possibility of external or natural threats will all influence the activities of law enforcement. Many police departments have long-term strategic
plans that attempt to evaluate these changes and challenges. In most cases, this planning is to
forecast budgets and predict the needs of the department (for example, the construction of
offices, detention facilities, and staffing requirements) decades into the future. ✦

government-funded agencies. There is a delicate balance between the need for a corporation to provide a safe and profitable environment and our desire for safety when shopping or purchasing goods and services. One of the challenges that ordinary citizens face, however, is that we seldom know when we are under surveillance by these corporations. While the asset protection and security staff are generally professional, we are at some risk of being victimized by these employees. One way that citizens can hold these corporations more accountable is to launch civil litigation if they have been harmed.

Conclusions

This book attempts to make sense of criminal justice systems in the United States. This task is made all the more difficult by the sheer size and diversity of criminal justice agencies. Each jurisdiction within the nation has overlapping levels of criminal justice enforcement, prosecution, and correctional control. While these agencies share more commonalities than differences, they each have a slightly different character. These agencies must respond to a number of controversial, problematic, or threatening issues, and we have addressed dozens of these challenges throughout this text—from the disproportionate confinement of minority group members to wrongful convictions and the police use of force. We examined these issues from numerous perspectives and found that there are no easy answers to many of these challenges.

To assist in our examination of crime control, we introduced Packer's (1968) concept of two competing models within justice systems: the crime control and due process models. While this approach is nearly four decades old, it is still a useful tool in analyzing the operations of justice systems. In this chapter, we introduced several alternative ways to examine criminal justice policy. Many of these approaches will be familiar from the theory classes that you have taken. One important thing to consider is that there are many ways of interpreting the world, and the one that seems best to you will probably determine the way that you perceive offenses, offenders, and criminal justice policies. We encourage each of you to go beyond looking at the world using only one approach and to see if others have merit or make sense to you.

Often people want "black-and-white" answers to complex problems—and responding to crime is an inherently complex challenge—but easy solutions seldom exist. Instead, policy formation often rests on complex negotiations between different stakeholders that result in policies that may be far different than the ones that were originally conceived. The police, court officials, and correctional staff members who are supposed to implement these laws or policies are frequently left with a poor policy that is seldom evaluated, and sometimes interest disappears with the next funding cycle or election. As a result, employees of criminal justice systems tend to be cynical about each new change or reform, and they typically take a "wait and see" attitude to decide whether these reforms will last. This presents another challenge of policy implementation.

In some cases, shifting cultural values and beliefs may influence offender behavior more than criminal justice systems. Changing attitudes toward drunk driving probably have had a more positive effect on reducing this behavior than police checkpoints or harsher penalties. In addition, some of the most effective solutions to crime and justice problems may lie outside justice systems. Sherman and his colleagues (1998) found that some social service interventions may have a greater role in prevention than more police, courts, or corrections. These are important findings, but are Americans willing to tolerate the intrusions of public health nurses and teachers into the lives of at-risk families in the name of future crime prevention?

We have outlined a number of controversies in criminal justice. Identification is the first consideration in problem-solving, and we are making progress in dealing with some of the most difficult challenges, such as disproportionate minority confinement, "driving while black," the differential treatment of women, how to respond to juveniles, and the police use of force. In all of these issues, we can see the tension between the due process and crime control approaches and by scrutinizing the activities of the police, courts, and corrections, advocates of both positions will work toward a healthy balance between civil liberties and crime control. Many challenges still remain, and many of the students reading this text will have the opportunity to confront these problems working within criminal justice systems. You will have the advantage of having much more insight into the operations of justice systems than your counterparts a generation ago.

Key Terms

black codes	Jim Crow laws	social construction
civil commitment	late modernity	social isolation
constructive perspective	old wine in new bottles	
critical criminology	pandemic	

Critical Review Questions

1. Place yourself in the role of a "police futurist." What do you think will be the biggest challenges to law enforcement in the next decade?

2. Can you think of ways that private forms of social control (such as corporate security and loss prevention) reduce the privacy in your day-to-day activities?

3. Where did you receive your knowledge about sexual offenders? Do all sex offenders pose the same level of risk? Do media accounts about sex offenders disclose that they have one of the lowest recidivism rates of all offenders?

4. How do our cultural values and beliefs shape the law-abiding behavior of individuals? We used the example of driving while intoxicated, but can you think of other issues where people's attitudes toward offenses have changed over time?

5. Can you think of ways that crime can be reduced without using the criminal justice system? (Hint: Are speed bumps a more efficient manner of slowing speeders than traffic enforcement officers?)

6. What do you think that scholars and social commentators mean by "social isolation"? Do you believe that social isolation has caused us to be more fearful and insecure about crime?

References

Baum, Katrina. (2006). *Identity Theft, 2004*. Washington, DC: Bureau of Justice Statistics.

Baumer, Eric, Janet L. Lauritsen, Richard Rosenfeld, and Richard Wright. (1998). "The influence of crack cocaine on robbery, burglary and homicide rates: A cross-city, longitudinal analysis." *Journal of Research in Crime and Delinquency* 35, 316–40.

Beckett, Katherine, and Theodore Sasson. (2000). *The Politics of Injustice*. Thousand Oaks, CA: Pine Forge.

Bohm, Robert M. (2006). "'McJustice': On the McDonaldization of criminal justice." *Justice Quarterly* 23 (1), 127–145.

Eschholz, Sarah. (2002). "Racial composition of television offenders and viewer's fear of crime." *Critical Criminology* 11 (1), 41–60.

Feeley, Malcolm, and Jonathan Simon. (1992). "The new penology: Notes on the emerging strategy of corrections and its implications." *Criminology* 30 (4), 449–474.

Garland, David. (2001). *The Culture of Control: Crime and Social Order in Contemporary Society*. Chicago: University of Chicago Press.

Government Accounting Office (GAO). (2003). *Uneven Implementation of Wireless Enhanced 911 Raises Prospect of Piecemeal Availability for Years to Come*. Washington, DC: Author.

Harries, Keith. (1999). *Mapping Crime: Principle and Practice*. Washington, DC: National Institute of Justice.

Hughes, Kristen A. (2006). *Justice Expenditure and Employment in the United States*. Washington, DC: U.S. Department of Justice, Bureau of Justice Statistics.

Kleiman, Mark, A. R. (2005). *When Brute Force Fails: Strategic Thinking for Crime Control*. Washington DC: U.S. Department of Justice.

Klinger, David A. (2003). "Spreading diffusion in criminology." *Criminology & Public Policy* 3 (2), 461–468.

Kraska, Peter B. (2004). *Theorizing Criminal Justice: Eight Essential Orientations*. Prospect Heights, IL: Waveland.

———. (2006). "Criminal justice theory: Toward legitimacy and an infrastructure." *Justice Quarterly* 23 (2), 167–185.

Langan, Patrick A., and David J. Levin. (2002). *Recidivism of Prisoners Released in 1994*. Washington, DC: U.S. Department of Justice, Bureau of Justice Statistics.

Lilly, J. Robert, Francis T. Cullen, and Richard A. Ball. (2001). *Criminological Theory: Context and Consequences*. Thousand Oaks, CA: Sage.

Maguire, Kathleen, and Ann L. Pastore. (2005). *Sourcebook of Criminal Justice Statistics, 2003*. Washington, DC: U.S. Department of Justice.

Meckler, Laura. (2005, Sept. 13). "Airport screening machines get smarter." *Pittsburgh Post-Gazette*. Retrieved January 1, 2007 from: *http://www.post-gazette.com/pg/05256/570687.stm*.

Morris, Allison, and Gabrielle Maxwell. (1998). "Restorative justice in New Zealand: Family group conferences as a case study." *Western Criminology Review* 1 (1), Retrieved July 5, 2006 from: *http://wcr.sonoma.edu/v1n1/morris.html*.

Muncie, John. (2005). "The globalization of crime control—the case of youth and juvenile justice: Neo-liberalism, policy convergence, and international conventions." *Theoretical Criminology* 9 (1), 35–64.

National Council of La Raza (NCLR). (2004). *Lost Opportunities: The Reality of Latinos in the Criminal Justice System*. Washington, DC: Author.

Norgren, Jill, and Serena Nanda. (2006). *American Cultural Pluralism and Law*. Portsmouth, NH: Greenwood.

Packer, Herbert. (1968). *The Limits of the Criminal Sanction*. Stanford, CA: Stanford University Press.

Putnam, Robert D. (2000). *Bowling Alone: The Collapse and Revival of American Community*. New York: Simon and Schuster.

Robinson, Matthew B. (2003). "The mouse who would rule the world! How American criminal justice reflects the themes of Disneyization." *Journal of Criminal Justice and Popular Culture* 10 (1), 69–86.

Ruddell, Rick. (2005). "Social disruption, state formation, and minority threat: A cross-national study of imprisonment." *Punishment & Society* 7 (1), 7–28.

Sample, Lisa L., and Timothy M. Bray. (2003). "Are sex offenders dangerous?" *Criminology & Public Policy* 3 (1), 59–82.

Schwartz, Barbara K. (2005). *The Sex Offender, Volume V: Issues in Assessment, Treatment and Supervision of Adult and Juvenile Offenders*. Kingston, NJ: Civics Research Institute.

Seagal, Debra. (1993, November). "Tales from the cutting-room floor: The reality of 'reality-based' television." *Harper's Magazine*, pp., 50–57.

Sherman, Lawrence W., Denise Gottfredson, Doris MacKenzie, John Eck, Peter Reuter, and Shawn Bushway. (1998). *Preventing Crime: What Works, What Doesn't, What's Promising*. Washington, DC: National Institute of Justice.

Singh, Anne-Marie. (2005). "Private Security, Crime Control, and the Coercion of Bodies." *Theoretical Criminology* 9 (2), 153–174.

Tyler, Tom R. (2006). *Why People Obey the Law*. New Princeton, NJ: Princeton University Press.

Ventura, Holly E., J. Mitchell Miller, and Mathieu Deflem. (2005). "Governmentality and the war on terror: FBI Project Carnivore and the diffusion of disciplinary power." *Critical Criminology* 13 (1), 55–70.

Winfree, L. Thomas, and Howard Abadinsky. (2003). *Understanding Crime: Theory and Practice*, second edition. Belmont CA: Wadsworth.

Recommended Readings

Kleiman, Mark A. R. (2005). *When Brute Force Fails: Strategic Thinking for Crime Control*. Washington, DC: U.S. Department of Justice. Kleiman takes a critical look at offender motivation and the operations of criminal justice agencies. He examines how offenders weigh the economic costs of crime using examples from recent crime control initiatives and makes some suggestions about increasing the performance of criminal justice agencies. This book can be downloaded from the NCJRS Web site at: *http://www.ncjrs.gov/pdffiles1/nij/grants/211204.pdf*.

Kraska, Peter. (2004). *Theorizing Criminal Justice: Eight Essential Orientations*. Prospect Heights, IL: Waveland Press. Most books on theory examine offenders and try to explain their criminal conduct. Kraska, by contrast, presents eight different approaches to understanding the operations of justice systems, including Packer's model of due process and crime control. Understanding theories of justice systems is a key component in research.

Sherman, Lawrence W., Denise Gottfredson, Doris MacKenzie, John Eck, Peter Reuter, and Shawn Bushway. (1998). *Preventing Crime: What Works, What Doesn't, What's Promising.* Washington, DC: National Institute of Justice. This lengthy report outlines crime prevention strategies and highlights programs that are effective, those that seem promising, as well as failures. Surprisingly, these investigators find that many of the successful interventions fall outside criminal justice systems. The entire 1997 report to Congress can be downloaded from the NCJRS Web site at: *http://www.ncjrs.gov/ works/ wholedoc.htm.* ✦

Case Index

Author Index

Subject Index